INTERVENTIONS
New Studies in Medieval Culture

Ethan Knapp, Series Editor

Answerable Style
The Idea of the Literary in Medieval England

Edited by
Frank Grady *and*
Andrew Galloway

THE OHIO STATE UNIVERSITY PRESS | COLUMBUS

Copyright © 2013 by The Ohio State University.
All rights reserved.

Library of Congress Cataloging-in-Publication Data
Answerable style : the idea of the literary in medieval England / Edited by Frank Grady and Andrew Galloway.
    p. cm. — (Interventions : new studies in medieval culture)
Includes bibliographical references and index.
  ISBN 978-0-8142-1207-3 (cloth : alk. paper) — ISBN 0-8142-1207-7 (cloth : alk. paper) — ISBN 0-8142-9309-6 (cd) (print)
  1. English literature—Middle English, 1100–1500—History and criticism. 2. Literature, Medieval—History and criticism. I. Grady, Frank. II. Galloway, Andrew. III. Series: Interventions : new studies in medieval culture.
  PR255.A57 2013
  820.9'001—dc23
                                    2012030981

Paper (ISBN: 978-0-8142-5632-9)
Cover design by Judith Arisman
Type set in Adobe Garamond Pro
Text design by Juliet Williams

contents

List of Illustrations — vii

Introduction The Medieval Literary
             ANDREW GALLOWAY — 1

PART I: The Literary between Latin and Vernacular

Chapter 1 Horace's *Ars poetica* in the Medieval Classroom and Beyond:
           The Horizons of Ancient Precept
           RITA COPELAND — 15

Chapter 2 Latin Composition Lessons, *Piers Plowman*, and the
           Piers Plowman Tradition
           WENDY SCASE — 34

Chapter 3 Langland Translating
           TRAUGOTT LAWLER — 54

Chapter 4 Escaping the Whirling Wicker:
           Ricardian Poetics and Narrative Voice in *The Canterbury Tales*
           KATHERINE ZIEMAN — 75

Chapter 5 Langland's Literary Syntax, or Anima as an Alternative to
           Latin Grammar
           KATHARINE BREEN — 95

Chapter 6 *Speculum Vitae* and the Form of *Piers Plowman*
         RALPH HANNA   121

Chapter 7 Petrarch's Pleasures, Chaucer's Revulsions, and the Aesthetics of
           Renunciation in Late-Medieval Culture
           ANDREW GALLOWAY   140

PART II: Literarity in the Vernacular Sphere

Chapter 8 Chaucer's History-Effect
           STEVEN JUSTICE   169

Chapter 9 Seigneurial Poetics, or The Poacher, the Prikasour,
           the Hunt, and Its Oeuvre
           FRANK GRADY   195

Chapter 10 Agency and the Poetics of Sensation in Gower's *Mirour de l'Omme*
           MAURA NOLAN   214

Chapter 11 *Troilus and Criseyde:* Genre and Source
           LEE PATTERSON   244

Chapter 12 The Silence of Langland's Study: Matter, Invisibility, Instruction
           D. VANCE SMITH   263

Chapter 13 Voice and Public Interiorities: Chaucer, Orpheus, Machaut
           DAVID LAWTON   284

Works Cited   307
Index   333

illustrations

Figure 1	Anima's speech of self-naming. Cambridge, Trinity College, MS B.15.17 (W), fol. 86v	101
Figure 2	Anima's speech of self-naming. Oxford, Corpus Christi College, MS 201 (F), fol. 61r	102
Figure 3	Ebstorf World Map, c. 1230–1250	109
Figure 4	*Speculum theologiae*. Table of the Ten Commandments. Robert de Lisle Psalter, London, British Library, MS Arundel 83 II, fol. 127v	112
Figure 5	*Speculum theologiae*. Table of the Seven Petitions of the Paternoster. London, British Library, MS Royal 1.B.x, fol. 4r	113

introduction

The Medieval Literary

ANDREW GALLOWAY

IN RECENT YEARS, scholars working in a range of periods have begun to talk about aesthetics, form, and "the literary" in reanimated ways. A new emphasis, if not a movement, has emerged, in which what counts as distinctly literary form and as the very category of literature is receiving attention with a focus and energy suggesting a major reorientation of a number of familiar approaches, including historicism, theory, and gender studies. Such developments have proven immensely productive, and have already begun to generate historical and theoretical reflections on the critical shift itself. With very few exceptions, however, the scholars building and mapping this new emphasis have paid scant notice to medieval literary scholarship, much less the Middle Ages.[1] This raises interesting theoretical and historical questions. Are, for instance, either the "premodern" materials or the ways in which they have been approached so stubbornly distinct from postmedieval things of all kinds? If so, one might wonder, is there any special value that such other-

---

1. See especially Marjorie Levinson, "What Is New Formalism?" *PMLA* 122 (March 2007): 558-69. As Grady's essay in chapter 9 below notes, mention of a single medievalist, Katherine O'Brien O'Keefe, appears in a bibliographical appendix, in a section entitled "Alternative Solutions to Problems Raised by New Formalism," found at sitemaker.umich.edu/ pmla_article. For a thoughtful reassessment of the role of earlier "literary theory" in this new emphasis, see also Jonathan Culler, *The Literary in Theory* (Stanford, CA: Stanford University Press, 2007).

ness—in approach and materials—might offer? Would a renewed emphasis on "the literary" (however we choose to define that) help us appreciate these earlier periods in new ways? Or should, perhaps, the methods currently available for postmedieval works treated in this vein be altered in some way to suit those materials? If so, how?

These are questions that this volume both directly and indirectly pursues. But this volume is also predicated on the point that these questions have already long been pursued by medievalists. Here we return to the question of why such inquiries have gone unremarked by scholars of later periods. Essays explicitly on the medieval ideas of "the literary" have increasingly appeared in recent years, often including a wide range of scrutiny of how focus on historicism or theory or gender studies can aid or occlude this attention. Moreover, those recent inquiries among medievalists are in turn building on decades of medieval scholarship that has aimed at some of the same topics. Indeed, since at least the 1970s—before the topic became central to Renaissance studies (and well before Stephen Greenblatt's provocative 1997 essay on the emergence of the literary in the Renaissance as a form of "cultural capital"[2])— medieval studies has centrally pursued ways of understanding "the literary" and the distinctive powers and implications of literary form. Yet here medievalists may share some responsibility for the invisibility of their attention to this topic, at least to critics of later periods. However legion the ingenious and wide-ranging work on this topic by medievalists, however deep the critical roots, no wide-ranging conference, monograph, or collection of essays has addressed this topic for medieval literature overtly or in any significant breadth of scope and theoretical approach. Given the potential interest for all concerned, it seems high time such a volume were assembled.

One reason medievalists have not done so before may be the very richness of their scholarly and critical lineage. Although the focus on this topic is explicit and pervasive in medieval literary essays in recent years, the lineage of attention to this in medieval literary criticism extends much further. The questions framed above have been with us in medieval studies for a long time, and what is "new" about this book is not simply its posing them. In fact, to offer a collection on this topic as if no earlier treatments of the issue existed in medieval criticism would be as misleading as the elision in postmedieval accounts of the current trends in medieval criticism. Scattered essays on "the medieval literary" continue to appear in numbers, but all such work proceeds with a sense of continuing and developing a set of questions, and refining a range of complex literary and nonliterary materials, that medievalists have

---

2. Stephen Greenblatt, "What Is the History of Literature?" *Critical Inquiry* 23 (1997): 460-81.

been working on for decades. This offers grounds not for announcing a new movement, but instead for taking stock of some major earlier tributaries to this focus, and for defining and demonstrating new possibilities.

Recalling a body of previous work on which literary criticism remains dependent, even while we are engaged in advancing these pursuits in new ways, is regularly necessary at moments of rapid disciplinary shift and growth. An important opportunity to pursue this dual goal for this topic was a conference organized by Steven Justice and Maura Nolan at the University of California, Berkeley, on "Form after Historicism," in honor of Anne Middleton on the occasion of her retirement as the Florence Green Bixby Professor of English. At this conference were first presented a number of the papers—many by those who have known or been taught by Anne—that were then substantially revised and rewritten for this volume. To this core were joined a number of other original essays from scholars making notable contributions to the topic of "the medieval literary," and who were moreover explicitly attentive to the debt their work owes to Middleton's approaches to this issue. The essays generally, though not exclusively, treat the later fourteenth-century poetry of Chaucer, Langland, and Gower, where this topic has been most often elaborated and where Middleton's own work has made the most significant contributions. The essays also and by design speak to a wide range through the premodern centuries, focusing on various interacting traditions and linguistic spheres. By these means it is hoped that this collection can be instructive for medievalists of all kinds as well as those working well beyond medieval contexts and medievalists' debates.

Middleton's work serves exceedingly well both as a guiding light and an opportunity for such a venture. The volume's title "Answerable Style" does not simply evoke Milton's meditation on the problem of a proper genre to describe the Fall (*Paradise Lost* 9.20); it also alludes to an early essay by Middleton on the stylistic responses to different purposes and audiences by the Old English homilist Ælfric.[3] By both lineages the term remains apt for considering the idea of the medieval literary, both as that has developed through a series of contextual pursuits and as that is now in the process of displaying new formations, answering to new developments, and posing new questions for further responses. For Middleton, "form" has long been central to literary study, as well as what may best be called a distinctive literary ethics, the "good" of literature. These elements reach deeply in her work into literary, legal, and other kinds of cultural spheres. Her emphases on "the liter-

---

3. "Ælfric's Answerable Style: The Rhetoric of the Alliterative Prose," *Studies in Medieval Culture* 4 (1973 [1968]): 83–91. The dissertation was "The 'English Ways' of Ælfric's Prose," Harvard University, 1966.

ary" and the idea of medieval literature have persistently posited a culturally wide reach, while opening up or returning to the central questions that now seem taken up everywhere in modern literary studies. In her work, attention to "the literary" typically unfolds it as a transmitter and emitter of meaning rather than some "reflection" or homology of its social contexts, for which literature serves, as she has repeatedly showed, as a focus of reinterpretation as well as a good in its own right.[4]

As should be clear already, her work is far from alone in defining this set of topics, nor is this volume inspired solely by her continuing body of writings. Other enduring reference points in this topic are studies by Lee Patterson, Ralph Hanna, and David Lawton, to name just a few of the most often cited critics—all three of whom present contributions here.[5] These and others have long focused on Middle English poetry as a place for querying and verifying the "good" of literature and the idea of the medieval literary as a general and long-term issue. Middleton, however, has pursued these topics with special richness and intensity. Her work's distinctiveness is not simply a particularly rich critical style but also a characteristically multisided mode of perception, by which she has consistently both brought the properties of literature to new focus and showed how those created and responded to cultural conditions. Her treatments of *Piers Plowman* are particularly notable contributions in this vein—helping bring into central view a poem that was declared (by a noted medievalist formalist) a singularly shapeless poem, the barometer of an "age of crisis"—to show, for instance, how its ambient energies for renewal of received didactic traditions lead to its repeated breakdowns and reassemblies.[6] Her distinctive mode of perception is similarly apparent in her many influential demonstrations of how form reflects generic innovation and combination, as in her influential focus on the use in *Piers* of a brief, lyrical mode, found in English as well as French poetry. She was the

---

4. See, e.g., Anne Middleton, "Chaucer's 'New Men' and the Good of Literature in the *Canterbury Tales*," in *Literature and Society*, ed. Edward Said (Baltimore: Johns Hopkins University Press, 1980), 15–56.

5. Patterson's first work on this may be epitomized by his book *Chaucer and the Subject of History* (Madison: University of Wisconsin Press, 1991); Lawton's may be epitomized by his essay "Dullness and the Fifteenth Century," *ELH* 54 (1987): 761–99. Hanna's key early studies, spanning a number of years, may be epitomized by his collection in *Pursuing History: Middle English Manuscripts and Their Texts* (Stanford, CA: Stanford University Press, 1996).

6. For Middleton's most overtly formalist essay, see "Narration and the Invention of Experience: Episodic Form in *Piers Plowman*," in *The Wisdom of Poetry: Essays on Early English Literature in Honor of Morton W. Bloomfield*, ed. Larry D. Benson and Siegfried Wenzel (Kalamazoo, MI: Medieval Institute Publications, 1982), 91–122, 280–83. The earlier comment is that of Charles Muscatine, *Poetry and Crisis in the Age of Chaucer* (Notre Dame, IN: University of Notre Dame Press, 1972), repr. in *Medieval Literature, Style, and Culture: Essays by Charles Muscatine* (Columbia: University of South Carolina Press, 1999), 111–38.

first to argue that Langland abstracted this into a formal device for continuously rethinking the traditional topics that his poetry took up.[7]

Middleton has made foundational contributions also to distinctive properties of "the literary" as a defining feature of late-medieval English culture in general. This is clear from what remains possibly her most famous essay, on "the idea of public poetry in the reign of Richard II," the period of Chaucer, Langland, and so many other major poets. Her comments there have so influentially shaped how we understand that period itself, as well as how any period can be linked to distinctive terms of "the literary," that it deserves quoting at length:

> The public poetry of the Ricardian period is best understood not as poetry "about" contemporary events and abuses, whether viewed concretely or at a distance, from the vantage point of a universal scheme of ideal order—it is rarely occasional or topical, and it is indifferent on the whole to comprehensive rational systems of thought or of poetic structure. Rather it is poetry defined by a constant relation of speaker to audience within an ideally conceived worldly community, a relation which has become the poetic subject. In describing their mode of address, the poets most often refer to the general or common voice, and the ideal of human nature that sustains this voice assigns new importance to secular life, the civic virtues, and communal service. The voice of public poetry is neither courtly, nor spiritual, nor popular. It is pious, but its central pieties are worldly felicity and peaceful, harmonious communal existence. It speaks for bourgeois moderation, a course between the rigorous absolutes of religious rule on the one hand, and, on the other, the rhetorical hyperboles and emotional vanities of the courtly style.[8]

These remarks, which take their departure from John Burrow's important book *Ricardian Poetry*, reach back to the perspectives of Jacob Burckhardt, Johan Huizinga, Leo Spitzer, Erich Auerbach, and Kenneth Burke, and outward to the culturally oriented art historical aesthetics of Michael Baxandall and others. Their direct and indirect ramifications extend to much recent work. Directly important for extending these views has been Lawton's key

---

7. "The Audience and Public of *Piers Plowman*," in *Middle English Alliterative Poetry and Its Literary Background: Seven Essays*, ed. David Lawton (Cambridge: D. S. Brewer, 1982), 101–23, 147–54. The notion there has been influential in many kinds of study of *Piers* as well as of other medieval English narratives; for its sustained further application to *Piers*, see, e.g., D. Vance Smith, *The Book of the Incipit: Beginnings in the Fourteenth Century* (Minneapolis: University of Minnesota Press, 2001).

8. Anne Middleton, "The Idea of Public Poetry in the Reign of Richard II," *Speculum* 53 (1978): 95.

essay on the uses of "dullness" in post-Ricardian literature to create a kind of literary discourse that, by denying its originality of artistry, particularly secured the domain of "the public sphere" described by the writers on whom Middleton focused.[9] So too, Patterson's work on Chaucer seminally attended to the formal ways in which Chaucer's narratives create room for subjectivity, self-criticism, and delay in the larger purposes of Christian and courtly ideologies, in an approach that owed much to Middleton's; and in recent years Patterson returned to focus in similar ways on the formal properties of poetry fully invested in particular ideologies and contexts, but capable of opening those up for wider uses.[10] In a different way, David Carlson has shown how the Latin poetry of the same period shows the principles of "public poetry" that Middleton described; other scholars have continued to extend the chronological horizons of these issues. As Lawton looked toward the fifteenth century, so David Matthews has described the national public sphere or "common voice" before Ricardian literature, focusing on the topical political writings in Latin, French, and English from the mid-thirteenth to the mid-fourteenth century.[11]

The ramifications of these topics also extend to something quite new in the proliferating approaches to these issues, and in the broad project of contemplating the "good" of literature in medieval culture. Smoothly as it emerges from prior work, that novelty can be glimpsed in the leaps in historical period being made—an approach that, for instance, James Simpson presents in a study joining Gower's late fourteenth-century *Confessio Amantis* to the twelfth-century *De Planctu Naturae* of Alan de Lille, that Carolyn Dinshaw proposes in a study linking medieval and modern approaches to how sexuality defines historical communities and the uses of literature, and that Paul Strohm suggests on theoretical grounds in general.[12] Other work

---

9. Lawton, "Dullness in the Fifteenth Century."

10. Lee Patterson, "Court Politics and the Invention of Literature: The Case of Sir John Clanvowe," in *Culture and History, 1350-1600: Essays on English Communities, Identities, and Writing*, ed. David Aers (Detroit: Wayne State University Press, 1992), 7–42, repr. in Lee Patterson, *Acts of Recognition: Essays on Medieval Culture* (Notre Dame, IN: University of Notre Dame Press, 2010), 56–83.

11. David Carlson, "The Invention of the Anglo-Latin Public Poetry (circa 1367–1402) and Its Prosody, Esp. in John Gower," *Mittellateinisches Jahrbuch* 39 (2004): 389–406; David Matthews, *Writing to the King: Nation, Kingship, and Literature in England, 1250–1350* (Cambridge: Cambridge University Press, 2010).

12. James Simpson, *Sciences and the Self in Medieval Poetry: Alan of Lille's "Anticlaudianus" and John Gower's "Confessio"* (Cambridge: Cambridge University Press, 1995); Carolyn Dinshaw, *Getting Medieval: Sexualities and Communities, Pre- and Postmodern* (Durham, NC: Duke University Press, 1999); Paul Strohm, *Theory and the Premodern Text* (Minneapolis: University of Minnesota Press, 2000).

has stressed how literary texts formally, psychoanalytically, and in other ways tend to resist simple historical placement—a principle that guides a wide range of essays in a volume edited by Elizabeth Scala and Sylvia Federico. On Gower, Malte Urban (like Maura Nolan, in the collection just mentioned) has argued for a shattering of historical context and teleology to match the disruptions of history that Gower's poetics presents.[13] Still other work has more directly emphasized the primacy of the aesthetic. Peggy Knapp has engaged the concerns of New Formalists to return to a careful reading of Chaucer in emphatically "aesthetic" terms, including his crafting of an imagined community as a work of art.[14]

Much other work on medieval texts and culture has sought to revive formalism as a subtle historical instrument, with a new mandate to identify the nature and conditions of the literary that result from works' social and historical visions and functions. If postmedieval literary studies have recently begun to assess "the literary in theory," in Jonathan Culler's apt phrase, many studies of medieval literature may be said to be seeking the literary in history.[15] The emphasis is clear in the burgeoning pursuits of medieval "literary theory" (both within and outside of literary works themselves) and the Latin commentary tradition. Study of the latter has been reinvigorated by Alastair Minnis especially, as well as by Rita Copeland, who contributes the opening essay here. Other studies have pursued the historical implications of poetry that seems to question and resist its historical contexts, dialectically positioning itself above as well as in conversation with its immediate social setting in a way deemed essential to the properties of the "literary" as we understand that, as Patterson found the short Chaucerian poem *The Boke of Cupide* by John Clanvowe to do in both inhabiting and criticizing the courtly traditions of literature. In similarly social but not merely "symptomatic" terms others have excavated the "poetry of praise," as John Burrow has; or pursued the "natural history of form," as Christopher Cannon does through the twelfth and thirteenth centuries to show the gradual remaking of a notion of English literary status after the shattering consequences of the Norman Conquest; or the "job" of poetry defined by Chaucer and his followers that, as David Carlson has argued, conditioned its contemporary and later readers to adapt to a world of new bourgeois domination yet continued servility to a steeply

---

13. Elizabeth Scala and Sylvia Federico, eds., *The Post-Historical Middle Ages* (New York: Palgrave Macmillan, 2009); Malte Urban, *Fragments: Past and Present in Chaucer and Gower* (Bern: Peter Lang, 2008).

14. Peggy Knapp, *Chaucerian Aesthetics* (New York: Palgrave Macmillan, 2008).

15. Culler, *The Literary in Theory*. See also his "Introduction: Critical Paradigms," to the special issue of *PMLA*, "Literary Criticism for the Twenty-First Century," vol. 125 (2010): 905–15.

hierarchical state; or the transformation of the idea of making literature as a form of "labor," as Kellie Robertson has explored that through Langland, Chaucer, and their contemporaries and followers, who blur the line separating intellectual from material endeavor in order to solidify the culture authority of their own writing and literature itself; or Lydgate's balancing of human agency with accidental contingency to create both "public culture" and a particularly "poetic form of ambiguity" across his writings, as Maura Nolan has shown; or again, Lydgate's establishment of a quasi-sacred force for vernacular "high style" in the *Life of Our Lady*, whose signal though fast-vanishing importance Robert Meyer-Lee has charted.[16] For these, and many others that might be mentioned, history is not some reductive explanation of the literary; rather, putting the literary into the historical is a means for rethinking both.

Middleton would not necessarily endorse all these positions, just as she would not necessarily grant the lineage in which I have loosely situated her work. Like all genealogies, histories of medieval criticism (to which Middleton herself has made important contributions[17]) are framed more or less self-consciously from the perspective of present viewers. In an important sense, this volume, like the conference at which its idea began, is a tribute to a scholar whose contributions have shaped the thought and vocations of many medieval literary scholars, including all those whose chapters are represented here. But, in a fuller tribute, this volume seeks to assess the impact of the ideas with which that scholar has been most associated, guided by a topic woven through both medieval and modern literary scholarship at present as it grapples with enduring questions of the critical enterprise.

THE VOLUME'S ESSAYS are divided into two broad categories. These are meant to evoke two basic medieval literary situations on which the volume's topic depends. The first, titled "The Literary between Latin and Vernacular," might be further glossed by Rita Copeland's title, "The Medieval Classroom

---

16. J. A. Burrow, *The Poetry of Praise* (Cambridge: Cambridge University Press, 2008); Christopher Cannon, *The Grounds of English Literature* (Oxford: Oxford University Press, 2004); David Carlson, *Chaucer's Jobs* (New York: Palgrave Macmillan, 2004); Kellie Robertson, *The Laborer's Two Bodies: Labor and the 'Work' of the Text in Medieval Britain, 1350-1500* (New York: Palgrave Macmillan, 2006); Maura Nolan, *John Lydgate and the Making of Public Culture* (Cambridge: Cambridge University Press, 2005); Robert J. Meyer-Lee, "The Emergence of the Literary in John Lydgate's *Life of Our Lady*," *JEGP* 109 (2010): 322–48.

17. Especially Anne Middleton, "Medieval Studies," in *Redrawing the Boundaries: The Transformation of English and American Literary Studies*, ed. Stephen Greenblatt and Giles Gunn (New York: Modern Language Association, 1992), 12–40.

and Beyond." The essays in part 1 of this volume take the basic relation between Latin and vernacular literary production as their starting point, and from there trace a wide range of forms and conditions of the medieval literary. The first two essays, by Copeland and Wendy Scase, take up most directly the schoolroom definitions and guides of "literature" in order to view from new angles what might be called the contact zone between learned, clerical culture and vernacular English poetry. Treating the most canonical guide in Western culture to ideas of "the literary," Copeland recovers the medieval reception of Horace's *Ars poetica,* pedagogically potent even as it was displaced in many of its roles by Geoffrey of Vinsauf's *Poetria nova.* Scase, going yet further beyond the "classroom" but keeping its intellectual impress clearly in view, explores the grammar-school arts of composition to establish the context for what she argues is a vernacular citational style used heavily by Langland's followers in the *"Piers Plowman* tradition"—in which his text may even have been treated as a work for memorization and other manipulations and interpretations adapted from the schooltext tradition. Scase thus uses rhetorical evidence to posit a remarkable new claim about this poem's authority in some settings.

The other essays in part 1 take up wider horizons of such Latin nurseries of the medieval literary and display a further range of methods, discoveries, and new implications. Traugott Lawler sets forth a detailed range of poetic instances of the contact between Latin and English in an astounding plethora of new discoveries showing Langland's renderings of Latin into English as a central principle of the composition of *Piers Plowman.* The transparency of the Latin materials through the English verse defines a mode of literary writing that speaks to and from a world whose "two cultures" are increasingly visible as continually interactive.

This linguistic interaction is central to other essays in this part of the volume. In an inquiry into the modality of voicing in Middle English, Katherine Zieman uses marginal Latin manuscript annotations to show medieval categories of poetic tropes and modes in Chaucer, especially that of the apostrophe, where the notion of Chaucer's "personal" voicing most fully tests the Latin apparatus. Yet as Zieman shows, the effects of such "personal" voicing remain elusive in modern critical frameworks as well. Extending the question of the resulting modality of such Latin-English translation, Katharine Breen argues that Anima in *Piers Plowman* stands as a kind of learning device cast in "sorry Latin," combining the resources of personification, language instruction, visual schemes of virtues and vices, and wider ethical systems to bring readers to synthesize Latinate and vernacular, secular domains into a literary mode at once stable and moveable, didactic and whimsical, which mixes gender roles as readily as languages and schemes when "practical" purposes demand. This argument offers a way to show how medieval "faculty" psychology and gendered literary motifs could be framed within the terms of basic doctrinal imagery and text, which Breen shows Langland to be exploiting here, in ways that parallel the peculiar visual presentations of the texts in the *Speculum theologiae*. In turn, Ralph Hanna takes up in more formalist terms another standard "didactic" Latin work highly likely to have influenced *Piers Plowman* directly: the *Speculum vitae,* whose reassembling, Hanna shows, constitutes another central key to Langland's intellectually "traditional" but ethically revolutionary reassessments.

The conclusions from such inquiries point toward an important variety of new methods as well as a range of new conclusions, some with rather different implications for further work. Whereas Breen sees the tools of basic Latin and doctrinal pedagogy as means to and instances of vital literary and intellectual production, Hanna argues that Langland approached the *Speculum Vitae* in a way that revived and reanimated an outworn ethical project by questioning its application to direct experience. Both essays show how didacticism served to produce a more surreally vibrant yet intellectually dense modality than at least some modern notions of "the literary" can accommodate. Finally, closing part 1, my essay takes up the relation between Chaucer's *Clerk's Tale* and Petrarch's Latin story of Griselda to ponder the strange pleasures of renunciation visible in both, a topic that Middleton opened over three decades ago.[18] The history of emotion, as Jonathan Culler has observed, offers a particularly promising direction for "literary criticism for the twenty-first century."[19] Here too, however, medieval scholars have provided foundational studies, although those foundations are fragmentary and submerged. Revisiting some of those, and outlining a historical phase of transition in the understanding of "need" and deprivation, I suggest that a late-medieval "aesthetics of renunciation" is key to the idea of the literary and the impetus for aesthetics generally, as those developed differently in Italian and English contexts.

The volume's second part turns to "the literary" outside the Latin sphere, here in the relations between English and other vernaculars, especially Italian and French, as these shaped medieval form and ideas of literary genre and literariness as such. This part, "Literarity in the Vernacular Sphere," returns in a different way to the question Greenblatt asked concerning what literary his-

---

18. Anne Middleton, "The Clerk and His Tale: Some Literary Contexts," *Studies in the Age of Chaucer* 2 (1980): 121–50.

19. Culler, "Introduction: Critical Paradigms," 912, referring to the essay in the same volume by Sianne Ngai, "Our Aesthetic Categories," *PMLA* 125 (October 2010): 948–58.

tory is, and whether its relations to formal or to cultural contexts should take priority. That question has been recently broached anew by Steven Justice,[20] and in his essay here Justice instances that concern again by showing how Chaucer's response to Dante's geographic realism in the *Troilus* allows a teasing rhetoric of uncertainty about the details of "character" and thus about history itself, though still returning to a history that is distinctively literary. In a similar reappraisal, Frank Grady turns to the major "alternative" tradition of alliterative poetry to show how the uneasy combination of "tragedie" and hunting in that poetry is part of a larger collection of strategies for emphasizing how "form" can be imposed on contingent phenomena, a mode of apparent literary transcendence of history that is sustained and helps sustain the social relations of medieval seigneurial culture.

As Middleton has repeatedly stressed, literary form is cultural meaning and power; and other essays in this second section on vernacular literature demonstrate and extend this proposition. Using Gower's French *Mirour de l'Omme*—representative of another key vernacular of medieval England—Maura Nolan shows that the historical and ethical formulations of "necessity" and "contingency," the concepts by means of which Gower routinely represents Fortune, also govern his poetic production in that poem and throughout his oeuvre. Patterson here revisits the question of what "tragedy" is in Chaucer's *Troilus and Criseyde* to argue for its origins in what Patterson shows is the Dantean mode, not the Boethian one, thus refuting the commonest assumption about Chaucer's poem and its genre: it is not tragedy in our sense but what we would call "epic," and therefore is a form of historical narrative whose sense of origins, beginnings, and causes are the central issues. Patterson's tracing of this genealogy opens up from a new perspective Chaucer's unsettling focus on the social world as a wide field of human agenda and choices rather than transcendental causes, and thus provides a key instance of how a particular literary form has defined literary criticism's fascination with the social implications of literature. Like Justice's essay, Patterson's essay shows how Chaucer creates literary history as a richly historical experience and from the inside out, in terms of narrative mode that defines the powers and limits of historical consciousness.

The volume's final essays extend other critical approaches to reassess the medieval literary, often directly based on the kinds of issues and strategies that Middleton established. D. Vance Smith discusses the silences in medieval literature concerning everyday economic life and the work of women,

---

20. Steven Justice, "Literary History," in *Chaucer: Contemporary Approaches*, ed. David Raybin and Susanna Fein (University Park: Pennsylvania State University Press, 2009), 195–210.

in order to show—against a wide range of domestic and grammar school history—that *Piers Plowman* stresses the limits of literary decorum where it breaks into that silence. Smith's essay thus treats in new ways the *limits* of the literary, its boundaries at domestic intimacy; yet he links this back to Dame Study's uneasiness with the violations of the traditional venues of Latin learning that Langland's own poem embodied. Finally, David Lawton extends the concern with "form" into an approach to "voicing" in a major response to and extension of the central theme of Middleton's essay, "The Idea of Poetry in the Reign of Richard II": he shows how complex the nature of voicing is in Middle English poetry, and he folds Chaucer back into this complex field from which Middleton had excluded him. Lawton's essay shows in sum how substantial Middleton's critical innovation was by extending it in many further directions, finding in "voice" the body both of a text and of a reciter (or musician), and using Chaucer's invocations of Ovid's Orpheus as a key to these and other aspects of how voicing both seeks flight from any form and carries bodily and material weight wherever it goes.

Many other categories and subcategories besides the two simple divisions used in this book might be used to chart the medieval literary, and certainly many other critical trajectories beyond Middleton's work are in fact kept in view in this volume. Yet in tandem these basic categories, with her influential and prescient work threading among them, provide a fuller and more varied assessment of "the medieval literary" than has elsewhere appeared so directly. It is hoped that so framed, the topic may become a major resource as much as a problem within and beyond medieval studies: a means of adding to as well as challenging our strategies for literary understanding and appreciation of any kind.

Part I.

The Literary between Latin and Vernacular

one

Horace's *Ars poetica* in the Medieval Classroom and Beyond
The Horizons of Ancient Precept

RITA COPELAND

WHEN DOES a classic of criticism become a classic? When, under what conditions, does it manifest those supposedly abiding characteristics that make it a classic, giving it the heft of a global pronouncement? Perhaps when it has outlived its familiar and daily usefulness.

Modern readers put Horace's *Ars poetica* in a category with Aristotle's *Poetics*, as a text that long served as an authority of evaluative standards, establishing the canon of classicism for humanist and Neoclassical critics (from Scaliger and Sidney to Boileau, Dryden, Pope, and others). Like Aristotle's *Poetics*, the *Ars poetica* became a founding text of a metadiscourse about literature across linguistic traditions, providing a critical standard of literary form and style, decorum, and moral function. It articulated a classical norm of canon-building through imitation and translation. It came to stand as an ancient cornerstone of what we now construct—retrospectively—as the "history" of literary theory. Beginning in the sixteenth century, commentators explicitly harmonized Horatian with Aristotelian doctrine, fusing the precepts of the two works in ways that seem at times wishful, and in so doing elevated Horace's work to a new philosophical status. This development has been much studied by historians of early modern and Neoclassical aesthetics.[1] The *Ars poetica* provided a key classical justification for the notion of poetry as an epistemology.

But as medievalists know, this was not how the *Ars poetica* was read and used during the first seven or eight hundred years of its post-classical history. From late antiquity to the thirteenth century, the *Ars poetica* was treated as a pragmatic classroom text, a source of practical information for students learning how to compose their own grammatical exercises, a fixture of the grammar curriculum. Simply put, it was a composition and style guide. It was also profoundly identified with Latinity in the most elementary sense of that term: it was used in contexts where the learning of Latin involved both acquiring a new language and acquiring the very skills of literacy, that is, where to become literate was to leave one's native language behind and take up Latin letters. Here, the *Ars poetica* served as a first passage into the mechanics of composition, an introductory textbook.

What was the event, or change of conditions, that transformed the status of the *Ars poetica* from quotidian school text and humble composition art to global theoretical authority? The unexamined response would be recourse to periodization paradigms: the humanists of the sixteenth century saw something in the *Ars poetica* that the Middle Ages had failed to see, and integrated it in a classical (or classicized) framework. This is not inaccurate, but neither is it the whole story; and I think the more interesting turn of the story is what happened to the *Ars poetica* in the Middle Ages to render it newly visible to scholars of later periods. Under what circumstances was the *Ars poetica* allowed to grow up?

One productive avenue to approach this question is translation of the *Ars poetica* into European vernaculars. The first translations are surprisingly late: the earliest was the Italian translation by Lodovico Dolce in 1535, followed by Jacques Pelletier du Mans' French translation in 1545, and Thomas Drant's English translation in 1567. This is especially curious given that some of its central doctrine concerns interlingual translation or imitation: indeed, along with Cicero's *De optimo genere oratorum*, the *Ars poetica* is a

---

1. R. Stillers, *Humanistische Deutung: Studien zu Kommentar und Literaturtheorie in der italienischen Renaissance* (Düsseldorf: Droste, 1988), 107–24; Daniel Javitch, "The Assimilation of Aristotle's *Poetics* in Sixteenth-Century Italy," in *The Cambridge History of Literary Criticism, vol. 3, The Renaissance*, ed. Glyn P. Norton (Cambridge: Cambridge University Press, 1999), 53–65; Glenn Most, "Classical Scholarship and Literary Criticism," in *The Cambridge History of Literary Criticism, vol. 4, The Eighteenth Century*, ed. H. B. Nisbet and Claude Rawson (Cambridge: Cambridge University Press, 1997), 742–57. The essays in Charles Martindale and David Hopkins, eds., *Horace Made New: Horatian Influences on British Writing from the Renaissance to the Twentieth Century* (Cambridge: Cambridge University Press, 1993), provide useful perspectives on reception, although not specific to histories of aesthetics and ideas.

founding text in the history of translation theory, quoted and memorialized by Jerome and Boethius.[2] Medieval commentators on the text were perfectly aware that there was a theory of translation embedded in Horace's advice about imitation, and duly record their understandings of these principles.[3] But if medieval *translators* from Latin into vernaculars, or between two vernaculars, consciously deployed the Horatian precept to avoid rendering *verbum verbo* like a *fidus interpres*, they saw no apparent use in translating the actual source of that precept; and this in an era that saw many translations of useful academic and scientific works—Ciceronian rhetorics in Italian, Spanish, and French, Aristotle's political, ethical, and scientific writings in French, translations of encyclopedias, even vernacular translations of the basic Latin grammar (the *Ars minor*) of Donatus.[4]

This is evidence that the *Ars poetica* in the Middle Ages was almost exclusively associated with Latinity, and despite its celebrated teaching about translation, its application did not extend beyond an all-Latin context. The late appearance of the first translations suggests that only when it was no longer necessary to this specific but ubiquitous Latinate function was it intellectually "available" to be translated into various vernaculars. In these vernacular milieus, its orientation was diffused and generalized. The French and English translations were affiliated with, or even gave rise to, the formation of vernacular literary circles—Pelletier du Mans' translation with the Pléiade group in France and Drant's with Sidney's Pembroke circle in England.[5] The fusion of Aristotelian and Horatian principles by humanist commentators began early in the sixteenth century and then progressed alongside the vari-

---

2. Jerome, *De optimo genere interpretandi* (*Ep.* 57), ed. G. J. M. Bartelink (Leiden: Brill, 1980); Boethius, *In Isagogen Porphyrii*, ed. Samuel Brandt, CSEL 48 (Vienna: Tempsky, 1906), 135; W. Schwarz, "The Meaning of *fidus interpres* in Medieval Translation," *Journal of Theological Studies* 45 (1944): 73–78.

3. See the texts edited in Margareta Fredborg, "*Difficile est proprie communia dicere* (Horats, A.P. 128): Horatsfortolkningens bidrag til middelalderens poetik," *Museum Tusculanum* 40–43 (1980): 583–97.

4. Virginia Cox, "Ciceronian Rhetoric in Late Medieval Italy," in *The Rhetoric of Cicero in Its Medieval and Renaissance Commentary Tradition*, ed. Virginia Cox and John O. Ward (Leiden: Brill, 2006), 109–43; Leopold Delisle, "Notice sur la Rhétorique de Cicéron, traduite par Maitre Jean d'Antioche, MS 590 du Musée Condé," *Notices et extraits des manuscrits de la Bibliothèque Nationale* 36 (1899): 207–65; Jacques Monfrin, "Humanisme et traductions au Moyen Âge," *Journal des savants* 148 (1963): 161–90; Brian Merrilees, "Teaching Latin in French: Adaptations of Donatus' *Ars minor*," *Fifteenth-Century Studies* 12 (1987): 87–98. For further examples of learned translation, readers may consult Roger Ellis, ed., *The Oxford History of Literary Translation in English*, vol. 1: *To 1550* (Oxford: Oxford University Press, 2008).

5. The best general account of this is still Elizabeth Jelliffe MacIntire, "French Influence on the Beginnings of English Classicism," *PMLA* 26 (1911): 496–527; see especially 508–10.

ous translation movements; clearly the heightened theoretical interest in the *Ars poetica* helped to extend its influence into vernacular circles.[6]

But herein lies a great historical paradox: the classicism with which the Renaissance newly invested the *Ars poetica* helped to propel it out of its classical form (Latin) into various vernaculars, where it assumed the mantle of classical metatext about the power of poetry. Once translated, it achieved the status of metadiscourse precisely because, as a classical authority, it could be "de-classicized" and stand for the ambitions of all vernacular poetics. The best example of this is the use that Joachim du Bellay made of it in his *Deffence et illustration de la langue françoyse*, written in 1549 (four years after Pelletier du Mans' French translation of Horace), which directs French poets to build their literary language on strong imitation of classical forms, just as Horace advised Romans poets to forge their canon by appropriating Greek models.

The roots of these important changes go back to the Middle Ages. Here I would like to look closely at some medieval approaches to the *Ars poetica* and consider the use that was made of its teachings on composition and style, as well as on imitation and translation. The medieval tradition of the *Ars poetica* has been a rather specialist enterprise: it must be tracked through glosses and commentaries, some of which have been known through modern editions since the late nineteenth century, while others have come into focus through more recent scholarship.[7] The Middle Ages enshrined the *Ars poetica* in the grammar-school curriculum, along with Horace's *Satires*, *Odes*, and other *Epistles*; it also survived as a curricular fixture of Latin learning well into the sixteenth century. When we look at the character of medieval commentary on the *Ars poetica*, we can see the horizons of its usefulness, the scope but also limitations of those horizons, and begin to understand how it took on a different function for later audiences.

The Horace that medieval readers encountered was not terribly different from the Horace that presented itself to the early humanist scholars. The whole textual corpus was often copied with scholia inherited from late antiquity (comprised of glosses from as early as the fifth century). This more-or-less coherent collection of glosses is now called the Pseudo-Acronian scholia, because humanist scholars attributed it to the second-century commentator

---

6. The key work on the importation of Aristotelian thought into Horace's *Ars poetica* and vice versa is Marvin T. Herrick, *The Fusion of Horatian and Aristotelian Literary Criticism, 1531–1555*, Illinois Studies in Language and Literature 32 (Urbana: University of Illinois Press, 1946).

7. Scevola Mariotti, ed., *Orazio: Enciclopedia oraziana*, 3 vols. (Rome: Istituto della Enciclopedia Italiana, 1996–98), especially vol. 3 on the receptions of Horace; for an overview see also Karsten Friis-Jensen, "Horace and the Early Writers of Arts of Poetry," in *Sprachtheorien in Spätantike und Mittelalter*, ed. Sten Ebbesen (Tübingen: Gunter Narr Verlag, 1995), 360–401.

Acron (whose glosses may or may not be represented in the existing corpus). Another group of glosses was associated with the third-century commentator Porphyrion, and although we no longer have these in their original form, they were incorporated into other groups of glosses, including the Pseudo-Acronian matter.[8] The earliest humanist commentators made use of these glosses in their treatments of the *Ars poetica*, but what they took from them was apparently quite different from what the medieval readers and teachers found in them. In particular, the tradition of the Porphyrion glosses was oriented to younger students, and focused on grammar and style. But much the same could be said of the Pseudo-Acronian scholia. The glosses tend to paraphrase the text and give synonyms for words used in an unusual sense or form. It is not surprising that these scholia were copied in so many medieval manuscripts of Horace, for they are relatively simple and explanatory in their purpose. It is interesting, therefore, that the humanist commentators used the same glosses to launch what were altogether more philosophical approaches to the *Ars poetica*, that is, incorporating those glosses into their new editions and explanations. Various other groups of medieval glosses, including a group of Carolingian glosses known as the *Scholia Vindobonensia* (the Vienna Glosses), and groups of glosses extending from the sixth century to the ninth century, developed along the lines of the Porphyrion glosses, and expanded their teachings on certain points in response to increasingly complex demands of pedagogical interpretation.[9]

To understand the kind of use that Horace's *Ars poetica* served in the medieval classroom, we can turn to one of the most developed glosses, less a gloss than a full-fledged commentary, from the middle of the twelfth century. The modern editor of this commentary, Karsten Friis-Jensen, named it the "Materia" commentary, after its opening word.[10] The "Materia" commentary is important to our understanding of the role that the *Ars poetica* performed in medieval classrooms, and how teachers adapted it to suit new

---

8. Otto Keller, ed., *Pseudacronis scholia in Horatium vetustiora*, 2 vols. (Leipzig: Teubner, 1902–4).

9. J. Zechmeister, ed., *Scholia Vindobonensia ad Horatii artem poeticam* (Vienna: C. Geroldum, 1877); H. J. Botschuyver, ed., *Scholia in Horatium codicum parisinorum latinorum 7972, 7974, 7971* (Amsterdam: Bottenburg, 1935); Botschuyver, ed., *Scholia in Horatium codicum parisinorum latinorum 10310 et 7973* (Amsterdam: Bottenburg, 1939); Botschuyver, ed., *Scholia in Horatium in codicibus parisinis latinis 17897 et 8223* (Amsterdam: Bottenburg, 1942). On these see Karsten Friis-Jensen, "Medieval Commentaries on Horace," in *Medieval and Renaissance Scholarship*, ed. Nicholas Mann and Birger Munk Olsen (Leiden: Brill, 1997), 51–73; and Suzanne Reynolds, *Medieval Reading: Grammar, Rhetoric, and the Classical Text* (Cambridge: Cambridge University Press, 1996), 13 and notes.

10. Karsten Friis-Jensen, ed., "The *Ars Poetica* in Twelfth-Century France: The Horace of Matthew of Vendôme, Geoffrey of Vinsauf, and John of Garland," *Cahiers de l'Institut du Moyen Âge grec et latin* 60 (1990): 319–88.

demands. Medieval grammar students were taught how to compose by imitating the examples from classical poetry, which they also expounded for grammatical usage. The *Ars poetica* served to reinforce these exercises, with its teaching on decorum, the faults of style, coherence of narrative, poetic license, and imitation of traditional materials. The "Materia" commentary exemplifies how medieval teachers went beyond the late antique glosses to link Horace's precepts to the compositional needs of their students. Its most distinctive feature is its opening, which develops Horace's advice about stylistic decorum and the corresponding faults of style into a simple, prescriptive list of six faults to avoid in composing poems. The teacher has rationalized and ordered Horace's advice in the opening thirty-seven lines into a coherent and virtually stand-alone doctrine (and indeed, this introduction on the six faults and their corresponding virtues also circulated independently of the whole commentary).[11]

> The material [*materia*] of the author in this work is the art of poetry. His intention is to give precepts concerning the art of poetry. The cause of this intention is twofold: one is general and one is specific. The general cause is that he might instruct any erring poets in the art of poetry. The particular cause, that is, the personal purpose, is so that he might instruct the Pisones, at whose request he undertook this work. . . . The precepts are given in two ways, first in showing which faults are to be avoided, and second which virtues are to be sought out. Thus he first teaches what is to be avoided, and with the errors of style purged, he then adds the rules and precepts of the art of poetry. For as he says in his Epistles, "Unless the vessel is clean, whatever you pour in turns sour."[12]
>
> There are six faults to be avoided in poetic composition; not that there are not others, but these are the chief ones.
>
> The first of these is the incongruous placing of the parts [*partium incongrua positio*]. The parts of a work are the beginning, the middle, and the end. Parts are placed incongruously when the beginning is discordant with the middle, and the middle is discordant with the end. Horace censures this by likening it to a picture, where he says: "If a painter chose to join a human head to the neck of a horse" (*AP* 1–2). For congruent placing

---

11. Translation in Rita Copeland and Ineke Sluiter, eds., *Medieval Grammar and Rhetoric: Language Arts and Literary Theory, A.D. 300–1475* (Oxford: Oxford University Press, 2009), 554–56, based on the Latin text in Friis-Jensen, "The Ars Poetica in Twelfth-Century France," 336–38. Translations from the *Ars poetica* are based on *Satires, Epistles, and Ars poetica*, trans. H. R. Fairclough, Loeb Classical Library (Cambridge, MA: Harvard University Press; London: Heinemann, 1926; repr., 1978).

12. *Epistles* 1.2.54.

of the parts is when the beginning accords with the middle, and the middle accords with the end.

The second fault is incongruent digression [*incongrua orationis digressio*]. One digresses by abandoning the course of one's speech for something else which does not pertain to the matter. Horace condemns this fault where he says: "Works with noble beginning and grand promises often have one or two purple patches so stitched on as to glitter far and wide" (*AP* 14–15). However, there can also be a congruent digression, when one strays from the theme for a useful purpose, digressing to another topic to the advantage of the argument. This was the method that Cicero followed in the *Verrines*. . . . This is also what Virgil does at the beginning of the *Aeneid*. . . . You will be able to recognize this method as a whole in the digressions of other authors.

The third fault is obscure brevity [*brevitas obscura*], which happens when one wants to speak concisely, but does not make clear the things that he ought to say. Horace criticizes this where he says "Striving to be brief, I become obscure" (*AP* 25–26). But there is also an appropriate form of brevity that explains clearly and does not produce obscurity.

The fourth fault is incongruous variation in style. There are three manners of speaking, which some call styles, others call types [*figurae*], and others call characters: the simple or low style, the middle style, and the grand style [*humilis stilus, mediocris et altus*]. The low style is when someone uses simple or humble words about people of low station, as in comedy. The middle style is when we treat people of middle status in words of a middle type, as in satire. The grand style is when we treat people of high status in grand words, as in tragedy. But each of these styles has its own corresponding fault which is very close to it. The middle style has the fault of drifting and of being loose [*fluctuans et dissolutum*]. . . . Horace criticizes this where he says: "Aiming at smoothness, I fail in force and fire" (*AP* 26–27). The high style has the fault of being turgid or inflated [*turgidum et inflatum*]. . . . Horace censures this when he says "promising grandeur, it is (in fact) bombastic" (*AP* 27). The simple style has the fault of being arid and bloodless [*aridum et exsangue*]. . . . Horace criticizes this where he says that one who is "overcautious and fearful of the gale, creeps along the ground" (*AP* 28). Here, however, we can point to no corresponding virtue, as we did for the other faults.

The fifth fault is the incongruous variation of material [*incongrua materie variatio*], which happens when one's subject matter is left aside and something else is introduced, but is found clashing, either by clumsy variation or by a discordant mode of exposition. Horace criticizes this where he talks about the one "who tries to vary a single subject in monstrous fashion" (*AP* 29). There is an acceptable form of varying the material, when a subject matter is left aside in favor of something else which embellishes it and which avoids clashes, as we see in Virgil, when he leaves aside his subject matter and invents the story of how Aeneas came to Dido. . . . And it is only appropriate to poets to vary their material, since they intersperse history with fiction. Whence they are called poets, that is, makers. For "*poire*"[13] means "to make." And this is the difference between variation of material and digression of speech: to vary the material is appropriate to poets only, but to digress from the speech is appropriate both to poets and historians.

The sixth fault is an incongruous incompleteness of the work [*incongrua operis imperfectio*], which happens when someone begins to write, but either from ignorance or negligence does not bring what was started to a close. Horace criticizes this by an extended comparison with a bronze-founder, where he says, "Near the Aemilian School . . . there is a craftsman who in bronze will mold nails and imitate waving locks, but is unhappy in the total result, because he cannot represent a whole figure" (*AP* 32–37) . . .

The utility of this work is the science of poetic composition, that is, making good verses. The title is "Here begins the book of Poetics of Horace," or "Here begins Horace's book on the Art of Poetry," which means the same thing. The meaning is: "Here begin the precepts on the Art of Poetry." For *poio, pois*[14] is "I make, you make." Whence *poesis* or *poetria*, i.e. a creation [*fictio*] or anything made [*figmentum*], and the poet is one who makes [*fictor*].

With these preliminary matters concluded, let us move to the literal exposition.

The "Materia" commentary gives the doctrine of poetic unity and self-consistency another kind of classroom cast: it reinterprets Horace's precepts in light of the teaching of the *Rhetorica ad Herennium* (4.8.11) about levels of style. In the *Ad Herennium*, the doctrine of the low, middle, and high styles represents distinctions among verbal styles. But among medieval commentators there was a growing tendency, marked from the mid-twelfth century onwards, to associate the three styles with levels of subject matter and social status (characters of low, middle, or exalted position).[15] In the "Mate-

---

13. A corruption of Greek *poiein*.
14. That is, Greek *poiô, poieis*.
15. See Friis-Jensen, "Horace and the Early Writers of Arts of Poetry," 375–78; and for background on the distinction between verbal and material (or social) conceptions of levels of style, see

ria" commentary, the treatment of "incongruous variation of style" is a mixture of Horatian criticism, prescriptive rhetoric, and a newer identification of stylistic register with social estates.

We know that this treatment of decorum and style was meant to reach a student audience, because its own reception history clearly links it to later pedagogical texts. Friis-Jensen's studies have shown the direct impact of the "Materia" commentary on the pedagogical genre that emerged around the turn of the twelfth century, the Latin *ars poetriae* or art of poetry. These were works aimed at students learning Latin and developing their compositional skills by imitating classical models. The importance of the "Materia" commentary for these medieval pedagogical arts is that its Horatian doctrine seems to have passed directly to some of them, notably the *Ars versificatoria* of Matthew of Vendôme (before 1175), Geoffrey of Vinsauf's *Documentum de modo et arte dictandi et versificandi* (ca.1199), and the *Parisiana poetria* by John of Garland (ca. 1230). These texts take over the simplified system of the six faults of style, showing how Horace's teaching could be reduced to an accessible, iterable, and thus highly practical scheme aimed at students at an intermediate level (as well as any level of student needing instruction in Latin composition).[16]

Horace's famous advice on imitation of traditional materials presented interesting difficulties to the earliest scholiasts. The lines in question are these:

> Aut famam sequere aut sibi convenientia finge. . . .
> Difficile est proprie communia dicere; tuque
> rectius Iliacum carmen deducis in actus,
> quam si proferres ignota indictaque primus.
> publica materies privati iuris erit, si
> non circa vilem patulumque moraberis orbem,
> nec verbo verbum curabis reddere fidus
> interpres, nec desilies imitator in artum,
> unde pedem proferre pudor vetet aut operis lex. . . . (119, 128–35)

Franz Quadlbauer, *Die antike Theorie der genera dicendi im lateinischen Mittelalter* (Vienna: Hermann Böhlaus, 1962), 34–39; and Douglas Kelly, *The Arts of Poetry and Prose*, Typologie des Sources du Moyen Âge Occidental, fasc. 59 (Turnhout: Brepols, 1991), 71–78. Edmond Faral finds the earliest move toward a material application of style in a Horace commentary that predates the eleventh century: see *Les arts poétiques du XIIe et du XIIIe siècle* (Paris: Champion, 1924), 86–88.

16. See the studies by Friis-Jensen, "The *Ars Poetica* in Twelfth-Century France" and "Horace and the Early Writers of Arts of Poetry."

Either follow traditional materials [*fama*] or make up [*finge*] something that is self-consistent. . . . It it hard to treat *proprie* [*"as your own"* or *"appropriately"*] those things that are *communia* [= either *"commonplace,"* i.e. *what has already been treated by others, or "communal," untreated or unclaimed material*].[17] You are doing better stretching into acts a song of Troy than if, for the first time, you were presenting something unknown and unheard. Public ground [*publica materies*] will be private property if you do not linger along the broad and open pathway, if you do not attempt to render word for word as a *fidus interpres* [= *"faithful translator"* or *"faithful interpretor/expositor"*], and if, as imitator, you do not leap into the narrow bind out of which either shame or the rule of craft will prevent you from stepping forth.[18]

The direction that this advice takes depends on how the term *communia* is read, and the tale of possible explanations for this contested passage is a long one. Charles Brink, whose annotation of the *Ars poetica* is a comprehensive resource on the text and its scholia tradition, assumes that the intended meaning of *communia* is "new" or "untried subjects," or by extension, "generalities," and that the advice should be taken to mean that it is hard and thus disadvantageous to attempt new or general subjects; one should rather follow traditional materials and make them one's own.[19] But unlike Brink, I am more interested in the way that this was received than in interpreting it correctly according to Horace's intention. The scholia of Porphyrion and the Pseudo-Acron interpreted *communia* in two ways: as "untried subjects," in which case it is better to appropriate well-known stories; or in exactly the opposite way, as "communal" or "familiar subjects," which the poet should appropriate as his own in spite of the difficulty that attends this enterprise. So either way, *communia* represent difficulty, because they are untold and untried, or because they are well worn.

The "Materia" commentary casts a wide net in its interpretation of this passage. It accommodates both positions inherited from the scholia tradition, and ultimately comes down in favor of imitating traditional material:

> Now "it is difficult to treat in a way that is *proprie*" subjects that have not been heard; which means "it is difficult to treat in a way that is *proprie*,"

---

17. See the discussion of this point below.
18. Latin text and translation (with minor alterations) from Fairclough, ed. and trans., *Satires, Epistles, and Ars poetica*.
19. C. O. Brink, *Horace on Poetry*, vol. 2: *The "Ars poetica"* (Cambridge: Cambridge University Press, 1963–82), 204–7.

that is, suitably [*competenter*], "things which are *communia*," that is, subjects that have not been heard. He says *communia*, because these subjects [i.e. untried themes] are available for development to everyone in common. "You are doing better." However difficult and thus praiseworthy it may be, it is nevertheless more praiseworthy to follow tradition. And this is the meaning of "You are doing better" etc. Or, this whole passage concerning the treatment of traditional material may be read in the following way. "It is difficult" etc., as if he'd said, "I talked about using traditional material or making up something self-consistent; however, it is more praiseworthy to use traditional and "common" material [*famam sequi et communia*], that is, matter that is familiar [*trita*] to all, and to "treat it suitably [*proprie*]": for this is difficult. . . And because it is difficult, it is praiseworthy.[20]

Where Horace seems to advise using traditional material because the alternative, making up something new, is fraught with danger, the medieval commentary makes a positive virtue out of imitation, because—on its reading—it is more challenging and rewarding to treat familiar material in a suitable or "proper" way. The medieval commentary seems to direct its advice to those who will be doing most of their work imitating established and familiar models, that is, intermediate students who will be producing their own compositions from assigned models and discovering their subjects in matter familiar from poetic tradition.

The commentary treats the next lines, "nec verbo verbum curabis reddere fidus interpres," in quite an uncontroversial way. It recognizes that this passage is about interlingual translation, and about the difficulties that might arise when seeking verbal equivalence:

> perhaps he would come upon some word that cannot be expressed adequately in both languages; and thus he ought not render word for word . . . it is as if he said that you should seek to translate the sense, not the words. One will be a *fidus interpres* if one should attempt to account for every word.[21]

However, we can learn a great deal by looking at how readers of the "Materia" commentary in turn interpreted the Horatian advice about the *fidus interpres*. Matthew of Vendôme's *Ars versificatoria*, written before 1175, is

---

20. My translation from the Latin text in Friis-Jensen, "The *Ars Poetica* in Twelfth-Century France," 353.
21. My translation from the Latin text in Friis-Jensen, "The *Ars Poetica* in Twelfth-Century France," 354.

clearly dependent on the "Materia" commentary, as Friis-Jensen has shown, and also finds its own way to the Horatian text. Matthew takes Horace's warning against the *fidus interpres* in a way that patently links its value to the schoolroom:

> We turn now to the treatment of material, in which certain ill-trained people habitually overstep the line and shamefully depart from preceptive guidlines. When paraphrasing poetic fables in school exercises, they render word for word, down to every figure of speech, as if they sought to produce a metrical commentary on the authors . . . One should not try to render word for word like a *fidus interpres*.[22]

Clearly Matthew understands the *fidus interpres* as "slavish expositor," not a translator. More importantly, he applies Horace's advice to the context where it seems Horace was most valued: the school exercises in poetic composition, the paraphrasing and imitating that had been the staple of the grammar classroom since Quintilian's day. For Matthew of Vendôme, Horace's precepts on literary imitation find their audience, not among enterprising poets, but among students struggling to master composition in a language not their own, in a setting where the acquisition of literacy means immersion in a foreign language. Horace's dictates serve to reinforce a grammar lesson and encourage students to demonstrate some ingenuity in their performance of routine compositional exercises.

Thus we have a picture of the role of the *Ars poetica* in the medieval classroom. But from the streamlining of Horace's teaching on style that we find in the "Materia" commentary, we can also see something of the pedagogical limitations or deficiencies of the *Ars poetica* for medieval teaching by the middle of the twelfth century. The teachers had to rationalize and systematize the rather diffuse teaching of the *Ars poetica*. The *Ars poetica* is elusive in its advice, it speaks to fellow poets rather than to students, and of course it assumes the nativeness of Latin as well as the Greek-Latin bilingualism of the Roman cultural outlook. It is arguably a work about the norms of judgment and taste, evaluating the Roman assimilation of the Greek literary canon. But for all of its sophisticated insight, the *Ars poetica* was becoming inadequate to fulfill the pedagogical purposes that it had served for many centuries. Grammar teachers were developing new ways of approaching the changing needs of their students, and looking for a more structured and consolidated approach to Latin composition, an approach that could go hand in

---

22. *Ars versificatoria*, ed. Faral, *Les arts poétiques du XII et du XIII siècle*, 180 (my translation).

hand with the teaching of Latin as a foreign language. This need was quickly filled by that highly successful pedagogical genre, the *ars poetriae,* those independent prescriptive treatises that adapted older teachings to new purposes, giving students clear and straightforward advice about how to compose. The core of this new genre can be seen in the opening of the "Materia" commentary, with its summary of six faults of style and their corresponding virtues: from that core the new genre of the *ars poetriae* spun out like an industry.

The most successful of the *artes poetriae* was Geoffrey of Vinsauf's versified treatise, the *Poetria nova,* written over the first decade of the thirteenth century. This treatise had a vast circulation throughout the later Middle Ages and well into the early modern period: it survives in more than two hundred manuscripts, and was used in nearly every corner of Western and Central Europe. It is, indeed, still the most anthologized of the medieval arts of poetry (there are three different modern English translations of it). So successful was it as a classroom text that it soon acquired its own commentary and gloss tradition. As the work of Marjorie Curry Woods demonstrates, the *Poetria nova* penetrated into every level of teaching and every kind of outlook: from elementary to advanced, from the late medieval cloister even to the humanist studium.[23] The title *Poetria nova,* which apparently was not Geoffrey's working title, was conferred on the text during the generations that followed Geoffrey's composition, pointing to its growing reception as a new "rival" to Horace's "old" poetics.[24]

This has important implications for the fortunes of the *Ars poetica.* The medieval arts of poetry, and especially Geoffrey of Vinsauf's *Poetria nova,* assumed many of the functions that Horace's text had played in medieval schools. Indeed, one way in which the *Poetria nova* took the genre of the *ars poetriae* forward was to move away from strict dependence on the text of Horace's *Ars poetica*. Where the earliest of the *artes poetriae,* Matthew of Vendôme's *Ars versificatoria* and Geoffrey's own *Documentum de modo et arte dictandi et versificandi*, gave much space to citation of Horace's *Ars* (and in the case of Geoffrey's *Documentum* made an explicit claim to covering the same matter as Horace[25]), the *Poetria nova* substitutes its own newly synthetic teaching, a combination of Horatian doctrine and the more ambitious precept of the *Rhetorica ad Herennium*. In what Martin Camargo has

---

23. Marjorie Curry Woods, *Classroom Commentaries: Teaching the "Poetria Nova" across Medieval and Renaissance Europe* (Columbus: The Ohio State University Press, 2009).

24. Martin Camargo, "From *Liber versuum* to *Poetria nova*: The Evolution of Geoffrey of Vinsauf's Masterpiece," *Journal of Medieval Latin* 21 (2011): 1-16. I am grateful to Professor Camargo for allowing me to read his article before its publication. See also Woods, *Classroom Commentaries*, 14 n. 62, 34, 99.

25. *Documentum de modo et arte dictandi et versificandi* 2.3.162, ed. Faral, *Les arts poétiques*, 317.

described as the "evolution" of the *Poetria nova* over the course of Geoffrey of Vinsauf's career as a grammar master, the poem came into being as a new kind of product, the sum of Geoffrey's experience not only in the classroom but as a composer of illustrative verse set pieces, which he substituted for the classical examples that he used in his earlier treatise.[26] In this way, then, the *Poetria nova* could present, not just a new extension of Horatian teaching, but a revisionist alternative to the ancient *Ars*.

The *Poetria nova* fulfilled many of the teaching aims of the *Ars poetica*, but in a way that was more systematic and user-friendly, and in a way that specifically addressed what students needed to know.[27] It gives substantial attention to the structure of a composition, and its advice about how to develop a narrative is geared to the classroom situation of working from a model text or a familiar subject: this is the purpose of its famous teaching about amplifying and abbreviating a theme. It also has a clear section on stylistic embellishment (*elocutio*), giving all the figures of speech, figures of thought, and tropes along with explanations of them and examples from classical poets.

Horace's *Ars poetica* certainly did not lapse into any kind of obscurity with the ascendancy of Geoffrey's *Poetria nova*. The *Ars poetica* continued to be copied, possibly as many times during the fourteenth and fifteenth centuries as up to 1300.[28] Sometimes the *Ars poetica* is found in the very manuscripts that contain the *Poetria nova*.[29] Clearly it continued to be read and valued, for its own sake as a classical text and for the authority that it lent to the modern works that were more immediately suited to day to day teaching in medieval schools. Woods comments that the appearance of the *Ars poetica* in manuscripts with Geoffrey's treatise suggests that the *Poetria nova* did not replace Horace's *Ars* but complemented it. I believe that such complementarity was surely the intention of the medieval copyists and schoolmasters. But the long historical impact of the new *artes poetriae* transformed the role and position of Horace's *Ars poetica*.

One index of the practical usefulness of the *Ars poetica* is its penetration into literary culture. We can judge this in large part by the extent to which it is cited. It is cited in the places where one would expect to find it, in other academic and pedagogical writings: surveys of canonical authors (e.g.,

---

26. Camargo, "From *Liber versuum* to *Poetria nova*."
27. See Woods, *Classroom Commentaries*, 12–14, 128.
28. "Nobody has seen all the manuscripts of H[orace]." Brink, *Horace on Poetry,* 2:1. Hilda Buttenwieser tabulated close to 300 Horace manuscripts, of which she says 250 were copied before 1300, and hypothesized many more after that date: "Popular Authors of the Middle Ages: The Testimony of the Manuscripts," *Speculum* 17 (1942): 54.
29. Woods, *Classroom Commentaries*, 14.

Conrad of Hirsau's *Dialogus super auctores*, from the middle of the twelfth century; Hugh of Trimberg's *Registrum multorum auctorum* from the later thirteenth century), academic commentaries on classical authors (e.g., Bernardus Silvestris' commentary on Virgil, with frequent citations), and even Dante's *De vulgari eloquentia*. It is also routinely invoked in Latin literary productions, along with Horace's other poems. If its impact on teaching was a continuing one, however, it might be expected to have left an imprint in the emergent vernacular literary cultures. But vernacular authors seem to be silent about the *Ars poetica*. Here Dante may be the exception that proves the rule. He cites the *Ars poetica* several times in the *Commedia*: for example, in *Inferno* 32, he invokes the reference to Amphion building the city of Thebes through poetic song (*AP* 391-401), and in *Paradiso* 26, in Adam's discourse about the origin of languages, he alludes to Horace's comments on linguistic change (*AP* 58-72). But these are literary rather than pedagogical allusions.

By contrast, Geoffrey of Vinsauf's *Poetria nova* makes some eruptive appearances in Chaucer, where Chaucer is playing with the very idea of a teaching text which offers rules that can be either observed or comically violated. The example of the former is the well-known passage in *Troilus and Criseyde*, where the narrator gives a word-for-word Englishing of Geoffrey of Vinsauf's advice about invention in order to describe Pandarus' mental preparations for the plot that he is constructing to bring the lovers together (lines 1065-71); the example of the latter, violation of principles, could be said to be the entire *Nun's Priest's Tale*, which is a willful, egregious transgression of all the rules of decorum that the *Poetria nova* distilled from Horace, and which also cites Geoffrey of Vinsauf's lament for Richard the I as a model of the device of apostrophe (VII 3347–54). In both these contexts, Chaucer is invoking a study template that teaches craft knowledge rather than any "philosophy" of art, and it is signficant that the work he invokes is the *Poetria nova*.[30] What this could suggest is that, by the mid to late fourteenth century,

---

30. In two important and related articles, Martin Camargo reevaluates the evidence about the *artes poetriae* in England from the late thirteenth to the late fourteenth century. Manuscript evidence suggests that the *Poetria nova* itself was not in common use as a textbook in the curricula of the schools. Camargo argues that it only returned to widespread use in the later fourteenth century under the influence of the Oxford Benedictines and their dictaminal teaching. Chaucer's direct knowledge of the *Poetria nova* would be part of this "renaissance" of rhetoric at the end of the century. As Camargo stresses, his analysis concerns England only, not the Continent, where (as indicated by manuscript copying throughout the century) the *Poetria nova* and other *artes poetriae* maintained a continuous presence. His findings do not imply that the *artes poetriae* exerted no influence in England during this period; rather, the preservation pattern of the manuscripts indicates that their immediate presence as textbooks during these years is doubtful, although the teaching they contain would have been encountered in other derivative forms. See Camargo, "Chaucer and the Oxford Renaissance of Anglo-Latin Rhetoric," *Studies in the Age of Chaucer* 34 (2012): 173–207, and "The Late Fourteenth-Century Renaissance of Anglo-Latin Rhetoric," *Philosophy and Rhetoric* 45.2 (2012): 107–33.

the *Poetria nova* (and the other kinds of teaching to which it gave rise) were coming to displace the *Ars poetica* itself as quotidian guides to the craft of composition. It does not suggest that Chaucer and others did not know the *Ars poetica*, but rather that they did not think of it in the category of standard preceptive manual. This role was gradually being assumed by the *artes poetriae*, and especially the *Poetria nova*.

One further indication that the *Poetria nova* and other *artes poetriae* assumed the role of the *Ars poetica* as a fixture of instruction in an exclusively Latin classroom context is that they were never translated (until modern times), not even in the late Middle Ages, when many kinds of learned works, both classical and medieval, were vernacularized. This does not mean that the *Poetria nova* had no influence on vernacular writers: whatever was learned from it in the Latin grammar schools would certainly have filtered into the project of vernacular writing, and as Chaucer shows, the *Poetria nova* could be invoked comically as an authoritative textbook. But as was the case earlier with the *Ars poetica*, so with the *Poetria nova* throughout its classroom career, the profound identification with a Latin grammar curriculum seems to have pre-empted translating it, as if this would be supererogatory.

Horace's *Ars poetica* was gradually superseded as a pragmatic teaching text by the altogether more useful *Poetria nova*. And here, I believe, lies an important reason for the new visibility that the *Ars poetica* began to receive. In effect, the late medieval industry of the *artes poetriae*, which modern readers find so uncongenial and reductive, liberated Horace's art from its identification with classroom teaching, and made it visible as a different kind of text, a poet's poem and a standard of literary judgment.

By the late fifteenth century, the humanist scholar Cristoforo Landino had set the stage for elevating the themes of the *Ars poetica* to a moral and philosophical status, drawing on the recent enlargement of the Ciceronian corpus to claim that the poet, like the orator, must be learned in all the arts.[31] But by the middle of the sixteenth century, commentators had further enlarged their dossiers to recruit Aristotelian thought to the understanding of Horace's precepts. The *Ars poetica* became a field of philosophical reflection informed by newly assimilated Greek thought. One notable example of this is the association of the Horatian notion of decorum or suitability (as in Horace's term *convenientia*) with the Aristotelian notion of verisimilitude, that is, the necessary and the probable in the structure of events or in the representation of character (*Poetics* 1454a 33–34). Read and reinforced in

---

31. Cristoforo Landino, *In Q. Horatium Flaccum commentaria*, in *Opera Q. Horatii Flacci Venusini, grammaticorum antiquiss. Heleni Acronis, et Porphirionis commentariis illustrata* (Basel: Heinrich Petri, 1555), 928. See Herrick, *Horatian and Aristotelian Literary Criticism*, 32.

this way through Aristotle, decorum became a principle not just of stylistic appropriateness but of an ethical and aesthetic sensibility.[32] Thus Thomas Drant's English translation of 1567 can render *convenientia* as "truthlyke." Similarly, the famous Horatian dictum on poetic representation, "ut pictura poesis," was infused with an Aristotelian epistemology and psychology based on the famous discussions of mimesis as a source of knowledge and pleasure at the beginning of Aristotle's *Poetics*.[33]

To account for these new approaches, we might predictably invoke humanist learning; and obviously sixteenth-century commentators had more direct access to Greek philosophy than medieval commentators. But medieval commentators were certainly no strangers to ancient philosophy, and if philosophical commentators during the Middle Ages had bothered much with the *Ars poetica*, they would have found ways to elaborate its meaning. Thus we must also look to the functions that Horace's *Ars poetica* played in the two cultures. Medieval commentators on Horace were schoolmasters, more humble and practical in their outlook than the learned scholars of the Renaissance. In other words, the function that the *Ars poetica* performed determined what kinds of commentators took it on. In the years between the thirteenth century and the sixteenth century, the work had ceased to be essential to pragmatic pedagogy, and once it was no longer inextricably linked with that world, it was available to a learned and philosophically oriented milieu.

A sign of its departure from the classroom was that it could achieve a new value as edifying recreation for adults. Queen Elizabeth's translation of a healthy portion of the *Ars poetica* dates from late in her reign, 1598, not from her youth (when she might have been expected to test her Latinity as a pedagogical exercise). Clearly for Elizabeth, thinking about the *Ars poetica* filled a need similar to the one filled by her 1593 translation of Boethius' *Consolatio*, a reprieve from burdens of state, something challenging enough to sustain voluntary attention to its complexities.[34]

Three decades earlier Thomas Drant could preface his translation of the *Ars poetica* with the argument that the *difficulty* of Horace's poem gives it greater worth than the silly love stories—the "flim-flames" and "gue-

---

32. The link is found in the 1550 commentary of Vincenzo Maggi (Madius); see Herrick, *The Fusion of Horatian and Aristotelian Literary Criticism*, 55; for further context, see Javitch, "The Assimilation of Aristotle's *Poetics*."

33. See Herrick, *Horatian and Aristotelian Literary Criticism*, 30–31.

34. Caroline Pemberton, ed., *Queen Elizabeth's Englishings of Boethius, "DCP" A.D. 1593, Plutarch, "De Curiosite," Horace, De Arte Poetica (part) A.D. 1598*, EETS o.s. 113 (London: Kegan Paul, Trench, Trübner, 1899). See Riccardo Scarcia, "Elisabetta I, traduttrice dell' 'Ars Poetica,'" in *I 2000 anni dell'Ars Poetica* (Genoa: D.AR.FI.CL.ET., 1988), 55–67.

gawes"—that printers find so profitable to market. Horace, he says, is "hard, and very hard," and much harder to translate than a "love booke, a shrill tragedye, or a smothe, and plat-levyled poesie. Thys can I trulye say of myne own experyence, that I can soner translate twelve verses out of the greek Homer, than six oute of Horace."[35]

Once liberated from the practical constraints of the Latin grammar curriculum, the *Ars poetica* was on its way to becoming a theoretical meta-discourse. And this was the role that it assumed when it finally reached vernacular literary audiences through the various translations. Our final case in point can be Joachim du Bellay's response to Horatian dicta on translation and imitation. In *Deffence et illustration de la langue françoyse*, written within a few years of the French translation of the *Ars poetica*, Du Bellay recognizes the agonistic stance that Horace takes on translation and imitation of Greek sources (the same stance that Cicero had taken in *De optimo genere oratorum*):[36] the imitator should be something of a greedy predator or plunderer on behalf of his own national culture, no subservient acolyte. Thus every literary imitation executed by a French poet is part of a collective effort to augment the capacities of French. Faithful translation is useful to give access to knowledge, but as a literary enterprise it has little or no value. Du Bellay's reading of Horace on translation is oriented to a completely different mission than that of the medieval school commentaries: it aims at building an entirely new literary language rather than developing an individual style within a mono-linguistic context. Du Bellay's outlook is explicitly cultural and historical, and his reading of the *Ars poetica* is sensitive to that cultural level of argument in Horace's text that the medieval school masters seemed to filter out as irrelevant to their purposes. Du Bellay elevates Horace's precepts to trans-historical status. Modern authors should follow the standard of combative imitation set by Cicero and Virgil, who were able to enrich their language by imitating

> les meilleurs auteurs grecz, se transformant en eux, les devorant; et apres les avoir bien digerez, les convertissant en sang et nouriture, se proposant, chacun selon son naturel et l'argument qu'il vouloit elire, le meilleur aucteur, don't ilz observoint diligemment toutes les plus rare et exquises vertuz, et

---

35. *Horace his arte of Poetrie, pistles, and Satyrs Englished, and to the Earle of Ormounte by Tho. Drant addressed* (London, 1567) [STC (2nd ed.) 13797], sig.*6r. See also Neel Mukherjee, "Thomas Drant's Rewriting of Horace," *Studies in English Literature 1500–1900* 40 (2000): 10.

36. Joachim du Bellay, *Deffence et illustration de la langue françoyse* (Paris: Crozet, 1839), 1.5; pp. 86–88.

icelles comme grephes, ainsi que j'ai dict devant, entoint et apliquoint à leur langue [1.7].

[the best Greek authors, turning themselves into them, devouring them; and after having digested them well, turning them into blood and nourishment, appropriating for themselves, each according to his nature and the argument he wished to select, the best author whose most rare and exquisite virtues they observed diligently, and these, like grafts (as I have said already) they joined and applied to their own tongue.]

Addressing those modern authors who occupy themselves with simply translating classical models, he asks:

si ces tant fameux aucteurs [i.e. Cicero and Virgil] se fussent amusez à traduyre, eussent-ilz elevé leur langue à l'excellence et hauteur ou nous la voyons maintenant? Ne pensez donques, quelque diligence et industrie que vous puissiez mettre en cest endroit, faire tant que nostre langue encores rampante à terre puisse hausser la teste et s'elever sur piedz [1.7].[37]

[if these authors, so famous, had passed the time with translating, would they have elevated their language to the excellence and loftiness where we see it now? Then do not think, whatever diligence and industry that you can bring to this purpose, to make it possible for our language, still creeping along the ground, to be able to lift its head up and rise up on its feet.]

For the *Ars poetica* to be "rediscovered" by early modern theorists as a rallying cry for a new ethic of translation and as a guarantor of a new sensibility of decorum, it had first to be dislodged from its long residence in the humble Latin grammar curriculum. Medieval school masters, searching for a better way to teach Latin composition, can be said to have given the *Ars poetica* its chance to become a classic of critical theory. Once it had outlived its usefulness they let go of it, and it became the property of humanist and Neoclassical critics, who at once classicized it and universalized it in their national languages. This is the route through which it comes before every modern student reading a history of literary criticism. For its canonical status in the modern tradition, its explanatory assimilation to the history of aesthetics from the humanist period onward, we have ultimately to thank those obscure medieval schoolmasters.

---

37. Du Bellay, *Deffence et illustration de la langue françoyse*, 89–90.

t w o

Latin Composition Lessons, *Piers Plowman*, and the *Piers Plowman* Tradition*

WENDY SCASE

"THE *Piers Plowman* tradition" is a widely used label for alliterative poetry which is unmistakably informed by *Piers Plowman*. The most prominent examples of the *Piers Plowman* tradition are *Pierce the Ploughman's Crede* (1393–1401), *Richard the Redeless* (c. 1400), *Mum and the Sothsegger* (c. 1409), and *The Crowned King* (after 1415).[1] Other composition in the tradition includes at least some of A-text passus 12, lines attributed to the self-proclaimed literary continuator calling himself "John But" and shorter pieces where scribes apparently make good perceived deficiencies in exemplars. It is with the stylistic relations between the model and *Piers*-tradition writing that the present essay is primarily concerned. I propose to offer a new contextual framework for analysing the ways in which the *Piers*-tradition poets use *Piers Plowman:* the arts of composition taught in the medieval classroom.[2]

---

* I am grateful to the members of the Medieval and Early Modern Centre at the University of Sydney for inviting me to read a version of this essay and for their questions and feedback. I also thank the anonymous readers for their feedback and suggestions, and the editors of this volume for their advice.

1. The dates are from Helen Barr, ed., *The Piers Plowman Tradition* (London: J. M. Dent, 1993), 9–10, 16, 23, 30–31. For reasons of space I shall omit *Crowned King* from analysis in this essay. All quotations of *Piers*-tradition texts in this essay are taken from this edition.

2. In the introduction to his essay collection *Middle English Alliterative Poetry and Its Literary*

There has been considerable discussion of the thematic and ideological relations between *Piers Plowman* and the major works in the tradition and it is widely recognized that these works are informed by *Piers Plowman* on every compositional level, from structure and narrative to the recycling of alliterative collocations, and in some cases to the quotation of lines and half-lines. Anne Middleton's fine essay on the "John But" passus (*Piers,* A 12) is a distinguished example of such work, and one to which this and previous essays of mine are indebted.[3] Recognition of these relations is of course long-standing. Skeat, for example, argued that *Richard the Redeless* must be by the same poet as *Piers Plowman,* and painstakingly listed stylistic parallels and textual correspondences between the two texts.[4] Recent critics have continued to examine stylistic relations between *Piers* and the tradition poems. Blamires praises *Richard* and *Mum* as an "extremely fine effort in the Langlandian idiom,"

Background (Cambridge: D. S. Brewer, 1982), David Lawton identifies the need for examination of "the medieval Latin background to Middle English alliterative poetry [including] . . . teaching of grammar" (15). Lawton deliberately excluded the topic from his collection, calling on scholars in medieval Latin to take up this work. Since Lawton wrote, much work has been done on medieval grammar by scholars of medieval Latin. The present essay seeks to use this scholarship to study a distinct corpus of alliterative poetry. My findings raise the question of how other works in the wider corpus relate to grammar teaching. There is a considerable body of work on alliterative meter: see, for example, Thomas Cable, *The English Alliterative Tradition* (Philadelphia: University of Pennsylvania Press, 1991); Thorlac Turville-Petre, *The Alliterative Revival* (Cambridge: D. S. Brewer, 1977), 48–68; Hoyt Duggan, "Alliterative Patterning as a Basis for Emendation in Middle English Alliterative Poetry," *Studies in the Age of Chaucer* 8 (1986): 73–104; and Duggan, "The Shape of the b-verse in Middle English Alliterative Poetry," *Speculum* 61 (1986): 564–92.

3. Anne Middleton, "Making a Good End: John But as a Reader of *Piers Plowman,*" in *Medieval English Studies Presented to George Kane,* ed. Edward Donald Kennedy, Ronald Waldron, and Joseph S. Wittig (Woodbridge, UK: D. S. Brewer, 1988), 243–67. Other important examples of work on the *Piers Plowman* tradition and its relations with *Piers* include Barr, *The Piers Plowman Tradition;* Barr, "The Relationship of *Richard the Redeless* and *Mum and the Sothsegger:* Some New Evidence," *Yearbook of Langland Studies* 4 (1990): 105–33; Barr, *Signes and Sothe: Language in the "Piers Plowman" Tradition* (Cambridge: D. S. Brewer, 1994); Alcuin Blamires, "*Mum and the Sothsegger* and Langlandian Idiom," *Neuphilologische Mitteilungen* 76 (1975): 583–604; and David Lawton, "Lollardy and the *Piers Plowman* Tradition," *Modern Language Review* 76 (1981): 780–93. Unless otherwise stated, all *Piers Plowman* quotations and references in the present essay are taken from the Athlone Press editions: George Kane, ed., *Piers Plowman: The A Version* (London: Athlone Press, 1960); George Kane and E. Talbot Donaldson, eds., *Piers Plowman: The B Version* (London: Athlone Press, 1975); George Russell and George Kane, eds., *Piers Plowman: The C Version* (London: Athlone Press, 1997).

4. Skeat argued that there could hardly have been two poets of such genius alive at the same time. W. W. Skeat, ed., *The Vision of William Concerning Piers the Plowman in Three Parallel Texts together with Richard the Redeless by William Langland* (Oxford: Oxford University Press, 1886), 2: lxxxiv–lxxxvi. The parallels are listed in W. W. Skeat, ed., *The Vision of William Concerning Piers the Plowman, together with Vita de Dowel, Dobet, et Dobest, Secundum Wit et Resoun, by William Langland, Part Three: Langland's Vision of Piers the Plowman, The Whitaker Text; or Text C,* EETS o.s. 54 (London: N. Trübner, 1873).

analysing that "idiom" in themes of themes and topics treated.[5] Helen Barr observes that the tradition poems she studies "quote lines of *Piers* verbatim" and include "quotations, or echoes"; that John But uses "selective readings of *Piers Plowman*"; and that none of the poems is "mindless pastiche,"[6] while *Mum* includes a "collage of episodes from *Piers*."[7] David Lawton states that *Pierce the Ploughman's Crede* "takes much of its colour . . . from *Piers* . . . developing these elements to serve its more immediate Lollard interests."[8] Thorlac Turville-Petre suggests that the tradition poems "show the influence of *Piers Plowman* . . . in their unadorned alliterative style."[9] To date, however, no investigation has been made of the compositional habits of the *Piers*-tradition poets in relation to the compositional techniques taught in the grammar school. The present study seeks to demonstrate that such an investigation may contribute substantially to our understanding of the *Piers*-tradition poets and to our knowledge of the cultural status and reception of *Piers Plowman*. At the end I shall make some proposals about the status of *Piers Plowman* among the tradition writers and reflect on its implications. By shedding light on the practices of the tradition writers, I hope to modify our understanding of the place of *Piers Plowman* in late medieval culture and in English literature.

Textbooks

There is abundant evidence for the textual resources used by schoolmasters. In the elementary stages of grammar-school education, the resources for teaching reading and composition seem to have been fairly uniform across medieval Europe.[10] Having introduced their pupils to Latin grammar and

---

5. Blamires, "*Mum and the Sothsegger* and Langlandian Idiom," 604.
6. Barr, *Signes and Sothe*, 13, 132, 21, 170.
7. Barr, *Piers Plowman Tradition*, 28.
8. Lawton, "Lollardy and the *Piers Plowman* Tradition," 787–88.
9. Turville-Petre, *Alliterative Revival*, 31–32.
10. My outline of medieval grammar teaching is indebted to Marjorie Curry Woods and Rita Copeland, "Classroom and Confession," in *The Cambridge History of Medieval English Literature*, ed. David Wallace (Cambridge: Cambridge University Press, 1999), 376–406; Douglas Kelly, *The Arts of Poetry and Prose*, Typologie des Sources du Moyen Âge Occidental, fasc. 59 (Turnhout: Brepols, 1991); Martin Irvine, *The Making of Textual Culture: "Grammatica" and Literary Theory, 350–1100* (Cambridge: Cambridge University Press, 1994); Martin Irvine with David Thomson, "*Grammatica* and Literary Theory"; J. J. Murphy, "The Arts of Poetry and Prose"; and Vincent Gillespie, "From the Twelfth Century to c. 1450," in *The Cambridge History of Literary Criticism, vol. 2: The Middle Ages*, ed. Alastair Minnis and Ian Johnson (Cambridge: Cambridge University Press, 2005), 15–41, 42–67, 145–235; Suzanne Reynolds, *Medieval Reading: Grammar, Rhetoric, and the Classical Text* (Cambridge: Cambridge University Press, 1996), esp. 7–11; and Eva Matthews Sanford, "The Uses of Classical

the construing of Latin using the *Ars Minor* of Donatus, teachers provided texts for their pupils that offered short units of proverbial or sententious material.[11] The first texts included the *Distichs of Cato* (a collection of proverbs traditionally but falsely attributed to Cato), the *Eclogue of Theodolus* (an allegorical dialogue), and the fables of Avianus.[12] Textbooks of English provenance from the fourteenth and fifteenth centuries often follow these texts with Alan of Lille's *Liber Parabolarum* (another collection of proverbs), *Facetus*, the *De Contemptu Mundi* (moralizing material), and materials attributed to "Seneca" and other authorities. For example, in 1358 William de Ravenstone, schoolmaster of the school of St. Paul's in London, bequeathed to the school many volumes, including texts of Cato, Theodolus, Avianus and other preliminary texts bound "in vno volumine," while another item in the same inventory is described as "librum Catonis cum aliis xij contentis infra."[13] Elementary work in grammar also included study of selected classical authors such as Virgil, Juvenal, Horace, and Ovid. A late-thirteenth-century book of school texts, Worcester Cathedral MS F. 147, for example, includes Cato, Theodolus, and other elementary reading texts together with Alan of Lille's *Anticlaudianus*, the *De Contemptu Mundi*, Perseus, Juvenal, Horace, and other classical authors.[14] Many of the manuscripts of the curriculum texts have glosses to assist the teacher.[15]

Given that all those who received a grammar-school education encountered this curriculum, it is not surprising that many vernacular authors, including Langland and his contemporaries, quote them or allude to them. Edith Rickert noticed that many of the classical writers with which Chau-

---

Latin Authors in the *Libri Manuales*," *Transactions and Proceedings of the American Philological Association* 55 (1924): 199–246.

11. Woods notes that "mnemonically effective tags of moral verse" constitute much of the material studied at the elementary level (Woods and Copeland, "Classroom and Confession," 385; cf. 381; cf. Gillespie, "From the Twelfth Century to c. 1450," 154).

12. A twelfth-century program of study attributed to Alexander Neckham prescribes "postquam alphabetum didicerit et ceteris puerilibus rudimentis imbutus fuerit, Donatum et illud utile moralitatis compendium quod catonis esse vulgus opinatur addiscat et ab egloga Theodoli transeat ad eglogas bucolicorum," quoted in George L. Hamilton, "Theodolus: A Medieval Textbook," *Modern Philology* 7 (1909): 175; for similar recommendations for elementary reading, see 176–79. The seminal study of the *Distichs of Cato* is M. Boas, "De librorum Catonianorum historia atque compositione," *Mnemosyne* 42 (1914): 17–46.

13. Edited in Edith Rickert, "Chaucer at School," *Modern Philology* 29 (1932): 266, 268.

14. Described in R. M. Thompson with Michael Gullick, *A Descriptive Catalogue of the Medieval Manuscripts in Worcester Cathedral Library* (Woodbridge, UK: D. S. Brewer, 2001), 101–2.

15. Irvine, *The Making of Textual Culture*, 355–58; Reynolds, *Medieval Reading*, 11; Richard Hazelton, "The Christianization of 'Cato': The *Disticha Catonis* in the Light of Late Medieval Commentaries," *Medieval Studies* 19 (1957): 157–73.

cer shows acquaintance were standards of the curriculum.[16] More recently, Jill Mann has shown that Chaucer refers to many elementary school texts: Cato, the *Facetus,* Alan of Lille's *Liber Parabolarum,* Maximian, and Claudian's rape of *Proserpina* among them.[17] Richard Hazelton observed that "Deschamps, Langland, and Gower . . . employ Catoniana in their verse to the same degree that Chaucer does."[18] It is well recognized that Langland makes use of quotations from or alludes to several school texts, most recently by Christopher Cannon in an important revisionary study of the material.[19] In the B-text of *Piers,* Langland draws on the *Liber Parabolarum* (B 18.408a), Avianus (B 12.259), the *De Contemptu Mundi* (B 17.321–22), on Cato in numerous places (B 6. 314–15; 7.72, 155–56; 10.194–201, 343–4; 11.404; 12.21–23; 19.296–97), and on "Seneca" (14.309, 20.275).[20] Covetousness has used a special "donet" (B 5.207), and "Grammer, þe ground of al" (B 15.372) translates Isidore's definition of grammar as "origo fundamentum liberalium litterarum"; Isodore's *Etymologies* is also used at B 15.37–39, 372.[21]

The *Piers*-tradition poets also use grammar-school texts as a point of reference, explicitly acknowledging or drawing on school texts. With opening lines referring to the cross and the a.b.c., *Pierce* aligns itself with the most basic primer of all. *Richard* includes unattributed, but presumably familiar, proverbial material (I. 153–54, II. 138). *Mum,* which includes an amusing vignette about "Sire Grumbald the grammier" (330), draws on *sententiae* and proverbs (51–53, 70–71, 422, 1473–74, 1703) and cites and quotes Cato (289–91, 875, 1404, 1514), *De Contemptu Mundi* (1623), "Seneca," and other school authors (304–45, 422a, 1141, 1530a, 1538a). John But follows *Piers* in quoting "Omnia probate quod bonum est tenete" (A 12.50–57; cf. B 3.339–43; also in C, not in A). This biblical tag (I Thess. 5:21) was a commonplace classroom illustration of contradictory imperatives.[22]

---

16. Rickert, "Chaucer at School."
17. Jill Mann, "'He Knew Nat Catoun': Medieval School-Texts and Middle English Literature," in *The Text in the Community: Essays on Medieval Works, Manuscripts, Authors, and Readers,* ed. Jill Mann and Maura Nolan (Notre Dame, IN: University of Notre Dame, 2006), 41–74.
18. Richard Hazelton, "Chaucer and Cato," *Speculum* 35 (1960): 370.
19. Mann, "'He Knew Nat Catoun,'" 64–66; Christopher Cannon, "Langland's Ars Grammatica," *Yearbook of Langland Studies* 22 (2008): 1–25.
20. It is not clear whether B IV.17 refers to Cato.
21. Cf. A. V. C. Schmidt, *The Clerkly Maker: Langland's Poetic Art* (Cambridge: D. S. Brewer, 1987), 21 n. 5.
22. It is quoted by Jerome (Epistle 119) in a letter expounding scripture to two monks, and (from Jerome) in *Sic et Non,* a teaching text by Abelard (d. 1142–43) written to support teaching of dialectic: Peter Abailard, *Sic et Non, A Critical Edition,* ed. Blanche B. Boyer and Richard McKeon (Chicago: University of Chicago Press, 1976–77), 103. Cf. K. C. Sidwell, *Reading Medieval Latin* (Cambridge: Cambridge University Press, 1995), 260–61.

Teaching the Arts of Composition

1. Translation

School Latin classes involved translation and glossing of school texts in the vernacular. John of Salisbury notes that translation into another language is one method by which the "splendor orationis" of a model can be understood.[23] Many glosses of school texts are in vernaculars.[24] A fair amount of Middle English composition looks to be translation of classroom texts, such as the translations of *Maximian, Pamphilus,* and so on.[25] Translations of Cato survive in many European vernaculars, including four in Middle English.[26] Translations of school texts in French, Anglo-Norman, and Spanish have been identified.[27] Students were required to construe Latin in vernacular language, and some of the bi- and tri-lingual collections of proverbs and distichs may be related to this kind of school exercise, which was probably usually Latin—English at the time *Piers* was composed (Anima regrets that pupils can no longer construe in French).[28] Langland and the *Piers*-tradition poets engage with the school texts in the manner taught in the classroom. *Piers* and the texts in the tradition provide many examples of the construing of short

---

23. C. I. I. Webb, ed., *Ioannis Saresberiensis Episcopi Cartonensis Metalogicon Libri IIII* (Oxford: Clarendon Press, 1929), 55.

24. The classic study, with many examples, is Tony Hunt, *Teaching and Learning Latin in Thirteenth-Century England*, 3 vols. (Cambridge: Cambridge University Press, 1991); cf. Reynolds, *Medieval Reading*, 62.

25. *Pamphilus* was an erotic dialogue featuring a deceiving go-between; Middle English versions include *Interludium de Clerico et Puella* and perhaps *Dame Sirith* (J. A. W. Bennett and G. V. Smithers, eds., *Early Middle English Verse and Prose*, 2nd ed. [Oxford: Clarendon Press, 1968], 77–95, 196–200). A Middle English *Maximian* is included in Oxford, Bodleian Library, MS Digby 86 and London, British Library, MS Harley 2253 (Carleton Brown, ed., *English Lyrics of the XIIIth Century* [Oxford: Clarendon Press, 1932], 92–100). For the Latin texts as beginners' school texts, see Gillespie, "From the Twelfth Century to c. 1450," 154–59. Gillespie notes that *Pamphilus* was dropped from the Oxford curriculum in the early fourteenth century (158). If this loss of favor was widespread, perhaps it would explain why there are no Middle English versions after 1340.

26. Hamilton, "Theodolus: A Medieval Textbook," 182.

27. See Ralph Hanna, Tony Hunt, R. G. Keightley, Alastair Minnis, and Nigel F. Palmer, "Latin Commentary Tradition and Vernacular Literature," in *The Cambridge History of Literary Criticism, vol. 2: The Middle Ages*, ed. Minnis and Johnson, 364–65, 369–71.

28. B 15.375–76. Examples of bilingual proverb collections occur in Oxford, Bodleian Library, MS Rawlinson D 328, ff. 140r–44v, ed. Sanford B. Meech, "A Collection of Proverbs in Rawlinson MS D 328," *Modern Philology* 38 (1940): 113–32; and in Manchester, John Rylands Library, MS Latin 394, ed. W. A. Pantin, "A Medieval Collection of Latin and English Proverbs and Riddles, from the Rylands Latin MS 394," *Bulletin of the John Rylands Library* 14 (1930): 81–114. These manuscripts appear to be mid-fifteenth century. Trilingual parallel texts of Cato and other proverbial material occur in the Vernon and Simeon manuscripts of c. 1390–1400: Oxford, Bodleian Library, MS Eng. poet. a. 1, ff. 309v–14r; and London, British Library, MS Additional 22283, ff. 118v–23r.

units of text in the vernacular. The quotations from Cato and other school authors are often translated in the following or preceding lines, as in the following example from the speech of Dame Study in *Piers*:[29]

> In ooþer Science it seiþ, I seiȝ it in Catoun,
> *Qui simulat verbis [nec] corde est fides amicus,*
> *Tu quoque fac simile; sic ars deluditur arte.*
> Whoso gloseþ as gylours doon, go me to þe same,
> And so shaltow fals folk and feiþlees bigile:
> (B 10.194–98)

The *Mum*-poet makes a rather elegant translation of a tag from Cato:

> And cleerly Caton construeth the same,
> And seyth soethly, I saw it in youthe,
> *Nam nulli tacuisse nocet, nocet esse locutum*
> That of "bable" cometh blame and of "be stille" neuer . . .
> (*Mum*, lines 289–91)

The *Mum*-poet neatly maps the chiastic structure of the Latin tag onto the alliterative line, and replaces the ornamental alliteration of the Latin (*Nam, nulli, nocet*) with structural alliteration, using the line to point up the key connections and antithesis (*bable, blame, be stille*).[30] It is possible that the *Piers*-tradition poets modeled their rendering of school texts in alliterative verse on the examples in *Piers Plowman*.

2. Imitation

Closely associated with translation in medieval and classical pedagogic thought, imitation was another important element in classroom study of curriculum authors and texts.[31] Bernard of Chartres, according to John of Salisbury, connected imitation with translation into another language in his teaching and is said to have recommended the educational benefits of imita-

---

29. Cannon, "Langland's *Ars Grammatica*," argues that the relationship between the Latin lines and their English equivalents in *Piers* should in some cases be understood in relation to the practice of "making Latins"—composing Latin lines on the basis of English prompts (19–25), but he also acknowledges that Langland is to be found translating Latin schoolroom texts (11).

30. He cites the first line of the distich at line 1404.

31. Rita Copeland, *Rhetoric, Hermeneutics, and Translation in the Middle Ages: Academic and Vernacular Texts* (Cambridge: Cambridge University Press, 1991), 10.

tion of texts heard in lessons.³² Pupils were expected to study closely small units of model text and to imitate them. Classroom texts were those thought to provide excellent and instructive models for composition. A preface to Vergil's *Aeneid* recommends the text for imitation, "Si quis vero hec omnia studeat imitari, maximam scribendi peritiam consequitur."³³ Classroom composition exercises—the *praeexercitamina*—required students to write on set themes in imitation of their model texts.³⁴

Imitation was associated with techniques of recycling material in new compositions. Isidore described the technique in book one of the *Etymologies*, "De Grammatica," when explaining the term *cento*:

> Centones apud Grammaticos vocari solent, qui de carminibus Homeri seu Vergilii ad propria opera more centonario ex multis hinc inde conpositis in unum sarciunt corpus, ad facultatem cuiusque materiae.³⁵

Cento means "patchwork," or "a garment of several bits or pieces sewed together."³⁶ Isidore gives the example of the *cento* of Proba, a late antique Christian poet who mixed lines from Vergil into a composition on biblical subjects. This work continued to be copied throughout the Middle Ages. In the thirteenth-century manuscript London, British Library, MS Harley 4967 it is found with texts associated with grammar teaching, including the *Liber Parabolarum* by Alan of Lille, and the fables of Avianus.³⁷ It also survives in a fourteenth-century manuscript from York, and in an anthology copied c. 1375 in the London area.³⁸ Clearly this example was available—perhaps

---

32. Webb, *Ioannis Saresberiensis, Episcopi Cartonensis Metalogicon Libri IIII*, book 1, chapter 24, p. 55; cf. Kelly, *The Arts of Poetry and Prose*, 51 ("And since memory is strengthened by exercise and cleverness is sharpened, he set for imitation those things which they had heard").

33. Kelly, *The Arts of Poetry and Prose*, 61 ("Certainly, if anyone applies himself to imitate all these things, the greatest knowledge of writing follows").

34. Kelly, *The Arts of Poetry and Prose*, 50.

35. W. M. Lindsay, ed., *Isidori Hispalensis Episcopi, Etymologiarum sive originum, Libri XX* (Oxford: Clarendon Press, 1911), vol. 1, book 1, chapter 39, line 25 (no pagination) ("Those used to be called patchworkers among grammarians who from the works of Homer or Vergil patched from many compositions into one in their own works in the manner of patchwork, to the enhancement of the subject-matter").

36. C. T. Lewis and C. Short, *A Latin Dictionary* (Oxford: Clarendon Press, 1894).

37. Ff. 169r–74v. For a description of the contents of this manuscript, see Christopher Baswell, *Virgil in Medieval England: Figuring the "Aeneid" from the Twelfth Century to Chaucer* (Cambridge: Cambridge University Press, 1995), 300–301.

38. London, British Library, MS Cott. Vesp. B. XXIII, f. 77v, owned by John Erghome, an Austin friar of York (d. 1386); see K. W. Humphreys, *The Friars' Libraries*, Corpus of British Medieval Library Catalogues (London: British Library in association with the British Academy, 1990), 124; London, British Library, MS Cotton Titus A. XX, ff. 69–78; for date and provenance, see A. G. Rigg, *A History of Anglo-Latin Literature, 1066–1422* (Cambridge: Cambridge University Press, 1992), 308. A further

to grammar teachers—while the technique (and its name) must have been known in the schoolroom through Isidore's mention of it. But the technique was also modeled by curriculum authors such as Juvencus, Avitus, Sedulius, and Arator. These authors imitated Vergil and other pagan epics, adapting their metre and figures to Christian subject-matter. Their works are commonly collected in manuscripts associated with the study of grammar.[39] These models of *cento* must have offered a specially extreme, virtuoso example of the kinds of imitative response to classical models which were taught in the schools. Although late medieval Latin poets do not often seem to have attempted to compose in this manner, it was not wholly defunct outside the classroom. Yeager has argued that John Gower's *Vox Clamantis,* as a Latin poem which patches together material from Ovid to create wholly new meanings, resembles the technique of *cento*.[40]

In the section on translation I suggested that it is possible that the *Piers*-tradition poets modeled their rendering of school texts in alliterative verse on the examples in *Piers Plowman*. But it is in their responses to lines, fragments, and short passages of *Piers* that the relevance of schoolroom pedagogy to their compositional practices is most marked. Just as schoolboys were taught to imitate their text-book models when composing on themes set by their schoolmaster, along the lines of Proba, Juvencus, Avitus, Sedulius, and Arator, so the *Piers-* tradition poets characteristically borrow fragments of *Piers* and redeploy them to develop their own distinctive themes.

In *Richard,* there are clear examples of whole lines from *Piers* being patched into new contexts with the minimum of adaptation required to align with the poet's own chosen topic.[41] "Trouthe hathe determyned the tente to the ende" (*Richard,* II. 97), takes over a line about the proper exercise of justice on transgressors in *Piers* "Til treuþe hadde ytermyned hire trespas to þe ende" (B 1.97; also in A and C), inserting it as a clause in a long sentence about truth's determining the intention of gifts in relation to law cases.[42] "But mesure is a meri mene though men moche yerne" (*Richard,* II.

---

late medieval English manuscript is Cambridge, Trinity College 0.7.7, ff. 28–37 (R. F. Yeager, *John Gower's Poetic: The Search for the New Arion* [Cambridge: D. S. Brewer, 1990], 55).

39. Irvine, *The Making of Textual Culture,* 160, 355–58.

40. Yeager, *John Gower's Poetic,* 48–62; cf. Bruce Harbert, "Lessons from the Great Clerk: Ovid and John Gower," in *Ovid Renewed: Ovidian Influences on Literature and Art from the Middle Ages to the Twentieth Century,* ed. Charles Martindale (Cambridge: Cambridge University Press, 1988), 83–97; and Andrew Galloway, "Gower in His Most Learned Role and the Peasants' Revolt of 1381," *Mediaevalia* 16 (1993): 329–47. Yeager struggled to explain Gower's evident knowledge of *cento,* not noticing its connections with the pedagogy of the grammar schools.

41. I am indebted to the identification of the sources of *Richard* provided in Skeat, *The Vision of William Concerning Piers the Plowman.*

42. I quote the B-text for comparison because the evidence points toward the conclusion that the

139) appropriates a line in which Holy Church advises Will to observe moderation in drinking alcohol, "Mesure is medicine þou3 þow muchel yerne" (B 1.35, also in A and C) to the topic of the king's unfairness to his subjects; he has not practised moderation, giving lavishly to some while dispossessing others. "For legiance without loue litill thinge availith" (*Richard*, I. 111) paraphrases Trajan's pronouncement on charity "'Lawe wiþouten loue,' quod Troianus, 'ley þer a bene!'" (B 11.171, also in C but not in A), adapting the line to the topic of Richard's oppressed subjects. There are several other examples of the patching in of whole lines with the minimal adaptation required for the new topic.[43]

By far the most usual kind of mixed-in material, however, is half-lines. The commonest kind of half-line intermixing is the recycling of *Piers* b-verses as b-verses in *Richard*. Examples include the b-verse in a line describing the king's crown, "It was full goodeliche ygraue with gold al aboughte" (*Richard*, I. 127), which redeploys the b-verse from Fauel's instructions "And bad gile '[go] gyu[e] gold al aboute . . .'" (B 2.145, also in A and C), and that in "Be preysinge of polaxis that no pete hadde" (*Richard*, I. 104), describing the behavior of royal officials, whose b-verse comes from "Or Poul þe Apostle þat no pite hadde" (B 10.430, also in A and C). There are many other examples. Other kinds of redeployment of *Piers* material are rarer. There are a few examples of an a-verse from *Piers* being redeployed as an a-verse in *Richard*. For example, the a-verse of a line about Lady Meed's bad influence, "*And* makeþ men mysdo many score tymes" (B 3.123, also in A and C) is patched into a line about the bribing of people with gifts of livery, "This makyth men mysdo more than oughte ellis" (*Richard*, III. 188).[44] On occasion the *Richard*-poet redeploys a b-verse from *Piers* as an a-verse. For example, when the reader is characterised as bewildered by the poem,

---

Richard (and *Mum*) poets knew *Piers Plowman* in this version. However, it is not the purpose of the present essay to offer a definitive pronouncement on the question of which versions the poets knew. For this reason, in each case I indicate the status of the appropriated material in all versions. For reasons of space and economy, I do not attempt to describe the precise status of the material. "Also in" on occasion refers to readings that are substantially but not entirely the same.

43. "And letith lyghte of the lawe and lesse of the peple" (*Richard*, III. 284), referring to governance, craftily adapts Wastour's contempt for the knight, "And leet li3t of þe lawe and lasse of þe kny3te" (B 6.168, also in A and C); "Tho ben men of this molde that most harme worchen" (*Richard*, III. 316), transfers to the topic of those who corrupt justice with bribery a *Piers* line about dishonest traders, "For þise are men on þis molde þat moost harm wercheþ" (B 3.80, also in A but not in C); "Comliche a clerk than comsid the wordis" (*Richard*, IV. 35) describes the way a clerk addresses parliament using a line from the knight's discussion with Piers, "Curteisly þe kny3t *þanne comsed* þise wordes" (B 6.33, also in A and C); here and below I use italics in quotations of *Piers* to indicate readings that I have restored from the manuscripts.

44. Other examples of a-verses redeployed in the same position include B 4.137 (also in A and C) in *Richard*, III. 124; and B III. 247 (in A but not in C) in *Richard*, III. 311.

"'What is this to mene, man?' maiste thou axe," *Richard*, III. 62, the *Richard*-poet adapts the slow-witted Will's question to Holy Church, "And seide 'mercy, madame, what is þis to mene?'" (A 1.11; B 1.11—in the unemended text; cf. C 1.11). Also rarely, two *Piers* lines are collapsed with carry over of the second *Piers* b-verse. When the positive figure of Wit/ Wisdom is exiled from court, his pursuit, "He was halowid and y-huntid and y-hotte trusse" (*Richard*, III. 228), is described in the same manner as that of the wicked Liar who is chased away from the king's court in *Piers*, "He was nowher welcome for his manye tales, Ouer al yhonted and yhote trusse" (B 2.220–21, also in A and C).

It is obviously not the case that the *Richard*-poet is simply using formulas that were also known to Langland. The many close correspondences between the two texts demonstrate that the poet has studied *Piers* closely (possibly in a B-text manuscript, given the data), adapting ready-made material to his own themes and topics. Furthermore, while some of the half-lines could be described as formulas or common expressions ("in lengthe and in brede" [*Richard*, I. 12, and II. 22] for example [cf. B 3.203]), many are distinctively Langlandian formulations, for example, "as his kynde wolde" (*Richard*, II. 142, cf. *Piers*, B 6.164).

Mum and the Sothsegger revisits many of the topics addressed in *Richard*, treating in particular the themes of corruption of justice and impediments to making complaint and speaking out about corruption. This text demonstrates similar practices to those observed in *Richard*, but in more highly developed form, making more intensive, varied, and creative use of verbal detail from *Piers* than is found in *Richard*.

As in *Richard*, there are several examples of *Piers* b-verses being redeployed as b-verses in *Mum*.[45] But redeployment of *Piers* a-verses is more in evidence here than in *Richard*. For example, "And yf ye willeth to wite what the wight hatte" (*Mum*, line 37), where the narrator addresses the reader and refers to the Sothsegger, uses the a-verse of "And if ye wilneþ to wite

---

45. Examples include "alle the foure ordres," used three times in *Mum* (lines 392, 494, 864), twice with "freres" in the a-verse, redeploying "I fond þere Freres, alle þe foure ordres" (B Prol.58, also in A and C); also from the *Piers* Prologue (B Prol.84, also in A and C) comes "siþ þe pestilence tyme," *Mum*, line 1369; "and waitid aboute" (*Mum*, line 1289) is used to end the dream vision as in B 7.145 (also in A and C); "as the lawe asketh," a b-verse from a passage where the narrator addresses the king about correct rule (*Mum*, line 1677) is unusually from a later portion of the poem, from Conscience's address to the needy king, "as þi lawe askeþ" (B 19.479, also in C, not in A); "malgre his chekes" (*Mum*, line 1300) is admittedly a common formula, but Langland gives many examples of how to use it in alliterative verse (B 4.50 (also in A, not in C); B 6.40 (also in C, not in A); B 6.158 (also in A, not in C); B 14.4 (B only)); "and y-hoote trusse" (*Mum*, line 174); uses a b-verse to describe how the Sothsegger is sent away, with "y-huntid" in the a-verse, as Liar is chased in *Piers*, and Wit/ Wisdom in *Richard* (as discussed above).

where þat [wye] dwelleþ," where *Piers* addresses the folk and refers to Truth (B 5.554, also in A; C 7.198 has "hoso wilneth"). In "For go to the gospel that grovnd is of lore" (*Mum*, line 76) the narrator uses an a-verse from Holy Church's address to the dreamer, "'Go to þe gospel,' quod she, 'þat god seide hymseluen'" (B 1.46, also in A and C). There are some striking redeployments of a-verses to new, sometimes radically different, topics and purposes. Another a-verse from Holy Church's speech, from a line about love, "And ek þe plante of pes, preche it in þin harpe" comes in an a-verse in the *Mum* narrator's naive defence of priests, "And eeke the plantz of pees and full of pitie euer" (A 1.137; B-text MSS here read "also"—Kane and Donaldson emend to "ek," B 1.152; C 1.148 rewrites the a-verse; *Mum*, line 703). An a-verse in the *Mum* dreamer's greeting to the gardener, "And halsid hym hendily as I had lernyd" (*Mum*, line 972) recycles an a-verse from Envy's insincere greeting of his neighbour, "I [hailse[d] hym hendely as I his frend were" (B 5.102; also in A but not in C).[46] The *Mum*-poet's practice of assembling materials from different parts and contexts of *Piers*, rather than simply minimally rewriting a long sequence, is particularly clear from the passage in which the narrator muses on the reliablity of dreams (*Mum*, lines 1309–1333). This passage shows clear knowledge of B 7.154–72 (also in A and C), likewise citing the examples of Joseph (Genesis, 40–1) and Daniel as accurate interpreters of dreams. Yet it is a new composition with much restructuring of material and amplification. A b-verse in the *Piers* passage, "Ac for þe book bible bereþ witnesse" (B VII. 157, also in C; the A-text seems to be corrupt and scribally repaired here) becomes an a-verse here, "The bible bereth witnesse, a boke of bileue" (*Mum*, line 1314). The b-verse "or ellis the boke lieth" (*Mum*, line 1326) mixes in a b-verse from B III. 251, "or þe boke lieþ" (also in A, not in C; some A and B manuscripts read "or elles").[47]

Again as in *Richard*, there are several examples of whole lines from *Piers* adapted and patched into *Mum*. Piers's assurance that he is on intimate terms with Truth, "'I knowe hym as kyndely as clerc doþ hise bokes'" (B V. 538, also in A and C) is patched into *Mum* twice, first in the speech of a clerk who explains why being a "sothsegger" is not likely to lead to preferment, as clerks "Knoweth this as kindely as clerc doeth his bokes" (*Mum*, line 109) and then in the speech of the beekeeper who explains how bees are instinctively able to identify wasters, "For thay knowen as kindely as clerc doeth his bokes" (*Mum*, line 1016). The reference to the brevity in which the proper

---

46. Other examples of *Piers* a-verses redeployed as a-verses in *Mum* include "And woneth at Westmynstre" (*Mum*, line 482, cf. B 3.12, also in A, rewritten in C); and "And thenne after oure deeth day" (*Mum*, line 1719, the speech of false executors; cf. B 7.118, also in A, not in C).

47. Cf. "or ellis þe bible lieþ" (B 6.231, also in A and C).

distribution of tithes can be described by the *Mum*-poet, "For in thre lynes hit [lith] and not oon lettre more" (*Mum,* line 655), re-writes minimally the line describing the pardon, "In two lynes it lay & nouʒt o lettre more" (A VIII.93; also in C; B MSS have "a leef" [B VII.111]; Kane and Donaldson emend to the AC reading.)[48] These examples show minimal adaptation (always remembering that we cannot know precisely the reading of the manuscript used by the poet). In other cases restructuring of a whole line takes place. "Sergeantz that seruen for soulde atte barre" (*Mum,* line 17) is rewritten slightly to dispense with the hesitancy of the *Piers* dreamer's "Sergeantʒ it [s]emed þat serueden at þe barre" (B Prol.212; some manuscripts and A and C read "seruen").

Sometimes the *Mum*-poet uses two or more *Piers* lines as a patchwork piece. For example, the lines in which a clerk addresses the narrator, drawing his attention to the practices of learned clerks, "And seide, 'soon, seest thou this semble of clercz, How thay bisien thaym on thaire bokes and beten thaire wittz'" (*Mum,* lines 366–7), adapt Holy Church's alerting of the dreamer to the moral meanings of his vision, "And seide, 'sone, slepestow? sestow þis peple, How bisie þei ben aboute þe maʒe?'" (B 1.5–6; in A, and in C which however names "Wille"). On occasion the *Mum*-poet creates a dense mixture of fragments from *Piers* that extends over several lines. One example is embedded in the narrator's warning about the consequences of suppressing truth:

> But hit be wel in his dayes we mowe dreede aftre
> Lest feerelees falle withynne fewe yeres.
> But God of his goodnes that gouuernith alle thingz
> Hym graunte of his grace to guye wel the peuple . . .
> (*Mum,* lines 221–4)

Patched into this passage are the *Piers* Prologue line which describes the evil which has resulted from the friars, "Manye ferlies han fallen in a fewe yeres" (B Prol.65, also in A and C), and the a-verse (and part of the b-verse) of "But [if] god of his goodnesse graunte vs a trewe" amplified over two lines (B 6.331; some MSS omit "if"; also in C but not in A).[49] The *Piers* Prologue

---

48. If, as the balance of the comparative evidence seems to suggest, the *Mum*-poet is using a B manuscript, this particular piece of evidence suggests that his copy of B was less corrupt than the B archetype. The evidence for the manuscript used by the *Richard*-poet also points to the use of a B-text. This evidence supports Barr's hypothesis that the same person wrote both *Richard* and *Mum* (Barr, "Relationship").

49. The a-verse is used elsewhere in *Piers;* see B 1.122 (not in A or C); B 6.138 (not in C).

line is also patched into a later passage, where it is amplified over two lines, "Y-write ful of wordes of woundres that han falle, And fele-folde ferlees wythynne thees fewe yeris" (*Mum*, lines 1736–7).[50]

3. Composing Rhetorical Figures

Amplification by means of rhetorical figures was one of the schoolroom exercises. An epigram from a classical text would be given to students, who were then required to amplify the theme in order to practise employing rhetorical figures such as *interpretatio* (exploring etymology), *frequentatio* (describing something in different ways) and *circumlocutio*.[51] The relation of *Pierce* with *Piers* is perhaps best categorised as one of amplification. In its entirety, *Pierce* effectively amplifies the encounter of the Dreamer with the pair of friars at the beginning of the "Vita de Dowel" section (A-text passus 9, B-text passus 8, C-text passus 10). Will's critical questioning of the friars about how to find Dowel becomes four meetings with friars, followed by an encounter with Pierce Plowman, as the narrator attempts to find someone who can teach him his creed. The sequence is an opportunity for much amplification of material drawn from various parts of the model. For example, the friar's suggestion that Meed finance a window in his church and have her name written there (A 3.47–49, B 3.48–50, C 3.51–54), is amplified with detailed description of the church that is under construction and the possible design of the window that will depict the narrator (*Pierce*, 118–29). The description of Piers when he dons his poor, practical plowman's clothing (A 7.54–56, B 6.59–61, C 8.58–60) is vastly amplified in a passage that describes in detail the plowman's clothing, and that of his wife, twin children, and baby (*Pierce*, 422–39). The devices of amplification in *Pierce* owe much to the virtuosity of description characteristically displayed by ambitious alliterative poets, but here they are appropriated for satirical and ironic purposes. Although Langland shares the interest of the alliterative long-line poets in specialised and wide vocabularies, he eschews the art of alliterative "thick description." By contrast, the *Pierce*-poet takes Langland's brief, compressed, complex suggestions and amplifies them in the more traditional alliterative manner. For example, we could compare the description of the plowman's clothing with, say, the description of the arming of Gawain in *Sir Gawain and the Green*

---

50. Another example in which *Mum* amplifies one *Piers* line over two lines is *Mum*, 574–75 "Til I wiste wittrely who shulde haue The maistrie, Mvm or the sothe-sigger"; cf. B 18.66 (also in C), where a dead body says that no-one knows whether life or death will prevail during the Harrowing of Hell.

51. Edmond Faral, *Les arts poétiques du XIIe et XIIIe siècle* (Paris: Champion, 1924), 64–85.

Knight, or the description of the Minorites' church with the description of the Castle de Hautdesert.⁵²

The *Richard*-poet may be using *Piers* as a model for structuring sequences of lines into rhetorical figures. One possible instance is the use of the "Rith as . . . Ryth so" collocation in *Richard:*

> Rith as the hous-hennes vppon londe hacchen
> And cherichen her chekonys fro chele of the wynter,
> Ryth so the hende Egle the Eyere of hem all,
> Hasteth him in heruest to houyn his bryddis . . .
> (*Richard*, II. 143–6)

This method of mapping a simile onto alliterative lines is regularly used in *Piers*. One particularly striking parallel occurs in the speech of Ymaginatif. Ymaginatif refers explicitly to the "ensamples" offered in the bestiaries, explaining how the peacock represents rich men:

> Right so þe riche, if he his richesse kepe
> And deleþ it noȝt til his deeþ day, þe tail[le is al of] sorwe.
> Riȝt as þe pennes of þe pecok peyneþ hym in his fliȝt,
> So is possession peyne of pens and of nobles
> To alle hem that it holdeþ til hir tail be plukked . . .
> Thus þe poete preueþ þat þe pecok for his feþeres;
> So is þe riche [reuerenced] by reson of hise goodes.
> (B 12.247–51, 262–63, in B only)

The parallel is particularly striking because *Richard* shares both bestiary material and the "right so" structure with *Piers* here. *Richard* draws extensively on bestiary material, here developing the example of the sharp-eyed and compassionate eagle as an image of Henry Bolingbroke, whose badge was the eagle.⁵³ But there are many other instances of this construction in *Piers* which the *Richard*-poet might have used as a model.⁵⁴

---

52. J. R. R. Tolkien and E. V. Gordon, eds., *Sir Gawain and the Green Knight*, rev. Norman Davis, 2nd ed. (Oxford: Clarendon Press, 1967), lines 566–99, 767–802. My suggestion that the poet amplifies in the style of the classic alliterative corpus is at odds with Turville-Petre's view that the *Pierce*-poet completely avoids "the high style of alliterative verse with its rich and elaborate diction and poetic expressions" and follows the plainer style of *Piers* (*Alliterative Revival*, 113–14). Turville-Petre's statement contradicts his own observation that "The Dominicans live in regal splendour, and their minster is described in all the detail we are by now accustomed to find in alliterative verse" (112).

53. Barr, *The Piers Plowman Tradition*, note to *Richard*, II. 8–9.

54. Examples include B 9.38, 42; 12.103, 104; 12.198, 202; 14.140, 143; 14.282, 284; 15.64,

4. Memorization

Memorization of texts was key to elementary classroom pedagogy.[55] Jill Mann notes that memorization began with basic devotional material (the Psalter, the Pater Noster, the Creed, etc.).[56] The *Distichs of Cato* were memorized, as well as being construed in the vernacular. Hazleton describes requiring schoolboys to memorize Cato as "a practice that seems to have been universal."[57] Cannon points out that memorization of a given prompt text would have preceded exercises in the classroom.[58] John of Salisbury, writing of the pedagogy of Bernard of Chartres, reports "hec . . . inculcabat mentibus auditorum," and "quoniam memoria exercitio firmatur, ingeniumque acuitur ad imitandum ea que audiebant . . . proponebatur."[59] Egbert of Liège created a collection of proverbs, fables, and short narratives for his eleventh-century pupils to memorize so that they could spend their time in profitable recitation when their teacher was absent.[60] There is evidence that some of the authors who imitated *Piers Plowman* were working on the basis of memorization of their model text. Examples of pastiche material suggest that the opening lines and other vision beginnings and endings were memorized and imitated by readers. For example, the person who patched together a version of the opening lines of *Piers* in a late fifteenth-century set of accounts was probably composing on the basis of memorized material.[61] John But may have fallen into this category of someone who had memorial knowledge of sections of *Piers*. It stands to reason that he did not have a manuscript of the complete poem to hand when he composed his completion of the A-text (otherwise he would not have needed to compose lines of his own). In general his work seems based on broad recollection of episodes rather than close verbal recall.[62] He does however on occasion mix in lines and half-lines from

---

65; 15.470, 471; 15.474, 476; 18.160, 161. None of these instances occurs in the A-version. If the poet is modeling his practice of simile on *Piers* it must have been on a later version of the poem.

55. Reynolds, *Medieval Reading*, 29.
56. Mann, "'He Knew Nat Catoun,'" 42.
57. Hazleton, "Chaucer and Cato," 360.
58. Cannon, "Langland's *Ars Grammatica*," 20.
59. Webb, ed., *Metalogicon*, book 1, chapter 24, p. 55; cf. Kelly, *The Arts of Poetry and Prose*, 51 ("he forced these things into the minds of his audience"; "And since memory is strengthened by exercise and cleverness is sharpened, he set for imitation those things which they had heard").
60. Mann, "'He Knew Nat Catoun,'" 52.
61. Kew, The National Archives (Public Record Office), E 101/516/9; for transcription and discussion, see Wendy Scase, "*Dauy Dycars Dreame* and Robert Crowley's *Piers Plowman*," *Yearbook of Langland Studies* 21 (2007): 187, and for the manuscript, see fig. 3 (186); for other examples and discussion, see 188–90.
62. For example, the continuation of Will's encounter with scripture, A 12.38–47, seems to be based on Will's encounters with Dame Study (cf. A 11.100–5) and Holy Church (cf. A 11.77).

the poem. For example, "Many ferlys me byfel in a fewe ȝeris" (A 12.58), is clearly an adaptation, for quite different purposes, of the Prologue line "Manye ferlis han fallen in a fewe ȝeris" (A Prol.62). In the Prologue this line is a chilling warning about where the friars' corruption may be leading. In passus 12 it prefaces But's account of Will's adventures. This is precisely the kind of redeployment of material that we have observed in *Pierce, Richard,* and *Mum,* and it seems he must have been working with memorized material.

5. Composition Theory and Ethics

It is possible that *Piers* transmitted to the *Piers*-tradition poets a vocabulary for aligning their vernacular practice with that of the schoolroom. In his definition of the *conpilator* in the *Etymologies,* Isidore associates the word *conpilator* with the word *pila,* meaning a mortar in which materials are crushed into small fragments and mixed, "Conpilator, qui aliena dicta suis praemiscet, sicut solent pigmentarii in pila diversa mixta contundere" ("A compiler, one who mixes the sayings of others with his own works, just as pigment-makers are accustomed to crush various mixtures into small fragments in a mortar").[63] Isidore notes that a Mantuan poet who mixed lines of Homer with his own verse was identified pejoratively as a *conpilator* and was accused of having committed a morally bad act, "Hoc scelere quondam accusabatur Mantuanus ille vates, cum quosdam versus Homeri transferens suis permiscuisset et conpilator veterum ab aemulis diceretur" ("With this vice, a certain Mantuan poet was accused, since transferring certain verses of Homer he mixed them with his own, and he was called by his rivals a mortar-mixer of the ancients.") Isidore also records the Mantuan poet's defence, "Magnarum esse virium clavam Herculi extorquere de manu" ("It is to be of great strength, to seize the club from Hercules' hand"). Ranulph Higden referred to and quoted from this story in his own defence at the beginning of the *Polychronicon.* Higden's first Middle English translator, Langland's contemporary John Trevisa, translated Isidore's "immiscuisset" ("he mixed") using the Middle English verb *medlen:* "he hadde i-take som of Omeres [verse], and i-medled among his."[64] This was Higden's defence for his practice of add-

---

63. Lindsay, *Etymologiarum,* book 10, line 44.
64. Churchill Babington, ed., *Polychronicon Ranulphi Higden Monachi Cestrensis together with the English translations of John Trevisa and of an Unknown Writer,* Rolls Series 41 (London: Longman, Green, Longman, Roberts and Green, 1865), 1:10–13. Cf. *MED, medlen,* 'to intersperse, mingle, intermingle,' http://quod.lib.umich.edu/m/med/ (accessed 10 September 2008).

ing to the writings of *auctours,* when he "somwhat putt to and eche [amplify] writinge of auctours" ("quippiam adjiciam laboribus auctores").[65] Middle English "meddling" with making, therefore, in Trevisa's translation of Higden, denotes the activity of extracting fragments from an authoritative model of composition and mixing them into a composition of one's own, and is associated with the traditional objection and defence disseminated in Isidore.

The challenge to Will by Ymaginatyf and Will's own defence of his poetic practice may recall this tradition. In the famous and much-discussed "meddling with making" passage, when Ymaginatyf accuses Will of "meddling" with making, "þow medlest þee wiþ makynges" (B 12.16), *Piers* arguably aligns this Isidorean vocabulary with the practice of vernacular alliterative poetry.[66] Here Langland may draw on the tradition of comparing the activity of redeploying small snippets of the work of ancient poets with grinding up small fragments of material and mixing them in a mortar. We can be sure that at least one *Piers Plowman* tradition writer used the Isidorean vocabulary in Langland's formulation to describe his own poetic practice. John But records of himself, "for he medleþ of makyng [because he is a mixer of verses] he made þis ende" (A 12.109).

Conclusion

In this concluding section I shall draw together the analyses of the previous section, drawing some conclusions and considering their implications. I have been suggesting that the responses of the tradition poets to *Piers Plowman* were informed by the processes of composition taught in the grammarschool. I have proposed that, translating and imitating snippets of school texts in the classroom manner, *Piers* may have modeled for them how the vernacular alliterative line could be a vehicle for the arts of composition taught in school composition classes. The poem may also have vernacularized a vocabulary for thinking about compositional practice and ethics and authorised its association with alliterative verse-making. The *Piers*-tradition poets, I have suggested, perhaps worked with memorized passages. Imitating and amplifying fragments from *Piers,* and sometimes redeploying them in the treatment of wholly new material, it is evident that they studied closely

---

65. Babington, *Polychronicon,* 1:14–15.
66. Ralph Hanna reads "meddle" here as "intermix," though he draws different conclusions from mine; see Hanna, "'Meddling with Makings' and Will's Work," in *Late-Medieval Religious Texts and Their Transmission: Essays in Honour of A. I. Doyle,* ed. A. J. Minnis, York Manuscripts Conferences: Proceedings Series 3 (Cambridge: D. S. Brewer, 1994), 85–94.

the operations of lines and half-lines and rhetorical figures in *Piers*. The *Pierce*-poet and John But focus in particular on amplification of *Piers*. *Mum* and *Richard* operate more in the manner of *cento*, transferring fragments of material from their model to their own chosen themes of governance, corruption, and truthful, uncensored expression.[67] All of these observations suggest that the *Piers*-tradition poets were responding to *Piers* as if it were a classroom text for memorization, close study, imitation, and a model for composition on new themes.

Aligning the art of the *Piers Plowman* tradition texts with elementary school exercises might encourage us to view these writers as immature and uncreative. But to do so would be to miss a crucial distinction. The tradition writers made an astonishingly daring and original move. They practised the arts of imitative composition, but unlike their other Middle English counterparts they did not imitate a Latin author or text. Their principal model for study and emulation was, as we have seen, *Piers Plowman*. The astonishing move of these writers was to promote the vernacular, alliterative *Piers* to the status of *auctoritas*. *Richard*, *Mum*, *Pierce* and the other tradition texts provide our earliest definite evidence of an identifiable alliterative Middle English text being studied and imitated as a literary model in the manner of the curriculum classics.[68]

This conclusion raises some further intriguing possibilities. Was the work of the tradition writers conducted with the *aim* of actually making *Piers* a classroom "classic"—a canonical curriculum text? Or—an even more startling possibility, but the question is unavoidable—were these writers even working, perhaps, in the knowledge that *Piers Plowman* actually *was* taught by some masters? Could some kind of use of *Piers* as a teaching text explain the widespread knowledge and diffusion of the poem, and the development

---

67. The art of the *Mum*-poet may have developed as he got to know and understand *Piers* in more depth. If, as Barr and others have suggested, the same poet wrote *Richard* and *Mum*, it would be reasonable to deduce that *Mum* was his second attempt at tackling the theme of good governance and corruption. The differences that I noted above between the response to *Piers* in *Richard* and that in *Mum* suggest that, if indeed the same poet is at work, by the time he wrote *Mum* he had much more detailed knowledge and understanding of the art of *Piers Plowman*, and he had become more adventurous and creative in his use of his model. For the case for common authorship, see Barr, "Relationship"; Day and Steele noted the *Mum*-poet's "advance" in his mastery of his medium (Barr, "Relationship," 129 n. 73).

68. Other Middle English alliterative poets must have learned their art from reading and hearing models, but the corpus does not—in the present state of our knowledge at least—provide evidence for the identification of specific vernacular texts as authoritative models. Whether Chaucer and Gower are treated in a similar way by their imitators remains to be explored. Chaucer was of course a "maister" for Hoccleve and the other poets who followed him, but his works taught them modes of response to models in Latin and other languages. Gower may have hoped—or expected—that the *Confessio Amantis* would provide a text for study, when he provided it with Latin glosses and comment in the scholastic manner.

of the tradition of imitation? Could this kind of use explain some of the oddities of the manuscript tradition? Could it, for example, explain the continuing and late copying of the A-text (more accessible and appropriate for the classroom, perhaps, than the longer text)? Might it perhaps explain the extract comprising a definition from Isidore, with Langland's alliterative amplification (C 16.182–201a) that is found on the fly-leaf of a manuscript written by John Cok, with the heading "nota bene de libero arbitrio secundum augustinum et ysidorum"—did the extract perhaps serve as an example of amplification using etymology? Could it possibly explain the presence of glosses to *Piers* and scholastic material in some of the manuscripts?[69] For now, these further possibilities must remain speculative. Before firmer conclusions can be drawn, further study is required of pedagogic practices in earlier fifteenth-century England, of the Latin and English literature of the schoolroom, and of responses to it by vernacular authors.

---

69. The Cok manuscript is Cambridge, Gonville and Caius College, MS 669*/646, p. 210. Many manuscripts have glosses and analytical notes such as "exemplum" (e.g., London, British Library, MS Cotton Vespaspian B XVI, f. 50v; and Cambridge, Cambridge University Library, MS L1.4.14, ff. 48v, 51r).

three

Langland Translating

TRAUGOTT LAWLER

> You have shown to all who shall hereafter attempt the study of our ancient authors the way to success, by directing them to the perusal of the books which those authors had read.... The reason why the authors which are yet read of the sixteenth century are so little understood is, that they are read alone; and no help is borrowed from those who lived with them or before them.
>
> —Samuel Johnson to Thomas Warton, July 16, 1754 (*The Letters of Samuel Johnson*, ed. R. W. Chapman)

I

This essay is meant to supplement my short discussion of Langland's translations in Roger Ellis's *Oxford History of Literary Translation in English*.[1] There I raised the question why some Latin quoted in *Piers Plowman* is translated and some not, and put forward the theory that the answer lies in the relation of speaker to listener: speakers who talk down translate. Most translation is done by tutor-figures—Wit, Study, Clergy, Patience—tutoring Will, but much also is done by Langland in his author-voice, tutoring us; but any speaker who thinks he is smarter or better-educated than his listener translates for him: Hunger translates for Piers and so does the priest, and of course everyone translates for Will, but Will and Piers almost never translate. The talking down is also evident in pronouns: if you translate for some-

---

1. Traugott Lawler, "William Langland," in *The Oxford History of Literary Translation in English, vol. 1: To 1550*, ed. Roger Ellis (Oxford: Oxford University Press, 2008), 149–59. I read an earlier version of the first part of this paper at the Langland Conference in Philadelphia in May 2007. Since Anne Middleton responded vigorously to it then, it pleases me to offer it to her now. I have not tried to suppress the marks of its original oral delivery.

one, you call him "thou," not "you." Only tutors translate, and tutors nearly always translate; studying this matter has made me conclude that Langland pays more attention to dramatic situation than has usually been thought. I also offered extended analyses of Langland's mode of translation, emphasizing his habit of making verbs, expanding, and specifying, and suggesting that improving his translations might have been one of his purposes in revising A into B and B into C.

I also made this remark: "Furthermore, more of [the] poetry than has been realized is not original composition but actual translation of particular sources. A single instance is B 15.332–41, lines that say that giving money to the rich is like adding trees to the forest or water to the Thames; this comes from a Latin proverb that goes back at least to Horace ("In silvam non ligna feras" [don't bring wood to the woods], *Satires* 1.X.34), which Langland probably drew from Peter Chanter's *Verbum adbreviatum*, ch. 48: "addere ligna silvis et aquas mari" [to add wood to the woods and water to the sea]" (151). That obiter dictum is the starting point for the present essay: I want in general to report on some new possibilities I have been pursuing about Langland's reading and translating, and in particular to uncover Latin sources for Langland's English that go beyond the Latin he actually quotes.

Like Anne Middleton, I am one of the authors of the Penn Commentary on *Piers Plowman*, though I am slower than Anne and much slower than Stephen Barney and Andrew Galloway.[2] My stint is C passūs 15–19, which is B 13–17—from the dinner party at Conscience's through Will's meeting with the Samaritan. I spent some time several years ago reading Peter the Chanter's *Verbum adbreviatum*, because I thought it might be the source of even more of *Piers Plowman* than has been acknowledged; among other things, I hoped to see if could shed some light on the little knot of Latin quotations at B 15.342:

Who parfourneþ þis prophecie of þe peple þat now libbeþ,
Dispersit, dedit pauperibus?
. . . .
Fele of yow fareþ as if I a forest hadde
That were ful of faire trees, and I fondede and caste
How I myȝte mo þerInne amonges hem sette.
Right so ye riche, ye robeþ þat ben riche

---

2. Andrew Galloway, *The Penn Commentary on Piers Plowman, vol. 1: C Prologue-Passus 4; B Prologue-Passus 4; A Prologue-Passus 4* (Philadelphia: University of Pennsylvania Press, 2006); Stephen A. Barney, *The Penn Commentary on Piers Plowman: vol. 5: C Passus 20–22; B Passus 18–20* (Philadelphia: University of Pennsylvania Press, 2006).

> And helpeþ hem þat helpeþ yow and ȝyueþ þer no nede is;
> As whoso filled a tonne ful of a fressh ryuer,
> And wente forþ wiþ þat water to woke [*moisten*] wiþ Temese.
> Right so ye riche, ye robeþ and fedeþ
> Hem þat han as ye han; hem ye make at ese.
> Ac Religiouse þat riche ben sholde raþer feeste beggeris
> Than burgeises þat riche ben as þe book techeþ,
>
> *Quia sacrilegium est res pauperum non pauperibus dare. Item, peccatoribus dare est demonibus immolare. Item, monache, si indiges et accipis, pocius das quam accipis; Si autem non eges & accipis rapis. Porro non indiget monachus si habeat quod nature sufficit.* (B 15.326–43)[3]

For reasons that will become clear, I have given here the dozen or so lines before the knot of Latin, but it was that knot that I was originally after: "Sacrilegium est res pauperum non pauperibus dare"; "Peccatoribus dare est demonibus immolare"; "Monache, si indiges et accipis, pocius das quam accipis, si autem non eges et accipis, rapis"; and finally, "Porro non indiget monachus si habeat quod naturae sufficit." The first three of these four statements had been identified in Peter Chanter (though not together), but the fourth had not. I thought I had an advantage that John Alford didn't have when he compiled his *Guide to the Quotations*:[4] online search engines, notably the *Patrologia latina* online and the CETEDOC Library of Latin Texts. And indeed I did find that fourth quotation in the *PL* online, not in Peter the Chanter but in Peter of Blois's Letter 102—and when I went to read that, I found all the others also, and "Dispersit, dedit pauperibus" at the start of Langland's passage as well, which suggested pretty strongly that Langland's source was not Peter Chanter at all, but Peter's older contemporary Peter of Blois.[5] But what was really interesting was what else I found—that not only was all the Latin there, but in between the "Dispersit" line and the knot of four remarks on wasting the patrimony of the poor, Peter of Blois says, "We are neither to give to the rich, nor to bring wood to the forest, nor to pour

---

3. I cite the B and C versions of *Piers Plowman* from the Athlone editions (I do not cite A): George Kane and E. Talbot Donaldson, eds., *Piers Plowman: The B Version; Will's Visions of Piers Plowman, Do-Well, Do-Better, and Do-Best* (London: Athlone Press, 1975); George Russell and George Kane, eds., *Piers Plowman: The C Version; Will's Visions of Piers Plowman, Do-Well, Do-Better, and Do-Best* (London: Athlone Press, 1997).

4. John Alford, *Piers Plowman: A Guide to the Quotations* (Binghamton, NY: Medieval and Renaissance Texts and Studies, 1992).

5. I therefore retract the statement in my translation essay ("William Langland," cited in n. 1 above), p. 151, that the source is Peter the Chanter.

water into the sea"—that is, what Langland has between his Latin quotations, lines that seem to be so English, so perfectly Langlandian, that no one has ever supposed that they are translations, are in fact translations of Peter's Latin. Here is Peter: "Ubi est ergo, quaeso, verbum illud Prophetae, 'Dispersit, dedit pauperibus'? Porro nec divitibus dare, nec nos ligna ferre in silvam, nec aquas in mare effundere oportebat. Verbum Beati Hieronymi est, sacrilegium esse res pauperum non pauperibus dare . . . " (*PL* 207.319).[6] And so on.[7] And here again is Langland:

> Who parfourneþ þis prophecie of þe peple þat now libbeþ,
> *Dispersit, dedit pauperibus?*
> . . . .
> Fele of yow fareþ as if I a forest hadde
> That were ful of faire trees, and I fondede and caste
> How I my3te mo þerInne amonges hem sette.
> Right so ye riche, ye robeþ þat ben riche
> And helpeþ hem þat helpeþ yow, and 3yueþ þer no nede is;
> As whoso filled a tonne ful of a fressh ryuer,
> And wente forþ wiþ þat water to woke wiþ Temese.
> Right so ye riche, ye robeþ and fedeþ
> Hem þat han as ye han; hem ye make at ese. (326–40)

This is Langland translating. It expands—Peter of Blois's twelve words become nine lines; it specifies—the sea becomes the Thames; and it makes verbs: Peter's two verbs (*ferre, effundere*) become seven. Indeed with hindsight one might have seen that the very inflation of it should suggest that it is translation.

I can't begin to say how much time this little discovery has caused me to waste. Now every time I see a line or passage that has a little fat in it,

---

6. All citations of the *Patrologia latina* are made by volume and column from the Chadwyck-Healey electronic version of the first edition: *Patrologiae cursus completus, series latina*, ed. Jean-Paul Migne et al., 221 vols. (Paris, 1844–55 and 1862–65).

7. The speaker is actually Hugh, Abbot of Reading. Peter of Blois cites a recent conversation with him, in which Hugh expressed his distaste for the high living associated with his office and his desire to return to the life of a simple monk. He laments especially the requirement of elaborate hospitality, in which it seems to him he is spending the patrimony of the poor on delicacies for the rich. Finally: "Where, I ask, is that phrase of the Prophet: 'He distributed and gave to the poor?' We are neither to give to the rich, nor to bring wood to the forest, nor to pour water into the sea. St Jerome said, 'It is a sacrilege to give what belongs to the poor to those who aren't poor.' And again, 'Giving to sinners and making sacrifice to devils are the same thing; and it is no less sinful to give to the wicked than to give for wickedness.'" And twelve sentences later: "Listen to Jerome: 'Monk, if you are in need and take, you should still rather give than take; if you aren't needy and take, you commit rapine. A monk isn't needy if he has what nature requires.'"

or seems by any chance, however remote, to contain hidden translation, I try to figure out what it might be in Latin and then go hunting in the online databases. I might as well be looking in the woods for a particular tree, or in the Thames for a particular drop of water. Well, actually it isn't that bad. I have made a few more little discoveries. "Alle myȝte god haue maad riche men if he wolde" (B 11.197; cf. 14.166–67, C 16.18–20) is St. Augustine, "Potuit enim Deus omnes homines divites facere."[8] "Double scaþe" (B 15.59) is "duplex malum."[9] Chaucer's "Diverse folk diversely they seyde" (*CT.* A.3857; cf. E.1469, F.202) is "Diversi diverse dicunt."[10] "Riȝt softe walkeþ" (B 14.211) is Paul's "caute ambuletis" (Ephesians 5.15) applied ironically by Langland to the rich man's burden of worry. "Cristes court" (B 15.17) is "aula Christi."[11] Will's question to Liberum arbitrium, "Is þat body bettere þen þou?" (C 16.179) plays on the topos "anima corpore melior."[12] The branches of the seven sins are "rami vitiorum" (part of the same metaphor as *radix vitiorum*).[13] "Grammer, þe ground of al" (B 15.372) is from Cassiodorus, repeated by Isidore and Bede: "Grammatica . . . origo et fundamentum liberalium litterarum," quoted in a commentary on Donatus as "fundamentum et origo omnium liberalium artium."[14] "Grace sholde growe and be grene þoruȝ hir goode lyvynge" (B 15.424): you'd suppose that one would surely be English, with the happy alliterating of grace, grow and green—and yet the idea of the greenness of grace, *viriditas gratiae*, is all over the place—I saw dozens of instances.[15] So I intend to keep on wasting my time—always hoping that I'm not wasting it—and perhaps I have reminded you that brilliant though Langland's poetry always is, more of it than we think may have its *fundamentum et origo* in somebody else's Latin. (I pass over the possibility that some of the Latin lines we can't identify, not even with our data bases, are by Langland, translating his English, making it more portentous by rendering it in Latin. I'm pretty sure that's true of B 13.45, *Vos*

---

8. Actually from a sermon, *De misericordia divina et humana*, attributed to Augustine, *PL* 39.2930. But cf. Augustine on Psalm 72, *PL* 37.1649–50, for an implicit reference to the same idea.

9. E.g., Bernard, *PL* 182.881.

10. In various phrases with various verbs. E.g., Augustine on Psalm 119: "in diversis codicibus diverse scriptum est" (*PL* 37.1600).

11. E.g., Alcuin (who particularly liked the phrase) in the poem "De sancto Amando episcopo Trajectensi": "Coetibus angelicis Christi subvectus in aulum" (*PL* 101.741a).

12. E.g., Augustine, *De immortalitate animae*, *PL* 32.1034.

13. E.g., Gregory, *Moralia*, *PL* 76.744.

14. Cassiodorus, *De artibus et disciplina liberalium artium*, *PL* 70.1151. Isidore, *Etymologiae*, *PL* 82.81. Bede, *De ratione temporum*, *PL* 90.305. The commentary on Donatus is *Expositio in Donatum majorem*, ed. B. Löfstedt, CCCM 40A (Turnhout: Brepols, 1977), 4. I found this by searching the Brepols Library of Latin Texts website.

15. E.g., Ambrose, *Hexaemeron*, *PL* 14.186.

qui peccata hominum comeditis, nisi pro eis lacrimas & oraciones effuderitis, ea que in deliciis comeditis in tormentis euometis, which translates lines 42–44.[16]

As for Peter of Blois: his letters were if anything more popular than the *Verbum Abbreviatum;* about 250 manuscripts survive. And he is a brilliant, readable writer, with a taste for satire. I don't see why Langland could not have been reading him, and found in Letter 102 not only some telling satire on lush monastic banquets, and the idea that monks should feast the poor instead, but his whole set of quotations, including "Dispersit, dedit pauperibus" as prophecy, and the woods and sea metaphors—and all much closer together than they are in Peter the Chanter. I'm actually inclined to think that Langland knew this material from both writers, since both say so much pertinent to his theme, but the compactness of the passage in Peter of Blois makes me feel sure he knew Letter 102. In any case, it seems clear that both of these Peters had a major place in Langland's reading, and deserve to have a place in our reading as well.

Let me end this portion of my essay with an anecdote that has a small surprise ending. In Peter of Blois's letter 102, down past the part that Langland clearly drew on, comes this statement: "Video in claustris coelestes homines, aut potius angelos terrestres, quorum conversatio est in coelis [Phillipians 3.20]" (*PL* 207.315), "In cloisters I see heavenly men, or rather angels on earth, whose conversation is in heaven." I read that and thought, "Oh my, this could lie behind that remark we all love in passus B 10, "If heaven be on this earth, and ease to any soul,/ It is in cloister or in school" (it's 10.305–6), which I had always thought of as a charming original opinion by Langland. So I tried the data bases, pairing "caelum" with "claustrum," but found nothing. But I remembered that Morton Bloomfield's book had a lot about Langland and monasticism, so I looked there—and duly discovered that the monastery as paradise is an old motif, and that Bloomfield in 1958 and Robert Kaske in 1957 had given ample evidence that Langland's couplet was a translation of Latin.[17] Kaske cited Benvenuto da Imola, the commentator on Dante, quoting someone he calls Petrus Ravennas (who is probably Peter Damian): "Si paradisus in hoc mundo est, in claustro vel in scolis est." What could be closer? And yet, how far from Langland. And Bloomfield cited Bishop Thomas Brinton, Langland's contemporary, who says "Si vita

---

16. See my "Harlots' Holiness: The System of Absolution for Miswinning in the C Version of *Piers Plowman*," *Yearbook of Langland Studies* 20 (2006): 188–89, and Katherine Kerby-Fulton, *Reformist Apocalypticism and "Piers Plowman"* (Cambridge: Cambridge University Press, 1990), 157.

17. Morton W. Bloomfield, "*Piers Plowman*" as a Fourteenth-Century Apocalypse (New Brunswick, NJ: Rutgers University Press, n.d. [1962]), 72, 197; Bloomfield, "*Piers Plowman* and the Three Grades of Chastity," *Anglia* 76 (1958): 229 n. 1); Robert E. Kaske, "Langland and the *Paradisus claustralis*," *Modern Language Notes* 72 (1957): 481–83.

angelica sit in terris, aut est in studio aut in claustro," and repeats it twice more (with "paradisus" once for "vita angelica").[18] There is also an article by Elizabeth M. Orsten in the *American Benedictine Review* for 1970.[19] Writing in ignorance of Bloomfield, Orsten cites Brinton's three places, then goes on to speculate whether Langland knew the Benedictine priory in Worcester. But she mentions something that Bloomfield does not, namely, that in Sermon 98 Brinton prefaces the remark with the phrase "juxta vulgare," that is, maybe, "as they say in English." So it's an English proverb? That seemed a little unlikely—and it isn't in Whiting—so I thought, better try the databases again, now that I know that the word is *paradisus*, not *caelum*—and I found it: "Juxta sententiam cordis mei, si paradisus in hac vita presenti est, vel in claustro est vel in scholis." It's by—guess who?—Peter of Blois, in his letter 13, writing to a novice monk urging him to stay where he is (*PL* 207.39).[20] So what do I make of all this? I doubt the sentence is original with Peter of Blois, because so much of what he writes is taken from others, but the immense popularity of his letters, added to the clear evidence that Langland knew Letter 102, leave me thinking: first, that Langland in Passus 10 was translating Peter of Blois; second, that Benvenuto's Peter of Ravenna, or Benvenuto himself, was remembering Peter of Blois; and third, that when Brinton referred to the phrase in English, he was thinking of Langland. How pleasant to imagine a bishop reading *Piers Plowman*.[21]

II

Thus far my Philadelphia talk (with a few changes and a lot of footnotes). I had intended to extend it for this essay by offering a few more examples

---

18. Sister Mary Aquinas Devlin, ed., *The Sermons of Thomas Brinton, Bishop of Rochester (1373–1389)*, Camden Society, 3rd Ser. 55–56 (London: Offices of the Royal Historical Society, 1954), 101 (Sermon 25); 118 (Sermon 29, with "paradisus"); 453 (Sermon 98).

19. Elizabeth M. Orsten, "'Heaven on Earth'—Langland's Vision of Life within the Cloister," *American Benedictine Review* 21 (1970): 526–34.

20. Bloomfield appears to have known this place, though he contents himself with mentioning Peter of Blois's name in a little list of "various manifestations of the image" of "the cloister as the earthly counterpart of heaven."

21. Galloway, *Penn Commentary*, 1:133–34, 139, has also suggested that Brinton read Langland—specifically that the traditional idea that Langland read the fable of the mice and rats in Brinton has the matter backwards. As for "paradise on earth," since Devlin places Sermon 24 definitely in 1373, seems to put Sermon 29 in that year also, and dates Sermon 98 as probably in 1378, and since the B-version was probably completed around 1376, it is entirely possible that the influence goes both ways: that Langland knew the phrase first from Brinton, and that Brinton then saw Langland's English before he used it again in 1378. In any case, if Devlin's dates are right, and the dating of B is right, the notion that Brinton read *Piers Plowman* provides a neat explanation of why he only says "juxta vulgare" the third time.

of hidden translation from Passus B 15. What I discovered when I tried to do that, however, was that between finding an exact hit and finding nothing there is a vast middle ground, so most of what follows—discussion of six passages—is examples of partial hits or semi-finds. (It's of course a little base of me to speak of "hits" and "semi-finds," as if my making discoveries were the only issue. The obvious explanation for a so-called "semi-hit" is that Langland is not simply translating but making English poetry. But he is also making English poetry even when he translates exactly. Nothing I have found has undermined in the least my sense of Langland's originality. I certainly want to show that he found more of his poetry in Latin books than we have been supposing, but it's also clear to me that, as I have spelled out in the Peter of Blois example, he always makes it his own, just as Chaucer makes his own what he borrows from Boethius or Jerome or the Bible. When Eliot translates Dante, as in "I had not thought death had undone so many," or Brunetto's "What! are *you* here?" (in *Little Gidding*), we thrill at the enrichment that comes from allusion. Langland's sources are more pedestrian than Eliot's, but his "translations" in fact bring a similar enlargement to the world of the poem. And it is precisely the fact that he makes what he borrows his own that has kept us from sniffing out these Latin sources.) Readers may well want to skim my six passages for what interests them, but I urge everyone to take a good look at the last one, which I thought particularly repaid my effort.

1. B 15.111–16 *Dunghill hypocrisy*

The first is a passage where Langland actually tells us his source is Latin:

> For ypocrisie in latyn is likned to a loþly dongehill
> That were bisnewed wiþ snow and snakes wiþInne,
> Or to a wal þat were whitlymed and were foul wiþInne;
> Right so, preestes, prechours and prelates manye,
> Ye aren enblaunched wiþ *bele paroles* and wiþ *bele* cloþes
> Ac youre werkes and wordes þervnder aren ful wolueliche.

The lines contain five elements: hypocrisy, dunghill, snow, snakes, and wall.
 A dunghill (Latin *sterquilinium*) is a refuse pile: it has trash and garbage as well as actual dung. The inevitable association for Langland is the book of Job, since in the Vulgate Job sits not "in the ashes" (2.8), as in modern Bibles based directly on Hebrew, but, following the Septuagint, "on the dunghill," *in sterquilinio*. The potsherd he uses to scrape the pus

from his sores he presumably found in the dunghill. His comforter Zophar associates the dunghill with hypocrisy: "gaudium hypocritae ad instar puncti . . . quasi sterquilinium in fine perdetur" ("The joy of the hypocrite [is] but for a moment . . . in the end he shall be destroyed like a dunghill," Job 20.5–7). This verse is cited often, e.g. by John of Salisbury, "Ecce quam miser est finis hypocritarum, qui, sacro testante eloquio, perdentur ut sterquilinium quo nichil immundius est" ("See how miserably hypocrites end up: as the sacred text says here, they will be destroyed like a dunghill, than which nothing is filthier," *Policraticus* 7.24, *PL* 199.701). It is also common to picture Job's dunghill as crawling with worms, though the Bible text does not say that, e.g. Aelred of Rievaulx, "Ecce sterquilinium in quo sedebat, sanies quam radebat, foetor quem exhalabat, vermes quibus scatebat . . . " ("The dunghill he sat in, the sores he scraped, the stench of his breath, the worms he was crawling with . . . ," *Dialogus de anima* 2.273–75);[22] Dhuoda, "(Job) solus in sterquilinio putredinum sedens, vermes ei ad cibum undique fluebant" ("As Job sat alone on the dunghill of filth, worms sprang up from everywhere to feed on him," *Liber manualis* 5.1.86–87);[23] Peter Chanter: "Recole penitentiam Job qui sedens in sterquilinio testa radebat saniem, et vermes scaturiebant de carne propria, uxoris et amicorum paciebatur obprobria" ("Remember Job's penance: he sat on a dunghill and scraped the sores from his head, and worms swarmed out of his flesh, and he endured insults from his wife and his friends," *Verbum abbreviatum, textus conflatus* 2.53.143).[24] To these can be added the fact that many species of snakes lay their eggs in a warm, moist place such as a dunghill; the association of snakes with dunghills is a commonplace: see the passages from Swift, Walton, South in the Appendix. Finally, see Matthew 23:33, where, in the passage in which Jesus accuses the Scribes and Pharisees of hypocrisy again and again, he calls them "You serpents, you brood of vipers." There is then a diverse background, much of it in Latin, for associating hypocrisy with dunghill and snakes.

The image of a hypocrite as a whitelimed wall comes from Acts, where Paul addresses the high priest Ananias, who should uphold Jewish law but has violated it by striking him, as "paries dealbate." Augustine: "Paries quippe dealbatus hypocrisis est, id est simulatio sacerdotalem praeferens dignitatem,

---

22. In *Aelredi Rievallensis Opera Omnia*, ed. A. Hoste and C. H. Talbot, CCCM 1 (Turnhout: Brepols, 1971), 713.

23. *Manuel pour mon fils*, ed. Pierre Riché and trans. Bernard de Vregille and Claude Mondésert, Sources Chrétiennes 225 bis (Paris: Éditions de Cerf, 1991), 266.

24. Peter the Chanter, *Verbum adbreviatum*, ed. Monique Boutry, CCCM 196 (Turnhout: Brepols. 2004), 812.

et sub hoc nomine tamquam candido tegmine interiorem quasi luteam turpitudinem occultans" ("A whited wall is hypocrisy, that is, a show of priestly dignity, and under the name of priest, as under a white surface, hiding a dirty inside," *De sermone Domini in monte* 1.1463).[25] But surely the much more famous image of the Scribes and Pharisees as whited sepulchers (Matthew 23:27), outwardly beautiful but within full of dead men's bones and all uncleanliness, is in both Augustine's mind and Langland's, since though a wall might be weak within, or rough-looking until whitewashed, it is not likely to be "foul within." Paul's image does not imply a foul inside, only the superficiality of the whitewash (and perhaps Ananias's inflexibility). Hypocrite and wall are connected to the dunghill by Peter Chanter: "De quibus etiam Job ait: 'Hoc scio, quod laus impiorum brevis est, et gaudium hypocritae ad instar puncti. Si ascenderit usque ad coelum superbia ejus, et caput ejus nubes tetigerit, quasi sterquilinium in fine perdetur (Job 20:[4–5]). Hic hypocrita sterquilinio comparatur, qui est paries dealbatus" ("Job says about them, 'This I know, that the praise of the wicked is short, and the joy of the hypocrite but for a moment.' . . . Here a hypocrite, who is a whited wall, is compared to a dunghill," *Verbum adbreviatum,* ed. Boutry 1.11.293–96, pp. 96–97).

As for the fifth element, snow, though it occurs several times in the Bible as an image of purity (e.g. Isaiah), it is not associated with hypocrisy either in the Bible or, as far as I have been able to find, in the patristic tradition. At 4 Kings 5:27, however, Giezi is "leprosus quasi nix" ("a leper as white as snow") and Peter Damian comments, "Nix enim alba, sed frigida; ypocrita nempe, qui se per sanctitatis adumbratae figmentum transfigurat in angelum lucis, nullis inferuet aestibus charitatis; atque ad instar nivis simul est albus et frigidus, quia piis quidem se deseruire operibus simulat, sed viscera solidae pietatis ignorat" ("Snow is white but cold; the hypocrite by pretending a holiness he doesn't have transfigures himself into an angel of light, but he certainly does not glow with any heat of charity, but like snow is white and cold, because he pretends that he devotes himself to good works but does not know genuine goodness from the inside," *Epistolae* 6.32, *PL* 144.426). Dan Michel of Northgate used the image of a snow-covered dunghill not for hypocrisy but for beauty: "Non uayr body ne is bote a huyt zech uol of donge stynkinde and ase a donghel besnewed" (A fair body is nothing but a white sack full of stinking dung, and like a dunghill with snow on it" (*Ayen-*

---

25. Augustine, *De sermone Domini in monte,* ed. Almut Mutzenbecher, CCSL 35 (Turnhout: Brepols, 1967), 68.

bite of Inwyt, 23b).[26] Samuel Singer's *Thesaurus proverbiorum medii aevi,*[27] s.v. Schnee 47–51, gives four French proverbs comparing pride or physical beauty to snow on a dunghill, and also gives Lydgate's Pride asserting that her mantle hides her foulness, "As snowh (who that loke wel) Maketh whyht a ffoul dongel" (*Pilgrimage of the Life of Man* 14541–42 [Whiting S441; cf. Deguileville 7999]),[28] but no Latin proverb; yet something like "hypocrisis est quasi sterquilinium tectum nive" may well have existed (indeed, I cite something close to that just below, though it is not a proverb). Under Frau 839–40 Singer cites Matheolus, *Lamentationes* 1973–75 on women: "Vestibus ornata mulier nive stercus opertum / Est; cum, sublata nive, vile sit id quod apertum/Est" ("A woman decked out in her clothes is like a dunghill covered with snow, since if the snow is removed what is revealed is vile"). The one text I know of that applies the image of a snow-covered dunghill to hypocrisy is already known to Langland scholars: the thirteenth-century *Summa virtutum de remediis anime,* edited by Siegfried Wenzel for the Chaucer Library and referred to by A. V. C. Schmidt in his note to B 15.11–13; it says that a hypocrite "est sterquilinium niue tectum in quo sal inutile est" ("is the dungheap covered with snow in which salt is useless, Luke 14").[29] Surely, however, no proverb nor learned authority would claim that snow on a dunghill hides snakes, since snakes hibernate in underground cavities, not in dunghills. Thus the idea of a dunghill with snow on the outside and snakes on the inside is actually quite improbable, though surely within the reach of the imagination.[30]

---

26. *Dan Michel's Ayenbite of Inwyt,* ed. Richard Morris and newly collated by Pamela Gradon, EETS o.s. 23 (Oxford: Oxford University Press, 1965), 81.

27. Samuel Singer, ed. *Thesaurus proverbiorum medii aevi,* 13 vols. (Berlin and New York: de Gruyter, 1995–2002).

28. Guillaume de Deguileville, *Pilgrimage of the Life of Man, Englisht by John Lydgate, A.D. 1426, from the French of Guillaume de Deguileville, A.D. 1330, 1355,* ed. Frederick J. Furnivall and Katherine B. Locock, EETS e.s. 77, 83, 92 (London: K. Paul, Trench, Trübner, 1899–1904); *Le pèlerinage de la vie humaine,* ed. J. J. Stürzinger (London: Printed for the Roxburghe Club by Nichols & Sons, 1893); Bartlett Jere Whiting with the collaboration of Helen Wescott Whiting, *Proverbs, Sentences, and Proverbial Phrases from English Writings Mainly before 1500* (Cambridge, MA: Harvard University Press, 1968).

29. Siegfried Wenzel, ed., *Summa virtutum de remediis anime* (Athens: University of Georgia Press, 1984). The salt reference is misleading. Luke quotes Jesus saying that salt that has lost its savor "is neither profitable for the land nor the dunghill" (14.35), but Jesus makes no connection to hypocrites or snow. The author of the *Summa* is able to apply the text to hypocrites by adding the snow. Schmidt's edition is William Langland, *The Vision of Piers Plowman: A Critical Edition of the B-Text Based on Trinity College Cambridge Ms. B.15.17,* 2nd ed. (London: J. M. Dent; Rutland, VT: Charles E. Tuttle, 1995).

30. Derek Pearsall in his *Piers Plowman: A New Annotated Edition of the C Text* (Exeter: University of Exeter Press, 2008), 16.266–68n, has noted the resemblance to Chaucer's *Squire's Tale* V.512–20,

This was an instructive place, tempering my confidence. I started out feeling sure that I would find a single source for the whole set of lines. What I found instead is that yes, every element in the lines is traditional, and we can even grant that individual words or phrases such as "dongehill" for "sterquilinium" or "wal that is whitlymed" for "paries dealbata" are translations—but finally what we have here is Langland composing, not Langland translating.

2. B 15.13 *Oon wiþouten tonge and teeþ*

I did not find the simple phrase "sine lingua et sine dentibus." But I did find that such oxymorons as "speaking without a tongue" and "eating without teeth" occur regularly in attempts to describe spirits. The passages quoted in the Appendix from Tertullian and Jerome are sarcastic rejoinders to those who deny the reality of Christ's flesh—as if he ate without teeth, spoke without a tongue, etc. Alcuin says to Pippin, "Quidam ignotus mecum sine lingua et voce locutus est, qui nunquam ante fuit, nec postea erit; et quem non audiebam, nec novi" ("Somebody without a voice or a tongue spoke to me: he never was and never will be, and I didn't hear him and don't know him," *De dialectica, PL* 101.978). Pippin guesses right: a dream. St. Bernard says of the Holy Spirit, "Docet vel monet sine lingua; praebet vel tenet sine manibus; sine pedibus currit et succurrit pereuntibus" ("He teaches and warns without a tongue, he offers or holds back without hands, without feet he runs to the aid of those who are perishing," *Sermo* 6, *PL* 183.803). And Richard of St. Victor, "O dulcis confabulatio Dei in anima, quae sine lingua et labiorum formatur strepitu, quae sine aure percipitur, sed sub silentio solus qui loquitur et cui loquitur audit illam, a qua omnis alienus excluditur!" ("O, the sweet talking of God in the soul, which takes form without a tongue or sound of lips, which is heard without ears: alone in silence the speaker speaks, and alone in silence the one spoken to hears the talking, and everyone outside him is excluded from it," *De gradibus charitatis, PL* 196.1206–7). In short, "speaking without a tongue or teeth" is a standard

---

in which the hypocritical tercelet is compared first to a snake hiding under flowers, then to a fair tomb covering a corpse. But the snake hidden in flowers is a much more common image, with clear overtones of the temptation of Eve in Eden—and what really makes Langland's image different from Chaucer's is the double hiding: the snow hides the putrid dunghill, and the dunghill hides snakes, not merely putrid but deadly. And at line 116 the snakes metamorphose into wolves. The image of snow on a dunghill is alive today in the myth that Luther called man redeemed a snow-covered dunghill, which is what you get if you Google the phrase.

way of describing a spirit: Langland here draws on a tradition so broad that he hardly needs to translate any particular text.

3. B 15.42–43 *Presul and Pontifex and Metropolitanus / . . . Episcopus and Pastor*

Will's riot of terms reads almost like a parody of the following passage: "Cesset ergo Eboracensis Ecclesia primatum Scotiae sibi vindicando appetere; quem si haberet, cum praesul Sancti Andreae summus pontifex Scotorum appelletur, summus vero non est nisi qui super alios est; qui autem super alios episcopus est, quid nisi archiepiscopus est, licet barbaries gentis pallii honorem ignoret? Si, inquam, super hunc, qui summus vocatur pontifex suae gentis, praelationem haberet praesul Eboracae, jam non tantum metropolitanus, imo primas esset alterius etiam regni. Quod nusquam legitur" ("Therefore let the church at York stop trying to claim pre-eminence in Scotland. If it had it, even though the bishop of St Andrew's is called the highest priest of the Scots—nobody is the highest who isn't above others. What is a bishop above other bishops but an archbishop, even if the barbarity of the nation ignores the honor of the pallium? If, I say, the bishop of York had pre-eminence over him who is called the highest priest of his nation, he would be not just the metropolitan but the primate of the other kingdom—which is unheard of," Nicholas of Worcester, *Letter to Eadmer; PL* 159.810).[31]

4. B 15.69 *Cristes counseil*

"Consilium Christi" is a fairly common phrase, used by Paulinus of Nola, but especially in Franciscan writers. Of 15 examples that come up in CETEDOC, two-thirds are by Franciscans: two by Bonaventure, one by John Pecham, one from the *Legend of the Three Companions,* and six by Peter John Olivi. Thus Langland's use of the phrase may support Lawrence M. Clopper's hypothesis that he had been a Franciscan novice.[32]

---

31. Printed also in A. W. Haddan and W. Stubbs, *Councils and Ecclesiastical Documents Relating to Great Britain and Ireland* (Oxford, 1869–78; repr., 1974), vol. 2, part 1, 202–4. For the controversy Nicholas is writing about, whether the archbishop of York or Canterbury was the metropolitan of Scotland, and for his letter, see Antonia Gransden, *Legends, Traditions, and History in Medieval England* (London; Rio Grande, OH: Hambledon Press, 1992), 14–15.

32. Lawrence Clopper, *"Songes of Rechelesnesse": Langland and the Franciscans* (Ann Arbor: University of Michigan Press, 1997), 325–33.

5. B 15.125 *Ac a Porthors þat sholde be his Plow,* Placebo *to sigge.*
(*Cf.* B 7.124 *"Of preieres and of penaunce my plouȝ shal ben herafter"*
and C 5.45–46, *"The lomes þat y labore with and lyflode deserue/
Is paternoster and my primer,* placebo *and* dirige.*"*)

Behind this cluster of lines, as behind the entire poem, is the rich agricultural imagery of the Bible and of Christian tradition.[33] Plowing appears as a metaphor in at least three biblical places: Job 4:8 and Osee 10:13, both on plowing wickedness, and in Jesus's remark at Luke 9:62, "No man putting his hand to the plow and looking back is fit for the kingdom of God." One large Christian tradition associates plowing and preaching; this was explored by Stephen A. Barney in his essay "The Plowshare of the Tongue."[34] But another is about plowing the field of one's own heart, discarding the rocks of sin and sowing the seeds of righteousness, and it is in that tradition that Langland's metaphor belongs. This plowing is penitential: the ground, it is assumed, has been infertile; the cutting action of the plowshare represents the painful work of cutting away sinful habits. Bede says of Luke 9:62, "Manum cuilibet in aratrum mittere est, quasi quodam compunctionis instrumento, ligno et ferro dominicae passionis, duritiem sui cordis atterere, atque ad proferendos operum bonorum fructus aperire" ("For anyone, to put the hand to the plow is as it were with a kind of tool of compunction, with the wood and steel of our Lord's passion, to wear down the hardness of one's heart, and to open it to bringing forth the fruit of good works," *PL* 92.461.) This definition is repeated by Rabanus (*PL* 110.513), by Gratian (*PL* 187.1567), and many others. Rabanus builds on it: "Arator crux, sive praedicationis officium, vel inchoatio bonorum operum, ut in Evangelio: Nemo mittens manum suam in aratrum, et respiciens retro, aptus est regno coelorum (Luc. IX[:62])" ("The plowman is the cross, or the office of preaching, or the beginning of good works, as in the Gospel: 'No man putting his hand to the plough, and looking back, is fit for the kingdom of God,'" *De universo* 19.1, *PL* 111.505).[35] If Bede's statement is not the exact basis of Piers's image in B 7.124, it is at least behind it—and Piers's image in turn lies behind both Will's in C 5.45–46, of his penitential psalms as his

---

33. I grant, of course, that it does not take a Latin tradition to call the key instrument of any trade a plow, as when the merchant in Chaucer's *Shipman's Tale* says that merchants' money is their plow (VII.288).

34. Stephen A. Barney, "The Plowshare of the Tongue: The Progress of a Symbol from the Bible to *Piers Plowman*," *Mediaeval Studies* 35 (1973): 261–93.

35. A rich sentence for the poem in general: the plowman is the cross, or the office of preaching, or the beginning of good works. Piers really takes up the plow when he abjures plowing for good works: he becomes most fully himself in his moment of conversion in passus 7.

tools, and the present one of the breviary as plow—with the implication that reading one's breviary is a penitential act.[36]

There is also an old play on "arare/orare." Cicero puns "ex oratore arator factus sit" ("from an orator he was made a plowman," *Orationaes Phillipicae* 3.22), and Quintilian quotes him in a passage praising witty plays on words (*Institutio oratoria* 9.3.71); Ordericus Vitalis asks, "Unde vivent oratores si defecerint aratores?" ("How would orators live if there were no more plowmen?," *PL* 188.250). Likewise many Christian writers link "orare" and "laborare," as in the traditional Benedictine motto "ora et labora"; however, the common belief that St Benedict's rule includes the dictum "laborare est orare" is erroneous,[37] and I cannot find anywhere an assertion from the Middle Ages that work is itself prayer. I remembered Barney's essay and wondered why I didn't get more, till I recalled that it is preaching he discusses, and I didn't want to go that route: I wanted collocations of plowing and praying, not plowing and preaching. I then remembered that "bubulcus" means one who plows with oxen, and I put aside "arator/aratrum" and "vomer" to search it, and found this: "De arantis allegorico officio: Bubulcus qui in bobus arat, debet habere duo, vocis suavitatem, qua mulceat laborem bonum operantium; et aculeum pungentem, quo torporem excutiat pigritantium" ("On the allegorical office of plowman: A plowman who plows with oxen needs two things: sweetness in his voice, to soothe the labor of good workers, and a stinging goad to stir the torpor of lazy ones," *Miscellanea* attributed to Hugh of St Victor, *PL* 177.745). The writer doesn't apply the allegory, but at least makes clear that plowing can be allegorized, and stresses voice. I also found Honorius's identification of the precentor with a plowman goading oxen; see Appendix. Now I had a definite connection of plowing and singing the office. Of course Langland's verb is "sigge," not "singe," and of course one would not sing from a portehors, which is a portable breviary. Nevertheless all this material suggests that Langland's thrice-used metaphor of praying and plowing has a tradition behind it.

---

36. See also Paulinus of Nola, Letter 39, to his farmer-friends Aper and Amanda, developing at length the image of cultivating the heart. At one point he says that the soul "cultivates itself with regular prayer" (*orationibus crebris semet excolat*) (*PL* 61.365; P. G. Walsh, *Letters of St. Paulinus of Nola* [Westminster, MD: Newman Press; London: Longmans, Green and Co., 1968], 2.198).

37. Marie-Benoît Meeuws, "'Ora et labora': Devise bénédictine?" *Collectanea cisterciensia* 54 (1992): 193–219. Meeuws claims it's not the motto of the Benedictines, but a nineteenth-century invention. But see some corrections in Marjorie O'Rourke Boyle, "William Harvey's Anatomy Book and Literary Culture," *Medical History* 52 (2008): 73–91, which establish that it is older, but offer no evidence that it goes back to Benedict, or even the Middle Ages.

6. B 15.148–50 A Pauline mélange

"What is charite?" quod I þo; "a childissh þyng," he seide:
"*Nisi efficiamini sicut parvuli non intrabitis in regnum celorum.*
Wiþouten fauntelte or folie a fre liberal wille."

My procedure really paid dividends in deepening my understanding of this definition of charity by Patience, and the development in lines 156–75 of "charite þat Poul preiseþ best" (156). It was clear from the start, of course, that Langland was asserting a paradox: charity is childish but not infantile. Its biblical basis is also clear enough in the passage, since Langland quotes both Jesus's "Nisi . . . efficiamini sicut parvuli" ("Unless you . . . become as little children," Matt. 18.3) and Paul's "hic in enigmate, tunc facie ad faciem" ("here darkly, then face to face,'" cf. 1 Cor 13:12, at line 162b) which evokes his (Paul's) contrast in the preceding verse between childhood and adulthood: "quando autem factus sum vir, evacuavi quae erant parvuli" ("but when I became a man, I put away the things of a child," 1 Cor 13:11). Searching "parvulus," however, made me see Paul's own expression of the paradox in the next chapter of 1 Corinthians: "Fratres, nolite pueri effici sensibus, sed malitia parvuli estote; sensibus autem perfecti estote" ("Brethren, do not become children in sense; but in malice be children, and in sense be perfect," 1 Cor 14:20); and searching "pueritia" (fauntelte) led me to the hardheaded view of boyish folly characteristic of Proverbs: "O children, how long will you love childishness, and fools covet those things which are hurtful to themselves, and the unwise hate knowledge?" (1:22); "Folly is bound up in the heart of the child, and the rod of correction shall drive it away" (22:15). Furthermore, various Latin writers (e.g. Augustine, *Contra Faustum* 12.35 [*PL* 42.272], Isidore, *Allegoriae sacrae scripturae* 98 [*PL* 83.113)] compare the Jews who mock Jesus on Calvary to the "puerilis stultitia" of the boys who mock Elisha's baldness and are eaten by two bears (4 Kings 2:23–24). That phrase, "puerilis stultitia," seems to lie behind Langland's "fauntelte or folie." And a still deeper sense of the biblical basis of the passage came to me when—again, thinking Latin—I read "He is glad wiþ alle glade" (169) and thought, that's Paul: "gaudere cum gaudentibus, flere cum flentibus" ("rejoice with them that rejoice, weep with them that weep," Romans 12:15)—a line Langland has already quoted at A 11.193. In the C version it is clearer that Langland is translating Paul: "He is glad with alle glade as gurles þat lawhen alle/And sory when he seth men sory" (C 16.302–3). So I turned to Romans 12—and realized that Langland's whole passage defining charity, B 15.148–74 (C 16.298–315, a little less clearly; see below) translates (not in order of verses, and with Langland's usual freedom) Paul's two meditations on charity, Romans 12:9–21 and 1 Corinthians 13. The use of 1 Corinthians 13 is maybe obvious enough, since Langland quotes it several times in the passage, but there is no Latin hint given of the reliance on Romans 12, even though more of the passage actually comes from there:

> 165 ne chaffareþ noȝt, ne chalangeþ, ne craueþ: "non quaerit quae sua sunt" 1 Cor 13:5; 166–68 As proud of a peny as of a pound of golde . . . scarlet: "non alta sapientes, sed humilibus consentientes" Rom 12.16; 169 glad wiþ alle glade: Rom 12:15 (as above); good til alle wikkede: "nulli malum pro malo reddentes" Rom 12:17; 170 leneþ and loueþ alle þat oure lord made: "si esurierit inimicus tuus, ciba illum, si sitit, potum da illi" Rom 12:20 (also "necessitatibus sanctorum communicantes" 12:13, "providentes bona" 12:17); 171 Corseþ he no creature ne he kan bere no wraþe: "benedicite persequentibus vos: benedicite et nolite maledicere" 12:14, "date locum irae" 12:19, "non irritatur" 1 Cor 13:5; 172 Ne no likynge haþ to lye ne laughe men to scorne: "non gaudet super iniquitate, congaudet autem veritate" 1 Cor 13:6; 173–74 Al þat men seyn, he leet it sooþ and in solace takeþ/And alle manere meschiefs in myldenesse he suffreþ: "omnia credit, omnia sperit, omnia sustinet" 1 Cor 13:7, "nulli malum pro malo reddentes" Rom 12.7, "non vosmetipsos defendentes" Rom 12:19; 175 Coueiteþ he noon erþely good, but heueneriche blisse: "non est ambitiosa, non quaerit quae sua sunt" 1 Cor 13:5 plus 8–14, all looking to "cum autem venerit quod perfectum est" (10).

The personification of charity, the re-ordering of the statements, and all the little vignettes and specifications disguise the translation; nor is every verse of Paul in either passage translated. Still the *fundamentum* of Langland's passage, the *fons et origo*, the ground of all, is Paul. Of course, someone else who knows the Bible better might have recognized the reliance on Paul without trying to smell out translated lines, but my method worked for me. I should also say that the revision of this passage in C, despite the one line I have already quoted that is closer to Paul, seems designed to make it a little less derivative. And yet even in the C version, Paul is still the ground.

What can I conclude from these six examples? First, that extended, point--for-point reliance on an unacknowledged source, such as shows up in the Peter of Blois passage, and that I had hoped (as if hunting for Easter eggs) to find more and more of, is probably very rare: even the extended reliance on Romans 12 in the definition of charity, though I can tick off the correspondences, is much more mediated by Langland's shaping and his inventive phrasing than the Blois passage. The other five have illuminated Langland's methods of composition precisely by refusing to yield a perfect match to me: each in its way shows how deeply intertwined his imagery and diction can be with Latin materials, but each also finally shows him composing freely, not working with any one identifiable text. They vindicate his independence, which the Blois passage might conceivably call into question (though I have argued that it does not). They give us a glimpse beyond a Langland learned in Latin to a Langland inventive in English. But the definition of charity lets us see deepest of all, lets us see how fruitful engagement with two of Paul's most eloquent passages brings Langland also to a new pitch of eloquence, makes him not less inventive but more. I have always thought that the definition of charity is a highlight of the poem, always felt a new surge in the verse; now it is hard for me not to see that surge as arising out of the thrill Langland must have felt at outdoing Paul with new diction, new imagery, even as he stays close to Paul's text. This is translation and transcendence at once.

Appendix of Illustrative Passages to #1, 2, and 5 Above

1. *Dunghill/hypocrite*

Swift's "Description of a Salamander," 29–31:

> I've seen a snake in human Form,
> All stain'd with Infamy and Vice,
> Leap from the Dunghill in a trice.

Walton's *Compleat Angler*, ch. 8: "The land-snake breeds and hatches her eggs, which become young snakes, in some old dunghill, or a like hot place."

From a sermon of 1845 by Robert South: "For as snakes breed in dunghills, not singly but in knots . . . " (*Sermons Preached Upon Several Occasions* (Philadelphia: Sorin & Ball, 1845).

2. *One without tongue and teeth*

Tertullian, *De carne Christi* 5: Quid dimidias mendacio Christum? Totus veritas fuit. Maluit, credo, nasci quam ex aliqua parte mentiri, et quidem in semetipsum, ut carnem gestaret sine ossibus duram, sine musculis solidam, sine sanguine cruentam, sine tunica vestitam, sine fame esurientem, sine dentibus edentem, sine lingua loquentem, ut phantasma auribus fuerit sermo ejus per imaginem vocis. (Why make out that Christ was half a lie? He was wholly the truth. He thought it better, I am sure, to be born than to be partially a liar, a liar too against himself, by wearing flesh without bones yet hard, without muscles yet firm, without blood yet gory, without a cloak yet clothed, flesh that hungered without appetite, ate without teeth, and spoke without a tongue, so that his discourse should be a phantasm conveyed to the ears by the ghost of a voice. [*Q. Septimii Florentis Tertulliani De Carne Christi Liber: Tertullian's Treatise on the Incarnation*. Ed. and transl. Ernest Evans (London: Society for Promoting Christian Knowledge, 1956)].)

Jerome, *Contra Joannem Hierosolymitanum, ad Pammachium* [Against John of Jerusalem, To Pammachius] (like the preceding, contradicting Marcion) (*PL* 23.387): Noli potentiam Domini Magorum praestigiis adaequare, ut videatur fuisse quod non fuit, et putetur comedisse sine dentibus, ambulasse sine pedibus, fregisse panem sine manibus, locutus esse sine lingua, et latus monstrasse sine costis. (Don't equate the power of the Lord with the tricks of magicians, so that he may appear to have been what he was not, and may be thought to have eaten without teeth, walked without feet, broken bread without hands, spoken without a tongue, and showed his side without ribs.)

3. Plowing

Honoratus of Marseilles, *Vita Hilarii* (*PL* 50.1223): Corpore infirmus, mente validus et robustus, sobolem novam spiritali adhortatione concipiens, instructione formans, orationibus procreans, in corde praeclari cespitis sanctum semen aratro fidei percolendum jaciebat peritus agricola, quod orationum perennibus donis et lacrymarum fluentibus rivis irrigabat. (Weak in body but strong and robust in mind, the expert farmer conceived a new shoot by spiritual exhortation, formed it by instruction, and brought it forth by prayer. He sowed in his bright heart of turf a holy seed to be cultivated by the plow of faith, and he irrigated it by constant gifts of prayers and flowing rivers of tears.)

Gregory, *Homilies on Ezechiel*, 3 (*PL* 76.813): Manum quippe in aratrum mittere est quasi per quemdam compunctionis vomerem ad proferendos fructus terram sui cordis aperire. (To put your hand to the plow is as it were by the plowshare of compunction to open the land of your heart to bear fruit.)

Galandus Regniacensis, *Libellus proverbiorum,* Proverb 99: Qui terrenam mentem suam penitentie uomere scindens eius occulta confitendo aperit, spiritalis arator est (A man who cuts the earth of his mind with the plowshare of penance and thus opens up his secrets by confessing them is a spiritual plowman.) Galand de Reigny, *Petit livre de proverbes.* Ed. Jean Chatillon, Maurice Dumontier, and Alexis Grélois. Source Chrétiennes 436 (Paris, Editions de Cerf, 1998), p. 142.

Honorius of Autun, *Gemma animae,* 1.17, *PL* 172.549–50 (describing a high mass with the bishop presiding): Legitur in Evangelio de servo arante, quod, peracto acto opere de agro, domum redeat, et post servitium Domino suo impensum ad convivium recumbat (Luc. 17). Ager Dei sunt corda fidelium, servus arans est ordo praedicantium; per lectorem Epistolae doctores exprimuntur, qui agrum Dei praedicando coluerunt; per responsionem, fideles qui per bonam operationem respondentes fructum justitiae protulerunt. Aratrum, est nostrum servitium. Boves hinc inde trahentes sunt utrinque totis viribus Domino canentes. Praecentor qui cantantes manu et voce incitat, est servus qui boves stimulo minans dulci voce bobus jubilat. . . . Cantores qui respondent primo canenti, vox est auditorum quasi evigilantium et Dominum laudantium. Versus, est arans servus per dulcedinem modulationis corda carnalium, quae se aperiunt more sulci in confessione vocis et lacrymarum. Arant qui aratro compunctionis corda scindunt, in lectione pascitur auditor quasi quodammodo bos. Bos ad hoc pascitur, ut in eo opus agriculturae exerceatur. Bos est praedicator, cantor, quodammodo bubulcus, qui jubilat bobus, ut hilarius aratrum trahant, scilicet instigat canentes ut laetius canant. Terra scinditur, quando corda auditorum compunguntur. Tales operarii cum de agro hujus mundi redeunt, aeternum convivium cum Domino suo ineunt.

(We read in the gospels of a servant plowing that when his work in the field is done he comes home and after further service to his Lord sits down to supper [Luke 17:7–8, bent to Honorius's needs]. God's field is the hearts of the faithful, the plowing servant is the order of preachers. The reader of the epistle stands for teachers who have cultivated the field of God by preaching; the response stands for the faithful who respond by doing well and thus have brought forth the fruit of justice. The plow is our service of worship. The oxen pulling back and forth are those singing on both sides of the choir with all their strength to the Lord. The precentor who leads the singers with hand and voice is the servant who even as he threatens the oxen with the goad calls joyfully to them in a sweet voice. . . . The singers who respond to the first singer—this is the voice of listeners as it were watching and praising the lord. The verse is the servant plowing hearts of the carnal with the sweetness of his modulation; the hearts open up just like a furrow, confessing with voice and tears. They plow who cut those hearts with the plow of compunction; in the reading the listener grazes in a way like the ox. The ox grazes so that he can do the work of cultivating the field. The ox is the preacher; the cantor, in a way like the plowman who calls joyfully to the oxen so that they will pull the plow more gaily, goads the singers to sing more joyfully. The earth is cut when the hearts of listeners are pierced with compunction. And all these workers, when they come home from the field of this world, go into endless supper with their Lord.)

four

Escaping the Whirling Wicker
Ricardian Poetics and Narrative Voice in The Canterbury Tales

KATHERINE ZIEMAN

IN THE LATE 1980s, Lee Patterson pointed to "Exegetics," the mode of criticism associated with D. W. Robertson, Jr., as "the great unfinished business of Medieval Studies. . . . Unable to absorb Exegetics and move on, Chaucer studies instead circles back almost compulsively to an apparently irrepressible scandal, a recursiveness that itself bespeaks a scandalous limitation to its own critical creativity."[1] In far less dramatic fashion, one might claim that the mode of criticism derided as "dramatic" or "psychological" reading has been similarly irrepressible. Often traced back to George Lyman Kittredge, dramatic readings take as their basic principle the idea that "the Pilgrims do not exist for the sake of the stories, but *vice versa*. Structurally regarded, the stories are merely long speeches expressing, directly or indirectly, the characters of the several persons."[2] If Robertson's Augustinian model of reading presumed that "charity" was the telos of Chaucerian representation, dramatic reading presumed it to be "character." In their most extreme forms, both hermeneutics stand accused of conveniently invoking disjunctive modes of signification—allegory, irony—in the service of

---

1. Lee Patterson, *Negotiating the Past: The Historical Understanding of Medieval Literature* (Madison: University of Wisconsin Press, 1987), 5.

2. George Lyman Kittredge, *Chaucer and His Poetry* (Cambridge, MA: Harvard University Press, 1946), 154–55.

their presumed end. Where exegetical criticism tended to see in Chaucer's romances and fabliaux ironic denunciations of *fol amor*, "dramatic" readings saw fallible narrators whose inept rhetoric or unsavory politics were satirized, but never embraced, by Chaucer.

Dramatic reading was in many ways the corollary of Exegetics. If Exegetics stressed (and overgeneralized) the alterity of the Middle Ages, dramatic reading presumed the continuity of modes of literary expression considered transhistorical. Validated by the New Criticism, above all by E. Talbot Donaldson's "Chaucer the Pilgrim,"[3] dramatic reading took for granted the unity of form and content that gave the literary object an autonomous existence to which interpretive gestures equally appropriate to Coleridge or Browning could be applied. Indeed, as Patterson pointed out, it was precisely against this perception of a universal literary that Exegetical critics were reacting with their brand of historicism.[4] While Donaldson's reference to "Chaucer the Poet" as a transcendent figure does seem old-fashioned, various forms of dramatic reading persist in scholarship and pedagogy, despite repeated critiques of such reading strategies. Though the debate over the nature of Chaucer's narrative voice(s) has never escalated to a degree one would call scandalous, its lack of resolution does suggest an impasse in modern scholarship—one that arises from the same seemingly contradictory imperatives that aggravated the scandal of Exegetics: the goal on the one hand, of defining the concepts and interpretive strategies that define literary study as a coherent discipline, and, on the other, the desire to attend to the contingencies and particular circumstances of past cultures.

Scholarship devoted to Chaucer's narrative voice has gone beyond Donaldson in providing both theoretical nuance and a sense of historical specificity, but with widely diverging results in terms of how we should perceive Chaucerian utterances. Patterson, following H. Marshall Leicester, Jr., reframed the issues raised by Donaldson by claiming that Chaucer was not so much interested in character as he was in subjectivity.[5] This shift to some degree changed the terms of the discussion by acknowledging that every "I" is constructed, yet it also subordinated the stylistic and structural issues of narrative voice to a thematic concern with subjectivity—a concern attributed to Chaucer himself. If such interpretations no longer focused on determin-

---

3. E. Talbot Donaldson, "Chaucer the Pilgrim," orig. published in *PMLA* 69 (1954), repr. in *Speaking of Chaucer* (New York: Norton, 1970), 1–12.

4. Patterson, *Negotiating the Past*, 6.

5. Lee Patterson, *Chaucer and the Subject of History* (Madison: University of Wisconsin Press, 1991); H. Marshall Leicester, Jr., *The Disenchanted Self: Representing the Subject in the "Canterbury Tales"* (Berkeley: University of California Press, 1990).

ing the presence of irony, they still relied on the presumed unity of the Tales' narrative voices, as well as the idea that distinctive features of these voices serve to tell us something about the subject who utters them.[6] In direct contrast, scholars such as David Lawton and, more recently, A. C. Spearing have drawn on ideas from Bakhtin and sociolinguistics to argue not simply against the idea that the voices of the tales reflect their tellers, but also against the very coherence of the narrative voices employed in the tales, claiming that the "I" of any given tale is best understood as a rhetorical effect produced by narration rather than as a fully psychologized character.[7] These divergent views represent only two positions in a range of possibilities for perceiving the narrative voice(s) of *The Canterbury Tales*. Nor is it a trivial distinction: how one understands the fictive origin of an utterance—as emanating from a particular pilgrim, from a rhetorically produced "I," or from Chaucer—has a highly significant impact on one's experience of the text.

Indeed, it is difficult to imagine a modern literary work for which there would be this kind of disagreement on such a fundamental issue. This is not to suggest that modern texts have stable voices or that we all interpret them in the same way, but that we come to them with a set of shared expectations, through training and broader cultural practice, that structures our experience—generic, rhetorical, and typographical conventions (e.g., quotation marks) that help us determine how we might experience evocations of the voice in written texts. It is, perhaps, because the matter of how to negotiate this historical distance has not been resolved at the level of methodology that dramatic reading remains a not uncommon practice, especially at the level of the high school and introductory college teaching. Dramatic reading, furthermore, has a certain expedience in that it creates an instantly enabling hermeneutic that offers the satisfactions of affective identification familiar from novel-reading and modern confessional culture. Yet pointing to the uncertainties of historical distance and the comforts of more modern strategies does not explain why Donaldson's hermeneutic was so powerfully enabling to readers of Chaucer when such New Critical strategies fell flat when applied to his contemporaries, such as Langland.[8] Nor does it explain

---

6. Leicester, for example, takes as the "proper method" of reading "to ascribe the entire narration in all its details, to a single speaker . . . and use it as evidence in constructing that speaker's subjectivity" (*Disenchanted Self,* 12).

7. David Lawton, *Chaucer's Narrators* (Cambridge, UK: D. S. Brewer, 1985); A. C. Spearing, *Textual Subjectivity: The Encoding of Subjectivity in Medieval Narratives and Lyrics* (Oxford: Oxford University Press, 2005).

8. This is not to say that such readings have not been attempted. See, for example, Jay Martin, "Wil as Fool and Wanderer in Piers Plowman," *Texas Studies in Literature and Language* 3 (1962): 535–48; Richard K. Emmerson, "'Coveitise to Konne,' 'Goddes Pryvetee,' and Will's Ambiguous Dream

why such cogent arguments against dramatic reading as those articulated by Lawton and Spearing have not been more fully elaborated in an alternative methodology.

I would like to begin addressing these question by moving the discussion away from determining the presence or absence of irony, and away from determining the presence or absence of particular subjective intentions, toward examining the excesses of Chaucerian literary language—the sense that Chaucer's language means more than it says. It is this sense of excess meaning that the concept of irony or the assignment of particular intentions or words to specific speakers have served (however inadequately) to organize. Indeed, some would say that it is a feature of all language we consider literary, yet the question remains as to how Chaucer goes about eliciting and managing such excess in his writings as well as to how his strategies might be seen as responding to the conditions of vernacular literary production in his historical moment. To that end I would like to situate Chaucer's *Canterbury Tales* as part of the experiment in "vulgar eloquence" that Anne Middleton defined as "Public Poetry,"[9] in other words, as a project that uses different structural and rhetorical means to responds to the same pressures and concerns that engaged writers like William Langland. With this configuration of the literary and the historical in mind, I will then turn to the *locus classicus* of Chaucer's fallible narrators, the Man of Law, to suggest that while Chaucer's own poetic experimentation produced a form of refracted, duplicitous discourse that allows dramatic reading, his interest lay more in the public than the subjective aspects of language and intention.

Public Poetry and the Problem of Noise

Middleton describes "public poetry" as a project in vernacular literary expression in which writers such as Langland and Gower sought to represent "a 'common voice' to serve a 'common good.'"[10] "Common" in this case is conceived as a social category roughly synonymous with the "third estate": a category defined partly by engagement in labor or productivity, however that might be understood, yet also by lack of membership in the estates tra-

---

Experience in *Piers Plowman*," in *Suche Werkis to Werche: Essays on Piers Plowman in Honor of David C. Fowler*, ed. Míċeál Vaughan (East Lansing, MI: Colleagues Press, 1993), 89–121; Joseph S. Wittig, "'Culture Wars' and the Persona in *Piers Plowman*," *Yearbook of Langland Studies* 15 (2001): 167–95.

9. Anne Middleton, "The Idea of Public Poetry in the Reign of Richard II" *Speculum* 53 (1978): 94–114.

10. Middleton, "Idea of Public Poetry," 95.

ditionally endowed with the sociopolitical power to engage in public discourse. The "common voice" was thus determined by a lack of institutional interest, even while the raw materials from which it was to be constructed were often derived from the institutional discourses of church and court. The shared interests that might be discerned from this extra-institutional position are rarely self-evident. Public poetry, to the contrary, often evinces myriad forms of self-interest and is characterized by speakers willing to game the system to make institutional language work on their own behalf. The public poet makes it his job to create a common voice "distilled out of all the disparate special languages of society's parts," yet he attempts to create this synthesis from within, as it were, eschewing not merely the *personae* of church and crown that he is not authorized to take on, but also those of prophet or poet: he "claim[s] no privileged position, no special revelation from God or Muses."[11]

In attempting to situate themselves outside the institutions that produced public language, Ricardian poets were in some respects bound to focus on what M. M. Bakhtin referred to as the "centrifugal forces" of language: the drive to appropriate language to one's particular interests that is always in tension with the "centripetal forces" that stabilize and generalize language—the unifying mechanisms of official language, such as documentary formulae and conventional verse forms.[12] It is these centrifugal forces that Chaucer represents so vividly in the *House of Fame*'s Whirling Wicker, the rickety structure that is simultaneously the repository of all human speech and the chaotic instrument of its publication. As an image, it captures the sense of "centrifugal" force better than the examples of carnivalesque reversal—parody, clowning, buffoonery—Bakhtin himself enumerates to exemplify it. With this representation, Chaucer shows an affinity for the aims of public poetry, but simultaneously shows its challenges and pitfalls. The Wicker is itself an allegorical, and perhaps parodic, representation of the "common voice," which plays on the idiomatic use of the phrase in Middle English to mean "gossip, rumor."[13] As utterances circulate in the Wicker's structures, it becomes clear that the difficulty in representing the common voice is not merely that it might reveal self-interest rather than common good, but, more fundamentally, that unless structured by some form of unifying authority,

---

11. Middleton, "Idea of Public Poetry," 98, 99.

12. M. M. Bakhtin, *The Dialogic Imagination: Four Essays*, ed. Michael Holquist and trans. Caryl Emerson and Michael Holquist (Austin: University of Texas Press, 1982), 271–73.

13. *MED*, "voice," 3c. It is, however, not absolutely certain that the idiom was a "buzz word" among Ricardian poets before the 1390s.

the constitutive elements of such a voice simply will not signify; the result will not be poetry but inconsequential rumor, gossip, and noise.

This vision of noise is shared by Chaucer's contemporaries. Figured in the street cries at the end of the prologue to *Piers Plowman* and, in more politically determined fashion, in the rebellious animals of Gower's *Vox clamantis*, noise represents the instabilities of a language not fully structured by institutions as much as it represents the social mobility of those who claimed it as an everyday language.[14] Institutions and the forms of training they made available provided not simply authorization, but the terms of generalizability and stable contextualization that allows utterances to have meaning beyond their immediate moment. Without such terms language cannot signify.[15] The House of Fame depicts precisely such a loss of meaning as Geffrey describes the amplification of the "tydynges" that fill the Whirling Wicker:

> "Nost not thou
> That ys betyd, lo, late or now?"
> "No," quod he, "telle me what."
> And than he tolde hym this and that,
> And swor therto that hit was soth—
> "Thus hath he sayd," and "Thus he doth,"
> "Thus shal hit be," "Thus herde y seye,"
> "That shal be founde," "That dar I leye"—
> That al the folk that ys alyve
> Ne han the kunnynge to discryve
> The thinges that I herde there,
> What aloude, and what in ere.[16]

---

14. On English as "noise," see John Ganim, "Chaucer and the Noise of the People," in *Chaucerian Theatricality* (Princeton, NJ: Princeton University Press, 1990), 108–20; D. Vance Smith, "Chaucer as an English Writer," in *The Yale Companion to Chaucer*, ed. Seth Lerer (New Haven, CT: Yale University Press, 2006), 87–88; on the sociopolitical aspects of English and "mobility," see Steven Justice, *Writing and Rebellion: England in 1381* (Berkeley: University of California Press, 1994).

15. This issue affects all vernaculars, particularly when first pressed into the service of self-consciously literary expression. Ngũgĩ wa Thiong'o wrote of a similar sense of chaos in his earliest attempts to write literature in his native Gĩkũyũ: "I would write a paragraph in the evening sure of how it read, only later to find that it could be read in a different way which completely altered the meaning. I could only solve the problem by severely controlling the context of words in a sentence, and that of sentences in a paragraph, and that of the paragraph within the entire situation of the occurrence of the action in time and space. Yes, words did slip and slide under my own eyes. They would not stay in place. They would not stay still. And this was often a matter of great frustration" (*Decolonising the Mind: The Politics of Language in African Literature* [Oxford: Currey, 1986], 75).

16. *The Riverside Chaucer*, gen. ed. Larry Benson, 3rd ed. (Boston: Houghton Mifflin, 1987), *House of Fame*, ll.2047–58. All quotations of Chaucer's works are from this edition.

Without a principle of generalization beyond the fact of their rehearsal, the *tydynges* that were proffered by the Eagle as the stuff from which poetry might be made overwhelm in their copiousness. Ultimately, they can only be represented by vague demonstratives in a series of repeated verbal gestures. Though they are said to grow, this growth does not involve the production of greater meaning, but rather a simple growth in intensity, envisaged as destructive rather than generative, "encresing ever moo, / As fyr ys wont to quyke and goo / From a sparke spronge amys, / Til al a citee brent up ys" (2077–80).

Insofar as content is considered, the chaos of the Whirling Wicker ensures its consistent corruption. The well know passage in which the "sad soth sawe" and the "lesynge" have their slapstick collision as they simultaneously try to escape the Wicker suggests that the very act of articulation introduces falsehood. It does so, furthermore, in language that seems to mock the very idea of a common voice:

"And here I wol ensuren the,
Wyth the nones that thou wolt do so,
That I shal never fro the go,
But be thyn owne sworen brother!
We wil medle us ech with other,
That no man, be they never so wrothe,
Shal han on [of us] two, but bothe
At ones."
(*HF,* 2098–105)

Expressed in the terms of an oath of fellowship (made by whom it is not specified), the duplicity of *tydynges* suggests that truth cannot be distilled from shared interest, but rather that it is precisely this commingling of particular interests that ensures the distortion of meaning.

The House of Fame famously stalls precisely as the mysterious "man of gret auctorite" arrives on the scene (2158), with all the promise of order and meaning he implies. Yet even in its stalling and denial, the poem at some level displays an interest in the project of transmuting *tydynges* into truth. As the experiments of his contemporaries show, the expression of truth in vernacular poetics is a complicated matter, one that they pursue less by explicitly philosophical and political debate than by structural experimentation, in part because they do not pursue truth as a series of propositions or pronouncements made from above, but rather as something that might emerge from the noise of everyday discourse. Put another way, the project was one of defining and mediating between proper and common[17]—of identifying those aspects of the contemporary and the local that might exceed their particular moments to become relevant to common interest. Ricardian poetry experiments with various forms of focalization to effect such mediation. In the end, the *House of Fame* arguably becomes a comic representation of a failed experiment, one in which vernacular talk simply fails to signify beyond its immediate context, let alone have any claim on public attention.

Even though the Whirling Wicker represents a failure, the *House of Fame* still participates in Ricardian experimentation at the level of voice and form. If the various modes of address that characterize this poetry can be considered in terms of their management of proper and common, the dream vision form of the *House of Fame* is chief among the formal techniques used for such management. With its dual Boethian and French pedigree, the dream vision offered these writers a narrative form that simultaneously invested narrated experience with the promise of visionary truth and allowed that promise to be perpetually deferred. This interest was often coupled with a predilection for estates satire, with its pretensions to represent social totalities. More important than the narrative forms themselves, however, was the "I" that mediated them. Whereas the vague cacophony of voices in the House of Rumor is figured as an ineffective navigation of the range between particularity and generalizability, the Ricardian "I" offered a formal solution to that problem. The "I" who narrates visionary experience has the capacity to modulate between the immediacy of particular experience and generalized reflection, whether on the part of the "I" or through an interlocutor. While the speaker is usually closely identified with the poet himself, often with forms of authorial signatures, the identification is a complex one.[18] Insofar as the "I" coheres as a stable *persona*, it is what David Lawton has called an "open *persona*," that which "looks outward in order to challenge an audience's responses, rather than a 'closed' *persona*, which turns inwards, hermetically seals the artifact, and requires an independent solution. . . . it operates on the level of response and relationship; it is conceived not as a kind of drama but as a rhetorical extension of the poem's narrative."[19] Though one could say a great deal about the kinds of cultural formations that give rise to such a rhetorical strategy, the "open" *persona* serves not to explore subjectivity as

---

17. The difficulty in defining what is appropriate to "common" interest is the correlative of the "crisis of the proper" that Middleton identifies in her discussion of Langland's authorial signatures ("William Langland's 'Kynde Name': Authorial Signature and Social Identity in Late Fourteenth-Century England," in *Literary Practice and Social Change in Britain, 1380–1530*, ed. Lee Patterson [Berkeley: University of California Press, 1990], 15–82).

18. Middleton, "William Langland's 'Kynde Name,'" esp. 24–37.

19. Lawton, *Chaucer's Narrators*, 6.

such, but rather to mediate narratives in a particular way. It contextualizes narrated events through the particularity of experience, while simultaneously broadening its scope by modeling perception and reflecting on it: "the first-person narrator is there not to concentrate attention but to generalize it."[20]

Though Lawton claims that both Chaucer and Langland make use of open *personae*, he, like most scholars, distinguishes between them in terms of their handling of the technique. There is of course reason to do so: whereas Langland's public poetry speaks "as if" to a larger audience conceived as the Christian community, Chaucer's "Geffrey" seems, in his earlier poetry at least, to address those familiar with him. Whereas Langland's rhetorical stance is drawn largely from penitential traditions, Chaucer's is indebted to French courtly poetry. Yet insofar as these distinctions have underwritten a critical notion of Chaucer as unremittingly ironic and Langland as perpetually earnest, they may distract us from the ways in which the projects of both poets converge as they both come to explore the mediation of proper and common, particularly in regard to experimentation with narrative voice. Langland's extension of his similarly stalled A Version of *Piers Plowman* takes the direction of making his open *persona* and its generalizability the subject of scrutiny and formal elaboration. As I have argued elsewhere, it is in the extension of Vision Three, with "Will's" complaint about the value of *clergie* and the inner dream that it initiates, that the Dreamer is resituated from an observer on the boundaries of the narrative to an actant within it, thereby creating the possibility of a more closed *persona*.[21] This possibility, however, is realized only strategically and partially and never becomes a structural element of the poem as a whole.[22] The exploration suggests, rather, that the distinction between "open" and "closed" *personae* might best be considered as a spectrum, analogous to the spectrum between proper and common, that Ricardian writers were interested in exploring.

In *Piers Plowman* this spectrum—in part because it is surveyed by means of the first person—fraught with ethical tension. D. Vance Smith discusses this problem in the context of the oft-quoted passage from Will's chastisement by Ymaginatif in the B Version of *Piers Plowman*: "And þow medlest þee wiþ makynges and myȝtest go seye þi sauter" (B 12.16). As Smith points out, vernacular making is for Langland defined as a kind of "meddling."[23] It involves Will's presumptuous, unauthorized intrusion into the language of

---

20. Lawton, *Chaucer's Narrators*, 9.
21. Katherine Zieman, *Singing the New Song: Literacy and Liturgy in Late Medieval England* (Philadelphia: University of Pennsylvania Press, 2008), 162–75.
22. See, however, the studies mentioned in n. 8 above.
23. Smith, "Chaucer as an English Writer," 111.

truth, his active wrangling of and within it, which is contrasted to the performance of the Psalter, a performance in which the "I" merely conforms to David's image and is assimilated to it. The Chaucerian "I" of the dream visions and the *Troilus* at best seems to play out this tension by means of an imperfect and ironized relation to the "authorities" on which his tales are based rather by questioning the value of his enterprise altogether, yet the image of the Whirling Wicker does seem to engage this tension more directly. Smith in fact reads the "meddling" of the "sad sothe sawe" and "lesynge" of the *House of Fame* as a direct response to the Ymaginatif episode. While one might be reticent to lay that much interpretive weight on a single repeated word, it is clear that a similar cluster of concepts involving the publication of truth and its problematic nature is at stake in both cases. Smith claims that for Chaucer, in contrast to Langland,

> meddling is simply what we begin with, a mixed relation between truth and falsehood that we encounter whether we turn to the primal scene of poetry, language, or fame or to the larger world. And Chaucer seems to be offering a way out of the Langlandian hall of mirrors in this passage, also. We have no choice but to turn to "tydynges" if we want to say anything at all. The utterance itself tells us that we humans are powerless to evaluate its truth claims, and moral indignation is quite literally beside the point.[24]

This is an insightful description of the workings of language in *The House of Fame*. At the same time, it also describes the Chaucer of much modern scholarship whose double-voiced discourse seems so often deployed to resist reduction to a single (moral) point of view.[25] Yet if Langland's "I" managed to encase itself in a hall of mirrors in his self-interrogations, it is not clear that the decontextualized "tydynges" that escaped the Whirling Wicker signify anything more successfully.

Chaucer's efforts in reworking the materials of the *House of Fame* in *The Canterbury Tales*, as I will discuss, suggest that his implicit claims about the impossibility of truth are not his final pronouncement on the potential of public poetry. Whereas his way out of the hall of mirrors may have involved some acknowledgment about the nature of language, his escape from the

---

24. Smith, "Chaucer as an English Writer," 111–12.

25. Thomas J. Farrell is one of the few scholars who have attempted to work against this point of view. He points out that critics like Jill Mann have limited the degree of irony with which they presumed the text to signify, then replaced that irony with an ethical ambiguity by stating that Chaucer always suspends judgment on his characters ("The Persistence of Donaldson's Memory," *Chaucer Review* 41 [2007]: 291).

Whirling Wicker involved transforming the narratorial voice of his poetry, replacing Langland's reflexive "I" with the "he" and "she" of *The Canterbury Tales*, who each perform *as* a particular, locatable "I," but are distinguishable from Chaucer's "I." This distancing of the voice from the poet's "I" does not forestall the ethical questions raised by the implicated speaker. If anything, it places the notion of intention and interest in sharper relief as inevitable aspects of performance. Though Chaucer criticism has tended to focus on the refracted, duplicitous speech that results as a source of irreducible irony, Chaucer's *Man of Law's Tale* suggests that public truths can emerge from such implicated speech.

Meddling with Makings and the Man of Law

While the Canterbury project as a whole can be said to rework the issues raised between *House of Fame* and *Piers Plowman*, it is in *The Man of Law's Tale* that the dialogue about *tydynges* and truth is continued most explicitly. Several scholars have noted the importance of *tydynges* to both poems: in *House of Fame*, as we saw, "tydynges" were put forth as the raw materials of vernacular poetry; similarly, in *The Man of Law's Tale*, the merchants' "tydynges" are figured as the source of the tale of Constance (*MLT*, 2.129–30).[26] Given the problems connected to *tydynges* in the House of Rumor, where they issued only in chaotic noise, one might claim that in *The Man of Law's Tale*, Chaucer figured out what to do with *tydynges*—how to make them signify.

To claim that *The Man of Law's Tale* resolves anything might seem odd, as few critics would place among Chaucer's more successful tales. Nor is there much agreement about it, particularly in terms of its narrative voice. The tale is, as I mentioned, a *locus classicus* for interpretations that rely on fallible narrators as well for scholars determined to eliminate the idea of the fallible narrator altogether. Possessing all the elements that cause interpreters to wonder about its status, it is not to the liking of modern tastes, either aesthetically or politically. It employs what most modern readers perceive as extravagant, even inelegant, rhetorical gestures to tell a tale that represents women as objects of exchange among men, much of it set in an orientalist

---

26. This connection has been noted by David Wallace, *Chaucerian Polity: Absolutist Lineages and Associational Forms in England and Italy* (Stanford, CA: Stanford University Press, 1997), 185–87; Carolyn Dinshaw, *Chaucer's Sexual Poetics* (Madison: University of Wisconsin Press, 1989), 95; Smith, "Chaucer as an English Writer," 112–13.

landscape.²⁷ For every reader who has distanced the tale from Chaucer by assigning its excesses and failures to the Man of Law, there is another critic who insists that the tale is "serious"—that its seeming excesses arose because Chaucer "deepened and thickened the rhetorical and moral texture of the story."²⁸ While such readings have valuable things to say about the sociopolitical import of the tale, the narrative *persona* they describe does seem suspiciously confected to organize our responses to its inconsistencies. It is perhaps no coincidence, then, that the tale is also a target for anti-dramatic critics, who have set forth compelling cases to show that the "I" of the tale is "no more than a product of the Tale's rhetoric" instead of a coherent *persona*.²⁹ All told, however, the collective ambivalence about the tale points to more fundamental matters of narration and voice that arguments about the presence or absence of a coherent narrative *persona*—open or closed—merely serve to obscure.

Examining these matters involves another look at how precisely the voice of the *Man of Law's Tale* is constructed. For most readers, the narrator's presence is felt most vividly—to put it kindly—in the tale's frequent narratorial intrusions. The tone of this speaker, however, differs from that of the *Tales*' other intrusive narrators, such as the Knight. Much of the difference in tone, as Lawton has noted, is due to repeated citations within the tale of Innocent III's *De miseria humane conditionis*.³⁰ The majority of the tale's narratorial intrusions are, in fact, direct quotations of this well-known text.³¹ With this gesture, Chaucer affiliates the tale's narrative voice with a penitential tradition more characteristic of Langland than the courtly stylings of his earlier work. This affiliation involves not simply the affective quality of its appeals, but also its rhetoric gestures, specifically the inter-

---

27. Graham D. Caie, "Innocent III's *De Miseria* as a Gloss on the *Man of Law's Prologue* and *Tale*," *Neuphilologische Mitteilungen* 100 (1999): 175–85, looks at the Man of Law's rhetorical failings; Ann W. Astell, "Apostrophe, Prayer, and the Structure of Satire in the *Man of Law's Tale*," *Studies in the Age of Chaucer* 13 (1991): 81–97, interprets the Man of Law's consistent use of *apostrophe* as an indication of his limited vision; Dinshaw, *Chaucer's Sexual Poetics*, discusses the tale's representation of the "traffic in women," whereas Susan Schibanoff, "Worlds Apart: Orientalism, Antifeminism, and Heresy in Chaucer's 'Man of Law's Tale,'" *Exemplaria* 8 (1996): 59–96, relates its misogyny to Orientalist discourse. For a critical history of interpretations of the tale and its narrator, see Spearing, *Textual Subjectivity*, 103–18.
28. C. David Benson, "Poetic Variety in the *Man of Law's* and the *Clerk's Tales*," in *Chaucer's Religious Tales*, ed. C. David Benson and Elizabeth Robertson (Cambridge: Brewer, 1990), 140.
29. Lawton, *Chaucer's Narrators*, 92; Spearing, *Textual Subjectivity*, 118; Robert M. Jordan, "Heteroglossia and Chaucer's *Man of Law's Tale*," in *Bakhtin and Medieval Voices*, ed. Thomas J. Farrell (Gainesville: University Press of Florida, 1995), 93.
30. Lawton, *Chaucer's Narrators*, 91.
31. Glosses in several early manuscripts, including Hengwrt and Ellesmere, show awareness of the tale's citational practices by adding marginal glosses that provide the quoted passages of *De miseria*.

ruptive use of the vocative to make those affective appeals. In this respect, however, *The Man of Law's Tale* distinguishes itself in important ways. *Piers Plowman* features frequent interruptive vocatives, but if public poetry in general is "defined by a constant relation of speaker to audience within an ideally conceived worldly community," these exclamations suggest that this relation is not a simple one. Indeed Langland's exclamations are often unsettling to modern readers insofar as the affective immediacy and intensity they are meant to create seems at odds with the mediations of the dream vision frame. In Vision Three of the B Version, for example, the speech of Clergy, who, according to the fiction of the vision, is lecturing Will, is interrupted (rhetorically, if not thematically) by an admonition addressed directly to the clerical offenders under discussion: "Forþi, ye Correctours, claweþ heron and correcteþ fyrst yowselue."[32] One could read such moments as narratorial intrusions and assign them to the poetic "I," since the change in address is one way to signal such a change in speaker. Yet the identity of this speaker matters less than the rhetorical gesture of direct address, which transcends the boundaries of the vision to speak truth. Nor is that truth addressed to the common itself, but rather to a particular group ("ye Correctours") that the common can agree require public censure. Whereas the fiction of the dream vision produces a generalized "I" that can mediate various interests, it is set alongside gestures of complaint that reach beyond that fiction to elicit a more collective response.

Chaucer's incorporations of passages from *De miseria* similarly seize upon the affective immediacy of *exclamatio,* but in a very different manner. Favoring the classical "O" over the Langlandian "ye" of complaint, the pure vocality of Chaucer's interruptions emphasizes the presence of the individual speaker as much as the addressee. It is likely, in fact, that Chaucer added the "O" to his translation of Innocent's text where it did not occur in the Latin to emphasize the intrusion of a speakerly presence.[33] That presence is further defined not simply by the use of *exclamatio,* but more specifically by *apostrophe*. Where Innocent laments that "sudden sorrow always follows worldly joy" ["Semper mundane leticie tristicia repentina succedit"],[34] the

---

32. William Langland, *Piers Plowman: The B Version,* ed. George Kane and E. Talbot Donaldson (London: Athlone Press, 1975), 10.289. All further quotations are from this edition.

33. It is, of course, possible that Chaucer worked with a version of the text that included these "Os" as well as the vocative forms discussed below. Robert E. Lewis's extensive research into versions of *De miseria* (see n. 34 below), however, has not turned up such a version, nor, in the end, does it matter whether the vocative "O" was Chaucer's own invention or not. The quotations from *De miseria* in marginal glosses of *Man of Law's Tale* manuscripts do not include vocatives.

34. *De miseria condicionis humane,* ed. and trans. Robert E. Lewis (Athens: University of Georgia Press, 1978), 1.21. All further quotations and translations of the text are from this edition.

narrator of *The Man of Law's Tale* apostrophizes that sorrow: "O sodeyn wo, that evere art successour/To worldly blisse" (*MLT,* 2.421–2). Where Innocent describes the shame of the beggar ("si petit, pudore confunditor"), the narrator addresses the beggar himself: "To asken help thee shameth in thyn herte" (*MLP,* 2.99–101). Jonathan Culler once described apostrophe as the essence of the literary, in that it is the trope by which the speaker both creates objects by addressing them and effectively creates himself as a speaking subject in relation to that object.[35] In this narrative, rather than lyric, context, however, it seems more useful to note that these apostrophes orient the speaker in relation to his narrative. In contrast to the exclamations of *Piers Plowman,* which speak across and trouble narrative boundaries, the apostrophes of *The Man of Law's Tale* articulate that very boundary, defining a stable locus of articulation from which the tale is narrated. To claim that these consistent intrusions serve to construct a *persona* is not by any means to claim that the tales are narrated by fully psychologizable, "closed" *personae;* it is, rather, to suggest that Chaucer was first and foremost interested in the poetic possibilities of refracted discourse that a *persona* creates. By arranging his narrative such that *tydynges* are performed from particular contexts, he is able to create resonance from noise.

That resonance results from the sense that discourse is not simply refracted but reiterated. The notion that words are repeated in varying contexts creates the possibility that they can be infused with new intentions with each new performance. *The Man of Law's Tale* emphasizes this possibility still further by assigning the narrator highly emotional intrusions that are quoted from a prior text.[36] If we imagine the intrusive narrator of the tale as a speaking subject defining himself in relation to his narrative, it is equally important to note that this "subject" is made from prior texts. The idea of the Man of Law as a fallible narrator, in fact, derives in part from his seeming corruption of the meaning of *De miseria.* The prologue's opening *apostrophe* to "poverty," drawn directly from *De miseria,* suggests precisely such corruption:

O hateful harm, condicion of poverte!
With thurst, with coold, with hunger so confoundid!
To asken help thee shameth in thyn herte;
(*MLP,* 2.99–101)

---

35. Jonathan Culler, "Apostrophe," in *The Pursuit of Signs: Semiotics, Literature, Deconstruction* (Ithaca, NY: Cornell University Press, 1981), 135–55.

36. In those cases where *De miseria* is not quoted, other texts lie beneath the surface. At 1. 295, Ptolemy is brought to bear on the story (and appears in the marginal glosses as well); at 1. 358, Semiramus is mentioned. The function of *apostrophe,* in other words, is to connect the tale to the "disparate special languages" of the *litterati.*

Pauperes enim premuntur inedia, cruciantur . . . fame, siti, frigore . . . O miserabilis condicio mendicantis! Et si petit, pudore confunditor. (*De miseria* 1.14)[37]

While the passage functions to establish the speaker's rhetorical temperament, it also focuses attention on the issues of material wealth that drive the tale's narrative as well as the odd moral the narrator seems to draw from Innocent's text in this context.[38] As several scholars have noted, Innocent's point in mentioning the plight of the poor is to chastise those who judge solely according to one's material wealth: "Secundum fortunam estimatur persona, cum pocius secundum personam sit estimanda fortuna" ["A person is valued according to his wealth, when wealth should be valued according to the person"] (1.14).[39] The Man of Law, however, stays with the former criterion of evaluation rather than the latter, and thus turns away from the poor to "riche marchauntz" with his next *apostrophe* (2.122), not only praising them for their wealth, but decreeing them "fadres of tidynges / And of tales" (2.129–30), and thus linking them and their goods to his narrative activity.

The misappropriation is so blatant that it is difficult imagine an unironic interpretation. The uses of *De miseria* in the tale itself, however, are more equivocal, nor is it clear what prompts the use of the text in the first place. The first example occurs as a rhetorical delaying tactic, by which the narrator, having described the sumptuousness of Constance and the Sultan's wedding feast, and having hinted at its horrible outcome ("But al to deere they boghte it er they ryse" [2.420]), prepares the audience for the horrific events that will ensue:

> O sodeyn wo, that evere art successour
> To worldly blisse, spreynd with bitternesse,
> The ende of the joye of oure worldly labour!
> Wo occupieth the fyn of oure gladnesse.
> Herke this conseil for thy sikernesse:
> Upon thy glade day have in thy mynde
> The unwar wo or harm that comth bihynde.
> (*MLT*, 2.421–27)

---

37. "The poor are indeed oppressed by starvation; they suffer . . . hunger, thirst, cold . . . O the miserable condition of a beggar! If he begs, he is confounded by shame."

38. On the importance of commerce in the tale, see Dinshaw, *Chaucer's Sexual Poetics*, 95–99; Wallace, *Chaucerian Polity*, 190ff.; Smith, "Chaucer as an English Writer," 112ff.; R. A. Shoaf, "'Unwemmed Custance': Circulation, Property, and Incest in *the Man of Law's Tale*," *Exemplaria* 2 (1990): 287–302.

39. Wallace, *Chaucerian Polity*, 200; Smith, "Chaucer as an English Writer," 112.

> Semper mundane leticie tristicia repentina succedit. Mundana igitur felicitas multis amaritudinibus est respersa. Extrema gaudii luctus occupat. Audi ergo salubre consilium: In die bonorum ne immemor sis malorum. (*De miseria*, 1.21)[40]

As Graham Caie has noted, the passage of *De miseria* left out of this quotation refers to the tragedy that befell Job when his children were killed by a storm while feasting in his brother's house (Job 1.18).[41] Although this omitted passage might explain how this part of Innocent's text came to be associated with this moment in the story, the connection is at best superficial. Caie, in fact, takes it as an indicator of the Man of Law's misplaced priorities: "Innocent advocates sobriety and wisdom in the face of tragedy and reminds us that all things work together for good for those who love God. The Man of Law is simply appalled by the disruption of a jolly good feast and equitable marriage bargain, throwing up his hands in despair and pronouncing the fatalistic and pessimistic view that all joy ends in sorrow."[42] Exaggerations aside, Caie's reading seems suspect to anti-dramatic readers because it uses psychological depth to compensate for the apparent superficiality of intertextual reference. Yet if the alternative is to interpret rather than compensate for this seeming disjunction of text and context, what are we to make of it?

Other examples are still less clear-cut. When the messenger returns from Alla, bearing the letter expressing the king's acceptance of the child he had falsely been led to believe was monstrous, the narrator addresses him as a personification of drunkenness:

> O messager, fulfild of dronkenesse,
> Strong is thy breeth, thy lymes faltren ay,
> And thou biwreyest alle secreenesse.
> Thy mynde is lorn, thou janglest as a jay,
> Thy face is turned in a newe array.
> Ther dronkenesse regneth in any route,
> Ther is no conseil hyd, withouten doute.
> (*MLT*, 2.771–77)

---

40. "For sudden sorrow always follows worldly joy. Worldly happiness is besprinkled indeed with much bitterness. Mourning takes hold of the end of joy. Listen then to a wise counsel: 'In the day of good things, be not unmindful of evil things'" (trans. in Caie, "Innocent III's *De Miseria*," 176; cf. *De miseria* 1.21).

41. Caie, "Innocent III's *De Miseria*," 177.

42. Caie, "Innocent III's *De Miseria*," 177.

Quid turpius ebrioso, cui fetor in ore, tremor in corpore; qui promit stulta, cuius mens alienatur, facies transformatur? "Nullum enim latet secretum vbi regnat." (*De miseria*, 2.19)[43]

Taken from Innocent's treatment of the seven deadly sins, the passage's performance in this context seems truthful in spirit only. The messenger's betrayal does not stem from weak knees or loose lips, but because he falls asleep (indeed, in the first instance, Donegild got him drunk *because* he revealed his errand, not vice versa). As previously, the *apostrophe* seems primarily motivated by concern for narrative pacing, as if it serves to enhance the audience's experience of the resumption of a tragedy seemingly averted by Alla's good will. If this is the case, the focus on drunkenness at best defers to an aesthetic in which penitential admonitions are never gratuitous or distracting. Whatever expectations may have been set up in the prologue, the Man of Law's various appropriations of *De miseria* in the tale itself resist reduction to a single coherent intention.

Part of the problem with readings that attempt to locate such coherence, however, is the narrow psychological understanding of intention (along with an implicit expectation of moral censure) that is brought to bear on the interpretation. In a culture that places more value and authority in institutionally-affirmed, shared texts than in the newly-forged utterances of individual persons—in a self-consciously intertextual culture, if you will—"intention" is a far more complex concept, one that needs to account for the myriad ways that textual performances can be said to bear meaning or desire.[44] In some respects, Chaucer's interest in the inevitability of "meddling" in the Whirling Wicker calls attention to this very complexity of intention and signification. With *The Man of Law's Tale*, arguably with the *Canterbury Tales* as a whole, he takes this interest further by examining particular instances of meddling that come to light in the context of specific performances.

From this perspective, the Man of Law's engagements with the *De miseria* exhibit textual commingling—impure and possibly self-interested mediation that does not signal an ethical or aesthetic failure, but presents a more grounded and specifically, if fictionally, contextualized structuring of rumor and the "commune voys" (2.155). This meddling results in various forms of

---

43. *De miseria* 2.19: "What is more repulsive than a drunkard, in whose mouth is a stench, in whose body a trembling; who utters foolish things, whose reason is taken away, whose face is transformed? 'For there is no secret where drunkenness reigneth'" (trans. based on Lewis, *De miseria*, 166–68).

44. For more on the complexities of intention in the late medieval period, see Zieman, *Singing the New Song*, 92–113, 121–27, *et passim*.

refracted discourse that are often described using the Bakhtinian term "heteroglossia," and there is value in acknowledging the dialogism that exists in both Chaucer's and Langland's writing. Yet whereas Bakhtin describes how novelistic discourse allows heteroglossia to enter a field perceived as unified, Ricardian poets seem rather to imagine heteroglossia in terms of the various building blocks out of which one forges a unified poetics—a common voice that has pretensions toward truth, though they create this voice in different ways. To return to the dialogue between Chaucer and Langland elucidated by Smith, one might say that while Langland continues to harbor the fantasy that he can escape his hall of mirrors to give voice to truth, Chaucer harbors his own fantasy that truth will out despite the meddling. It is not simply the Man of Law's narration that represents this desire, but the structure of the narrative itself. Beginning with "tydynges," the story proceeds by a series of verbal mediations, none of them pure or disinterested. The Man of Law gets his tale second-hand from merchants (2.133); the Sultan hears the "common voys" about Constance second-hand, also from Merchants (2.155, 176–84); the marriage between the Sultan and Constance, we are told, is then arranged, "by tretys and embassadrie,/And by the popes mediacioun" (2.233–34); Custance is betrayed again and again by waylaid and miscommunicated messages and letters; much is made at the end of the tale of the rumor that the son Maurice was the messenger who arranges Alla's dinner with the Emperor and thus Custance's reunion with her father (2.1086–92). Whereas some of these impure mediations stem from evil intentions, such evil intentions seem an almost necessary condition to publish Custance's truth to several nations.

The meddling of impure verbal mediation has been viewed by other scholars in terms of commercial exchange and the inevitable corruptions of language.[45] Set against these figures of corruption is Custance, who, however much she may be moved around, is always stable in her signification. She is figured as the bearer of truth, "an icon of the originary power of the proper name,"[46] who in turn is a willing and welcoming recipient of "goddes sonde," whatever it might be (2.524, 760, 825, 903). While there is little question that this opposition of pure and corrupt communication is the central opposition of the tale,[47] there is perhaps a more fitting figure of Chaucer's

---

45. E.g., Shoaf, "'Unwemmed Custance.'"
46. Shoaf, "'Unwemmed Custance,'" 288.
47. In Shoaf's dramatic reading, the unrealistic desire for the purity of Custance and her transcendent meaning is assigned to the Man of Law, which in turn grants Chaucer the ability to realize the impossibility of this position. Like many dramatic readings, the assigning of particular viewpoints and positions to a narrator is often merely an expository or conceptual expedient that perhaps does not configure the ideas of the tale as effectively as it might, but nonetheless identifies important aspects of the tales.

poetic embedded in another instance of divine communication. When the spurned young knight who has falsely accused Custance of murder swears false witness against her on the gospel, he is promptly and directly "smoot" by the hand of God (2.669–72). Less a "communication" than a non-discursive gesture, this action would not seem to require comment. Nonetheless a heavenly gloss—the only representation of the *vox Dei* in all of Chaucer's works—descends from the heavens:

> A voys was herd in general audience,
> And seyde, "Thou hast desclaundred, giltelees,
> The doghter of hooly chirche in heigh presence;
> Thus hastou doon, and yet holde I my pees!"
> (*MLT,* 2.673–79; cf. Ps 49.21: "haec fecisti et tacui")

With his use of Psalm 49, it would appear that God too engages in meddling. And while such a gesture should establish beyond a doubt that "meddling is simply what we begin with," it is a particular kind of meddling: the act of verbal reiteration, which becomes the figure of both divine communication and vernacular poetics. The power of the Psalter may for Langland (or, at least, for Ymaginatif)[48] lie in its call to the "I" who utters it to assimilate himself to the text, yet for that text to enter into the discourse of lived experience, it must lend itself to multiple contexts. It is in that multiplicity that the surplus of meaning we associate with the literary resides.

One might then say that with the Canterbury pilgrims, Chaucer was more interested in exploring a discourse of self-conscious citationality than in representing character or subjectivity and that his positioning of the narrative voice of the tales was the primary mechanism through which he did so. The crafters of the Ellesmere manuscript also appear to have picked up on the importance of narrative intrusions in fixing that position. At several points throughout the *Tales,* including in *The Man of Law's Tale,* intrusions beginning with the vocative "O" are marked with the word "auctor."[49] The

---

48. Langland's recasting of this episode in the "autobiographical insertion" of C 5, where he speaks of liturgical texts as "þe lomes þat y labore with" (C 5.45), suggests that he has continued to involve himself in "meddling." See Zieman, *Singing the New Song,* 150–81.

49. These glosses have been noticed as a general phenomenon in the Ellesmere manuscript by Andrew Galloway, "Authority," in *A Companion to Chaucer,* ed. Peter Brown (Oxford: Blackwell, 2000), 28; and Stephanie Trigg, *Congenial Souls: Reading Chaucer from Medieval to Postmodern* (Minneapolis: University of Minnesota Press, 2002), 78–79. The glosses occur in other manuscripts, including Hengwrt, but less extensively. Similar glosses also occur in Oxford, Bodleian Library, MS Rawlinson poet. 163, a manuscript of the *Troilus,* where they also mark narratorial intrusion (see C. David Benson and Barry A. Windeatt, "The Manuscript Glosses to Chaucer's *Troilus and Criseyde,*" *Chaucer Review* 25 [1990]: 40, 43, 44, 46, 48, 49, 51).

gesture is similar to and possibly derived from glosses in manuscripts of the *Roman de la Rose,* which use the term "auctor" or "actor" and "amant" as speech markers that distinguish between the "I" who narrates and reflects on the action and the "I" who acts within the narrative.[50] That readers should desire to distinguish between the two shows their awareness of positionality and its rhetorical effects. That the makers of the Ellesmere should also interest themselves in the moments where the "I" is so positioned suggests that they were more interested in calling attention to the pilgrims as narrators than as individual characters at those junctures. In this respect, it might indeed be fair to claim that the narrators of the *Tales* are a product of the tales' rhetoric, yet to deny that there is any connection between specific pilgrims and their tales risks overlooking the very particularity that allowed them to be situated as narrators.[51] Though it is not a question of aligning every irregularity with a character trait of unified subject, I would suggest that interpreting tales like the Man of Law's involves considering the complex range of intention and desire and its expression in language that can span from the individual and subjective to the institutional or communal. With that, we should also consider the greater implication that it is through exploring that range in its full complexity that Chaucer imagines a common voice might be found.[52] At the very least, such considerations might encourage scholars of Chaucer to seek more flexible and historicized conceptual vocabularies of intention, intertextuality, and irony that could better analyze Chaucer's Canterbury project.[53]

---

50. Sylvia Huot, "'Ci parle l'aucteur': The Rubrication of Voice and Authorship in 'Roman de la Rose' Manuscripts," *SubStance* 17 (1988): 42–48.

51. See Lawton, *Chaucer's Narrators.*

52. Largely out of considerations of space, I have refrained in this essay from considering the politics of such a common voice. Given the palpable presence of "other" voices in *The Man of Law's Tale* in particular, however, it is safe to say that such an examination would be equally complicated.

53. David Lawton, "Donaldson and Irony," *Chaucer Review* 41 (2007): 231–39, touches on the poverty of vocabulary on irony in his attempt to bring Donaldson's reading of Chaucerian irony in line with theories of the Chicago school. Farrell ("The Persistence of Donaldson's Memory") also points out that most discussions of Donaldson's criticism tend to oversimplify it, as I, too, may have done in conflating his work with "dramatic" readings in general.

five

Langland's Literary Syntax, Or Anima as an Alternative to Latin Grammar

KATHARINE BREEN

Anima's Many Names

This essay will examine Langland's second B-text iteration of Anima as a newly constructed and deliberately hybrid tool for abstract thought—an instance in which the combination of English and Latin surpasses either language alone. It begins, however, with what the Augustinian canon John Mirk calls "sory Laten": Latin used by and for those who have not mastered it as a subject of academic study.[1] At the low end of the continuum, sorry Latin extends to Mirk's imagined worst-case scenario of a lay baptizer pressed into service *in extremis* but able to manage only the "pa of patris. fi of filij. spi of spiritus sancti" (1. 579). Stripped not just of the case endings that mark grammatical relationships, but also of their own medial consonants—not to mention the rest of the baptismal formula—*pa, fi,* and *spi* clearly derive most of their meaning from their non-Latin context. Nevertheless, Mirk holds that a midwife who pronounces this version of the baptismal formula scrapes together just enough Latin to be efficacious, as long as the syllables are pronounced in the correct order and the speaker has a genuine intent to baptize. High-end users of sorry Latin include the Lord in John Trevisa's

---

1. Gillis Kristensson, *John Mirk's "Instructions for Parish Priests"* (Lund: Gleerup, 1974), line 570.

Dialogus inter dominum et clericum, who can read and speak and understand Latin but asks for an English translation of Higden's *Polychronicon* because he does not possess the advanced tools of "studyinge and auysement and lokyng of oþer bokes."² Like the midwife's truncated baptismal formula but on a more sophisticated level, the Lord's Latin relies on a vernacular context for a significant portion of its meaning. By definition, then, sorry Latin is situated within a vernacular grid that substitutes for the syntactic and intertextual connections that are integral to full-fledged clerical Latinity. In order to account for this hybrid Latin's many forms, however, "vernacular" must be understood to encompass the wide range of "languages" that can be understood without specialized professional training, a list that includes verbal language, image, gesture, *mise-en-page,* and all of their combinations and permutations.³

Anima, I would like to suggest, serves as a particularly clear manifestation of sorry Latin's vernacular grid, designed for readers who fall between Mirk's lay baptizer and Trevisa's Lord on the continuum of latinity. My own opportunity to experiment with a comparable set of readers has been with undergraduates, though wiser heads warned against teaching *Piers*—and especially the *Vita*—at that level. In multiple iterations of my *Piers* course, Anima's enigmatic appearance in passus fifteen, deep in the *Vita,* prompted some of the most productive class discussions. As my students were quick to point out, Anima is one of the strangest characters in the poem for a number of distinct but interlocking reasons. Most obviously, he pushes against the conventions of personification that we had painstakingly compiled earlier in the quarter. Personification allegory generally makes abstract nouns easier to grasp by assigning them human bodies, along with mothers, fathers, spouses, children, and wardrobes that situate them within a social and conceptual sphere. Anima, in contrast, visibly resists physical description. "A sotil þyng wiþ alle" and "Oon wiþouten tonge and teeþ," he is so unknown and unknowable that Will is reduced to conjuring him as though he might be a devil, "If he were cristes creature [for cristes loue] . . . to tellen" (B

---

2. See Ronald Waldron, "Trevisa's Original Prefaces on Translation: A Critical Edition," in *Medieval English Studies Presented to George Kane,* ed. Edward Kennedy, Ronald Waldron, and Joseph Wittig (Cambridge: D. S. Brewer, 1988), 285-99, lines 59-60. Ralph Hanna discusses this passage in "'Vae octuplex,' Lollard Socio-Textual Ideology, and Ricardian-Lancastrian Prose Translation," in *Criticism and Dissent in the Middle Ages,* ed. Rita Copeland (Cambridge: Cambridge University Press, 1996), 244-63, esp. 244-45.

3. This expanded definition is implicit in Fiona Somerset and Nicholas Watson's anthology, *The Vulgar Tongue: Medieval and Postmedieval Vernacularity* (University Park: Pennsylvania State University Press, 2003), x-xi, which defines *vernacular* as a relative rather than an absolute quality; the anthology includes Harvey Hames, "The Language of Conversion: Ramon Llull's Art as a Vernacular," 43-56.

15.12–15).[4] At the same time, Anima tests the limits of Langland's vernacularity, not least because he is the only acting and speaking character in the B text with a purely Latin name.[5] But neither is Anima's name proper Latin, because it associates a grammatically feminine noun with a figure who is elsewhere referred to by the masculine pronouns "hym" and "he" (B 15.14–15).[6] In Latin as well as in English, then, Anima can only make himself known through the fracture of language rather than through its normal operation: just as he brushes up against the limits of personification allegory, so he also brushes up against the limits of linguistic expression. Finally, as my students noted, Anima is the literary equivalent of a mulligan since he supersedes but does not replace Langland's earlier, conventionally feminine personification of Anima as a lady in a tower in B 9. The very fact that the poem contains two full-fledged representations of Anima renders each one partial and provisional, opening the door for the second Anima's replacement by Liberum Arbitrium in the C text. Thus the grammatical and rhetorical tools that should allow Will, and through him the reader, to get a grip on Anima instead emphasize his difficulty. Even a trope whose function is to provide bodies can barely make Anima tangible, and he constantly threatens to slip through the cracks of both English and Latin.

All these different currents converge in Anima's extended act of self-naming in B 15.23–36, and this is the passage on which my undergraduates concentrated their attention. In doing so, they followed in the footsteps of late medieval scribes and readers, who often marked this passage with a red or blue paraph mark and used rubrication, variations in script, annotations, and other signs to flag it for particular attention:

---

4. All citations of the B and C texts of *Piers Plowman* refer to the Athlone Press editions: George Kane and E. Talbot Donaldson, eds., *Piers Plowman: The B Version*, rev. ed. (London: Athlone Press, 1988); George Russell and George Kane, eds., *Piers Plowman: The C Version* (London: Athlone Press, 1997).

5. As A V. C. Schmidt notes, the only such example in the C text is Anima's replacement, Liberum Arbitrium. Schmidt distinguishes these figures from Langland's many non-speaking and non-acting personifications with Latin names as well as from entities such as Fides/Faith/Abraham and Spes/Hope/Moses that are named in both English and Latin, attributing Anima and Liberum Arbitrium's anomalous status to a lack of appropriate English equivalents for their names; see A. V. C. Schmidt, "Langland and Scholastic Philosophy," *Medium Ævum* 38 (1969): 152.

6. Anima is not the only personification whose represented gender clashes with the grammatical gender of the underlying noun (see e.g. "*Latro*, luciferis Aunte," B 5.476, and the pairing of the feminine Fides and Spes with the masculine Abraham and Moses). He is, however, the only figure who virtually forces the reader into a solecism, since he is prominent enough to warrant discussion and lacks any other nomenclature. On *Latro*, see Helen Cooper, "Gender and Personification in *Piers Plowman*," *Yearbook of Langland Studies* 5 (1991): 45.

> "The whiles I quykne þe cors," quod he, "called am I *anima;*
> And whan I wilne and wolde *animus* ich hatte;
> And for þat I kan [and] knowe called am I *mens;*
> And whan I make mone to god *memoria* is my name;
> And whan I deme domes and do as truþe techeþ
> Thanne is *Racio* my riȝte name, reson on englissh;
> And whan I feele þat folk telleþ my firste name is *sensus,*
> And þat is wit and wisdom, þe welle of alle craftes;
> And whan I chalange or chalange noȝt, chepe or refuse,
> Thanne am I Conscience ycalled, goddes clerk and his Notarie;
> And whan I loue leelly oure lord and alle oþere
> Thanne is lele loue my name, and in latyn *Amor;*
> And whan I flee fro þe flessh and forsake þe careyne
> Thanne am I spirit spechelees; *Spiritus* þanne ich hatte."

Italicized in Kane and Donaldson's edition, Anima's Latin names are specifically emphasized in B text manuscripts, where various combinations of red lettering, larger lettering, red and black underlining, and red boxes define them alternately as keywords and as Latin interlopers in Langland's English text (figures 1–2).[7] By highlighting the relationship between Anima's many Latin names and the alliterating English lines that surround them, the sheer density of such rubrication draws attention to the complex relationship between Latin and vernacular in Langland's characterization of Anima, demanding that the reader slow down, take heed, and seek to remember. More than five hundred years later, through the medium of A. V. C. Schmidt's modern edition, American undergraduates are still obeying these instructions. After a substantial discussion of what it might mean for a single personification to have so many names, I gave one set of students their first-ever pop quiz—and was astonished by the result. Every single student in a class of twenty-eight could provide a working English definition of each one of Anima's Latin names, distinguishing Anima from Animus, Mens from Memoria, and so on. And when I reversed direction, asking them to move from English to Latin, 80 percent of the class still got a perfect score, correctly translating "spirit spechelees" as *Spiritus,* "lele loue (loyal love)" as *Amor* and all the rest. These percentages are all the more striking since none of my students had any formal training in Latin, though a few reported liturgical exposure through, as one of them put it, "years and years and years in

---

7. On the paraph marks and annotations, see C. David Benson and Lynne Blanchfield, *The Manuscripts of "Piers Plowman": The B-Version* (Cambridge: D. S. Brewer, 1987).

Catholic school"—a formation analogous, perhaps, to some medieval laypeople's experience of attending mass.

Wholly unscientific as it is, this anecdotal evidence suggests that Anima is offered in part as a language-learning tool. That is to say, while Will—and through him the reader—is learning what kind of a multi-faceted thing the soul is, he is also mastering a Latin vocabulary that enables the necessary fine distinctions. For Anima's act of self-naming is arranged roughly in the manner of a glossary, with Latin nouns equated with short definitional phrases in English and accompanied by English synonyms in the relatively few cases where these are available.[8] Even when the synonyms are present, however, the English noun doesn't seem to be sufficient in and of itself. It must be rendered more specific, and usually elevated, in order to function as a reliable equivalent of the Latin. Thus "loue leelly our lord and alle oþere" becomes "lele loue" and finally Amor, while "spirit spechelees" becomes Spiritus. The English terms and definitions provide an adequate periphrastic account of the meaning of Anima's various aspects, but the Latin transforms them into tools for thought—more specifically, into tools for self-knowledge, for the analysis of one's own soul. When it comes to the nuts and bolts of thinking, short names are more useful than long, compound ones, and a handle like Amor can be manipulated—subjected to a whole range of grammatical and conceptual operations—in ways that "loue leelly our lord and alle oþere" and even "lele loue" simply cannot. Certainly this generalization holds true for Langland's signature device of personification, where Piers Plowman's son, "Suffre-þi-Souereyns-to hauen-hir-wille- / Deme-hem-noȝt-for-if-þow-doost-þow-shalt-it-deere-abugge- / Lat-god-yworþe-wiþ-al-for-so-his-word-techeþ," cannot be anything more than a nonce coinage, and even short phrases like Do-wel and Do-bet cause all manner of problems as they slide between proper names, imperatives and—as Anne Middleton famously pointed out—examples of positive, comparative, and superlative grammatical forms (B 6.80-82).[9]

When I suggest that Anima is a language-learning tool, however, I do not mean that he teaches anything that resembles real Latin. If he did, every reader who grasped his self-naming would also be able to understand the chunk of undigested Latin that follows and authorizes it, a passage that is

---

8. Anima's glossarial nature is reflected in Schmidt's critical response, which he presents as a schema rather than continuous text; see Schmidt, "Langland and Scholastic Philosophy," 151–52.

9. Anne Middleton, "Two Infinites: Grammatical Metaphor in *Piers Plowman*," *ELH* 39, no. 2 (1972): 169–88. Benson and Blanchfield note that some scribes treat Do-wel, Do-bet etc. as imperatives, while other treat them as proper names and rubricate them accordingly; see Benson and Blanchfield, *The Manuscripts of "Piers Plowman*," 19.

based on Isidore of Seville's *Etymologies* and is plainly a different kettle of fish:

> *Anima* pro diuersis accionibus diuersa nomina sortitur: dum viuicat corpus anima est; dum vult animus est; dum scit mens est; dum recolit memoria est; dum iudicat racio est; dum sentit sensus est; dum amat Amor est; dum negat vel consentit consciencia est; dum spirat spiritus est. (B.15.39a)[10]

> *Anima* selects different names for different actions. As it gives life to the body it is *anima* [the soul]; as it wills, it is *animus* [intention]; as it knows, it is *mens* [mind]; as it recollects, it is *memoria* [memory]; as it judges, it is *racio* [reason]; as it senses, it is *sensus* [sense]; as it loves, it is *Amor* [love]; as it denies or consents, it is *consciencia* [conscience]; as it breathes the breath of life, it is *spiritus* [spirit].

Instead, Anima offers a limited number of abstract nouns, all presented in the nominative case and the singular number: a technical vocabulary having to do with the soul and the practice of introspection. In contrast to the *Etymologies*, these nouns are presented in a context that frees the reader from responsibility for declension, agreement, and conjugation—precisely the categories that most sharply distinguish Latin from English and make Langland's C.3 grammatical metaphor all but impenetrable. Anima's nouns can thus be assimilated to English in much the same way that one would assimilate any new vocabulary item, and they produce genuinely hybrid or macaronic thinking—an in-between status reflected in the manuscript tradition when Oxford, Corpus Christi College MS 201 (F) presents Anima's names as a bi-colored compromise between ordinary black text and the red of full-fledged Latin quotations (figure 2). A reader who accepts Anima's invitation to self-interrogation will thus do so with Latin nouns and English verbs and prepositions, achieving much of the sophistication and precision of Latin even if he does not know Latin grammar, even if—to borrow a category of economic privilege invoked by both Langland's Will and Trevisa's Lord—he did not have family or friends to fund his education.[11]

Implicitly, then, Anima imports a certain number of abstract Latin nouns in order to remedy a deficiency in English, which does not have the right nouns, with the right shades of meaning, to represent adequately the human

---

10. As Mary Carruthers notes in "Allegory without the Teeth: Some Reflections on Figural Language in *Piers Plowman*," *Yearbook of Langland Studies* 19 (2005): 34n, Amor and Conscience have been added to the seven qualities outlined in *Etymologies* 11.1.13. All translations are my own.

11. *Piers Plowman*, C 5.36; *Dialogus*, lines 67–68.

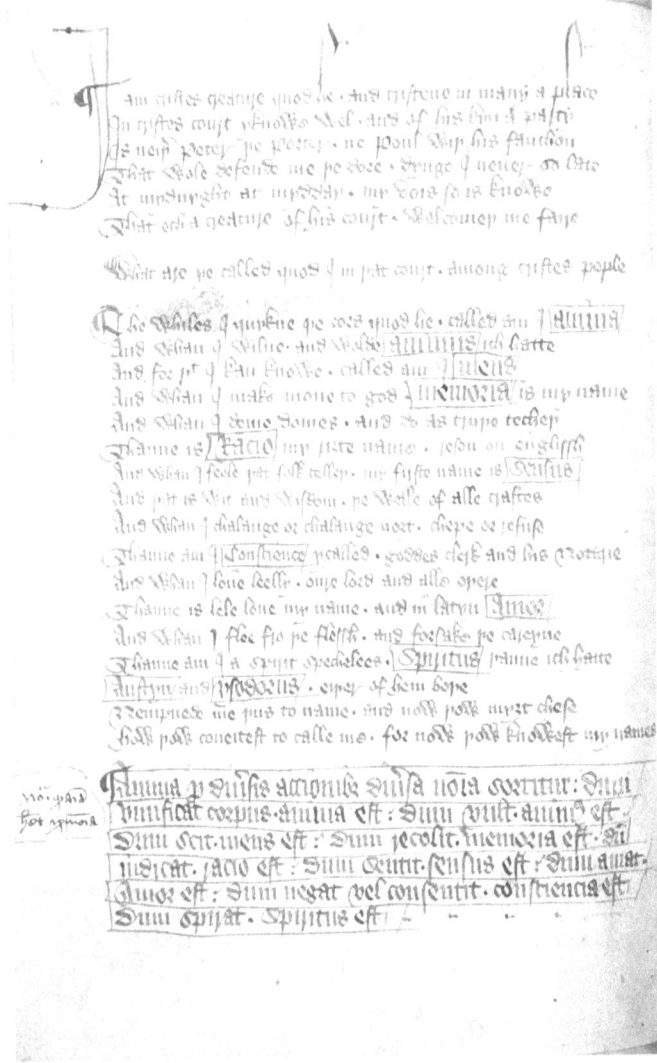

Figure 1. Anima's speech of self-naming. Cambridge, Trinity College, MS B.15.17 (W), fol. 86v. By permission of Trinity College Library.

soul. The evidence for this phenomenon lies not only in the careful qualification of phrases like "lele loue" but in the one English term that stands alone in Anima's speech, without a Latin equivalent. *Conscience* ultimately derives from Latin, probably via French, and is a close cognate of the Latin *conscientia*. By Langland's time it was already well established in English,

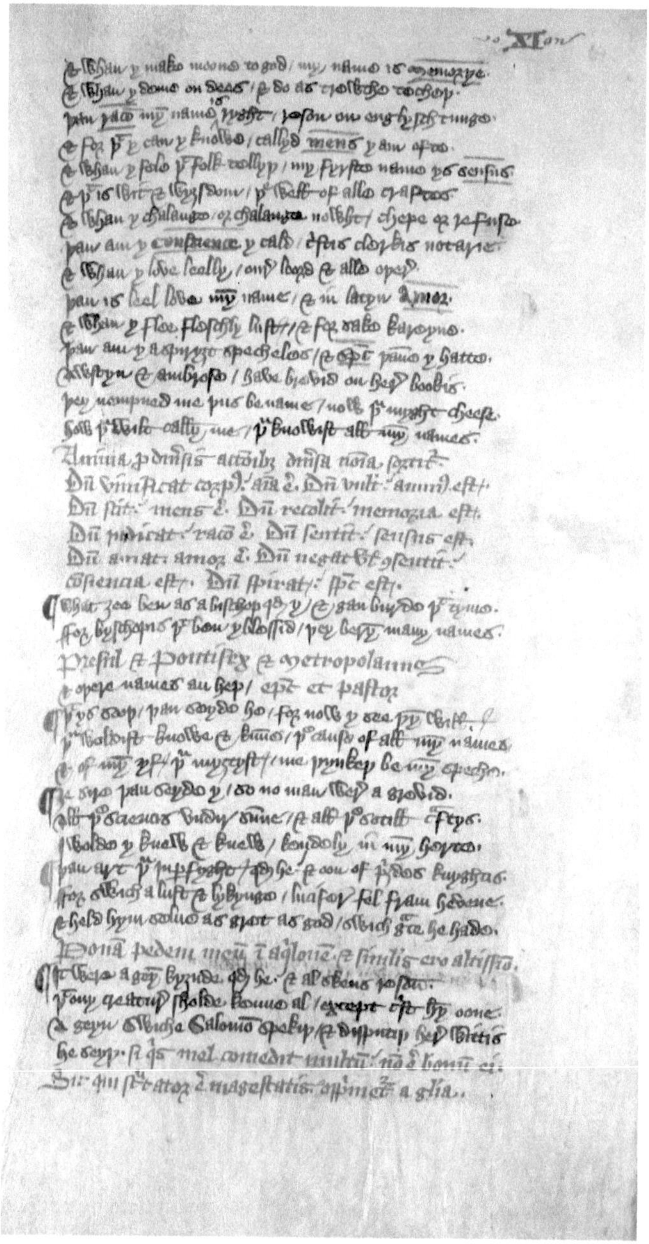

Figure 2. Anima's speech of self-naming. Oxford, Corpus Christi College, MS 201 (F), fol. 61r

with the first *Middle English Dictionary* citation in Anima's specific sense of "the faculty of knowing what is right" deriving from the *Ancrene Wisse*.[12] Anima's decision to use *conscience* rather than *conscientia*, then, is an important indicator, because it suggests that his respect for Latin is largely pragmatic: he breaks into Latin when no appropriate English word is available but does not seem to value Latin *per se*. Where many grammarians and educational theorists considered Latin to be intrinsically superior because of its sacred history or claims of privileged rationality, Anima is mainly interested in what Latin can do. Anima's position in B is all the more marked because it contrasts with the C text, where either Langland himself or a scribal tradition substitutes "Conscientia" for "Conscience" (C.16.192).[13] Implicitly, the fact that most of Anima's names were Latin created an expectation that they should all be Latin; by resisting that expectation, Anima presents himself as deliberately hybrid.

If Anima has no intrinsic preference for Latin words, then, why does he seek out translations for words like *love* and *spirit*, whose meanings are very close to their Latin equivalents? Once again Anima's use of *conscience* offers a clue, since it implicitly supersedes Langland's use of the venerable Anglo-Saxon term *inwit*, personified as the protector of the damsel Anima earlier in the poem. Although the *Middle English Dictionary* entries for *conscience* and *inwit* are practically indistinguishable—and *Ancrene Wisse* explicitly uses one to define the other—their generic associations in *Piers Plowman* could not be more different.[14] Sire Inwit is a secular figure and a relatively straightforward personification. A knight and a constable, he defends the feminine Anima, enclosed in her castle of flesh, against the assaults of a proud adventurer, Princeps huius mundi or "Prince of this world." The tools at Inwit's disposal, figured as his sons and associates, are not aspects of the soul like *memoria* and *spiritus* but concrete senses put to good use in the world: "Sire Se-wel, and Sey-wel, and here-wel þe hende, / Sire werch-wel-wiþ-þyn-hand . . . / And sire Godefray Go-wel" (B 9.20–22). Thus, although Inwit is arguably assigned a Latinate task, in the sense that he must preserve one Latin concept from contamination by another, his means of doing so are resolutely vernacular. Indeed the entire scene, with Anima as the beloved of an absent

---

12. *MED* s.v. *conscience* (n), sense 2a.
13. W. W. Skeat's edition gives Conscience in B but *Conscientia* in C; see W. W. Skeat, ed., *The Vision of William Concerning Piers the Plowman in Three Parallel Texts* (Oxford: Oxford University Press, 1886), B 15.32, C 17.192. The Athlone editions give Conscience in both instances, listing *conscientia* as a variant in eight C manuscripts. The scribe of F reorders the components of Anima's name and gives *memoria* as the English *memorye* (figure 2). If nothing else, Anima is clearly a site of slippage between languages.
14. *MED* s.v. *inwit* (n), sense 4.

Kynde, besieged by a "proud prikere of Fraunce" and defended by one Dowell, "duc of þise Marches," draws heavily on the conventions of romance, a genre whose very name is tightly linked to the vernacular (B 9.8, 11).[15]

In this context, the poem's implicit progress from *inwit* to *conscience* seems to depend less on the terms themselves than on the company they keep. Anima's use of *conscience*, though not Latin, is markedly Latinate. It derives from and in turn supports a conception of the soul that emerges from the thoroughly Latin realms of etymology and faculty psychology and from the scholastic tradition of *distinctio*. *Conscience* is held in place, its meaning fixed, by the Latin terms that surround it, even as it performs the same service for them. *Inwit*, in contrast, is ultimately inadequate to the description and defense of the soul because the largely French and English genre of romance is itself inadequate. A standard image that also appears in Grosseteste's *Chateau d'Amour* and the Middle English *Cursor Mundi* and *Castle of Perseverance*, the conceit of the soul besieged in her castle of flesh provides a more or less instructive representation of the soul's origins and place in the world, but it does not offer vernacular readers new tools for carrying out that defense.[16] If Anima is saved it will be, as at the end of the *Castle of Perseverance*, because of God's surpassing mercy—not because of the individual efforts of Sire Inwit, Sire Se-Wel, or the vernacular reader. Thus even before Langland's first representation of Anima fails, in the sense that it leaves room for and even invites a second representation of the same concept, it already sets itself up as engaged in a losing battle. It is a convention of romance that impregnable castles are never actually impregnable, and the conventions of romance themselves have already proved incapable of teaching Langland's readers what they really need to know.

Piers Plowman's second Anima supersedes the first in another way, one that specifically privileges its Latin-English hybridity over either of those languages alone. The highly compressed romance at the beginning of B 9 depends on the femininity of Anima. That is, it depends on a correlation

---

15. The French term *romanz* can be used at various levels of specificity to signify French, Romance language, or any vernacular language, usually in implicit or explicit contrast to Latin, while in English *romance* more specifically signifies French. Both British and French romance writers, including the *Gawain*-poet, Marie de France and Chrétien de Troyes, privileged the Welsh March as a setting for their tales. See Frédéric Godefroy, *Dictionnaire de l'ancienne langue française et de tous ses dialectes du IXe au XVe siècle* (Paris, 1880–1902), s.v. *romans* (n), sense 1; Alan Hindley, Frederick Langley, and Brian Levy, *Old French-English Dictionary* (Cambridge: Cambridge University Press, 2000), s.v. *romanz*; *MED* s.v. *romaunce* (n), sense 3.

16. On the traditional imagery of the soul in a castle, see Roberta Cornelius, *The Figurative Castle: A Study in the Medieval Allegory of the Edifice with Especial Reference to Religious Writings* (Bryn Mawr, PA, 1930).

between the grammatical gender of the Latin word *anima* and the represented gender of the corresponding personification. Anima is female here just as Philosophia is female for Boethius and Natura is female for Alan of Lille.[17] Like these authors, Langland relies on Anima's femininity to activate a host of gender-inflected plot lines and stereotypes that he can put to work immediately, sketching the entire story of the lady in the tower in just a few sentences. As a woman, Anima is equipped to enter into a hierarchical, heterosexual union with God but must depend on her loyal retainers to protect her from knights errant. In contrast, Langland's second version of Anima is resolutely formless, and presumably lacks not only tongue and teeth but sex characteristics as well.[18] After this carefully neutral introduction, Anima *is* assigned a gendered personal pronoun—an assignment that, according to Morton Bloomfield's definition of personification allegory, is necessary to prevent him from sinking back into the mass of ordinary common nouns.[19] Like the name Anima itself, however, this gender seems to be a label that Will assigns for his own convenience in order to humanize the creature he encounters and thus make him understandable. Anima does not identify his own gender, instead using first person pronouns and the modest and universal term "creature," nor does he—in contrast to the passage from the *Etymologies*—privilege any one of his many names over the others. Some of these names, moreover, are masculine and some feminine according to the rules of Latin grammar. Langland's second Anima thus does not become masculine in the way that the first Anima was feminine, nor does his gender immediately suggest a plotline or dictate a sequence of behavior.[20] Instead, Anima's

---

17. Beginning with Joseph Addison in the eighteenth century, critics have often claimed that the grammatical gender of a noun determines the gender of the corresponding personification, with the fact that most abstract nouns are feminine in Latin and the romance languages accounting for the preponderance of female personifications. More recently James Paxson and Barbara Newman have argued convincingly (though from very different perspectives) that the feminine gender of most personifications is in fact overdetermined. Newman notes specifically that a feminine embodiment of the soul has little grammatical justification: the masculine noun *animus*, with its emphasis on higher intellectual and spiritual functions, is if anything more semantically appropriate than *anima*. See James Paxson, "Gender Personified, Personification Gendered, and the Body Figuralized in *Piers Plowman*," *Yearbook of Langland Studies* 12 (1998): 65–96; and Barbara Newman, *God and the Goddesses: Vision, Poetry, and Belief in the Middle Ages* (Philadelphia: University of Pennsylvania Press, 2003), esp. 35–38.

18. Paxson suggests, however, that Anima's mouth without tongue or teeth is a euphemism for the human vagina; see Paxson, "Gender Personified," 85.

19. Morton Bloomfield, "A Grammatical Approach to Personification Allegory," *Modern Philology* 40 (1963): 161–71.

20. Many critics note in passing that Anima changes gender between B 9 and B 15, including Joan Baker and Susan Signe Morrison, who consider the later Anima as strongly masculine, in contrast to the earlier lady in the tower; see Joan Baker and Susan Signe Morrison, "The Luxury of Gender: *Piers Plowman* B 9 and the *Merchant's Tale*," in *William Langland's "Piers Plowman": A Book of Essays,*

deliberately indeterminate gender seems to serve as proof that he constructs himself according to English rules of grammatical gender (which allow such behavior, if only barely) rather than according to Latin ones (which prohibit it completely). He can exist beyond or between genders—and thus provide a more powerful, and nuanced, vision of the soul—precisely because he is governed by a Latin vocabulary but an English grammar.

All of this has been by way of arguing that Anima's extended act of self-naming in B 15 is a true Latin-English hybrid, drawing on the strengths of both languages to illustrate a concept that is possible within the confines of neither. English does not have an appropriate vocabulary, so Latin supplies that, along with traditions of faculty psychology and scholastic *distinctio*. But English syntax, with its limited requirements for the agreement of case, gender, and number, allows Langland to depict a personified soul that, by its own account, participates in neither bodily sex nor grammatical gender, thus marking its distance from everyday modes of thinking and being. The personification of Anima holds this difficult concept together, and in fact serves its own grammatical function. That is to say, Anima's speech of self-naming makes sense only because the character Anima is saying it. In the quotation from Isidore of Seville, there is no gender ambiguity because the entire passage refers back to a single definition, like a dictionary entry. In Langland's hybrid passage, in contrast, Anima's gender ambiguity can persist because the referent is not described but speaks, using the gender-neutral first person pronoun. At the same time, the task of simultaneously adding eight new Latin terms to an English vocabulary is feasible only because all the terms refer back to a single, already-imagined entity. Instead of memorizing Anima's names as a list, my students remembered them because they describe aspects of a personification they had already spent some time trying to get their minds around. Although Langland's description of Anima is negative in the sense that it mostly describes what Anima is not, it is strange and striking enough to lend itself to memory work.[21] More prosaically but more fundamentally, the personification of Anima provides a structure around which the different aspects of the soul can be organized, and without which they would not easily cohere. Linked to each other and to

---

ed. Kathleen Hewett-Smith (New York: Routledge, 2001), 44. Paxson and Masha Raskolnikov look at this transformation more closely, noting the indeterminacy of the second Anima's gender, though both finally consider the B 15 Anima to be masculine. See Paxson, "Gender Personified," 83–84; and Masha Raskolnikov, "Promising the Female, Delivering the Male: Transformations of Gender in *Piers Plowman*," *Yearbook of Langland Studies* 19 (2005): 81–105, esp. 95–101.

21. On the importance of striking images in memory work, by now well established, see, e.g., Mary Carruthers, *The Book of Memory: A Study of Memory in Medieval Culture*, 2nd ed. (Cambridge: Cambridge University Press, 2008).

Anima, the aspects of the soul signify more richly than they would if presented as a simple list.

Indeed, for Langland the B 15 Anima seems to serve as a new kind of grammatical unit or unit of thought. Anima's cultivated ambiguity represents not only a carefully adumbrated vision of the human soul, but also a self-conscious revision of the earlier Anima as a lady in a tower. Here, the poem seems to promise, we have a new and better way of thinking about the soul's workings, its capacity for judgment, and its relationship to God. By resisting positive description, moreover, the B 15 Anima reveals the Dreamer's most basic efforts at linguistic classification to be arbitrary and inadequate. As we have seen, Will uses a single name and masculine pronouns to gesture toward a personification who insists on many names and uses "I" and "creature." In assigning a masculine pronoun to an entity he calls Anima, Will also commits a solecism that must have grated on Langland's most Latinate readers, including his coterie readers in London and Westminster. Like the annotations and rubrication that flag Anima's self-naming in the manuscripts, this dissonance alerts such readers to pay careful attention to the relationship between Latin and English and the strengths and limitations of each. Having established that Anima exceeds both languages, Langland then uses them to create a new language whose basic unit is the personification—a language that, by its very difference from both Latin and English, allows Langland's readers to understand, and work to improve, something as ineffable as their own souls. Anima thus calls on both high-end and low-end readers to exercise ever more acutely the skills they have been developing over the course of reading *Piers Plowman*. Having watched Liar dissolve back into the local population of friars and pardoners at the end of passus two, readers become accustomed to thinking of personifications as conceptual tools rather than imaginary beings, and so it becomes possible to think of them as grammatical units as well.

Anima's Many Shapes

In emphasizing Anima's status as a personification allegory—albeit one that tests the limits of the form by testing the limits of human and grammatical gender—I have been in some respects deliberately obtuse. In 2005, Mary Carruthers asserted that Anima is nothing of the kind. Instead, Anima is an instance of another sub-type of allegory, *pictura* or *depinctio*, whose function is "to summarize major subject matters, to organize these for study, and to find one's way through their complications." As Carruthers sees it, "*Ani-*

ma's role is to introduce and dispose in summary fashion the matters upon which human knowledge rests, namely the powers of the soul." Anima thus responds to Will's stated desire to know Do-wel with a narrative map that outlines the cognitive terrain he must traverse in order to find the answer to his question. From this angle, Anima's closest cognate in *Piers Plowman* appears to be the allegorical itinerary to Truth that Piers provides to the pilgrims, which Carruthers likens, in turn, to the common practice of using pilgrimage routes to organize sermons and other texts so that each topic is formally "located" at a stop along the way. From here it is a small step to the visual rather than narrative *picturae* of a work like the *Speculum theologiae*, which consists of a series of three-dimensional grids connecting, for instance, the ten commandments with the ten plagues of Egypt and the ten offences against Mosaic law (figure 4). According to Carruthers's reading, Anima thus remains a cognitive tool but of a quite different kind than previously supposed. It belongs not with Langland's other personifications but with a series of inanimate maps and diagrams made up of imagistic language, captioned images, and every conceivable combination of the two.[22]

Although Carruthers's careful distinctions offer a valuable corrective to current, often muddled discussions of medieval allegory, I think that in the case of Anima she overstates her position. By the time we reach passus fifteen of *Piers Plowman*, Will's habit of encountering personified interlocutors—specifically, interlocutors who more and more closely resemble his better self—is too ingrained to be discarded without more narrative upheaval.[23] Instead, I propose that Anima is at once a *pictura* and a personification, in much the same way that the destroyed Ebstorf *mappamundi*—with the head, hands, and feet of Christ marking its four compass positions—is at once a representation of the deity and a map of the world (figure 3). (As if to confirm this double nature, the place where Christ's navel should be on the Ebstorf map corresponds to the position of Jerusalem as the *umbilicus mundi*.) On a less exalted plane, we can recognize that Langland's Anima is a cognitive map without ceasing to see him as a personification. Indeed, it is a measure of the reader's progress through the first fourteen passus of the poem that Anima can be both kinds of allegory either sequentially or simul-

---

22. Carruthers, "Allegory without the Teeth," 34.

23. Lavinia Griffiths argues that Langland's personifications are influenced by the nature of the "prevalent codes" that surround them. That is, "one personification tends to give rise to more personifications. They appear in branching complexes, and by a sort of metonymy confer a status similar to their own on those around them." While she speaks here of local groupings, such as Meed's wedding party, the same logic applies on a larger scale to *Piers Plowman* as a whole. See Lavinia Griffiths, *Personification in "Piers Plowman"* (Cambridge: D. S. Brewer, 1985), 15–16.

Figure 3. Ebstorf World Map, c. 1230–1250

taneously. Like a viewer manipulating the hinged belly of a *vierge ouvrante*, the reader can move back and forth between views as best suits his or her reading trajectory and Langland's didactic purposes. Such manipulation in fact classifies Anima as a sub-type of *pictura* consisting of moving rather than static images, a category that includes Hugh of St. Victor's *Archa Noe* and the image of the confessional cherub often attributed to Alan of Lille. Carruthers considers both of these moving images to be machines for invention, *ars inveniendi*, rather than mere schemas, and the same holds true for Anima.[24]

What, then, does the personified Anima look like when we open him up—just as one literally opens a *Madonna lactans* to reveal the Trinity, or imaginatively opens Christ on the cross to reveal the Ebstorf map of the world? Following up on one of Carruthers's suggestions, we may compare Anima to the *Speculum theologiae*, a collection of diagrams or cognitive maps compiled by the Franciscan John of Metz in the last quarter of the thirteenth century. A kind of visual anthology, the *Speculum theologiae* incorporates well-known diagrams such as the Tree of Virtues and Tree of Vices, the Bonaventuran Tree of Life, and the confessional cherub (probably produced by the Augustinian Clement of Llanthony rather than Alan of Lille), placing them alongside at least one moral diagram of John of Metz's own devising and often a smattering of scientific images.[25] The *Speculum theologiae*'s originality lies not in its raw ingredients but in its work of re-contextualization, in extracting diagrams from the treatises they originally accompanied and arranging them as a catechetical or meditational series.[26] Thus abstracted, the diagrams enjoyed considerable popularity. Lucy Freeman Sandler lists thirty-eight manuscript copies from France, Germany, Switzerland, the Low Countries, and all parts of England (I note one more in the British Library).[27] An accurate census is hard achieve because the *Speculum theologiae* carries various titles and author attributions—or more frequently none at all—and was sometimes added as prefatory material to existing Bibles, Psalters, and the like.[28] That was the case with Robert de Lisle's Psalter, which he gave to his

---

24. Carruthers, "Moving Images in the Mind's Eye," in *The Mind's Eye: Art and Theological Argument in the Middle Ages*, ed. Jeffrey F. Hamburger and Anne-Marie Bouché (Princeton, NJ: Dept. of Art and Archaeology, 2006), 287–305.

25. On the diagrams of the *Speculum theologiae*, see *inter alia* Lina Bolzoni, *The Web of Images: Vernacular Preaching from Its Origins to St. Bernardino da Siena*, trans. Carole Preston and Lisa Chien (Aldershot, UK: Ashgate, 2004), 41–81; Lucy Freeman Sandler, *The Psalter of Robert de Lisle in the British Library*, 2nd ed. (London: Harvey Miller Publishers, 1999); Michael Evans, "The Geometry of Mind," *Architectural Association Quarterly* 12 (1980): 32–55; and Fritz Saxl, "A Spiritual Encyclopedia of the Later Middle Ages," *Journal of the Warburg and Courtauld Institutes* 5 (1942): 82–134. On the cherub and the Tree of Life (or Lignum Vitae) in particular, including the attribution of the former to Clement of Llanthony, see Carruthers, "Moving Images," 295.

26. Of course, medieval diagrams that accompany texts do not necessarily illustrate them in a straightforward way. On such diagrams as independent works, despite superficial appearances to the contrary, see Evans, "Geometry of Mind"; and Evans, "An Illustrated Fragment of Peraldus's 'Summa' of Vice: Harleian MS. 3244," *Journal of the Warburg and Courtauld Institutes* 45 (1982): 14–68. On the treatise *De sex alis* as a brief aide-memoire, subordinate to the diagram of the cherub, see Carruthers, "Moving Images," 296.

27. Sandler, *Psalter of Robert de Lisle*, 107–15. The new *Speculum theologiae* manuscript is London, British Library Additional 17,358.

28. More generally, Evans notes that diagrams are "more widespread in medieval manuscripts than is usually realized, but difficult to locate through catalogue entries, since their neglect by art historians

daughters Audere and Alborou in 1339, and after their deaths to the priory at Chicksands where they most likely lived as nuns. It was also the case with a much less beautiful and considerably more typical fifteenth-century example prefixed to a thirteenth-century Bible, along with Peter of Poitier's diagrammatic *Arbor historiae* and various reading aides, including a concordance to the Gospels and list of lections according to Sarum use.[29] These two manuscripts contain overlapping but not identical sets of diagrams that encompass the basic elements of the archiepiscopal syllabi drawn up after the Fourth Lateran Council: the twelve articles of the faith, the ten commandments, the seven virtues and seven deadly sins, the seven sacraments, the Lord's Prayer, and so on. Both also include diagrams of a more naturalistic or scientific nature that cohabitate with the explicitly religious material much as the "realistic" local detail of the Ebstorf map cohabitates with its sacred content. While the De Lisle Psalter diagrams are, among other things, exquisite works of art (figure 4), I will focus on the Bible manuscript, London, British Library Royal 1.B.X, in part because its palette, restricted to black and red, captures some of the visual and structural similarity between these diagrams and the visual representations of Anima in manuscripts of *Piers Plowman*.[30]

As measured by the sheer frequency with which it appears, the core of the *Speculum theologiae* is the syllabic material, and this material shares not only Anima's status as *pictura* but also, and more specifically, his role as a hybrid of Latin and vernacular. This assertion might seem unlikely, since except for what seems to be a one-off translation of one of the diagrams into early-fifteenth-century German, the text of the *Speculum theologiae* is entirely Latin. A closer look at the Royal 1.B.X Paternoster diagram should make this claim seem more reasonable, however (figure 5). The table is made up of four main columns which are labeled "7 Petitiones (seven petitions [of the Paternoster])," "7 dona spiritus sancti (seven gifts of the Holy Spirit)," "7 Virtutes (seven virtues)" and "7 vicia et infirmitates (seven vices and infirmities)"—this last a list of the deadly sins coupled with the diseased states they were thought to provoke, with greed causing leprosy, sloth causing paralysis, and so on. This material is fairly basic Latin, though not quite as basic as in Anima's self-naming: the vices and virtues, gifts and maladies are mostly single words, though some knowledge of grammar would be needed to puzzle out the rest. Even this requirement, however, is not as onerous as it might seem since so many of the elements in the diagram would have been familiar, indeed explicitly memorized—if not as a part of childhood religious

---

is generally matched by that of librarians, who omit them from codicological descriptions" ("Geometry of Mind," 35).

29. I follow Sandler's date (*Psalter of Robert de Lisle*, 109) rather than that of the Royal catalogue.
30. For a discussion of this manuscript, see Evans, "Geometry of Mind," 39–49.

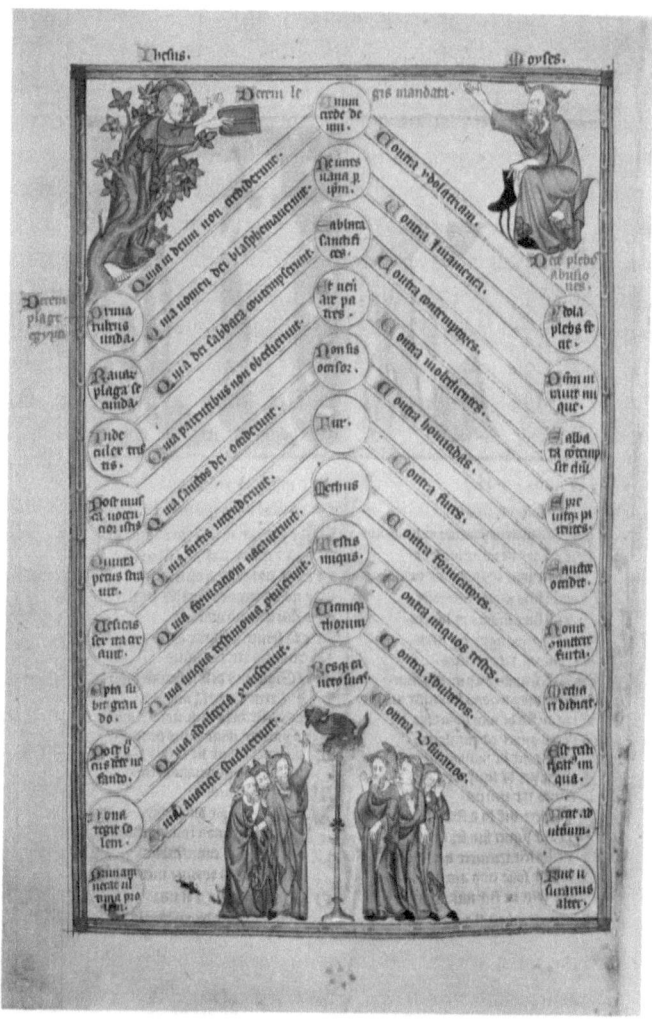

Figure 4. *Speculum theologiae.* Table of the Ten Commandments. Robert de Lisle Psalter, London, British Library, MS Arundel 83 II, fol. 127v. By permission of the British Library.

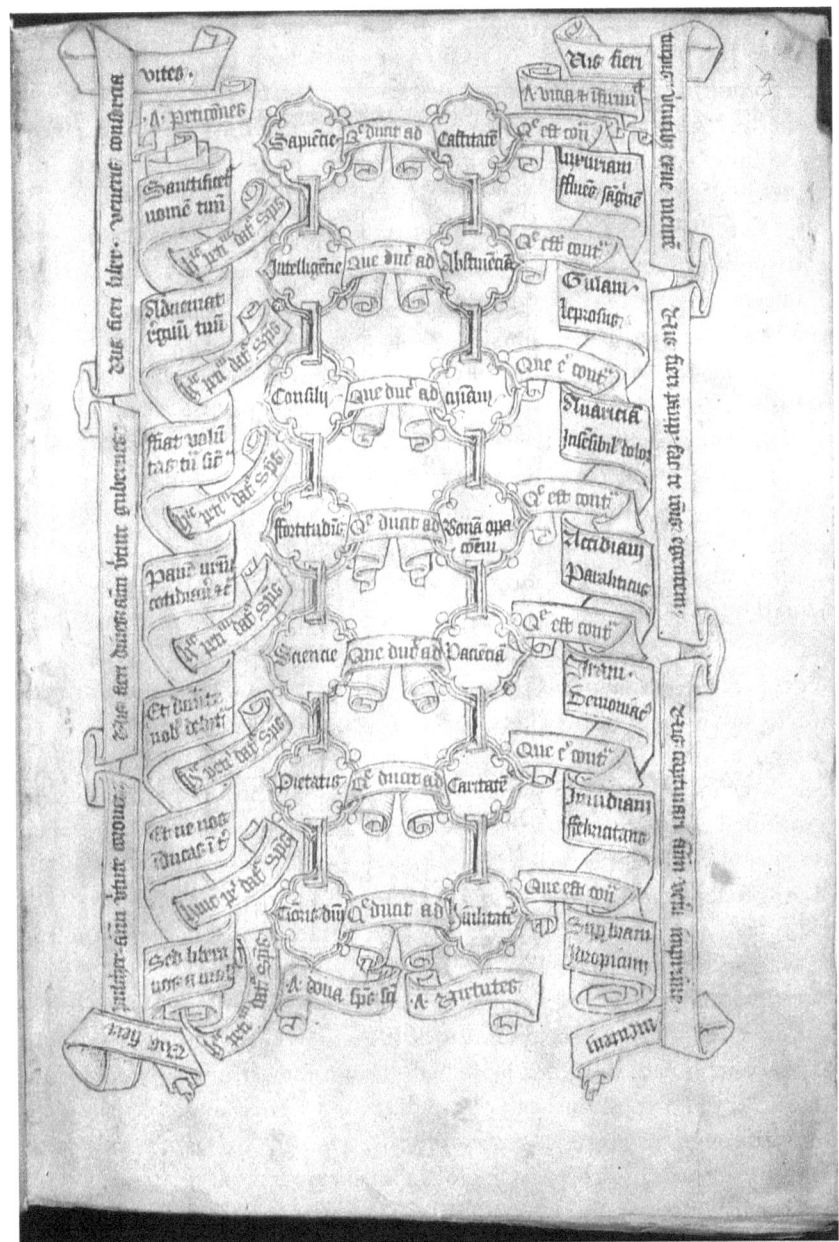

Figure 5. *Speculum theologiae.* Table of the Seven Petitions of the Paternoster. London, British Library, MS Royal 1.B.x, fol. 4r. By permission of the British Library.

education, then as a task imposed by a confessor. As a result, one does not read so much as recognize. Even for someone possessing only sorry Latin, the point of a diagram like this is not so much what it says as what it connects. It takes the dutifully memorized catechetical lists and literally gives them another dimension by connecting them to other, parallel lists in a three-dimensional grid.

The scribe's seemingly inverted use of rubrication in this diagram tends to confirm my hypothesis about its intended function. For aside from the traditional red of the column titles, only the phrases that connect the columns are written in red ink. In a narrative, this would be equivalent to rubricating all the nonlexical connecting words and leaving the nouns and verbs and adjectives in black. The diagram-maker's practice is all the more initially puzzling because the connectors in each column say the same thing. The first row reads: "'Sanctificetur nomen tuum': huic petitioni datur spiritus Sapiencie que ducit ad Castitatem que est contra Luxuriam/Fluens sanguinem ('Hallowed be thy name': [in response] to this petition is given the spirit of Wisdom, which leads to Chastity, which is against Lechery/Emitting blood)." In the second row the text changes to "'Aduenriat regnum tuum': huic petitioni datur spiritus Intelligencie que ducit ad Abstinenciam que est contra Gulam/Leprosus ('Thy kingdom come': [in response] to this petition is given the spirit of Understanding, which leads to Abstinence, which is against Greed/Leper)." So the diagram continues, with the same syntactical elements linking each set of petitions, gifts, virtues, and vices. If these rubricated connecting phrases do not serve a differentiating function, what do they do? Most obviously, they encourage the viewer to read across the lists as well as within them, in much the same way that the placement of the rubricated column titles encourages the viewer to read from bottom to top as well as from top to bottom. Beyond that, however, I believe that the red lettering, together with the elaborate scrolls on which it is inscribed, serves a syntactical function. The grammar of the sentences read from left to right is overdetermined, since it is presented once in the usual way through conjugations and prepositions and case endings and then again, more conspicuously, through the visual language of rubrication and scroll work. In keeping with the Derridean understanding of supplementation, moreover, this visual grammar both supports the traditional grammatical links and threatens to supplant them, in the process making a reasonably complex set of associations between petitions, gifts, virtues, and vices available to an audience located somewhere on the continuum of sorry Latin. To put this another way, the diagram vernacularizes its own Latin text. Like Anima's act of self-naming, it translates what would otherwise be an indigestible chunk of Latin into a collection of known or knowable Latin substantives set within an easy-to-understand, non-Latinate framework. That, I think, is the point of these strongly emphasized connectors, and by extension of the diagram as a whole. It allows viewers to move beyond the rote memorization of lists required of all lay people to attain a complexity and depth of understanding usually associated with Latinity—and if in the process it teaches some viewers a bit more Latin, so much the better.

That, at least, seems to have been the intention. In practice, the language of the diagram in MS Royal 1.B.X is *itself* sorry Latin.[31] Since the syntax of the diagram is so over-determined, none of its irregularities are actually confusing, but they easily could be in another context. In the examples cited above, the phrase "huic petitioni" is in the dative case where one would expect an ablative and the sins and infirmities are an inconsistent mishmash of nouns and adjectives, nominatives and accusatives. The latter problem probably arises because the maladies were not part of the original conception of the diagram, but rather were an addition inspired by Grosseteste's *Templum dei*, which includes a diagram with the same collocation of vices and maladies, each joined to its analogue by straight lines.[32] As a result, the *Speculum theologiae*'s sins are accusative, part of the original horizontal "sentence," while the maladies are nominative because that is how they appear in the source text. The maladies are visually integral to the diagram, combining with the sins to balance out the Paternoster petitions on the other side of the page, but grammatically they make no sense, suggesting that the diagram's visual language trumps its Latin. Attempts to correct this disjunction seem only to have made it worse, so that where the *Templum dei* reads "Fluens sanguine" and, later, "Ydropicus," Royal 1.B.X reads "fluens sanguinem" and "Idropicum," presumably by attraction to the accusative endings of the sins—thus rendering the list of maladies as a whole even more irregular. Collectively, these inconsistencies suggest that the Royal 1.B.X diagram upholds Mirk's contention that the endings of Latin words cannot carry religious significance, if only because few people are capable of getting them right. In addition, the rubricated connecting phrase at the center of each line, "que

---

31. I am grateful to Richard Kieckhefer for his help in thinking about these irregularities.

32. Robert Grosseteste, *Templum dei*, ed. Joseph Goering and F. A. C. Mantello (Toronto: Centre for Medieval Studies, 1984), 5.6. Grosseteste's much less visually elaborate diagram contains, in addition to the sins and maladies, the entity offended by each sin (God, one's neighbor, or one's self), the astrological sign that governs it, the sin's executor (Demons, World, or Flesh) and the wound or symptom associated with each sinful malady. It lacks the gifts and the virtues of the *Summa theologiae* diagram, which are associated with the petitions of the Pater Noster in Grosseteste's next diagram, 6.5. It is quite possible that the relationship between the *Templum dei* and the *Speculum theologiae* diagram is one of shared parentage or indirect rather than direct influence.

ducit ad," should modify a feminine noun, and in the examples given above it does. But in the third and seventh rows "que ducit ad" modifies the neuter *consilium* and the masculine *timor*. Implicitly, the *Speculum theologiae* lies beyond grammatical gender in much the same way as Langland's Anima. The diagram's Latin text is crucial, but it is subsumed within and transformed by the diagram's visual structures to produce a Latinate space that becomes the new and primary unit of analysis.

A glance at the disposition of *Speculum theologiae* manuscripts seems to corroborate the work's status as a hybrid of Latin and vernacular.[33] To be sure, many copies of the *Speculum theologiae* are preserved in traditionally Latinate contexts, rubbing shoulders with academic, medical, historical, and devotional texts.[34] This last category is by far the largest, and many such *Speculum theologiae* manuscripts can be traced to monastic libraries. In addition, various of the *Speculum theologiae*'s constituent diagrams survive as wall paintings in exclusively clerical spaces, including a confessional cherub in the chapter house of Westminster Abbey.[35] An important number of copies of the *Speculum theologiae*, however, address audiences somewhere on the continuum of sorry Latin. Judging from its context, the Royal 1.B.X diagram I have been focusing on seems intended as an aid for preaching, part of a program for updating a thirteenth-century Bible and making it

---

33. I used Sandler's handlist of *Speculum theologiae* manuscripts and, wherever possible, the catalogues and other sources she lists to compile lists of contents and indications of provenance for each manuscript. I am grateful to my research assistant, Jenny Lee, for her invaluable contribution to this undertaking.

34. Chambéry, Bibl. Municipale, MS 27 contains the *Speculum theologiae*, six treatises by Aristotle, one each by Boethius and Porphyry, and a short love poem. Florence, Bibl. Mediceo-Laurenziana, MS Plut. 30.24 is a computistic miscellany; London, Wellcome Historical Medical Library, MS 49 contains medical and anatomical drawings; London, Gray's Inn, MS 9 contains works on the history of England. For *Speculum theologiae* manuscripts containing devotional material and associated with monastic houses, see Aarau, Kantonsbibl., MS Wett., fol. 9; Darmstadt, Hessische Landesbibl., MS 535; Munich, Bayerische Staatsbibl. MSS Clm. 8201, 11465, 16104a; New Haven, Yale University, Beinecke Rare Book and Manuscript Library, MS 416; Paris, Bibl. Mazarine, MS 924; and Paris, Bibl. Nationale, MS lat. 14289. Other manuscripts that preserve the *Speculum theologiae* in a clerical and Latinate context but without clear institutional provenance include Cambridge, Jesus College, MS 24 (Q.B.7); Rome, Bibl. Casanatense, MS 1404; and Karlsruhe, Badische Landesbibl., MS St. Peter perg. 82.

35. Miriam Gill discusses the Westminster Cherub in "The Role of Images in Monastic Education: The Evidence from Wall Painting in Late Medieval England," in *Medieval Monastic Education*, ed. George Ferzoco and Carolyn Muessig (London: Leicester University Press, 2000), 117–35, arguing that "such art was not a substitute for a book, but reproduced the form and content of an illuminated manuscript on a monumental scale for simultaneous communal study. The bookish quality of this art not only characterizes and justifies its display in a monastic context, but also functions as an extension of monastic *lectio*" (125). While this may generally be true, such reading was not limited to monks. Bolzoni, *Web of Images*, 119, mentions in addition Trees of Life in the chapter house of the Church of San Francesco in Pistoia and the refectory of the monastery of Santa Croce in Florence.

more usable. It thus remained in clerical hands but served a mixed clerical and lay audience. This pattern is typical of an important subset of *Speculum theologiae* manuscripts, many of them bilingual or trilingual: Cambridge University Library MS Gg.IV.32 is a priest's personal miscellany containing syllabus prayers in English, French, and Latin and Paris, Bibliothèque de l'Arsenal MS 937 is a preaching anthology with texts in French and Latin. London, British Library MS Arundel 507, seemingly compiled by the monk Richard of Segbrok, associates the *Speculum theologiae* with Latin theological tracts but also with John Gaytryge's English translation of the syllabus of basic religious knowledge compiled by John Thoresby, Archbishop of York, in 1357.[36] Yet other copies of the *Speculum theologiae* survive in contexts that suggest they were used as visual aids for preaching, classroom instruction, or both, along the lines of the confessional cherub diagram St. Bernardino of Siena apparently used to illustrate a sermon in 1423.[37] This may have been the purpose, for instance, of Cambridge, University Library MS 111.56, a roll containing the Peter of Poitier's *Arbor historiae* on the recto and *Speculum theologiae* images on the verso, or of the similar but more extensive Paris, Bibliothèque de l'Arsenal MS 1234.[38] London, British Library MS Additional 17,358 is a *vademecum* small enough to fit into the palm of the hand, containing the *Speculum* and the *Arbor* alongside calendar and almanac material. With its pages opened out six-fold for instruction or private study, it becomes quite literally a portable sacred space, space that a preacher or reader can take with him wherever he goes. On a more monumental scale, John of Metz's Tower of Wisdom is painted in the church portico of Averara in Italy, where it was accessible to the public and presumably served as a preaching aid.[39] Collectively these pastoral tools invite lay viewers to join the clergy in a Latinate conceptual domain. Indeed, the fact that the *Speculum theologiae* was at times a purely monastic and clerical text seems to constitute

---

36. Other preachers' miscellanies containing the *Speculum theologiae* include Paris, Bibl. Nationale, MS lat. 3445, and possibly MSS lat. 3464 and 3473 as well.

37. Bolzoni, *Web of Images*, 132–33. Bolzoni carefully distinguishes between sermons that use the seraph as a rhetorical figure and those that seem to require the display of an actual image, placing Bernardino's 1423 sermons in the latter category.

38. Oxford, St. John's College, MS 58, an easily portable pamphlet of eleven folios containing the *Arbor historiae* and the *Speculum theologiae*, seems to have served a similar purpose.

39. Bolzoni also mentions a Tree of Life in the nave of the Basilica of Santa Maria Maggiore in Bergamo but notes, "What is so striking about the Tower of Knowledge in Averara . . . is the fact that a schema as intellectually challenging and complex as this could have been addressed to a wide public, very few of whom would have been capable of deciphering the Latin inscriptions. It may be inferred that many analogous examples in other towns have been lost, or remain hidden under frescoes executed in the sixteenth or seventeenth centuries" (*Web of Images*, 119). The destruction of such images would have been even more likely in England than in Italy.

part of its appeal, since it guarantees that the diagrams move beyond the syllabus required of lay people into a higher realm of knowledge.

Beyond these preaching texts, a number of *Speculum theologiae* manuscripts address themselves directly to readers who, because of their gender or lay status, would most likely have commanded only sorry Latin. As mentioned above, the most famous copy of the *Speculum theologiae* belonged to an aristocratic layman, Robert de Lisle, and was later intended for his two daughters who were nuns.[40] Assuming that de Lisle's instructions were carried out, this copy would ultimately have functioned as a kind of "nun's Latin," bridging the gap between religious vocation and supposed feminine weakness.[41] As such, it perhaps occupied the same domain as the Vernon manuscript, which contains a Paternoster diagram similar to the one in the *Speculum theologiae* as well as an A text of *Piers Plowman*.[42] Another small but significant subset of the audience of the *Speculum theologiae* would have spoken sorry Latin only temporarily, as a step toward full grammatical mastery. One of the preacher's volumes already mentioned, the fourteenth-century Paris, Bibliothèque de l'Arsenal MS 937, includes a grammatical tract written in both French and Latin and thus presumably designed for boys who were not yet fully Latinized.[43] Finally, a pair of manuscripts introduce vernacular elements into the *Speculum theologiae* itself. Paris, Bibliothèque Nationale MS français 9220 adds to the usual contents of the *Speculum*

---

40. Sandler, *Psalter of Robert de Lisle*, 12–13. Other aristocratic copies of the *Speculum theologiae* include the Howard Psalter and Hours of the Passion, now bound with the De Lisle Psalter in London, British Library, MS Arundel 83 and containing the arms of John Fitton of Wiggenhall (d. 1326) and an obit for Theodore of Malinton, Baron of Wemme (d. 1405). In Paris, Bibliothèque de l'Arsenal, MS 1037, the *Speculum theologiae* is paired with instructions for using an *adresceoir*, an instrument for measuring time, and inscribed to a "tres haute dame," presumably an aristocratic laywoman, while Paris, Bibliothèque de l'Arsenal, MS 1100, a fifteenth-century miscellany including the *Speculum theologiae* and material on the abbots of Cluny, is inscribed to Dame Alfons Mansoys; the binding is stamped with the arms of the convent of the Minimes de la Place Royale.

41. Ralph Hanna refers to French as used in religious establishments as "nun's Latin" in "Augustinian Canons and Middle English Literature," in *The English Medieval Book: Studies in Memory of Jeremy Griffiths*, ed. A. S. G. Edwards, Vincent Gillespie, and Ralph Hanna (London: British Library, 2000), 36. I consider the diagrammatic "language" of the *Speculum theologiae* to function analogously.

42. See *The Vernon Manuscript: A Facsimile of Bodleian Library, Oxford, MS. Eng. poet. a.1* (Cambridge: D. S. Brewer, 1987).

43. David Thomson's *A Descriptive Catalogue of Middle English Grammatical Texts* (New York: Garland, 1979) finds that only elementary grammar books were written in the vernacular, and that at least one author produced beginners' work in English and a more advanced grammar school treatise in Latin (43). There is a more circumstantial case for thinking that Oxford, Bodleian Library, MS Laud Misc. 156 may have been a school text. Containing the *Speculum theologiae* and a Bible dictionary, it belonged to the library of the Hospital of St. John Baptist in Exeter, which included an important regional grammar school.

theologiae diagrams with explanatory verses in French and Latin, while Jenkintown, PA, Alverthorpe Gallery, Rosenwald Collection MS 3 includes two copies of the Tower of Wisdom, one German and the other Latin. The Tower is one of the most text-heavy of the *Speculum theologiae* diagrams, and this may be why a translation was considered helpful. If so, it suggests a reader who felt comfortable with short, familiar snippets of text but not with longer, unpredictable ones. More broadly, all of these manuscripts suggest an audience that sought to rise toward perfection but had not satisfied the traditional clerical prerequisites. With its multiplication of trees, paths, grids, and ladders, the *Speculum theologiae* thus becomes, both literally and metaphorically, a scaffold for making the ascent as well as a locus for meditative dwelling. It serves as a new kind of common language—a *lingua franca* if not a vernacular—that defines a community of devout laypeople, religious women, and traditionally Latinate clerics.

Both Anima's act of self-naming and the *Speculum theologiae* diagrams thus participate in Nicholas Watson's category of "vernacular theology"—but with a twist.[44] For while neither text nor diagram is fully Latin, neither is fully vernacular either. Although the *Speculum theologiae* is arguably the more elementary of the two, it presents the fundamentals of the faith in a way quite distinct from, say, the aggressive vernacularity of the Wycliffite *Pierce the Plowman's Creed*, which culminates in and authorizes a stand-alone English version of the Creed. In contrast, the *Speculum theologiae* diagrams demand that their viewers project themselves into a markedly Latinate and sacred space. Just as, according to Paul Gehl, a grammar student "translate[s] himself, or at least his active intelligence ... into the original language of the great inherited texts," so a viewer of the *Speculum theologiae* translates himself—projects himself—into the diagrams.[45] The caveat is that the space of the diagrams, like the space created by Langland's Anima, is Latinate without being rigorously Latin. Both kinds of *pictura* work to separate the language itself, with all its grammatical complexity, from the religious complexity, or religious seriousness, it traditionally denotes. Each *pictura*—and, by extension, the works that contain them—purports to be a kind of portable cloister available to lay people as well as clerics, to part-time as well as full-time religious. Almost incidentally, they assert that the category of "part-time religious" is a perfectly acceptable and coherent one.

---

44. See Nicholas Watson, "Censorship and Cultural Change in Late-Medieval England: Vernacular Theology, the Oxford Translation Debate, and Arundel's Constitutions of 1409," *Speculum* 70 (1995): 822–64.

45. Paul Gehl, *A Moral Art: Grammar, Society, and Culture in Trecento Florence* (Ithaca, NY: Cornell University Press, 1993), 103.

I do not claim that Langland's Anima is reducible to a diagram like the one in MS Royal 1.B.X, or even to a diagram like those in the De Lisle Psalter—though the Psalter, like *Piers Plowman,* has an inescapable, even virtuoso, aesthetic dimension. I do claim, however, that the function of vernacular literature in late-fourteenth-century England—here encapsulated in Langland's aesthetically and conceptually complex allegory of Anima, the human soul—overlaps that of a work like the *Speculum theologiae.* Both Anima and the *Speculum theologiae* are tools for advancing upon the basic spiritual knowledge required of laypeople without requiring a concomitant advancement in formal education or curricular knowledge. Instead, they seek to define their own languages at the intersection of Latin and vernacular, languages that quite literally open up a new dimension, another axis along which to think and progress. Even though Langland's literary language is clearly distinct from the *Speculum theologiae*'s visual language, the logic governing them is additive rather than zero-sum. Collectively, the new languages seek to create a self-consciously "higher" meditative or imaginative realm open to all serious-minded Christians. At once Latinate and vernacular, religious and secular, serious and recreative (that is, capable of being done in one's spare time rather than as a vocation), this new cultural space is very much the space of "public poetry" as Anne Middleton so magisterially defined it.[46]

---

46. Anne Middleton, "The Idea of Public Poetry in the Reign of Richard II," *Speculum* 53 (1978): 94–114.

six

Speculum Vitae and the Form of *Piers Plowman*

RALPH HANNA

CONTRIBUTING to this collection is undertaking a dangerously imitative act. I'm going to try, as "þe wakkest, I wot, and of wyt feblest," to imitate something I hope our honoree would think worthy to read. This is certainly a shabby substitution, in which an act of homage equally presumes to emulate what has formed, guided, and educated its perpetrator over so many years. One can only entertain such a challenge in the hope that the homage is somehow going to mitigate the presumption.

The preceding paragraph is not just a "modesty topos," but also adumbrates my topic. In an intensely postmodern world, Anne Middleton's work persistently recalls to us a few home truths about the literary and why talking about it, teaching and thinking it (rather than something else), is for us neither simply a business nor a postmodern form of self-display but a persistent delight.

Imitation/mimesis is the most basic literary act: the poem presumes to find a form in words that communicates a shaped verbal understanding, appropriate to its occasion, its place and time, that reconstructs the "real." It seeks to subordinate randomly verbalized perception to principles, a form. Today, this is an impossibly "old-timey" formulation, so it is appropriate, rhetorically and otherwise, to begin with something equally passé, an annotator's footnote. This I offer only as a moment of siting that will provide a

121

springboard into something of a little more interest, in this case formal, the kind of verbal construction Langland undertakes in *Piers Plowman*.

I

Among the books hanging around the poet's library was certainly one inescapable piece of continental French, an international religious classic. This was Lorens of Orleans's *Somme le roi;* Lorens was a royal confessor and wrote the book for his patron Phillip IV about 1279. Robert Frank long ago signaled many general analogies between the *Somme* and Langland's typical argumentative moves, but the French work may be seen as more precisely generative of Langland's imaginative thinking. For example, he certainly alludes to the bravura passage in which Lorens establishes his pattern of septenary moral instruction in a central episode, "Herte highte þe herber" ("Tree of Charite," 16.15).[1]

Yet no one seems to have internalized that Langland knew *La Somme* multiply, not simply as a French text but an English one. One of Lorens's very interesting innovations on the generally Peraldan materials that he is reformulating is a very small section of his discussion of Avarice, its "ninth branch." This is designed to outline professions of their nature sinful (and thus to be avoided); through them people seek financial reward for acts that are immoral, valueless, waste time, or provoke sin in others. Lorens is brief and circumspect and cites only three examples—whores, heralds who flatter the great, and professional thugs (hitmen, hired guns). This succinct treatment normally appears in the numerous Middle English versions of the *Somme*.[2]

---

1. See Édith Brayer and Anne-Françoise Leurquin-Labie, eds., *La Somme le Roi par Frère Laurent* (Paris: Société des anciens textes français, 2008), chap. 50, pp. 201-6; for a literal translation see *The Book of Vices and Virtues*, ed. W. Nelson Francis, EETS 217 (London: Oxford University Press, 1942), 92–97. Langland, it must be added, also clearly knows and uses Lorens's source in the ordinary gloss to Cant. 4. *La Somme*'s description of the garden of virtues does not occur in the text that I introduce two paragraphs below, and thus was certainly known to Langland from the French. See Robert W. Frank, Jr., *"Piers Plowman" and the Scheme of Salvation*, Yale Studies in English 136 (New Haven, CT: Yale University Press, 1957), 1–2 and *passim*, e.g., 63–65 nn.

All citations of *Piers Plowman* are taken from the Athlone Press editions and, unless explicitly marked otherwise, from the B Version: George Kane, ed., *Piers Plowman: The A Version* (London: Athlone Press, 1960); George Kane and E. Talbot Donaldson, eds., *Piers Plowman: The B Version* (London: Athlone Press, 1975; rev. 1988); George Russell and George Kane, eds., *Piers Plowman: The C Version* (London: Athlone Press, 1997).

2. The discussion is brief enough to be cited in full here: "La noviesme branche d'avarice est en mauvés mestier. En ce pechent mout de gent en mout de manieres, comme ces foles fames qui por un pou de gahaing s'abandonent a pecchié; ausi comme cil heraut et cil champion e mout d'autres qui pur

Normally. Walter Skeat, who of course *did* know everything, realized that this formulation does not cover all cases and carefully signalled the fact, but did not follow it up, in one of his exemplary notes. The most widely dispersed of all English translations of *La Somme,* in at least forty-five surviving copies and fragments, is the poetic version called *Speculum Vitae.* In this passage, that translation innovates on the French source. The *Speculum,* work of an anonymous Yorkshire cleric c.1350–70, expands Lorens's half-dozen lines into over 140 octosyllabic verses and offers more or less extended discussion of nine "crafts of foly," "sinful professions." Three of these, presented consecutively—and this is what Skeat recognized—sound particularly resonant in the context of *Piers Plowman:* Faytours (*Speculum* 7123–32), Sneckedrawers (7133–62; "Som men calles þam 'robertmen,'" line 7134), and Herlotes, "minstrels" in the broadest Hawkin sense of the term (7163–82).[3]

Certainly, this discourse represents some form of Middle English slang/invective, and it has to have been dispersed enough to have been both legally and poetically comprehensible. Nonetheless, *Speculum Vitae* is the only site, literary or otherwise, in which Langland could have found this material, could have found it organized together, and most importantly, could have found it within an analytical framework. The evidence for such an assertion may be easily assembled through the consultation of historical dictionaries, and it is, as Skeat pointed out, quite unequivocal, since it involves more than simply reliance on the same vocabulary. Langland shares with the poet of *Speculum Vitae* an elsewhere unattested understanding of the connotations or implications of this terminology.

Skeat's customarily economical discussion of Prol.44 "Roberdes knaues" alone should constitute definitive proof. He pointed out that the word is presented as an alternative synonym in *Speculum* for "sneckdrawers"—an otherwise unparallelled fourteenth-century Northern compound; Langland uses the southern equivalent "lacchedrawers" twice (C 8.286, C 9.193). Leaving

---

deniers ou pur preu temporel s'abandonent a mestier deshoneste qui ne peut estre fez senz pechié, et de ceus qui le font et qui les sostienent"; chap. 36; Brayer and Leurquin-Labie, eds., *Somme le Roi,* 145. Compare *The Book of Vices and Virtues,* 41/10–18, which refers to "wikkede craftes" and "wikkede craftes and vnsittynge"; and *Dan Michel's Ayenbite of Inwyt,* ed. Richard Morris and newly collated by Pamela Gradon, EETS o.s. 23 (Oxford: Oxford University Press, 1965), 45/5–13, with "kueade creftes" and "crefte naȝt oneste."

3. Walter W. Skeat, ed., *The Vision of William Concerning Piers the Plowman in Three Parallel Texts* (London: Oxford University Press, 1886), 2:7. I cite this poem from Ralph Hanna, ed., *Speculum Vitae: A Reading Edition,* EETS 331–32 (Oxford: Oxford University Press, 2008), 1:237–42.

I have previously taken up issues germane here; see, on the function of marginals, "Will's Work," in *Written Work: Langland, Labor, and Authorship,* ed. Steven Justice and Kathryn Kerby-Fulton (Philadelphia: University of Pennsylvania Press, 1997), 44–53; and on time wasting, *London Literature, 1300–1380* (Cambridge: Cambridge University Press, 2005), 148–53, 258.

these usages aside, the terms occur only twice before *Piers* C, on both occasions in parliamentary statutes, and on both occasions, as in *Speculum Vitae*, as if synonyms.[4] The statutes lack any precision about what the words signify (although the inclusion of the term "wastours" in the first usage is suggestive). But both Langland's uses at Prol.44 and C 8.286 indicate that he envisioned behaviors like those described in considerable detail in the Yorkshire poem. There "sneckedrawers" do rob, in that they try to sneak into houses (testing the "snecke" or latch first), but their main interest is not in making off with items of value, but pilfering food ("wasting," since not the product of their own labor). "Sneckedrawers/robertmen" are prepared, if interrupted, to offer lengthy extenuations of their derelict behavior, in hopes simply of a handout.[5]

Skeat's persuasive findings may be further extended in an examination of the other two terms—and of the congruence of the two poets' customary usage of them. The most usual Middle English sense of the noun *faitour* (and of its derivative verb *faiten*), is "deceiver, imposter," a sense-development apparently shared only with Anglo-Norman. It customarily describes only deceitful vagrants, viewed as capable of a range of nefarious behaviors.[6] Never outside *Speculum* and *Piers* does the term explicitly (and narrowly) mean something on the order of "sturdy (and thus feigning) beggar," nor is the word ever accompanied by such a description as this:

> Lithir wyles can þai fynde
> To make þam seme crokid or blynde
> Or seke or mysays to mens sight.
> So can þai þair lyms dight
> For men suld þam mysays deme,
> Bot þai er noght swilk als þai seme. (*Speculum Vitae* 7125–30)

---

4. See *Statutes of the Realm*, 10 vols. (London: Eyre and Strahan, 1810–28), 1:268, 2:32–33 (5 Edward III, c.14; 7 Richard II, c.5), with "Robertsmen Wastours et Draghlacche" and "Roberdesmen et Drawlacches," respectively. Both statutes reaffirm the earlier 13 Edward I, c.4 ("The Statute of Winchester"; see 1:97) and concern the responsibility of nightwatchmen in towns for apprehending, and detaining overnight, suspicious persons—in the original statute only those "estrange," from outside the municipal walls.

5. The association of Rob-names (Robin [Hood], as well as Robert) with such behaviors goes back to at least early thirteenth-century legal documents and simply represents a derivative of the proper name. See *MED*, Robert n., sense 1 (a), and compare Langland's penitent thief, "Roberd þe robbere" (5.461).

6. Thus, one of the limited number of pre-Langlandian citations, "faiturs and ypocrites and iogolors þat desayues men" (Rolle, *Psalter* 30.16) or the four times repeated collocation "faitours et vagerantz (de lieu en lieu currantz)" of the 1383 statute I have cited in n.4.

—a definition that certainly resonates with a number of Langland's descriptions, perhaps most provocatively 6.120–28 and 7.90–106.

The term "harlot" is a bit trickier, since it has a lengthy English history. But the great majority of uses, from the early thirteenth century on, follow the sense of the Anglo-Norman etymon and mean simply "rogue, base fellow, vagabond." This general sense Langland, of course, knows, but a considerably narrower usage "entertainer," e.g., "Sholde noon harlot haue audience in hall ne in chambre" (13.433), is also well attested in the poem. "Entertainer" is actually the only sense of the word the *Speculum*-poet knows, and the lexical evidence would indicate that this extended usage originated, about 1300, as a Northernism (and thus a natural term for this poet).[7] And *Speculum Vitae* also includes two lengthy passages germane to Langland's discussion of "God's minstrels"; these insist upon the active charity due the poor, rather than to "harlots" (8573–98, 15697–722). Indeed, the notion of a cleanly or godly *geste* (13.446) is inherent in the prologue to the *Speculum*—and even more explicit in the early text it there imitates, the opening of *Cursor Mundi*.[8]

I think, although a catalogue of unique and precise connections might be extended, this forms an adequate demonstration of Langland's knowledge of and reliance on the earlier poem. In the remainder of this study, I address the obvious corollary to this demonstration: what difference does it make that Langland had read *Speculum Vitae*?

II

In the most general terms, this poem provides useful background for imagining the English literary landscape, the world of Edwardian poetry (or of Thorlac Turville-Petre's Middle Middle English), into which *Piers Plowman* intrudes. As a preliminary assay at this issue, I put "the crafts of folly"

---

7. Compare, most flamboyantly, *Cursor Mundi* 27927, 27922–23 (ed. Richard Morris, EETS 68 [London : K. Paul, Trench, Trübner, 1874–93], 1546–48):

Þat man may se be lichur state: . . .
Harlot[s] sagh, speche o disur,
Rimes vnright, gest of iogolur.

See similarly, Rolle, *Form of Living* 369 (in *Prose and Verse from MS. Longleat 29 and Related Manuscripts*, ed. S. J. Ogilvie-Thomson, EETS o.s. 293 [Cambridge: Boydell & Brewer, 1988], 12), incorporated within a lengthy Rolle citation at *Speculum* 5689.

8. See especially lines 115, 123, 251–56 (ed. Morris, EETS o.s. 57 [London : K. Paul, Trench, Trübner, 1874–93], 14 and 22).

temporarily to one side and consider the grossest formal attributes of *Piers*, that it is a dream-vision and that it proceeds, uniquely among such works, by multiplying visions. This initial formulation highlights Langland's decision to inflect whatever a handbook source like *Speculum Vitae* provided him against a considerably more secular model, at least in the first instance dependent upon imitating *Winner and Waster*.[9]

But however foreign to morally instructive literature dream-vision may appear, there are certain formal carryovers of conception, in this case addressing Langland's unparalleled decision to write a poem composed of multiple dreams. In the overall context of *Speculum Vitae*, describing "crafters of foly" is a vibrant and attractive piece of writing. Indeed, the passage stands out because this is precisely not how *Speculum Vitae* normally proceeds. The poem provides an immense filing system (and I doubt that it is to be a read poem, but a consulted one). It is formed of a largely static pattern of *distinctiones*—following Lorens, the poet splits out a subject from what he imagines a totality (vice/virtue), subdivides it, lists its constituent parts, and analyses each in turn. Thus, *Speculum* mainly defines topics, for example this (complete) discussion of Wanhope, the eighteenth branch of Sloth:

> Wanhope comes þan alderlast,
> In whilk þe fende haldes a man fast.
> For when a man in Wanhope es broght,
> In Goddis mercy ne traystes he noght,
> For hym thinke so mykell his mysse
> Þat he may neuer haf heuen-blisse.
> And in þat he may parchaunce
> Sla hymself thurgh þe fendes combraunce.
> Þus may þise sex vyces brynge
> A man vntil ane ille endynge. (5249–58)[10]

Presentations of the "crafts" resemble this passage only incidentally. The poet of *Speculum* is pretty obviously involved in category proliferation (as in the received division of Sloth into eighteen [!] parts). But equally, he cat-

---

9. For example, Langland's direct evocation, at the opening, of the earlier poem:

As I went in the west, wandryng myn one
Bi a bonke of a bourne, bryghte was the sone. (31–32)

I regularly cite from Thorlac Turville-Petre, ed., *Alliterative Poetry of the Later Middle Ages* (London: Routledge, 1989), 41–66; for "Middle Middle English," see his *England the Nation* (Oxford: Clarendon Press, 1996).

10. A similar discussion of Wanhope as a sin against the Holy Spirit appears at 4355–62.

egorizes and synthesizes some quite diverse behaviors into types reflecting Avarice. Unlike Wanhope, however, the presentations of the "crafts of folly" describe, not an inner *habitus,* but external acts alleged to express it. In these descriptions, one gets narrativized "sin," but at least partially fixed through identification of a type, the "vocation"/"craft." These descriptions, then, vacillate between type and represented behavior, the often complex activities of these perps. Thus, the "crafts" resemble Langlandian personification simply conceived, ceaseless repetition of the same vignette, yet a vignette always mobile/motile, subject of a consuetudinal narrative, and one that engages not simply "allegorical" type but also social practice.[11]

The "crafts" may stand out as different. But *Speculum* resolutely follows the definitional turn exemplified by Wanhope and through this choice, the English poet subverts much that he found in Lorens. For while *La Somme* is equally "mechanistic" in shape, it includes a certain "dynamism," an insistence on ascent, rising in virtue to meet divinity. *Speculum Vitae* only retains Lorens's persistently ascendant patterning in its praise of the last "degree," Temperance (14613–844). But both methods of argument, French and English, could be connected with normal forms of catechesis.

Frank indicated amply enough Langland's imaginative fascination with such topics—as well as his obvious irritation with them and his sense that they did not constructively engage his needs. They constitute the "bokes ynow" and friar teachers (Lorens was a Dominican) to which Ymagynatif directs the dreamer (12.16–19). The *Speculum,* an extremely sophisticated example of the genre, shows the problem: it is really like getting home from IKEA with a box full of wooden planks and finding that the (underexplanatory) instruction sheet is not there. (The problem is, of course, intensified here by the proliferation of "parts" and "branches" of the various sins and virtues—lots and lots of planks.)

Somme and *Speculum* may construct good Christians, but they do so by providing lists of "don't do this" alternating with lists of "instead do that."

---

11. Compare J. V. Cunningham, "The Literary Form of the Prologue to *The Canterbury Tales,*" *Modern Philology* 49 (1952): 172–81, who argues a similar coalescence of personification and vocational type, that Chaucer's "estates" portraits imitate the allegorical figures painted on the garden wall in *La roman de la rose.* Certainly, *Winner,* with its depiction of allegorizable armies nonetheless including professional types (friars on Winner's team, for example), provides a further local analogy.

Of course, Langland's having noticed a piece of English expansiveness limited to a brief space in a very long and extensive French text might itself be recognized as a formally generative perception. It implies the author's at least double attentiveness: (a) "vernacular" English, of which *Speculum Vitae* forms a strident example, as always "translated," alluding to a frequently unvoiced polylingual surround; (b) the malleability and power of local argumentative detail, an awareness played out in the poetic operations of "revision."

Readers are supposed to gain from reading these a checklist of those actions recognizably evil (vices), so they can identify them, and then replace each from a list of actions recognizably good (virtues). Or, in the technical argot of hamartiology and of "Herte þe herber," "pull up the weeds of vice in the garden of your soul and plant seeds of the virtues." This had been the catechetical model, and the absorbing center of religious writing, for a century and a half, ever since the need for this kind of specifically parochial instruction had been promulgated at the Fourth Lateran Council in 1215.

The real problem with this is that you obtained your planks, identifiable pieces of salvation, with some recognition tokens as to what they are. But although you have the information that should allow you to recognize bad planks (or actions), whether you could do so, as you were about to perform them, seems to me moot. Further, while the rhetoric of catechesis assumes the efficaciousness of proliferating branches/planks—it is supposed to allow increasingly fine-grained and meticulous confessional self-examination—that is not necessarily its only effect. It may simply generate chaos, confusion, or Wanhope, a sense of sin's ubiquity (cf. 14.323–26).[12] Worst of all, you are missing the instruction sheet about how to change those deviant planks out or what you would do to put them into the orderly form of the spiritual IKEA cabinet.

In their formal structure, *Somme* and *Speculum* imply that getting saved is mechanically automatic. In essence, you are presented with a series of discrete acts, bad and good, and asked open-endedly to make the latter into rules of spiritual conduct. The only problem comes when you ask, as Will does, "How?" (1.84), when you turn the issue from spiritual act/conduct into a question about spirituality. Of what would that instruction consist? To what in you would it appeal? And if the going catechetical model is as I describe, Ymaginatyf's advice probably deserves about the same restive response as Langland's dreamer gives it. It's surely "true" in a veridical sense, but it's not Truth, a spiritual explanation.

Piers Plowman is certainly unique in the imaginative drive it brings to this question, the need to formally innovate to remake Christian edification. But the poem is far from unique in wanting to engage the issue. The salient contribution of Nicholas Watson's well-known article on vernacular writing is its demonstration that the type of vernacular works that passed from the scene after 1409 were large catechetical handbooks of instruction.[13] For

---

12. Compare, for example, the tumble of Rolle's *Form of Living* 323–98 (ed. Ogilvie-Thomson, 11–13), cited at *Speculum* 5575–834, as a literal "form" for organizing one's confession.

13. See Nicholas Watson, "Censorship and Cultural Change in Late-Medieval England: Vernacular Theology, the Oxford Translation Debate, and Arundel's Constitutions of 1409," *Speculum* 70

Watson, here engaged in provocateurism, this demise of genre depends upon an external disruption, Arundel's interventions designed to restrict vernacular discussion. I would suggest a different formulation, that few people were writing catechetical materials like *Speculum Vitae* after 1409 because precisely of generic demise. One "genre/kind" of instruction had successfully performed that literary labor that, within its generic limits, it was capable of performing; or, stated otherwise, the genre had exhausted the questions that it appeared capable of answering. As a result, those seriously engaged needed to explore alternative ways to pose religious issues, to innovate generically. The problem is one internal to a particular form of literary representation—and of authors' and readers' response to a representation deemed insufficient, no longer addressing perceived concerns, and thus requiring replacement.

Viewed this way, it is informative that *Speculum Vitae* may be exactly contemporary with the last great Middle English catechetical endeavor, archbishop John Thoresby of York's catechism of 1357.[14] Around Langland, and some of it certainly known to him, are species of religious writing that try to translate, as I've put it, "What?" into "How?," catechetical instruction in spiritual conduct into instruction in spirituality. Lollardy, with its intense interest in personal responsibility for internalizing biblical injunction, always takes top billing, but it, too, is very far from unique. Already in the 1340s, Rolle's *Form* and Latin *Emendatio Vitae* attempt to redirect conduct inwardly; instructively, to find an overt model, Rolle had to regress, to move back beyond Lateran IV, to twelfth-century Victorine theology.

Rolle's impulse was followed, in Langland's imaginative lifetime, by Walter Hilton and *The Cloud*-author.[15] But similar activities were equally prominent in London, where one can find about 1370 a laicized version of *Ancrene Riwle* (another archaic text revivified); and in the 1380s, production of the innovative *Chastising of God's Children* and *Cleansing of Man's Soul*. Similar efforts occurred in Langland's West Midland homeland, most immediately evident in the texts gathered in Oxford, University College, MS 97.[16] Langland is a great deal more *au courant* than either Gower or

---

(1995): 822–64. The argument is unduly sweeping and, to an extent, factually inaccurate, as the two mid-fifteenth-century redactions of the full *Speculum Vitae* would indicate.

14. See Anne Hudson, "A New Look at *The Lay Folks' Catechism*," *Viator* 16 (1985): 243–58.

15. It is no accident that persistent critical strains seek to connect *Piers* with (or assess it within) such circumambient generic innovations: for example, Pamela Gradon, "Langland and the Ideology of Dissent," *Proceedings of the British Academy* 66 (1980): 179–205; or Malcolm Godden, *The Making of "Piers Plowman"* (London: Longman, 1990). In terms of my argument here, such efforts confuse the analogue with the object.

16. See A. I. Doyle, "University College, Oxford, MS 97 and Its Relationship to the Simeon Manuscript (British Library Add. 22283)," in *So meny people longages and tonges: Philological Essays in*

Chaucer, both cranking out yet more catechetics (*Le mirour de l'omme, The Parson's Tale*) that rely mainly on thirteenth-century handbooks.

But whatever the degree of contemporary spiritual innovation, these efforts equally inherited the formal problems I have been describing, not unique to *Somme* and its derivatives and congeners. Were one to prejudice the issue no further than to call *Piers Plowman* "extended narration" or "long poem," one should realize that composing through the mechanical segmentation of a topic (following Anne's intervention at her own day-conference, "constructing an array") provided the only circumambient narrative mode available to Langland. It is that followed in such predecessor texts as Robert Manning's *Handling Sin, The Northern Homilies, The South English Legendary,* or *The Prick of Conscience.* All impose on their subjects a mechanical shaping structural device, in the case of *The Homilies* and *Legendary,* for example, the liturgical year, and then develop the constituent chunks the organizational category throws up.

As a result, these poems, like *Speculum Vitae,* work by segmented narrative blocks. They may reach temporary, episodic climaxes (the triumph in martyrdom of a saint in the *Legendary,* for example), but then they stop, they refocus and repeat (what is fundamentally the same with different names), return to the same ground-zero opening. Quite universally, these might be described as jerk-start narratives, lacking at major structural junctures transitions, rhetorical flagging, or overt cross-reference. One might notice—but only for a brief moment—the analogy of such works with *The Canterbury Tales,* which also engages in segmentation and only unifies its parts under a claim for the multiplicity of the imagination. Thus, the prevailing model for "long poem" when Langland initiated his project was one of multiple allegedly analogous narrative segments, no single one achieving something like final closure (but only repetition or reiteration), and laid end to end to form "long poem." Suspiciously similar, it must be said, to many descriptions of the eight-dream form of Langland's poem.

There did, however, exist an alternative to such iterative structuring, one whose effects and influence Anne Middleton has provocatively argued out.[17]

Scots and Medieval English Presented to Angus McIntosh, ed. Michael Benskin and M. L. Samuels (Edinburgh: n.p., 1981), 265–82; and Jill C. Havens, "A Narrative of Faith: Middle English Devotional Anthologies and Religious Practice," *Journal of the Early Book Society* 7 (2004): 67–84.

17. See Anne Middleton, "Narration and the Invention of Experience: Episodic Form in *Piers Plowman,*" in *The Wisdom of Poetry: Essays in Early English Literature in Honor of Morton W. Bloomfield,* ed. Larry D. Benson and Siegfried Wenzel (Kalamazoo, MI: Medieval Institute, 1982), 91–122. Further provocative comments on the subject appear throughout D. Vance Smith, *The Book of the Incipit: Beginnings in the Fourteenth Century,* Medieval Cultures 28 (Minneapolis: University of Minnesota Press, 2001).

This is the directed and progressive unfolding of romance. As genre, romance deals with action as a kind of voluntary discipline; it assumes a relatively transparent self, that mind is legibly measured by external behavior, and that the hero comes to his own (his country, his inheritance) through a sequence of implicitly educative, yet largely repetitive adventures.[18] Of course, romance poets assume what may be true as well of the repeated visions of Langland's poem, that a suitable *habitus* of virtue only achieves clear formation through progressively less errant reiterations of the same.

But this alternative clashes strikingly with the presumptions of *Speculum Vitae* and a range of similar English narratives, dating back so far as the 1280s (in Anglo-Norman to the 1230s or 1240s). As I have indicated, the Northern poem resolutely excises a progressive structure resembling that of romance—Jacob's ladder as the way to Heaven. In *La Somme*, each rung is scaled by the eradication/extirpation of one vice and its replacement by the corresponding virtue.

Speculum Vitae's excision follows rigorously upon the poet's rejection—common in predecessor and companion writings—of romance as a fit narrative mode altogether. For the poet, mindful of Matt. 12:36 and its commonplace glosses, the genre represents merely "waste"—the misuse of spiritual and intellectual talents better reserved for pursuing virtue directly. Romance is what, in their most august moments, Herlotes, one of the "crafts of folly," transmit. Moreover, *Speculum Vitae* includes the most compulsively detailed analysis of time-wasting available in any language.[19]

But the *Speculum* also complicates seriously the notion of "timely" narration. One might contrast the "crafts of folly" with a second passage, also an original narrativization in this poet's treatment of Avarice. This expansive description of Okir (usury), like that of the "crafts," avoids described inner *habitus* in favor of meticulous description of social practices. The discussion, monumentally swollen from the rendition in *La Somme*, describes for 200 lines highly realized rural market behaviors, price manipulations gener-

---

18. For provocative studies outlining such structural features, see R. W. Southern, *The Making of the Middle Ages* (New Haven, CT: Yale University Press, 1953), 219–57; Larry D. Benson, *Malory's "Morte Darthur"* (Cambridge, MA: Harvard University Press, 1976), 73–80; Susan Wittig, *Stylistic and Narrative Structures in the Middle English Romances* (Austin: University of Texas Press, 1978); Carol Fewster, *Traditionality and Genre in Middle English Romance* (Cambridge: D. S. Brewer, 1987).

19. The topic is already implicit in Chretien's *Yvain*, with its interest in self-indulgent/wasteful and public/managed time. In *Speculum*, devoted from the outset to avoiding *vayne carpynge* (line 36), discussions of this issue appear at at least 447–68, 3651–54, 5039–60, 6445–50, 7269–96, 7610–18, 8557–90, 9621–30, 9882–94, 10357–64, 10421–72, 13171–204, and 15199–206. The topic equally intrigues Langland; compare, for example, his framing of the C version "biographical passage" at 5.27–28 and 92–101 (and B 1.138–41); or Study's diatribe, replaying a number of *Speculum Vitae* concerns, 10.30–80.

ally associable with trade in grain and livestock (6163–6340). This portrayal simply inverts the complaints against "crafts of foly," because this tricky price-fixing relies upon oppressively careful attention to time and season, commodifying time as form of profit.

One could see this as that "projective use of time" that Will invokes at C 5.93–98 as "ofte chaffarynge." But the real difficulty there, and with Will's formulation generally, concerns whether this "useful time," as Langland renders it in *Piers Plowman*, has itself been subsumed by spirituality's opposite. This social discourse of avidly pursuing "profit" turns out to be the grammar of Coveitise, his *donet* (5.207). In the poem, the effects of this language become particularly dire when they disrupt clerical instruction, sending clerics off to be clerks (Prol.83–111). From *Speculum Vitae*, I think Langland might have intuited that great joy and frustration of his poem, that narration itself might always engage one in a double-bind of use and uselessness, profit and waste.

III

Iterative structure and a definitional bent are not the only properties of pre-*Piers Plowman* instructional literature or dream vision. To return to the latter, one may identify some narrower formal constituents, peculiarly inflected in *Piers Plowman*. Poems associable with this formal structure may be characterized by a shared interest in described landscape, in meeting an interlocutor (*Piers* most usually follows its predecessor *Winner* in constructing these as contentious conversations), and in frequently describing the (allegorized) abode such a figure inhabits.

One recognizes the unusualness of Langland's handling here. His poem and its title-figure, especially, are not associated with the Frenchy *locus amoenus*, but with a largely undifferentiated landscape, initially a field only plane, flat, or level ("fair," Prol.17).[20] As I have already indicated in discussing the

---

20. See Elizabeth Salter, "*Piers Plowman* and the Visual Arts," in *English and International: Studies in the Literature, Art, and Patronage of Medieval England*, ed. Derek Pearsall and Nicolette Zeeman (Cambridge: Cambridge University Press, 1988), 256–66, 340–42. The undifferentiated open locale again reflects *Winner and Waster*, where the speaker awakes

> One a loueliche la(u)nde þat was ylike grene (48),

bordered by two contending hosts. And just as in Langland's landscape, in the distance

> At the creste of a clyffe a caban was rerede (59),

"cabin" here carrying its usual alliterative sense "pavilion," with suitable heraldry. As in Langland's first vision, the sight conveys a promise of royal judgment ("and [wende] to wiete or I went wondres ynewe"

vacillation between type and action in *Speculum* portraits, the character of the interlocutor in the poem has been programmed to shift between allegorical abstraction and socially realized figure (e.g. Wit in passus 9, fat friar [yet more specifically William Jordan?] in 13). And the poem at least toys with a dream as an educative experience, the speaker seeking instruction in various allegorical houses, alleged to offer definitive information (down to "feiþ in a fenestre" 18.15 and Dowel's "inne" 8.4).

Piers Plowman's dream in multiplicity allows a continuity in a mazily repeated, yet potentially highly specific, mode that is not the property of many earlier long narrative poems. *Piers* achieves this effect through its one constant, the presence of its inquiring, *How?*-seeking dreamer. From the start, he is a figure invested in a search for a new (spiritual) language—a task initially enunciated in the thoroughly unpointed and potentially self-indulgent "wondres to *here*" (Prol.4). This figure has been conceived as a mirror to the incipient narratives describing "crafters of folly" in *Speculum* "portraits." One might compare, for example, Langland's evocation of the trio "lyar/lollere-lachedrawer-lewd hermit" at C 8.286 and 9.193.

From this perspective, the poem opens in a starkly definitional mode, one that might be associated with beginning a search for an adequate spirituality. The speaker assumes the "habite" of the "heremite vnholy" (Prol.3) and, in so doing, opens a space in which the re-invention of holy language might occur. "Shoop me" (Prol.2) refers, not simply to a literal habit, perhaps a shrouding of identity, but to creating/constructing a speaker. Necessarily, whatever the newness of self-invested "habite," the poem's creative process must derive from discourses that pre-exist the speaker, the verbal "wondres" he hopes to encounter. Yet the fair field the dreamer immediately views (and is sucked into) functions as a tabula rasa, a blank slate, onto which he can literally (as Chaucer's Knight has noticed in his lines 886–88) plough/write his reordered version of the languages he has received.[21]

The ensuing prologue functions exactly as such a textual entry should, as a "pre-nouncement," both of method and of theme. Like the "heremite vnholy," it plays between the discipline one might associate with the spiritual life and a considerably more inchoate and possibly troubling set of procedures. On the one hand, the method of the Prologue is remarkably inovert

---

84). See R. V. W. Elliott, "The Topography of *Wynnere and Wastoure*," *English Studies* 48 (1967): 134–40; and Smith, *The Book of the Incipit*, 143–44, particularly noting the expansive description of A 2.40–48.

21. For the trope (the dreamer, after all, sustains his dream by verbal inquisition, before it is complete enough for him to wake and write it down), see Stephen A. Barney, "The Plowshare of the Tongue: The Progress of a Symbol from the Bible to *Piers Plowman*," *Mediaeval Studies* 35 (1973): 261–93.

and shrouded, a rambly and inconsequential imitation of the arbitrariness of visual notice: "And somme" 33, "faste aboute yede" 40, "I sei3" 50, "I fond" 58, etc. Through such rhetorical gestures, the speaker deliberately undoes, and frees his poem from, the hypercategorized forms of catechesis.

Yet, with the model of "crafts of folly" in mind, one may perceive beneath these surface moves at least allusions to a carefully considered program. The description begins with the most conventional of detail, a bow to the traditional "three estates" (with the new aristocracy of mercantile wealth as a pendant fourth group, lines 20–32). But it then immediately evokes *Speculum*'s "crafts," Herlotes, Faitours, and Robertmen (33–45); in the process, the poet alludes ("Faiteden . . . fou3ten" 42), to the poem's grounding in forms of verbal aggression. These figures are succeeded by their more commonplace (and more plausibly respectable) by-forms in the poem, lollerish fake pilgrim/hermit and fake mendicant instructor (46–67), the latter rendered socially visible by the failure of available catechetics (described at 83–111).[22] Finally, the speaker provides a foretaste of the poem's central scene and abiding emphasis, the conception of "pardon" (68–82). This poem will emphasize acting, rather than schematizing, penitential self-abnegation.

The prologue thus achieves legibility by its precision of reference to a precedent text. This paradoxically unstructured specificity in turn implies a literary community; the poem requires an audience capable of recognizing a shared text, and presumably neither thoroughly surprised nor baffled by what follows. Langland's unmarked allusiveness does presuppose an audience to whom the text is legible (perhaps given surmises about Langland's target cadre, as an inflection of "Statute discourse," over and above the poetic source).

Further, the Prologue emphasizes and identifies as that problem driving the poem a crisis about instructional language. Those best qualified to offer such materials, clerks at least moderately learned (and thus, widely employable), desert their teaching posts. They have been replaced by friars, latterday Lorenses who fail to attend to the efficacious spirit of the gospel. Moreover, the poem's language is absolute in condemning what is simultaneously ubiquitous ("wiþoute noumbre," 20.270) and dissolute ("alle þe foure ordres, / Prechynge . . . for profit," Prol.58–59). Into this vacuum, the speaker, a "crafter of foly," errant and visible to the world, like the friar, inserts himself.

Langland relies here upon two features of the "crafts"—both their open availability and their narrativity. First of all, the three "crafts" in which Lang-

---

22. For *lolleres*, see Anne Middleton's discussion of the term as indicating publicly ostentatious religious display: "Acts of Vagrancy: The C-Version 'Autobiography' and the Statute of 1388," in Justice and Kerby-Fulton, *Written Work*, 242–43, 276–88, 291.

land is most invested are predicated upon having a public presence (which "competent" instructors deny potential hearers). In *Speculum Vitae*, Faitours, Herlotes, and Sneckedrawers all practice outdoor trades. They, like the "hermits that inhabiten by the heigh way" (C 9.189, 204), alternative to the patient poor, invisible in their cotes and deprivation, are out there to draw attention. They require, not furtive sinfulness, like the Okirer's canny contracts, but ceaseless open, public display. Only in this way may they "continue," attract the living they seek (cf. C 5.39 and 104).[23]

Second, the "crafts" of *Speculum* are ceaselessly engaged in activities necessitated by the failure of catechesis, forms of self-composition. If useful spiritual language does not appear publicly current, then it has to be constructed from resources at hand, and in *Speculum Vitae*, this is a language ostensibly personal or biographical. Substantial energies in this "crafty" account get invested in complex "back-stories." The crafts, Herlotes most overtly so, are committed to narrative self-dramatization in the interests of sympathy (and pay).

Although Herlotes tell tales, romance lies and waste, professionally, those tales composed by Faitours and Sneckedrawers are considerably more interesting, accounts of being "forced by circumstance." In essence, both groups pretend to (confessional?) biography, but their self-authored accounts of themselves are persistently queried in *Speculum* as every bit as fictive as Herlotes' romance. These accounts represent the very opposite of contrite efforts at veridical self-revelation, for they offer yet more lies, narratives that didn't happen. *Speculum Vitae* groups the thoroughly explicit Heralds here, since they are really no better than Herlotes; they invent panegyric accounts of what their masters should have done (but didn't).[24] Similarly, Faitours write their stories, of debilitating accidents or genetic defects, on their bodies; Snecke-/Latch-drawers or Robertmen offer accounts of their social victimization to extort food from the intimidated or the unwary. But all, at some point or another, use unprogrammed outdoor wandering as a form of self-composition, and in their backstories, they double one narrative form already persistently doubled.

---

23. Compare faitours "to mens sight" *Speculum* 7127 (they require public display and thus being out and about), or the sneckdrawer/robertsman at the door in 7135–36; or

> Herlotes walkes thurgh many tounes
> With specked mantels and burdouns,
> And at ilk mans hous ga þai in
> Þare þai hope oght for to wynne (7163–66; ultimately, they must "stand on þe flore" 7169 to perform).

24. Interfacing with the discussion of God's minstrels, 13.421–59.

After all, the very form of dream-vision itself relies upon a doubled timescheme. It presents a narrative simultaneously present to both writer and reader and yet also a memory of the past. Truly "romynge in remembraunce" (C 5.11), dream poems only repeat (and perhaps clarify) the imaginative urge—the "back-story"—that initially willed them into existence.

Here, the most provocative figure—and the one most closely interfacing with Will's career in the poem—is Robert the Robber, the Sneckedrawer.[25] In the *Speculum* account, these "robertmen" are playing with latches in hopes of finding unlocked houses where they might pilfer food. But, shameless souls, they are thoroughly capable, when caught where they don't belong, to offer elaborate accounts of past wrongs inflicted upon them in hopes of coercing charity (rather than the stocks they might deserve).

At some level, this vignette has thoroughly constructed the narrative form of *Piers Plowman*. The poem, unlike those circumambient poetic objects I have mentioned, describes only one thing and is focused, whatever the apparent vicissitudes of its surface narrative, through an Aristotelian "single dramatic action." This is coming in from sleeping rough—and not so coincidentally, dreaming, fantasizing pasts, both biographical and throughly imaginative—and rambling, getting your foot in the door somewhere.[26]

---

25. On Ʒeuan-ʒelde-Aʒeyne, generated as Robertsman's double in C 6.308–10, see Ralph Hanna, "Robert the Ruyflare and His Companions," in *Literature and Religion in the Later Middle Ages: Philological Essays in Honor of Siegfried Wenzel*, ed. Richard G. Newhauser and John A. Alford, Medieval and Renaissance Texts and Studies 118 (Binghamton, NY: Medieval and Renaissance Texts and Studies, 1995), 83–85. Our honoree's still unpublished Gayley Lecture draws attention to other possible affiliations underlying Evan's Welshness. There she cited 4 Henry IV, c. 27: "Mischiefs which hath happened before this Tyme in the Land of Wales, by many Wastours, Rhymers, Minstrels, and other Vagabonds" (*Statutes of the Realm*, 2:140). According to this regulation, such individuals should not be fostered, nor allowed to make "commorths." Middleton argues that, in the statute (and perhaps *Piers Plowman*), wastour represents a Welsh term gwestwr (< gwest-gwr "hospitality man"), a vagrant who exacts free room and board, the commorth, from well-to-do houses and who might go about as a publicist, political prophet, or bearer of tidings. See further R. R. Davies, *The Revolt of Owain Glyn Dŵr* (Oxford: Oxford University Press, 1995), esp. 91–92, 285, on bardic "commorth" and capacity to spread sedition.

26. One might, in this regard, consider the behavior of the poem's least ironized personification, Pacience, introduced as he

> in þe paleis stood in pilgrymes cloþes
> And preyde mete, *pur charite*, for a pouere heremyte. (13.29–30)

Deferentially, he is not *at* the door, but at a remove (in the palisaded courtyard), and his prayer is not entirely for himself, but for the benefit "charite" will confer on the giver. Unlike "crafters of folly," Pacience has no back-story, only an indifferentiable succession, a true *habitus*, of "angres"/anguish borne sweetly, and he only stands, a reminder that many of the poem's greatest actions, Piers's response to tearing the Pardon, for example, involve no motion at all. (I am further reminded of Rolle's "I haue loued for to sit" [*Form* 829, ed. Ogilvie-Thomson, 23]; cf. the figure of poetic competence, Ymaginatyf, at 12.1–2.) But the real proof of the pudding might be the disruption of conventional

This narrative is the one promised from the poem's opening by Langland's favored Psalter verse, "Domine, quis habitabit . . . ?" (Ps. 14:1). (In this modality, the projected narrative should depend upon an outcry no "crafter of folly" would appear to consider undertaking, penitential tears [see 5.595–604].) Yet simultaneously, the topic underwrites the extraordinary deliberation of Langland's climax, Jesus's gospel life most compellingly narrativized as The Light at the Door of passus 18 (the hero another wandering Faytour-figure, Incarnation as fleshly disguise of poverty, with one hell of a back-story behind it).[27]

Obviously, Langland's presentation has been predicated upon Jesus's identification of himself as "the door" in John 10. In this gospel parable, Jesus is the true priest/good shepherd, both exemplary model and exemplary process of a teaching proper to salvation. He is the door that allows others to enter, but also the proper way of entering a ministry, an appropriate life of Christian instruction. This is a passage conventionally in the later Middle Ages deeply imbricated in antimendicant debates, in which these orders are identified as hireling shepherds, mercenary teachers, and confessors. They attempt to sneak in, intrude themselves by any entry except the proper door. Language that allows an entry through the door, the perhaps self-indulgent new narratives composed by "crafters of folly," provides the poem's hopefully licensed alternative (as at C 5.50, rewriting the suspicious C 5.29). Examples so fill the poem (and with the flexibility of metaphorical, or analogically metaphoric narrative) as to scarcely require exemplification.[28]

Langland's poem thus oscillates between two discrete formal functions. First, the Aristotelian "single dramatic action" of the poem is to enter, get in the door, "get straight." Without its gospel connotations, it is analogous to the conventional action of, for example, Chaucerian vision, like *The House*

---

catechesis Pacience enacts in the following passus, and the entire performance resembles another outcry "piercing" a palisade (10.468), a *pater noster*, which is the full narrative subject of *Speculum Vitae* (see 14.47–50).

27. And a not so covert allusion to another, fully human, narrative of errant readiness (to receive grace), the parable of the wise and foolish virgins (Matthew 25:1–13), subjected to expansive treatment at *Speculum* 10455–60, 10783–800, 11832–48, 11909–22, and 12053–54.

28. Most obviously, in the poem's evocation of a trip to Truth's tower, but equally a journey into your "herte-herber," where Truth also dwells (5.605–8). Passus 20 indicates the alternative version, in which the house is the self and the soul within (cf. 9.1–60). Thus, incursion is also the path Sin takes, as witness the pernicious instructional figure *penetrans-domos* (20.340), for whom see Penn R. Szittya's discussion of William of St Amour, *The Antifraternal Tradition in Medieval Literature* (Princeton, NJ: Princeton University Press, 1986), 3–10. For the poem's reliance on metaphoric narrative, see particularly J. A. Burrow, "The Action of Langland's Second Vision," *Essays in Criticism* 15 (1965): 247–68; and a number of Jill Mann's papers, perhaps especially "Eating and Drinking in Piers Plowman," *Essays and Studies* n.s. 32 (1979): 26–43.

of Fame (the house where all is allegedly explicated). Yet equally, the method of the poem, directionless wandering, "a wikkede wey but whoso hadde a gyde" (6.1), established by the quality of the speaker and by the position of asking "How?," is enabled by a form of self-creation in provocative disguise and banishment. Through this form, the poem addresses both the lost IKEA instructions, the limits of catechesis, as well as the more pressing social problem, the absent responsible clerical instructor. *Speculum Vitae* thus suggests a way of qualifying what has conventionally been taken as poem's fundamental narrative ground since Elizabeth Salter's important intervention.[29]

Speculum's "crafters of foly" animate the imagined and focused voice that produces *Piers Plowman*. After all, there is nothing inherently criminous about these houseless or homeless figures Langland appropriates. Indeed, the "crafts" manage to blur considerably one's notion of wrong-doing. Southwark whores, after all, were protegées of their bishop;[30] tollgatherers and hangmen are necessary legal officials; and figures like heralds and champions, potentially valued and valuable members of lordly retinues. In *Speculum* and its handbook ilk, they become pariahs because they fall outside that organizational schema that defines "proper Christian life."

Rhetorically, these books, as I have described them above, claim for themselves an exclusive and totalizing schema that includes all possible proscription and positive injunction. But there is one feature the three figures who so fascinate Langland share: their verbalism. This certainly, because predefined as nothing but "waste" and "lies," represents a voice that speaks from outside any account *Speculum* would claim as worthy of notice. But—and I return to the idea of forced entry, breaking the door, again—that feature also allows these voices to interrogate what lies inside the catechetical scheme but can speak no language that is really therein intelligible, except as an already excluded negative.

The vivacity of "crafters of folly" provides an entry into something else, something that is not the category thinking of catechetical instruction. These

---

29. Elizabeth (Salter) Zeeman, "*Piers Plowman* and the Pilgrimage to Truth," *Essays and Studies* n.s. 11 (1958): 1–16. Pilgrimage represents the poem's limit-case, not its norm (and Salter joins many unduly idealizing readers), as directed type of the more basic feature "wandering," following Prol.19, the ground-form of the poem. Moreover, in its most striking iteration in the text (the site of Burrow's intervention), the pilgrimage/plowing of passus 6 comes to bear a suspicious resemblance to unfocused wandering. Medieval fields got ploughed in a centrifugal circle or spiral (working away from any stable or fixed central point); see George C. Homans, *English Villagers of the Thirteenth Century* (Cambridge, MA: Harvard University Press, 1941), 44–50. In any event, as model this is qualified by Piers's apparent rejection of works alone in passus 7 and replaced at 19.332–35 by a much more indefinite sense of where Piers plows, "as wide as þe worlde is" (see Prol.4 and 20.380–81).

30. See John B. Post, "A Fifteenth-Century Customary of the Southwark Stews," *Journal of the Society of Archivists* 5 (1977): 418–28.

are figures outside the injunctive or proscriptive force of catechetical language; all they can speak, whether it is Will or passus 20's lawless Need, is pure affect, the desire to "continue." Yet simultaneously, they bear a voice that speaks against "bokes ynow." What Langland learned from texts like *Speculum Vitae* is the appropriate deployment of such a voice. In the poem's account, it remains recognizably what it has been in pre-existing discourse, the social wheedle that seeks a handout on the basis of some claim to a self-indulgence licensed by past indignities suffered (something like, say, C 5.35–43a). But equally, this voice raises some legitimate query as to why "crafts of folly" are possibly questionable things to be/have been doing, the accrual of the personal debt of sin. Like Robert and and his C version mate ȝeuan-ȝelde-aȝeyn, the voice comes to recognize, to see the bad plank from the IKEA box while it's being pulled it from the carton, and then voices how, if one so desired, one would find the restored plank, live out some penitential alternative.[31]

Inflecting Langland's form against its partial inspiration in *Speculum Vitae* uncovers some of *Piers Plowman*'s distinctive narrative moves. Quite against C. S. Lewis's Olympian dismissal, "fragments but not a poem," Edwardian segmented narrative forms constructively underwrite a great deal of the poet's enterprise. Equally, his poem is representative of its historical moment in its decentering invocation of a voice alternate to the overtly catechetical, its reliance on those ostracized in one of its direct Edwardian sources.

---

31. Alternatively, one could inflect this conclusion in the spirit of Anne's contributions in "William Langland's 'Kynde Name': Authorial Signature and Social Identity in Late Fourteenth-Century England," in *Literary Practice and Social Change in Britain, 1380–1530*, ed. Lee Patterson (Berkeley: University of California Press, 1990), 15–82; and "Langland's Lives: Reflections on Late-Medieval Religious and Literary Vocabulary," in *The Idea of Medieval Literature: New Essays on Chaucer and Medieval Culture in Honor of Donald R. Howard*, ed. James M. Dean and Christian K. Zacher (Newark, DE: University of Delaware Press, 1992), 227–42: the construction of a model life somewhere between the extremes promised by *The South English Legendary*, the preternaturally holy youth or les enfances of Judas or Pilate.

seven

Petrarch's Pleasures, Chaucer's Revulsions, and the Aesthetics of Renunciation in Late-Medieval Culture

ANDREW GALLOWAY

CHARTING THE HISTORY of emotions has a foundational role in medieval studies, but it cannot be considered a steadily developing one. This is clear from Johan Huizinga's most influential but controversial book, known to the English-speaking world since 1924 as *The Waning of the Middle Ages*. First appearing in Dutch in 1919, *Herfsttij der Middeleeuwen* (literally, 'the autumn of the Middle Ages'), later revised (1921) then variously abridged and further revised in successive French, English, and German versions, Huizinga's study was built on a theory concerning the intensity of late-medieval emotional experience, compressed between potent aesthetic and other sensual pleasures, and pervasive constraints on and condemnations of those. "For medieval man," Huizinga declares—in one of his many controversially sweeping statements—all enjoyments of life were sinful. Thus were conjured "all the horrifying ideas about decomposition," including "disgustingly varied notion of the naked corpse": cramped hands and feet, gaping mouth, worms writhing in the intestines. In the Dutch version only, Huizinga wonders, was this "the reaction of an all too intense sensuality that can only awaken itself from its intoxication with life in this manner?" Or is it the "mood of disappointment and discouragement of one who has fought and won and now would prefer a complete surrender to that which is transcendent, but somehow is still too close to earthly passion to be able to make that surrender?"[1] In the end he favors the idea that "in all of this [there was] a spirit of tremendous materialism that could not bear the thought of the passing of beauty without despairing of beauty itself" (160).

Huizinga's emphasis on the lurid and emotive as the signature mood of late-medieval culture has given his study a bad name in many recent scholarly quarters. But in its original form, his study supplies some topics worth reviving. The comments I have quoted above, for example, from the original Dutch differ fundamentally from the English translation of 1924. In the latter, the discussion of corpse images simply moralizes: "these preachers of contempt for the world express, indeed, a very materialistic sentiment, namely, that all beauty and all happiness are worthless because they are bound to end soon. Renunciation founded on disgust does not spring from Christian wisdom."[2]

With the Dutch edition now available in English, it can now be seen that Huizinga's study articulated theories about not only the complex status of pleasure in medieval art and literature but also about the history of emotions as a history of the aesthetic—and how renunciation or "contempt for the world" functioned as a key element in both. Indeed, a section framing his entire study, but dropped from the 1924 English translation, proposes a broad, analytical view of the shifting status of the aesthetic as defined by the varying boundary of renunciation or "contempt of the world." In this passage, wholly absent from the popular English version, Huizinga speculates that in medieval culture, licit aesthetic pleasure "lay, in the best of cases, right after reading; the enjoyment of reading could only be sanctified through striving for virtue or wisdom" (40). The Renaissance "managed to free itself from the rejection of all the joy of life as something sinful," but established no clear principle dividing higher and lower pleasures; thus it yielded to the rigors of Puritanism, whose condemnation of "the beautification of life" reawakened a medieval tradition, allowing only forms of beauty that "assumed expressly religious forms and sanctified themselves through their use in the service of faith." With the fading of Puritanism, a new distinction between licit and illicit aesthetic pleasure appeared, which Huizinga considered the basis for "spiritual attitudes" up to the present. A decisively secular version of renunciation reemerged within the aesthetic itself. In this episteme, which he con-

---

1. Johan Huizinga, *The Autumn of the Middle Ages*, trans. Rodney J. Payton and Ulrich Mammtzsch (Chicago: University of Chicago Press, 1996), 159. Further citations in the text, unless noted, are to this edition. The history of the text is discussed by Payton and Mammtzsch, ix–xviii.

2. Johan Huizinga, *The Waning of the Middle Ages: A Study of the Forms of Life, Thought, and Art in France and the Netherlands in the Fourteenth and Fifteenth Centuries*, trans. F. Hopman (London: E. Arnold, 1924), 136.

sidered to obtain henceforth, "anyone attempting to draw the dividing line between the high and lower enjoyment of life according to the dictates of ethical consciousness would no longer separate art from sensuous enjoyment, the enjoyment of nature from the cult of the body, the elevated from the natural, but would only separate egotism, lies, and vanity from purity" (40–41).

These ambitious claims suggest that the aesthetic, initially rejected, gradually became the encompassing field for both emotions and ethics, with, moreover, the impulse for renunciation serving as a central impetus to both. Perhaps Huizinga judged this perspective too abstract or severe for the American audience he sought in 1924 (whose desires for "This Here, and Soon" Huizinga privately sneered at)—though the passage was also missing from the 1938 French abridgment.[3] At any rate, the absence from his book's popular English version of a more complex view of the changing emotional and ethical place of the aesthetic in terms of the varying categories of "purity" and renunciation may partly explain why for decades so few medieval scholars pursued the history of emotion. A key but fleeting exception was Lucien Febvre. Febvre's essays on "histoire et sentiment" (1941 and 1943) focus on Huizinga's study (using the French abridgment) and, though objecting to Huizinga's claim that the late Middle Ages was uniquely fraught with emotion, approve the idea of using literature, art, and moral writings to begin "une vaste enquête collective sur les sentiments fondamentaux des hommes et leurs modalités."[4] Such interdisciplinary scope defines the grand agenda of the "Annales" school of history that Febvre helped found. But the focus on emotion as such, much less the aesthetic as its focal point, almost never emerged in that journal or its intellectual tradition.

The seed, however, sprang up most richly on the post-medieval side of cultural history, often based on a supposition that emotions were raw forces that had to be controlled and "civilized," a process that (as in Norbert Elias's influential work) explicitly occurred *after* the "Middle Ages," which by definition were the period of unconstrained passions—as if emotions were best seen as simply "there," gushing forces to be channeled or unleashed depending on situation.[5] By now, histories of emotion have deployed more varied methods and reached many more periods and topics, to explain, for

---

3. The abridged and revised French is *Le déclin du Moyen-Âge*, trans. Julia Bastin (Paris: Payot, 1938).

4. Lucien Febvre, "La sensibilité et l'histoire: Comment reconstituer la vie affective d'autrefois?" *Annales d'histoire sociale* 3 (1941): 18.

5. See the excellent overview by Barbara H. Rosenwein, "Theories of Change in the History of Emotions," in *A History of Emotions, 1200–1800*, ed. Jonas Liliequist (Ithaca, NY: Cornell University Press, 2012), 7–20. Rosenwein describes Elias' approach as based on the "hydraulic" theory of emotions.

instance, the "irrationality" of economic behavior, or the sociology of religion.[6] Focus on affect has gained particular visibility in twentieth century studies, where it is greeted as an important new strategy for pondering the nature of "the aesthetic."[7] Indeed, the rebirth of this topic is due to modern cultural historians such as Raymond Williams, but also, though much less visibly outside their own fields, to a growing number of medievalists. These, as if in direct opposition to Huizinga's sweeping propositions, have usually preceded in tightly focused scope and phenomenological detail, seeking the distinctive cultivation and privileging—rather than simply the unleashing—of specific emotions and postures, attempting to locate these within specific spiritual strategies and local political meanings, even within quite narrowly specific "emotional communities."[8]

This sharpening of focus and method is invaluable. Yet a broader view has seemed to recede from medievalists' grasp. As Barbara Rosenwein, a major contributor to the reemergence of a medieval history of emotions, observes, in spite of all the important results of recent studies, "we do not gain [from them] a sense of the general shape of emotions' history over the long haul."[9] Huizinga's recently translated thoughts on broad shifts in the boundaries between illicit and licit aesthetic emotion from the late fourteenth through the sixteenth century, and especially the moving boundary between affirmation and denunciation of the "pleasures of life," may, therefore, still be useful for reopening the relation between late-medieval aesthetics and renunciation, as situated within particular but larger cultural terms.

---

6. George Lowenstein and Scott Ricks, "Economics (Role of Emotion in)," in *Oxford Companion to Emotion and the Affective Sciences,* ed. David Sander and Klaus R. Scherer (Oxford: Oxford University Press, 2009), 131–33; Ole Riis and Linda Woodhead, *A Sociology of Religious Emotion* (Oxford: Oxford University Press, 2010).

7. See, e.g., Sianne Ngai, *Ugly Feelings* (Cambridge, MA: Harvard University Press, 2005).

8. Raymond Williams's early exploration of "structures of feeling" as "social experiences in solution" remains the crucial starting point: *Marxism and Literature* (Oxford: Oxford University Press, 1977), 128–35. For the adoption of such concerns in medieval inquiries, see, e.g., Barbara H. Rosenwein, ed., *Anger's Past: The Social Uses of an Emotion in the Middle Ages* (Ithaca, NY: Cornell University Press, 1998); and the important range of essays in Piroska Nagy and Damien Boquet, eds., *Le sujet des émotions au Moyen Âge* (Paris: Beauchesne, 2008); for Chaucer, see John Hill, *Chaucerian Belief: The Poetics of Reverence and Delight* (New Haven, CT: Yale University Press, 1991); for Gower and others, see Andrew Galloway, "The Literature of 1388 and the Politics of Pity in Gower's *Confessio Amantis,*" in *The Letter of the Law: Legal Practice and Literary Production in Medieval England,* ed. Emily Steiner and Candace Barrington (Ithaca, NY: Cornell University Press, 2002), 67–104. See also Sarah McNamer, *Affective Meditation and the Invention of Medieval Compassion* (Philadelphia: University of Pennsylvania Press, 2009). The phrase "emotional communities" derives from the important study of sixth- and seventh-century Gaul by Barbara H. Rosenwein, *Emotional Communities in the Early Middle Ages* (Ithaca, NY: Cornell University Press, 2006).

9. Rosenwein, "Theories of Change in the History of Emotions," 19.

The Griselda story presents an especially "passionate" focus for the fusion of aesthetics and renunciation on a European-wide scale. This account of a woman impassively accepting her husband's tormenting "testing" of her stoic vows of obedience to him, which circulated widely between the fourteenth and seventeenth centuries, has indeed already elicited some important hints at an inquiry of the kind suggested above, in Anne Middleton's 1980 essay, "The Clerk and his Tale: Some Literary Contexts."[10] In the context of the present interest in such studies, those hints deserve to be revisited and expanded. In her essay, Middleton drew attention to the strange pleasures of Francesco Petrarch, the looming source of Chaucer's version of this tale, including the emotional reactions that, he claims, his recitations of the tale provoked. In his prefatory letter to his Latin translation of Boccaccio's story of patient Griselda in the *Decameron*, Petrarch, writing in 1373, a year before his death, declares that the story

> ita michi placuit meque detinuit ut, inter tot curas pene mei ipsius que immemorem me fecere, illam memorie mandare voluerim, ut et ipse eam animo quociens vellem non sine voluptate repeterem, et amicis ut fit confabulantibus renarrarem.
>
> [so pleased and detained me that, among so many concerns that made me almost unmindful of myself, I wished to commit it to memory, so that I might repeat it in my mind often, not without pleasure, and retell it to friends with whom I happened to be speaking.][11]

So too, as Petrarch goes on to declare, when he allowed the tale to be read by a friend from Padua, "a man of the highest intellect and broad knowledge,"

---

10. Anne Middleton, "The Clerk and His Tale: Some Literary Contexts," *Studies in the Age of Chaucer* 2 (1980): 123; hereafter cited in the text.

11. Until the completion of the *Res Seniles* from the series VII Centenario della Nascita di Francesco Petrarca (Florence: Casa Editrice Le Lettere), the fullest critical edition of this portion of the *Res Seniles* (17.3) remains Thomas J. Farrell and Amy W. Goodwin, eds. and trans., in *Sources and Analogues of the "Canterbury Tales," vol. 1*, ed. Robert M. Correale and Mary Hamel, Chaucer Studies 28 (Cambridge: D. S. Brewer, 2002), 108–29, here at 109–11. Further quotations of Petrarch's letter to Boccaccio retelling the Griselda story are from this edition, cited by page in the text. Translations of all texts here are mine unless noted. The most complete editions of Petrarch remain the sixteenth-century editions, e.g., *Petrarchi Opera Omnia* (Basel: Henricus Petri, 1554), 3 vols., more readily available because of Google books than most of the modern editions of the Latin. Modern critical editions of various portions of Petrarch's letters and other writings are cited below. Those seeking English translations are more fortunate: see Aldo Bernardo, trans., *Letters on Familiar Matters*, 3 vols. (Baltimore: Johns Hopkins University Press, 1982–85; repr., New York: Italica Press, 2005); and Aldo S. Bernardo, Saul Levin, and Reta A. Bernardo, trans., *Letters of Old Age*, 2 vols. (Baltimore: Johns Hopkins University Press, 1992; repr., New York: Italica Press, 2005).

this man repeatedly "stopped, being overcome by sudden weeping," and after several attempts had to pass the work to another person to finish reading it. This Petrarch judges to be a better response than that of another reader who said he *would* have wept had he believed that the tale could be true, but he was able to persist dry eyed by the conviction that women such as Griselda could not exist. Such inability to conceive of an extreme response merely shows that "there are some who consider whatever is difficult for them, impossible for everyone," judging everyone simply "by their own measure."[12]

Observing these emotional strands linking the story's circulation, Middleton notes that Petrarch's framing of the tale, with these mentions of its further readers, defines a process not of textual interpretation in the medieval clerical vein but a confirmation of a new kind of literary vocation and its participants: "the ideal of the lettered life as a vocation, an international community of the elect, whose changing moods and various tasks are to its secular devotees as fast, meditations, prayers, and self-examinations are to the vowed religious" (127–28). It is thus "justification of . . . refined style and thought as a way of life at once secular and otherworldly, an *apologia* for the life of the untonsured and unbeneficed clerk" (133), which "constitutes Petrarch's chief invention" (149). The historical point neatly foreshadows subsequent critical comment on Petrarch, such as Giuseppe Mazzotta's discussion of Petrarch's "ethics of writing" as a new "theory of culture that is rooted in leisure, *otium,* which is [both] the core value of monastic contemplation and is the ideal of classical humanism."[13] Middleton, focusing on the new status of secular literary production, further argued that the *Clerk's Tale* invokes and extends the ideals of Petrarchan literary vocation and community, challenging the simple dichotomy of "serious" and "playful" kinds of literature. Instead, the tale is offered as refreshment of a new kind, by which literary play tests the "noble heart and the refined feelings," using a style "to be judged by the standards proper to poetic fable, and . . . tested by its adequacy to that affective rhetorical end" (135). In Chaucer, the Clerk's bookish demonstration of this affective testing challenges the Host's more traditional ideas of the extremes of clerical performance as either humor or didacticism. Against those options, Middleton says, the Clerk instead purveys a new kind of Petrarchan "serious entertainment" (147).

Subsequent decades have seen much attention to Chaucer's confrontation with Petrarchan modes of literature and aesthetics. David Wallace's

---

12. *Seniles* 17.4, *Letters of Old Age,* 2:669.
13. Giuseppe Mazzotta, *The Worlds of Petrarch* (Durham, NC: Duke University Press, 1993), 92, 148.

studies have been particularly suggestive and influential. Wallace takes the
Clerk's Tale as a key to a conflicting movement across Chaucer's writings
between two literary and political paradigms: that of the "absolutist" outlook of Petrarch, whom Wallace (in vigorous resistance to other Petrarchan
criticism) takes as a misogynist tool of autocrats, and that of a more associational, mercantile world epitomized by Boccaccio.[14] Yet even Wallace's major
contributions to our understanding of what Petrarch and Chaucer did with
this tale have not pursued the affective and aesthetic implications of renunciation on which Middleton fleetingly remarked. In both Petrarch's and Chaucer's versions of the tale, affect is so mobile and self-contradictory that it
invites fuller examination. Contemplating the passionate responses by those
who read the tale he wrote, for instance, Petrarch immediately recalls Juvenal
(*Satire* 15, lines 131-32),

>   mollissima corda
> humano generi dare se natura fatetur . . .

>   [Nature admits
> She gives the human race the softest hearts . . .]

The irony, unstated by Petrarch though informing everything he says about
the tale, is that this trait is precisely what Griselda does not display.

Indeed, part of the force of the tale is that the contradictory emotions
it presents and evokes are exchanged and shared by all those encountering
Griselda's impassivity, beginning with those around her in the story itself
and extending out to the narrator and his portrayed readers. Pleasure mixed
with distress seems to slide as easily into Gualterius's tears of sympathy when
he expels Griselda from his house to make way for a new bride (actually her
returning daughter, whom he himself had abducted) as it does into the joy
he has "proving" Griselda's "hardness" in the face of the torments he inflicts
on her. Griselda's nearly silent victory over fortune and necessity may define
a severe form of pleasure, that of executing a form with perfect control over
self. Yet she gains this victory by not providing even a glimpse of her pain
for others to witness and share. *Not* openly sharing emotion is her triumph,
the challenge she places before her husband Gualterius as well as the succes-

---

14. David Wallace, *Chaucerian Polity: Absolutist Lineages and Associational Forms in England and Italy* (Stanford, CA: Stanford University Press, 1997), esp. 261–98; and Wallace, "Griselda before Chaucer: Love between Men, Women, and Farewell Art," in *Through a Classical Eye: Transcultural and Transhistorical Visions in Medieval English, Italian, and Latin Literature in Honour of Winthrop Wether-bee*, ed. Andrew Galloway and R. F. Yeager (Toronto: University of Toronto Press, 2009), 206–20.

sion of moved male readers and redactors—an exceedingly non-Aristotelian premise for literary efficacy.

Such pleasures as Griselda's history offers her readers and, implicitly, herself is, of course, deeply ascetic, in the sense of denying the "normal" emotional attachments and their expressions. But the story, in Petrarch's and then Chaucer's hands, provides a means for probing more deeply the affective complexities that secular asceticism involves, and moreover for tracing how those features might have resonated with different ideological and discursive strands in Italy and in England. By "ideology" I mean what is unconscious or at least assumed as a beginning point for thought; by "discursive" I mean widespread terms and notions that could gain meanings or lose credibility, even survive as or be inverted into something like their opposite. In these terms there is what we may consider a cultural rather than simply immediately material history of deprivation and need.[15] Hans Baron's studies of Petrarch's varying dedication to philosophies praising some form of severely Spartan livelihood, if never harsh poverty, Franciscanism or Stoicism, situate this issue in late-medieval intellectual culture in general and Petrarch's Italy in particular.[16] Such work can spur further cultural, psychological, and aesthetic inquiries into how need as such is figured in both authors in relation to aesthetics, and in turn to the broader cultural contexts they inhabit.

Petrarch's version of the story emphasizes the good of redirecting desire away from the worldly benefits that Fortune controls. But Petrarch's account also suggests Gualterius's longing for identification with a glacially remote figure who incarnates such an ideal state of being, and this in turn appears to spur Gualterius's repeated effort to dominate and control Griselda utterly. Political postures directly follow from this complex power relation. David Wallace suggests that Petrarch, as a despotic supporter of tyrants and covert misogynist, finds a surrogate or calque in Gualterius as tyrant. Theories of gender identities and dynamics are also significant. Wallace shrewdly notes Petrarch's tendency to "play the woman"—in the sense of using conciliatory and intellectually flirtatious rhetoric—in his dealings with other men.[17] Wallace elsewhere amplifies this to suggest that the patterns of identifica-

---

15. See Andrew Galloway, "The Economy of Need in Late Medieval English Literature," *Viator* 40 (2009): 309–31.

16. Hans Baron, "Franciscan Poverty and Civic Wealth in the Shaping of Trecento Humanistic Thought: The Role of Petrarch," and "Franciscan Poverty and Civic Wealth in the Shaping of Trecento Humanistic Thought: The Role of Florence," both in *In Search of Florentine Civic Humanism: Essays on the Transition from Medieval to Modern Thought* (Princeton, NJ: Princeton University Press, 1988), 1:158–225.

17. Wallace, *Chaucerian Polity*, 365.

tion in Petrarch's address to Boccaccio move in many directions: "within the restricted, all-male environs of this tale-world, . . . any one man can play all the parts, imagine himself into all the subject positions: Petrarch is Walter and Boccaccio Griselda; Galeazzo Visconti is Walter of Salerno and Petrarch is simple-hearted, poor-loving Griselda; and so on."[18]

But renunciation, especially the refusal to make one's own need an object of others' control, has further properties not entirely subsumable to gender or politics. The capacity to derive pleasure from a mastery of pain and need, by oneself or another, may be pondered through the psychosocial operations that Friedrich Nietzsche—founding figure, surely, in the psycho-historical study of emotion—describes for asceticism. Nietzsche asserts that, in Christian culture, primal impulses to violence and aggression are transformed into asceticism in order to provide those impulses a sense of meaning.[19] This focus on inverted and redirected violence is certainly apt for this tale's pretended deaths, pretended divorce, and constant and real competition: a swarm of aggressive energies brought to an apotheosis in the self-inflicted violence of Griselda's immunity to any emotional reaction. Her domestic ascesis serves as the epitome of redirected violence in the secular realm, whereby she is made a marvel for and an aggressive challenge to all around her.

Nietzsche's terms may moreover help us proceed further into the principles of aestheticism as well as asceticism. If ascetics is one form of violence redirected, aesthetics based on renunciation is logically another. A zeal for formal control and emotional discipline suggests a principle of the aesthetic particularly suited to late-medieval culture in the terms that Huizinga suggested, especially if considered—as it briefly will be below—against the new forms of renunciation and status of neediness developing in England and Italy. As Petrarch presents Gualterius, the latter's affirmation of Griselda's *sculpting* of herself—behaving with perfect grace under endless torments, displaying decorous restraint for its own sake beyond any interest in the immediate elements of her various kinds of social dependency—smoothly rebounds to Gualterius's own profit. His project of "testing" her seems designed to restore his own faith in the human capacity to make the needy self into a transcendently valuable entity. Such testing also, incidentally, proves his discernment in seeing her as a prospect for demonstrating this: "because he had recognized so clearly the extraordinary virtue concealed

---

18. Wallace, "Griselda before Chaucer," 213.
19. Friedrich Nietzsche, "Third Essay: What Do Ascetic Ideals Mean?" *The Genealogy of Morals* (1887), in *The Birth of Tragedy and The Genealogy of Morals*, trans. Francis Golfing (New York: Doubleday, 1956), 231–99.

by her poverty, his prudence was widely praised" (*vulgo prudentissimus habebatur;* pp. 118–19).

Such pleasure in sculpted, renunciatory subjectivity is clearly tied to the Boethian and stoic tradition, and on this score Petrarch and Chaucer had much in common. Petrarch's *voluptas*, he says, derives from being 'recalled to himself' by reading and frequently meditating on the story of Griselda, amid so many cares that he had nearly forgotten himself (*inter tot curas pene mei ipsius que immemorem me fecere;* p. 111). Until he stumbled onto this tale, he was "angry" with himself and with the things distracting him (*et illis et michi, ut sic dixerim, iratus;* p. 111). Apart from its emphasis on self-inflicted anger, Petrarch's introduction follows the opening of Boethius's *De consolatione*, when Philosophia first arrives to guide the lachrymose narrator toward learning to be *sibi ipse sufficiens*, sufficient unto himself. As with Petrarch's frame for his tale, Boethius begins with Philosophia's efforts to bring Boethius's attention back from cares in which he has forgotten himself:

Sui paulisper oblitus est; recordabitur facile, si quidem nos ante cognoverit. Quod ut posit, paulisper lumina eius mortalium rerum nube caligantia tergamus.

["He has for a little forgotten himself. He will soon recover—he did, after all, know me before—and to make this possible for him, let me for a little clear his eyes of the mist of mortal affairs that clouds them."][20]

Self-sufficiency in the face of fortune's blows is a pervasive if not banally common late-medieval ethical and literary ideal. Yet this may be seen not as a simple goal to have an uncaring immunity to necessity or need, but as a constantly induced struggle, deliberately solicited by constant reminders of the state of contingency that threatens the self and its ideal self-possession. Thus, as J. Allan Mitchell says, Boethian *fortuna* is "more than a figure to be discarded on the way toward philosophical enlightenment": Fortune presents a "fundamental *datum* . . . without which enlightenment will not come in the *Consolation*."[21] The most dynamically staged encounters with need and with the opportunities for renunciation that Fortuna provides appear more

---

20. *De Consolatione Philosophiae*, I. metrum ii.1–5; prosa.ii.9–16. Text and translation (the latter modified for a more literal sense) are from *Boethius: The Theological Tractates and the "Consolation of Philosophy,"* ed. and trans. H. F. Tester, E. K. Rand, and S. J. Tester (Cambridge, MA: Harvard University Press, 1978); hereafter cited in text.

21. J. Allan Mitchell, *Ethics and Eventfulness in Middle English Literature* (New York: Palgrave, 2010), 16–17.

commonly in works by secular than religious writers in the later Middle Ages. This emergence of secular asceticism, a regularly enacted affirmation of "refined style and thought as a way of life at once secular and otherworldly" as Middleton says, may be a chief reason for the Griselda story's popularity. Certainly, new ideals of secular asceticism are found in England as well as Italy, as in the range (some politically dangerous) of kinds of self-denial explored by the English nobility, from ostentatiously austere funerals to flirtations with Lollardy. So clear is this refined asceticism that the mysterious 'S-S' in the Lancastrian livery might even refer to the Boethian ideal of *sibi ipse sufficiens*, most likely in the English nobility's French, "soi suffisant."[22]

The ideal, even its place in secular noble culture, is faithful enough to Boethius's work, whose narrator must learn to set aside emotional attachments in the midst of past or present wealth (which makes you more needy), glory, even pride in his children, in favor of an acceptance of his own free choice yet the perfect perspective of a God who stands outside of any agonies of hope or despair, or any temporal frame at all. Thus Boethius's argument avoids either imposing "necessity" on our free choices or, "to shift the force of necessity over to the other side," as Boethius's Philosophia says (*necessarium hoc in contrariam relabi partem*), imposing necessity on God himself, by making him the helpless perceiver of actions we carry out. And just as God is perfectly self-sufficient, not subject to need or necessity, so we can seek some measure of that by contemplating without fully grasping God's perfect understanding, which gives him foreknowledge "in some way" concerning "even those things which have no certain occurrence" (V.pr.v). All this, so familiar in Petrarch's and well as Chaucer's writings, reformulates the Stoic position, especially as that appears in Seneca, but with important refinements. One is that acceptance of and submission to Fortune's mutability as such is precisely an expression of free-will. A further implication is that such submission may allow self-sufficiency even while enjoying the goods of this world, so long as their basic limit—that we cannot truly possess them the way we can always possess ourselves—is recognized.[23] Boethian self-

---

22. On aristocratic asceticism at funerals, see Jeremy Catto, "Religion and the English Nobility in the Later Fourteenth Century," in *History and Imagination: Essays in Honor of H. R. Trevor-Roper*, ed. Hugh Lloyd-Jones, Valerie Pearl, and Blair Worden (New York: Holmes and Meier, 1981), 43–55; on their connections to Lollardy, see Anne Hudson, *The Premature Reformation: Wycliffite Texts and Lollard History* (Oxford: Clarendon Press, 1988), 110–17; on the mysterious 'S-S' badge (without the suggestion made here), see Doris Fletcher, "The Lancastrian Collar of Esses: Its Origin and Transformations down the Centuries," in *The Age of Richard II*, ed. James Gillespie (Phoenix Mill, UK: Sutton, 1997), 191–203.

23. For the intellectual lineage of both Stoicism and Platonism behind these issues in Boethius,

sufficiency does not *require* full deprivation of worldly goods: a point that is crucial for the success of this outlook in affluent late-medieval courtly worlds. Such self-possession is a dynamic encounter with need, not a state of grinding indigence. Its performance involves a rigor both ascetic and aesthetic, marked by "trials" of self-control which thus affirm a worldly but inner self's transcendent value.

Certainly Griselda's self-sufficiency is dynamically sustained in Petrarch's narrative, a matter of her overcoming again and again the force of "hard necessity," as she rises to unheard of heights then falls, then rises again. The good and bad fortune that randomly descend on her, *negotium inopinatum*, the "necessity" or "hard necessity" of obeying that confront her as it does Gualterius's other servants (*necessitas parendi; dura parendi necessitas*), and the increasingly frequent descriptions of Gualterius's own tormenting demands as springing from his "hard" will or "inhuman hardness" (*inhumana duricia*)—all these provide opportunities for her and her readers to revel in indomitable self-possession, which trumps Gualterius's or necessity's hardness with even greater hardness. The climax in Petrarch is when she hears of Gualterius's supposed plan to marry a new wife and send her away: "Que fama cum ad Griseldis noticiam pervenisset, tristis, ut puto. Sed ut que semel de se suisque de sortibus statuisset, inconcussa constitit" ("who, when such news had come to Griselda, was sad, as I suppose. But just as she had stood fast once before concerning the fortune allotted to herself and her children, so she stood unbowed"; 123).

An early and otherwise authoritative manuscript of Petrarch's *Epistolae Senilis*, Cambridge, Peterhouse College MS 81, here reads "as she had stood *senilis* [mature]" as a variant for *semel* ("once and for all") found in the other manuscripts (123). That reading, though probably not authorial, suggests contemporary awareness of the key terms and issues. For the textual variant in question echoes Petrarch's frequent elaboration of "maturity" as a label for the ability to feel deeply yet rise to control the self fully, and indeed to forge want and its lack into a subtle instrument for defining and to some extent controlling identity. Petrarch introduces Griselda by mentioning her "virilis senilisque animus" ("manly and mature soul"; 115), and Petrarch's own ideal as the writer of "mature letters," *Epistolae Senilis*, link this to himself directly. Griselda's manly, *senilis* soul is trained like that of a Spartan warrior by her hard upbringing: "Hec parco victu, in summa semper inopia educata, omnis inscia voluptatis, nil molle nil tenerum cogitare didicerat,

---

see John Magee, "The Good and Morality: *Consolatio* 2–4," in *The Cambridge Companion to Boethius*, ed. John Marenbon (Cambridge: Cambridge University Press, 2009), 181–206, esp. 185–86.

sed viriles senilisque animus virgineo latebat in pectore" ("with little food, raised always in the worst poverty, entirely ignorant of pleasure, she learned to think of nothing soft or tender, but a manly and mature soul lay hidden in her virginal breast"; 115). She even turns her "manly and mature" zeal for competition onto her supposed rival, Gualterius's proposed new bride. In response to his final demand that she prepare the wedding feast for his new bride by whom Griselda herself thinks she is being replaced, she proclaims her final triumph: "Unum bona fide te precor ac moneo," she tells Gualterius before the wedding, "ne hanc illis aculeis agites quibus alteram agitasti. Nam quod et iunior et delicatius enutrita est, pati quantum ego auguror non valeret" ("yet in good faith I ask and pray for one thing: do not sting her with those goads that you have used on another woman. For she is younger and more delicately raised, and I imagine that she cannot endure so much"; 127).

Petrarch's Griselda has a fully "needy" thus fully worldly and contingent self, but she protects and affirms the value of that by her mastery of that self and world, including an aggressive competition to *be needed* more than she herself needs. This goal, involving display and manipulation of those viewing and seeking, is consistent with Petrarch's other strategies of conferring value on his own intellectual and literary production. He often deploys remarkably subtle control—remarkable for a period before any sense of copyright—of how his writing is kept scarce, or seemingly scarce. It is Petrarch's regular practice to drive up his texts' value by coy reluctance or delays or apparent negligence in purveying his works, by gestures of destroying or threatening to destroy them, and by insisting that he has no need for mere worldly goods, including the writings he continually produces. He claims to be outraged, for instance, when someone to whom he has sent a passage from his *Africa* has secretly made a copy of it, and disseminated it before Petrarch says he was ready.[24] These Griselda-like strategies are clear as early as Petrarch's claim at the beginning of his *Epistolae rerum familiarum* that he has assembled the cumulative body of his letters and prose and verse out of the fragments of what he was too tired to throw into the fire. The gesture of his value beyond any material value continues to his final sentence in his *Testament,* that "Ego Franciscus Petrarca scripsi, qui testamentum aliud fecissem, si essem dives, ut vulgus insanum putat" ("I, Francesco Petrarca, have written this, who would have drawn up a different testament if I were rich, as the insane rabble believes me to be").[25]

24. *Seniles* 2.1; *Letters of Old Age,* 1:38–39.
25. *Petrarch's Testament,* ed. and trans. Theodor E. Mommsen (Ithaca, NY: Cornell University Press, 1957), 92–93.

Such supposed disinterest in worldly literary glory in order to provoke and incite others' need for him might be seen as a form of profiteering, whose commodities are both his works and his own capacity to generate them, all framed by his often violent gestures of depriving any readers of them:[26]

> Itaque cunta passim occursantia uno impetu vastanti et ne his quidem— ut tunc erat animus—parsuro, vestrum alter ad levam, alter ad dextram adesse visus, et apprehensa manu, ne fidem meam et spes vestras uno igne consumerem, familiariter admonere. Hec illis evadendi precipua causa fuit; alioquin, crede michi, cum reliquis arsissent.
>
> [Therefore, as I was about to destroy everything that came to hand with one impulse and certainly not planning on sparing these [works that I am now sending]—for such was my intention—one of you two [friends] seemed to appear to me to my right, and the other to my left, just as my hand was raised, and to admonish me that I not destroy in a single blaze both my promise to you and your faith. This was the main reason why these works were spared; otherwise, believe me, they would have burned with the rest.][27]

Such threats, like Petrarch's more casual use of delays or long silences, seem designed to evoke further desire for the philosophical and literary "goods" he possesses and only reluctantly purveys (e.g., closing a letter, "my book, *De vita solitaria*, which you request as solace for your solitude, I cannot send for the present, for I had only two copies and no more, to begin with").[28]

This complex manipulation of scarcity and need, his own and others', and violence against himself as well as others, all redirected to the pursuit of a uniquely prestigious secular literature, pose some complications to the view that Petrarch's understanding of and commitments to need were "traditional." Thus for Baron, Petrarch tended to restrain his "wavering ideas on poverty and avarice" to more traditionally anti-civic conclusions and a "philosophy of withdrawal" from the relations of wealth and power in urban Italian life, from which he finally retired near the end of his life to take up a

---

26. This claim stands in contrast to the view of David Wallace in *Chaucerian Polity*, who presents Petrarch in stark opposition to Boccaccio's use of "story-telling as commerce" (365). My view of Petrarch's "absolutist" mode is fundamentally indebted to Wallace's arguments, but I do not see this mode as inconsistent with the ethic that subtends mercantile and capitalist culture.

27. *Epistolae de rebus familiaribus* 1.1; Latin text from *Pétrarque: Lettres familières 1-III / Rerum familiarum I-III*, ed. Ugo Dotti and trans. (in French) André Longpré (Paris: Belles Lettres, 2002), 21.

28. *Res Seniles* 10.1; *Letters of Old Age*, 2:357.

life as rural and "simple" as he had had in his early years.²⁹ Rather than only slightly testing the limits of traditional intellectual commitments to poverty and renunciation, Petrarch's emotional performances can be read as generating a novel if paradoxical affirmation of a self-interested scale of values, a continual manipulation of want and deprivation that generated supple ways of creating a sense of value in his writings as commodities, and in renunciation itself as a form of abundance, profit, and aestheticism. As Gur Zak argues, Petrarch's goal is not to "renounce the self" but rather "elucidate the truth about his condition and assimilate and internalize it to establish the self as an authority over itself, over the passions and the fluctuations of fortune."³⁰

As this logic suggests, secular asceticism participates in other cultural mechanisms and issues, especially what is commonly identified as "singular profit" or self-interest. Both Italy and England included many voices asserting that such appetites were a major, indeed growing, problem, and both cultures energetically sought to contain the values of self-interested economic pursuits, especially mercantilism, within larger rationalizations. The idea of need is central to these. Thus as the Italian Dominican Thomas Aquinas wrote in the 1270s, drawing on Aristotle's *Politics*, there are only two kinds of exchange: one is "natural and necessary, by means of which one thing is exchanged for another, or things for money to meet the needs of life"—an exchange carried out not by traders but by "household managers or statesmen, who have to provide a family or a state with the necessaries of life." The other is that of "money for money or of things for money, not to meet the needs of life, but to acquire gain." The first, serving "natural needs" and possessing a "necessary end," is virtuous; the second is categorically dishonorable, because it serves the desire for gain, which, unlike natural need and necessity, knows no limits. For Aquinas, a system based on the pursuit of profit inevitably entails endless desire, a condition he assumes would be enacted in the hearts of individual participants. Traders may direct their gains to "some necessary end," such as for the support of a household "or even to help the needy," and only then is gain justified.³¹

In England, by the fourteenth and early fifteenth centuries an elaborate social contract was sometimes spun out of the idea of need. Thus *Dives and Pauper*, a prose English dialogue between a "Rich man" and a "pauper" writ-

---

29. Baron, "Franciscan Poverty: Petrarch," 177, 180.

30. Gur Zak, *Petrarch's Humanism and the Care of the Self* (Cambridge: Cambridge University Press, 2010), 116. Though Zak's ideas are consistent with the arguments here, Zak makes only passing mention of the story of Griselda, and in a different connection (156–57).

31. *Summa Theologiae*, 2a2ae q.77 art. 4. resp.

ten 1405–10 in East Anglia and extant in four copies, draws fully on Aquinas but goes further to define need as the central principle of social cohesion:

> *Diues.* 3if alle meen weryn as pore as þu art, þu shuldist fare wol euele. *Pauper.* 3if alle meen weryn as ryche as þu art, þu shuldyst faryn mechil wers. Qhoo shulde þanne tylþin þin lond? Whoo shulde heldyn þyn plow? Qhoo repyn þyn corn? Qhoo kepyn þinne beestys? Qhoo shapyn þinne clothis or sowyn hem? What myllere wolde þann gryndyn þyn corn? Qhat baxtere bakyn þyin bred? Qhat broustere brewyn þin ale? Qhat cook dyghtyn þin mete? Qhat smyth, qhat carpenter, amendyn þin hous and othere thynggys necessarye? Þu shuldist moun goon sholes and clothles and goon to þin bed meteles. Al muste þu þanne doon alone . . . þerfore sey3t Seynt Austyn quod diues et pauper sunt duo sibi necessaria. The ryche man and the pore been too thynggys wol needful iche to other. And, as I seyde ferst, the ryche man hat3 more nede of the pore mannys helpe þan the pore of the ryche.[32]

As so detailed an elaboration suggests, this theory of social and economic relations seeks to acknowledge and discipline ever-wider ranges of individual and this-worldly need. The Thomistic solution is luxuriously expanded into an entire economy, although it thereby risks losing any claim to be a strictly ethical or spiritual analysis.

Indeed, from the mid fourteenth century on is found the notion of neediness as a particularly worrisome affirmation of personal, subjective registers, in which "need" was not an objectively claimed category to be defined in others, but an affect affirmed by the subject—*I need.* This inversion of all objective morality opened "need" into "want," in the sense of unverifiable, unlimited desires.[33] The ambiguity visible in the word itself points to something fundamentally destabilizing in the notion of need in late-medieval culture. Whether "need" is an objectively or subjectively asserted condition became both crucial and impossible to know.

Many instances in England might be marshaled to show this ambiguity or inversion in the notion of need.[34] In the last quarter of the fourteenth century, for instance, *Piers Plowman,* throughout focused on the pursuit of a just economy, ends by dwelling on the figure Need who is personified and

---

32. *Dives and Pauper,* ed. Priscilla Heath Barnum, 2 vols. in 3, EETS 275, 280, and o.s. 323 (London: Oxford University Press, 1975–2004), vol. 1, pt. 1, 63; see also the patristic (or pseudo-patristic) sources cited in note at 2:15.

33. Galloway, "Economy of Need." For another word for economic value undergoing paradoxical changes in the period, see Jill Mann's survey of Middle English "enough": "Satisfaction and Payment in Middle English Literature," *Studies in the Age of Chaucer* 5 (1983): 17–28.

34. See Galloway, "Economy of Need," 328–30.

thus, daringly, speaks for itself: by linguistic literalism, this figure must, paradoxically, argue for all the personal advantages of claiming need—unraveling by this strategy alone the discourse of mutual need as an objective, socially impersonal principle of economics, salvation, or social relations. One can look further toward the dissolution of this as a social ethic. In the fifteenth century, un-ironic paeans to profit eclipse the issue of need as the basis of a social contract still further.

This increasing instability in England in the status and limits of need as a principle of social relations meant that new kinds of disciplinary structures were required that might answer to the new pressures to govern and define need. Moralists and historians of the period tended to declare themselves horrified by the sudden deterioration of morality in all social realms and the inversion of communal ethics into instantaneous self-interest, especially among populaces displaying new forms of social identity and political and economic self-consciousness, frequently marked (as in the sumptuary laws) by the rise of a luxury market in clothing.[35] The visible signs of a stable hierarchy of mutual need persisted, but its substance became unnervingly volatile; each estate, many English writers of this period claim or imply, adopted the forms of clothing of the estate above it—all seemed possessed by what Ranulph Higden, an influential mid-fourteenth-century chronicler, described as the English propensity for *varietas*. The socially undecipherable "variation" of new luxury fashions, whereby members of each estate hungered for the trappings and appearance of their betters, seemed to show the transformation of an objective scheme of a hierarchy based on mutual need into a swarming pursuit of self-interest. For Higden and many of his translators and adapters, this opened a dangerous new chapter in history, keyed to social changes for once rather than *Heilsgeschichte* and the Apocalpyse: this new world of untrammeled self-interest and personal wants foretold the coming destruction of the English by the Scots—the most devastating in a series of conquests that the English had had to endure.[36] Given the inversion

---

35. See, e.g., *Knighton's Chronicle, 1337–1397*, ed. and trans. G. H. Martin (Oxford: Oxford University Press, 1995), 508–9.

36. Ranulph Higden, *Polychronicon, together with the English Translation of John Trevisa* . . . , ed. Churchill Babington and Joseph Lumby, Rolls Series 41 (London: Longman, Green; Longman, Roberts and Green, 1865–86), 2:174. For the implications and some of the immediate followers of Higden's discussion of this, see Andrew Galloway, "Latin England," in *Imagining a Medieval English Community*, ed. Kathryn Lavezzo (Minneapolis: University of Minnesota Press, 2003), 45–73. The degree of pressure on the idea of proper clothing recalls the period's expansions of and contradictions in the idea of *habitus*—as a sphere of authorized thought as well as the distinct professional religious clothing—discussed by Katharine Breen, *Imagining an English Reading Public, 1150–1400* (Cambridge: Cambridge University Press, 2010).

of "need" from an impersonal articulation into self-centered discourse, no wonder satire against friars, with their professional insistence on indigence, grew so rampant in England, and could even, as in *Piers Plowman,* become apocalyptically inflected. A new and unplumbed age seemed at hand in the simple emergence of a first person subject bespeaking need, shifting *there is need* to *I need.*

This English context might be set next to Baron's richer but similar view of a major break in Florentine intellectual culture around 1400. At that point, Baron argues, a "traditional" if "wavering" commitment by fourteenth-century moralists and intellectuals to principles of poverty and renunciation gave way in Italy to a "sudden intellectual transformation."[37] Baron attributes the change to growing awareness of the heretic implications of the views of the Fraticelli, and to the increased prosperity of Humanist intellectuals themselves. But the breadth of this change suggests that a broader view might be valuable. For all of the "advance" of Italy over England in the movement toward "modernity," some pervasive instability rippled through social values and social relations in England and Italy alike. In both, it brought a new valuation of self-imposed and invisible renunciation, an implied demonstration of the needy self yet a sharply controlled—*aestheticized*—management of that need. In due course, a new ideology of the legitimacy or potential legitimacy of profit emerged, as part of a new ideal of carefully managed need and renunciation, which may be seen as already shifting the boundary of renunciation deep into secular culture and discourse.

Many critics have recognized that the narrator of Chaucer's *Clerk's Tale* finds more of a problem in Walter's act of testing and witnessing Griselda's fortitude than Petrarch ever seems to. Indeed, Chaucer's narrator frequently can barely contain his revulsion at what he describes, regularly interrupting his narrative to query Walter's "testing" of Griselda, and denouncing his source's claims to confer some hyperintellectual fruits:

> What neded it
> Hire for to tempte, and alwey moore and moore,
> Though som men preise it for a subtil wit?
> But as for me, I seye that yvele it sit
> To assaye a wyf whan that it is no nede,
> And putten hire in angwyssh and in drede.
> (457–62)[38]

---

37. See Baron, "Franciscan Poverty: Petrarch," *passim,* and "Franciscan Poverty: Florence," 192.
38. Quotations of Chaucer, hereafter in the text, are from *The Riverside Chaucer,* gen. ed. Larry D. Benson, 3rd ed. (Boston: Houghton Mifflin, 1987).

The logic-chopping inquiry into *necessitas* is rejected as mere self-indulgent teasing of "subtil" issues, where more immediate sympathy for the emotional consequences would be more appropriate. This passionate repudiation is anti-academic in style, yet still deeply "clerical" in the secular sense that Middleton suggests. In turn, Walter's "hardness" is shown to be an all-too-human effort to usurp providential or fortuitous authority, driven by efforts to prove that his social supremacy over her is justified by her emotional vulnerability. He too cannot fully master his emotions; against his rising frustration, such competitive self-justification is in vain:

> For now gooth he ful faste ymaginyng
> If by his wyves cheere he myghte se,
> Or by hire word aperceyve, that she
> Were changed; but he nevere hire koude fynde
> But evere in oon ylike sad and kynde.
> (598–602)

In Chaucer's narrative, emotions cannot be regulated, sorted, and dismissed nearly as cleanly as in Petrarch's emphasis on Griselda's "mature patience." For one thing, in Chaucer's tale, an "official" emotion, serving official social duties, typically covers others, implicitly less honorable ones. Amid Walter's most triumphant claims to a perfect knowledge of Griselda's is a sour note; his words of victory are undercut by multiple currents of doubt and regret. "Now knowe I, dere wyf, thy stedfastnesse," Walter finally declares (1056), adding with a visible effort to defend the purity of his own motives,

> "I have doon this deede
> For no malice, ne for no crueltee,
> Bur for t'assaye in thee thy wommanheede . . .
> Til I thy purpose knewe and al thy wille."
> (1073–78)

But the narrator makes it clear that Walter has failed utterly to understand the mind and heart—the "purpose" and "al thy wille"—that he sought to control and possess, and identify with. When Walter reveals the safety of her children to her, Griselda is, as in Petrarch, unresponsive, but in Chaucer this is not because of her own more triumphant mental detachment. Instead, she is unresponsive because of trauma, in our psychological sense:

> she for wonder took of it no keep;
> She herde nat what thyng he to hire seyde;
> She ferde as she had stert out of a sleep,
> Til she out of hire mazednesse abreyde.
> (1058–61)

At the same time, her ability to survive such a state, and to do so able to return in full control of her own reaction, is a skill she has been forced to learn from early in life, thanks to hard circumstances. For Petrarch, that impoverished background is displayed as proper training for her competitive edge in self-control. For Chaucer, it is an indication of reflexive response to circumstances, with, at first at least, no basis for triumph. It holds a hint of deep misery that no social elevation can touch, in Griselda's one warning to Walter: "ne prikke with no tormentynge / This tendre mayden, as ye han doon mo; / For she is fostred in hire norissynge / Moore tendrely, and . . . / . . . koude nat adversitee endure / As koude a povre fostred creature" (1038–43). By the end of the tale, however, as for instance in this slyly sharp late rebuke, Griselda seems to recover enough to control and shape her need in socially self-conscious terms. The aesthetic shaping of her own need is clear in the punctilious deflection of self-interest. She could have said "as ye han doon *me*." Even the difference of one letter shows her ability to shape and wield her need.

Walter's feelings in Chaucer's version unfold far more clearly than in Petrarch as undisciplined appetites to know fully, and thus identify somehow with, a mind capable of shaping its own desires so firmly. Walter can only feebly aspire to her freedom from emotions. His desire not to desire, his violent need not to need, provokes him seemingly uncontrollably to ever greater sadism in his drama of playing *fortuna*. His experiment in trying to control or at least directly glimpse her emotions concludes with defeat. He displays not Petrarchan joy in witnessing perfect passionlessness but barely repressed frustration at not bringing out any uncontrolled feelings in her, though that self-restraint is precisely what he has demanded of her. Amid such perversely contradictory impulses and frustrations, any guilt he might feel for the pain he has inflicted dissipates. Thus he manages to frame his feelings into noncommittal sympathy for another's distress, the most he can achieve in the direction of her supreme self-control:

> And whan this Walter saugh hire pacience,
> Hir glad chiere, and no malice at al,

> And he so ofte had doon to hire offence,
> And she ay sad and constant as a wal,
> Continuynge evere hire innocence overal,
> This sturdy markys gan his herte dresse
> To rewen upon hire wyfly stedfastnesse.
> (1044–50)

The effort to shape his aggression into sympathy is explicitly conscious self-cultivation: he "gan his herte dresse / To rewen." With all her family present, the only remaining attempt he can make to force her to display uncultivated signs of need is to offer back the children he has abducted. Yet even in the literally stunning shock of discovering that her children are alive, in Chaucer's description she shapes her most effusive emotional display in the tale to conform strictly to what circumstances demand and no more. Recovered from her blinding faint, she immediately takes up the actions and emotions explicitly proper to a mother, "tendrely kissynge / *Ful lyk* a mooder" (1083-84; my emphasis). However conditioned by poverty, however goaded by Walter, her control over herself returns, supreme and supremely aesthetic. Given her children back at last, Griselda addresses not them but God "and youre benynge fader" to thank those for preserving unexpectedly their lives. In one of the many penetrating touches Chaucer adds to undercut this punctiliously perfect self-control, the children themselves must be pried from her arms by the court attendants: "with greet sleighte and greet difficultee / The children from hire arm they gonne arace" (1102–3).

Both the need she suppresses, and the aesthetic control she uses to suppress it, are the means for creating the "full" though scripted and sculpted self that in Chaucer she achieves, the self-possessed identity that is the goal of an aesthetics of renunciation. But in Chaucer, as not in Petrarch, the dynamic struggle and thus *price* of this goal is fully visible. In Griselda's abnegation of need and artistic perfection is a coldly aggressive defense, as in Walter's desire to prove that abnegation (or rather the desire to prove its failure) is an aggressive sadism. As Wallace stresses, Chaucer's criticism of Petrarch's political affiliations to absolutist modes constantly assimilates Petrarch to Walter.[39]

Chaucer's Clerk also challenges Petrarch's aesthetic values, indeed, as vehemently as his absolutist ones. The Clerk's narrative reveals how the public elements of authority—including the "heigh stile" that, he emphasizes, Petrarch wrote this in—are carefully manufactured and deployed commodi-

---

39. Wallace, *Chaucerian Polity,* 44, 74, 213, 261ff.

ties, denying direct social and physical experience, even the writer's own. In Chaucer's tale, Petrarch's pleasures reside strictly in claims to rhetoric, clothing, and other such tools of controlling human natural existence, though natural death will claim Petrarch in the end: "He is now deed and nayled in his cheste; / I prey to God so yeve his soule reste!" (29–30). Like the clothing Griselda is given whose constant changes Chaucer's version stresses—with an ironic invocation of the period's constant anxieties about the inappropriately luxurious clothing worn by the lower estates—such literary properties as Petrarch has transmitted are granted value only as any commodity might be.[40]

In this sense Chaucer's *Tale* seems to challenge Petrarch's view of the aesthetic as framed in these terms of renunciation as deflected aggression. Chaucer's narrator seems to simmer with resistance to Walter's plan unfolding throughout. Yet the only direct aggression Chaucer's narrator himself displays is against the tale's luxuriant opening. Here surely lies a key to Chaucer's dynamic grappling with Petrarchan ideas of the aesthetics of renunciation as deflected indulgence, deflected aggression and passion. Chaucer's narrator rehearses but denigrates Petrarch's long initial passage describing the path of the Po down to Venice:

> I seye that first with heigh stile he enditeth,
> Er he the body of his tale writeth,
> A prohemye . . .
> . . . The which a long thyng were to devyse.
> And trewely, as to my juggement,
> Me thynketh it a thyng impertinent,
> Save that he wole conveyen his mateere.
> (52–55)

Though repeating while repudiating Petrarch's long opening passage—and showing, like Griselda, that perfect obedience to authority can also be utter renunciation of that authority's power—the Clerk calls the passage twice a "thyng," as if the material trappings of its rhetoric lacked any intrinsic value, merely clothing the essence or "body" of the *Tale*. "Thyng" suggests that Petrarch's flourish is a mere empty token of value, a bit of frippery like the elegant clothing that Griselda adopts and discards so impassively.[41] The

---

40. For Chaucer's elaboration of and emphasis on Griselda's changes of clothing, but assessed to a different end, see Kristine Gilmartin Wallace, "Array as Motif in the *Clerk's Tale*," *Rice University Studies* 62 (1976): 99–110.

41. On "thing," see Ad Putter, "The Poetry of 'Things' in Gower, *The Great Gatsby* and Chaucer,"

treatment thus coheres with Chaucer's general handling of the *Tale*'s issues. The anger it displays is both an unwillingness to accept literary form as an end in itself, and a higher degree of such control of form, through renunciation as the apotheosis of the aesthetic. By assailing Petrarch's rhetorical indulgence as hypocritical, Chaucer's narrator makes the aggression within the aesthetic of renunciation more visible, but he also makes a bid for the rewards of that struggle. Chaucer's Griselda's deployment of those ideals defines an untouchable sufficiency of identity and selfhood; she stands in the end, if in infinitely discreet and decorous ways, as a triumphant political and rhetorical agent of the overwhelmingly oppressive context she inhabits, which presents itself as if its many forms of violence were good form itself. Chaucer does not "medievalize" the tale's Italian values, but out-absolutizes Petrarch's, defeating him in a bid for emotional and moral control and sovereignty by means of the very values of self-subordination that he proposes. Chaucer's narrator shows that the final aesthetics of renunciation must be the renunciation of aesthetics.

Yet Petrarch's use of that opening passage of the Po is itself no simple flourish. Its flaunted writerliness—one of Petrarch's most visible additions to the story in Boccaccio—was resisted by other literary respondents besides Chaucer. An anonymous late-fourteenth-century French translator of Petrarch's narrative, for instance, simply omits it.[42] Given the zeal for deprivation in the rest of Petrarch's narrative, this opening indeed constitutes a remarkably contrasting indulgence:

> Est ad Ytalie latus occiduum Vesulus ex Appennini iugis mons unus altissimus, qui, vertice nubile superans, liquido sese ingerit etheri, mons suapte nobilis natura, Padi ortu nobilissimus, qui eius a latere fonte lapsus exiguo, orientem contra solem fertur, mirisque mox tumidus incrementis brevi spacio decurso, non tantum maximorum unus amnium sed fluviorum a Virgilio rex dictus, Liguriam gurgitem violentus intersecat; dehinc Emiliam atque Flamineam Veneciamque discriminans, multis ad ultimum et ingentibus hostiis in Adriaticum mare descendit.
>
> [On the western side of Italy, a lofty mountain named Vesulus reaches its peak out of the Apennines and into the rarified air above the clouds. This mountain, famous in its own right, is most renowned as the source of the

---

SPELL: Swiss Papers in English Language and Literature 22 (2009): 63–82. Putter, however, does not discuss this instance or tale.

42. See Amy Goodwin, "The Griselda Story in France," in Correale and Hamel, *Sources and Analogues of the "Canterbury Tales,"* 1:140–41.

Po. The river falls from a small spring on the mountainside and, carried toward the rising sun, is quickly swollen in a brief space by numerous tributaries. Thus it becomes not only one of the great streams but (as Virgil calls it) the king of rivers. It rushes through the Ligurian rapids; from there it bounds Emilia, Flaminia, and Venice and finally descends to the Adriatic Sea in a great delta.] (p. 110)

Petrarch's relief at returning from Milan to the rural world of Carrara may be recalled in this effusion, by which natural simplicity is recognized and re-valued by (his) narrative into luxury.[43] Petrarch's luxurious description here of the Po also likely has other, and more learned associations and roots. Near the end of *De consolatione,* for example, Boethius's Philosophia presents the notion of *casum inopinatum,* unexpected chance, as a thundering confluence of waters which yet has some complex order:

Rupis Achaemeniae scopulis ubi versa sequentum
    Pectoribus figit specula pugna fugax,
Tigris et Euphrates uno se fonte resolvunt
    Et mox abiunctis dissociantur aquis.
Si coeant cursumque iterum revocentur in unum,
    Confluat alterni quod trahit unda vadi;
Convenient puppes et vulsi flumine trunci
    Mixtaque fortuitos implicet unda modos,
Quos tamen ipsa vagos terrae diclivia casus
    Gurgitis et lapsi defluus ordo regit.
Sic quae permissis fluitare videtur habenis
    Fors patitur frenos ipsaque lege meat.

[Among the crags of the Achaemenian cliffs, where turned in flight
The fighting Parthian's arrows pierce his pursuers' breast,
The Tigris and Euphrates rise from one spring,
Next they separate and their waters divide;
If they should come together, into one course brought back again,
If all that the water of each stream bears should flow into one,
Their ships would meet, as will tree-trunks torn up by the river,
And their mingled waters in chance paths will twist and turn.
Yet these chance wanderings the very slopes of the land
And the down-flowing nature of the slipping stream control.

---

43. Baron, "Franciscan Poverty: Petrarch," 177–80.

So too that chance which seems slack-reined to roam
Endures its own bridle, and itself moves by law.] (V.m.i)

That this is a subtext in Petrarch's text is supported by Petrarch's use of the same section from Boethius in a letter of 1367, just a few years before translating the Griselda story. In the earlier letter, Petrarch also stressed the power of the human spirit over "fortune," using the example of the despotic ruler of Liguria, Galeazzo Visconti II, who had ruled Milan as a dictator (and nearly destroyed Florence) just before Petrarch's own patron from the same family, Giovanni Galeazzo, had assumed power. In Petrarch's view, Galeazzo, crippled by gout, "views his tortured and aching body as if it belonged to some unknown stranger," as Petrarch writes to the physician Tommaso del Garbo. The violent Galeazzo displays a patience with his own pain so great that it "amazes bystanders that, like a veritable prodigy, a man of delicate constitution, reared in the utmost luxury . . . endures not only with dry eyes but an untroubled brow what makes healthy men sad and groan just to see." The character of Griselda that Petrarch later elaborates is limned here; the aggressively competitive Galeazzo's self-sustaining and self-defining patience—at least as Petrarch confers that image on him—displays the pinnacle of theatrical subjectivity. A supreme good for its possessor, sustained by constant performance, such self-possession is also an object of wonder and pleasure to its many voyeurs.

Other texts and themes regularly invoked by Petrarch are likely also at play in the description of the coursing Po, suggesting deeper meanings to the passage and, if anything, overdetermining its appearance in the narrative. In his famous letter about his ascent of Mt. Ventoux on April 26, 1336 (though the immediacy of that letter is part of its fiction: it was likely written at least sixteen years later, a decade after the death of its supposed addressee), Petrarch had said that at the summit, he scanned the Rhone river laid out before him, then opened his ever-present pocket copy of Augustine's *Confessiones,* only to cast his eye on the words, "men go to admire the high mountains and the great flood of the seas and the wide-rolling rivers . . . and they abandon themselves." The words do not humble him as they did Augustine; quite the contrary, they "stunned" him into considering how "nothing is admirable except the soul, beside the greatness of which nothing is great."[44] Nearly as eighteenth-century writers would describe the "sublime"—and indeed the performance of neediness, self-loss, then self-

---

44. *De rebus familiaribus* IV.1. On the date and choice of nominal addressee, see the excellent edition, commentary, and translation by Rodney Lokaj, *Petrarch's Ascent of Mount Ventoux: The Familiaris IV, I* (Rome: Edizioni dell'Ateneo, 2006), 30–33.

re-making anticipates that much-celebrated later phenomenon—Petrarch's opening vista of the Po Valley as a Boethian metaphor of the world's "concurring causes" spurs his appreciation of an inner grandeur, one he will pursue through his fashioning of Griselda's virile self-assertion against "hard necessity." Against this vista, self-assertion overcoming the force of necessity is not only affirmed, it is apotheosized.

Nor does this exhaust the possible subtexts, the subterranean energies and associations, in the river's description. Petrarch's deep and long familiarity with Augustine's *Confessiones* is a clue to another likely basis and allusion, this one affirming narrative as well as psychic fecundity. In the *Confessiones*, Augustine proposes that Scripture, in all its complexities of metaphysical and literal assertions of God's and creation's goodness should be seen as a torrent, whose joyous and pleasure-giving uses are infinite, limited only by the human beings who exploit it according to their needs and abilities:

> Sicut enim fons in parvo loco uberior est pluribusque rivis in ampliora spatia fluxum ministrant quam quilibet eorum rivorum, qui per multa locorum ab eodem fonte deducitur, ita narratio dispensatoris tui sermocinaturis pluribus profutura parvo sermonis modulo scatet fluenta liquidae veritatis, unde sibi quisque verum, quod de his rebus potest, hic illud, ille illud, per longiores loquellarum anfractus trahat.

> [For as a fountain though pent within a narrow compass is more plentiful, and with his streams serves more rivers, over larger spaces of ground, than any of those rivers do, which after traversing wide regions, is derived out of the same fountain: even so this narration of that dispenser of thine, which was to benefit many who were to preach upon it, does out of a narrow scantling of language, overflow into streams of clearest truths, whence every man may draw out for himself such truth as he can upon these subjects, he, one observation, and he, another, by larger circumlocutions of discourse.][45]

Against this text, so familiar to him, Petrarch can be seen to present both Boccaccio's narrative and his Latin retelling—a still purer distillation of the *fluenta liquida veritatis*—as a potent affirmation of literature: it is a form of secular scripture. Here narrative creation epitomizes personal control, and invites consumption without limit, offering Petrarch himself as the purveyor of an endless and infinitely valuable resource for everyone's use like the

---

45. *Confessiones* 12.27; text and translation are from Augustine, *Confessions*, 2 vols., ed. and trans. William Watts (Cambridge, MA: Harvard University Press, 1999).

unceasing Po. That this claim transposes Augustine's description of the Bible onto a contemporary literary product, and onto a contemporary rather than biblical literary producer—none other than Petrarch himself—affirms present human subjectivity and contemporary literary creativity far more than can be sustained by the socially capacious ideology of mutual need, certainly more so than the form generated, even when it is satirically unraveled, by Chaucer and late-medieval English writers.

Perhaps only an absolutist politics can sponsor so strong a pleasure in pure subjectivity and endlessly valuable literariness. Perhaps only an equally pure commitment to mercantile principles—the sparing allocation of a valuable resource whose scarcity keeps its users and viewers always desirous—can create so freely surplus a pleasure in the aesthetic. Both depend on the deflected aggression of renunciation, though in a mode that can look much more like purified and elite indulgence of the self and the literary. Only after both absolutism and mercantilism are fully dominant (if irreconcilable) principles can there be a full shift from an emphasis on need as an explanation for worldly life, toward the more banal assumption that profit, surplus, and demand are central to everyday, non-aestheticized social relations. Primary among the ways in which this transition unfolded was the aesthetics of renunciation, in whose disciplining and refashioning the story of Griselda so productively figured.

Part II.

Literarity in the Vernacular Sphere

eight

Chaucer's History-Effect

STEVEN JUSTICE

THE POINT of this essay is to explain a compositional device Chaucer invents in the *Troilus and Criseyde*. Later it will argue that by this device Chaucer constituted himself as an object of investigation, but the essay's best rationale is that the device has never been fully explained or even recognized. Chaucer stages its introduction at the beginning of book 2. Approaching Criseyde on Troilus' errand, Pandarus apologizes for interrupting the parlor entertainment:

"But I am sory that I have yow let
To herken of youre book ye preysen thus.
For Goddes love, what seith it? tell it us!
Is it of love? O, som good ye me leere."

"Uncle," quod she, "youre maistresse is nat here."
With that they gonnen laughe . . .[1]

Criseyde's one-line reply caps this bit of the exchange. But what is her reply, exactly? The drift is tolerably clear, the specific content is not: she seems to

---

1. Quotations from Larry D. Benson, ed., *The Riverside Chaucer*, 3rd ed. (Boston: Houghton Mifflin, 1987).

respond, with either regret or rebuke that might be serious or humorous, to suggestions, either flirtatious or self-pitying, that she finds or pretends to find in her uncle's words. The laughter that begins the next stanza clarifies a bit—oh, it's a *joke*—but the moment of clarification acknowledges that the joke cannot be confidently experienced with clarity: the audience can read the characters' laughter as a clue, but cannot laugh with them. Criseyde's sentence is not formally obscure: the blank over which it is pleased to make readers stumble is not a difficulty of syntax or semantics. And there is no obscurity at all for her or Pandarus: the stanza break and the ingressive force of *gonnen* combine to suggest their laughter's fluent simultaneity. The problem is not what the sentence means, but what Criseyde means by it, and what her uncle understands. But asking what a character means or understands tacitly concedes that the character has a mind that can do these things; just by being asked, the question commits the questioner to believing in a subjectivity that conceals at least one item of unexpressed mental content. Further, the idea of a mind with *only* one thought unexpressed is incoherent and, more important, unimaginable: a mind that has one thought has countless others—already, in Criseyde's case, shadowed forth by the several guesses a dutiful reader could make about her meaning. With this, Chaucer begins an experiment in using ordinary structures of narrative inference to create the mirage of subjective depth. He disrupts the easy comprehension of the characters' words with a question which offers too many answers and too few grounds for assessing them, and which takes the shape of a routine and subliminal desire for understanding (*what does she mean?*). That desire in its turn smuggles along as its premise, as if it were a habit already formed, the unexpressed mental contents that must be the object of such investigation. The simultaneity of Criseyde's and Pandarus' laughter, following the connective "with that," shows it to be an immediate and involuntary response. The poem is full of such moments of reflex response.[2] When Pandarus finally is ready to propose Troilus as a lover, he grows serious and asks Criseyde to "take well" what he is about to say. Talk briefly and abruptly breaks off, again signaled by the consequential "with that": "With that she gan hire eighen down to caste, / And Pandarus to coghe gan a lite" (2.252–53). His nervous cough and her lowered eyes mark a shared and involuntary reaction to stimulus. The question of what causes their awkward self-consciousness implies that they have selves to be conscious of. It does not need to have an answer: its job is done once it gets this premise through the door. By its

---

2. This is one reason it is a rich source for Burrow's study of nonverbal communication; John A. Burrow, *Gestures and Looks in Medieval Narrative* (Cambridge: Cambridge University Press, 2002).

means Chaucer can conjure a psychic richness and presence that he may, but need not, elaborate. This illusion, in its turn, enables the intrigue that has kept Chaucer critics so long in the business of guessing at the characters' minds: what does Criseyde want; how much does she understand; how and how far does she consent, and when, and for what reasons; and what satisfaction does Pandarus get from it all? The very texture of personality the poem evokes is the byproduct of this basic puzzle, the puzzle that makes the reader wonder what the characters mean by sentences that rely for their precision on things unsaid because already known to them, and therefore assume that there are minds to rummage in for the answer.

That is the device, a machine for making character. It has been a while since the mainstream of Chaucer criticism, or of any criticism, has said much about character as richly individuated subjectivity. It took a nasty spill—certainly, in Chaucer studies, from Marshall Leicester's brilliant 1980 attack on the neat discrimination of voices in the *Canterbury Tales,* but more generally and fatally from the critical disposition that Leicester's essay represented.[3] It was submerged as a topic in the poststructuralist years, but had been a source of disciplinary nail-chewing for longer than that. The tendency to prefer talk about characters as enabling functions of narrative structure is the most recent form of a pressure that academic literary criticism has long and repeatedly put on itself.[4] Even the most serious and independent work on character in medieval narrative has shied from any hint of treating characters as selves encountered as having depth, even when the sense of that depth is their salient fact.[5] The worry was understandable: the fetish of character has too often assumed a prurient *bonhomie* with narrative protagonists instead of understanding them, and too often reduced literary criticism to literature-appreciation. The fault of counting Lady Macbeth's children was the fault of treating characters as *explanantia* rather than *explananda,* as the sources rather than the products of the literary discourse. But correcting the fault does not require pretending that the effects do not exist or

---

3. H. Marshall Leicester, Jr., "The Art of Impersonation: a General Prologue to the *Canterbury Tales,*" *PMLA* 95 (1980): 213–24. Precisely because it fit more snugly into that critical disposition, the argument of this essay seems to have been more influential than the conclusions Leicester drew from it in H. Marshall Leicester, Jr., *The Disenchanted Self: Representing the Subject in the "Canterbury Tales"* (Berkeley: University of California Press, 1990); there the discrimination of subjectivity from "speakerhood" produced what amounted to a splendid discussion of characters.

4. Diagnosed with great wit by Stanley Cavell, *Must We Mean What We Say?* (Cambridge: Cambridge University Press, 1976), 267–71.

5. Notably Warren Ginsberg, *The Cast of Character: The Representation of Personality in Ancient and Medieval Literature* (Toronto: University of Toronto Press, 1983), esp. 98–133; and Elizabeth Fowler, *Literary Character: The Human Figure in Early English Writing* (Ithaca, NY: Cornell University Press, 2003).

matter: if the products of discourse and the devices that produce them cannot be thought about, our discipline does not have much on which to train its thinking, and there is something pointless about wishing away the experience that most peremptorily seizes most readers. The subjective presence of character *is* there in the *Troilus*, as an effect that emerges from the logic of the narrative's discourse. The three elements—characters' status as effects of discernible causes, their discursive character, and the possession by the narrative of a describable logic—can be combined to make characters vivid, and can be analyzed to make that vividness available to understanding. The characters are not "real" (in the sense that all grownups know that characters are not real), but the *feeling that* they are real is. If criticism has been shy about talking of character, it has never been shy talking about imprecision: the sense that, in one way or another, poems are not to mean but to be suggests at the least that literary status is achieved by resisting clarity, and is one axiom that remains almost invariant through different moments and theoretical idioms.[6] But clear thought about how the indeterminacy is produced and how it calls forth its effects has been less common.[7] The *Troilus* confronts its readers saliently with the experience of character. Any account of the poem that does not allow that experience cannot account for much. My explanation ties that sense to the imprecisions that Chaucer cultivates. It has three advantages over most of the discussions that have appeared heretofore. First, it needs to imagine no entities (like "social persons") apart from the inferential procedures initiated by the narrative itself. Second, it can treat a specific kind of indeterminacy without being itself indeterminate, can precisely describe a technique of imprecision.

---

6. In Chaucer criticism, breadth and multiplicity of possibility seem almost to define Chaucerianness as such; classically, e.g., E. T. Donaldson, "Chaucer and the Elusion of Clarity," *Essays and Studies* 25 (1972): 23–44. Outside it, what is shared by, say, W. K. Wimsatt, Jr. ("The Structure of the 'Concrete Universal' in Literature," *PMLA* 62 [1947]: 262–80), Mikhail Bakhtin (*Problems of Dostoevsky's Poetics*, trans. Caryl Emerson [Minneapolis: University of Minnesota Press, 1984]), Wolfgang Iser ("Indeterminacy and the Reader's Response in Prose Fiction," in *Aspects of Narrative: Selected Papers from the English Institute*, ed. J. Hillis Miller [New York: Columbia University Press, 1971], 1–45), and Roland Barthes (*S/Z*, trans. Richard Howard [New York: Hill and Wang, 1974]) shows how resilient is the sense that indeterminacy makes literature and with what precision that sense can be deployed.

7. A major exception to this generalization was Barthes, *S/Z*; see 22–23, 75–76, 144–45, 178–82. Its influence on my more pedestrian argument here will be clear enough. The nearest approaches I know of to the particular account I offer are found in A. D. Nuttall, *Overheard by God: Fiction and Prayer in Herbert, Milton, Dante, and St. John* (London: Methuen, 1980), 128–43 (concerning St. John's gospel); in Peter R. Schroeder, "Hidden Depths: Dialogue and Characterization in Chaucer and Malory," *PMLA* 98 (1983): 374–87; and in the superb discussion in Karla Taylor, *Chaucer Reads the "Divine Comedy"* (Stanford, CA: Stanford University Press, 1989), 80–83.

And third, it can explain Chaucer's development of character without making it, or worry that it might make it, a way-station on the road to the novel. Chaucer devised the trick of character to do a job peculiar to the *Troilus,* to produce an erotic intrigue that arises less from what characters either say or avoid saying than from what they do not need to say, from what seems clear to them but not to us. The mystery about Chaucer's characters lies in what they do not need to think about, what comes without prompt and goes without saying—in what they presuppose. The poem's most engaging indirections are not those that characters execute against each other, but those the reader encounters as if by accident. It is an experiment peculiar to the *Troilus,* and so therefore is the device of characterization he crafts to enable it; there is nothing quite like either in the *Canterbury Tales.* (Indeed, he seems rather to have lost interest in it.) It was an experiment that we may call, in shorthand, the subjectivity-effect.

It was, as I say, without direct issue; it was nearly without precedent as well. Familiar as the device became in prose fiction (Flaubert would scarcely exist without it), character in classical and medieval narrative most often expresses itself rhetorically, complexities of thought and motive laid out exhaustively in direct discourse and explicit narration. Manifesting character in rhetorical performance—the soliloquies and the epigrammatic dialogue of the *Metamorphoses* distill one style of it—elaborates character as the momentary or developing realization of narrative situations and of thoughts already spoken. Understanding the narrative does not require guessing at what goes unreported, but in making the incremental adjustments that the reports require. This way is not second-best: it gives us Virgil's Aeneas and Ovid's Narcissus and Chrétien's Lancelot. It gives us also Chaucer's source for the *Troilus,* itself hardly naïve: Boccaccio's youthful *Filostrato* is a work whose rough but manifest genius comes largely from embracing and elaborating the explicit rendition of character, using it to construct a narrative of erotic intrigue very unlike the one Chaucer will build on its frame. Boccaccio's is the intrigue of those whose thoughts and affects stretch only as far as what they can say about them. The pathos of the erotic in the *Filostrato* is not its depth but its shallowness: love is a flesh wound that kills by infection and without dignity, that cuts deeper into its characters than their characters go. The story offers the intrigue of those who can only know what they say, and who develop personhood only by being brought to say it. The toughest puzzle of Chaucer's story—what does Criseyde know and when does she know it?—is not even a question in Boccaccio, whose Criseida knows seduction when she sees it and dickers over its terms; the questions about his Criseida do not begin until she begins to pose them. When she and Troiolo and Pandaro conceal things, they conceal them unconcealedly, you might say. Chaucer's intrigue, by contrast, is made not from what his characters avoid saying, but from what they do not need to say or avoid.

Which is not to say that his Pandarus and his Criseyde do not conceal; only that the mysteries about them do not lie there. But their deceptions and indirections do stage the process by which gaps and abruptions prompt desire. As Pandarus prepares his niece to hear the proposition he brings, he deploys a silence whose purpose is to provoke curiosity: "And with that word" ("with that," again),

> he gan right inwardly
> Byholden hire and loken on hire face,
> And seyde, "On swich a mirour goode grace."
>
> Than thought he thus: "If I my tale endite
> Aught harde, or make a proces any whyle,
> She shal no savour have therin but lite,
> And trowe I wolde hire in my wil bigyle;
> For tendre wittes wenen al be wyle
> Theras their kan nought pleynly understonde;
> Forthi hire wit to serven wol I fonde."
>
> And loked on hire in a bisy wyse,
> And she was war that he beheld hire so,
> And seyde, "Lord! so faste ye m'avise!
> Sey ye me nevere er now? What sey ye, no?"
> "Yis, yis," quod he, "and bet wol er I go!
> But be my trouthe I thoughte now if ye
> Be fortunat, for now men shal it se." (2.264–80)

The repetition of *loken* at either edge of Pandarus' silent strategizing ("he gan . . . /loken on hire face"; "And loked on hire") frames his thought as an obbligato played silently upon a suspended gaze.[8] The gaze is mutual: Pandarus can look "inwardly . . . on hire face" only if she is looking back at him, and the adverb suggests the intentness of investigation, an effort fixed on divining the others' thoughts. Pandarus' thought (about which he lies in the

---

8. B. A. Windeatt, ed., *Troilus & Criseyde: A New Edition of "The Book of Troilus"* (London: Longman, 1984), *ad loc.*, notices the effect of the repetition.

final lines) is indeed directed to what she will think; and Criseyde's redundant insistence "What sey ye, no?," pointlessly pressing him to answer a rhetorical question, suggests how unnerved she is by reflections whose presence is evident but whose content is not. Criseyde's urgency about specifying the unreported thought that has stopped Pandarus speaking is an intradiegetic operation of Chaucer's diegetic device. Its mechanism works like this: confront your audience with an abruption that does not disturb the speaker (Pandarus is not puzzled by his own silence) and the connection unmade asks to be made, engages uncompleted inference as desire and inquiry. Now the fact that Chaucer represents Pandarus and Criseyde in this concrete instance of the dynamic of enigma does not in itself prove that the idea of it is available to him in a form abstract enough to be deployed and analogized on other scales, in different registers, and as an instrument of his own narrative technique, but the poem does show it in operation elsewhere. We can see it in the narrator, as I will observe later, and we can see it in his protagonist: as one critic astutely observes, it seems to be Criseyde's paradoxical air of simultaneous withdrawal and defiance during the festival, striking a note of subjective presence, fetching and promissory, that calls out Troilus' love.[9]

In fact, the abstract idea of this dynamic was formally and familiarly available to the middle ages. That an urge to interpretation is provoked by an utterance that acts as though it makes a sense which is not apparent to its hearers is a notion bequeathed to it by the second book of Augustine's *Christian Pedagogy:* a passage that formally promises a meaning that it fails to deliver or trammels up in enigma—by passages that have the form of meaningful utterances but do not seem to communicate meaningfully—poses a problem to the reader, draws him by a desire to understand, until he finds the account that pieces the puzzle together and which rewards him with delight. The obscure and enigmatic expressions of Scripture work to call back the intellect from a disgusted satiety ("ad . . . intellectum a fastidio revocandum"), stimulating the mind to a "labor" that yields "discoveries more pleasing": "nemo ambigit . . . quaeque . . . cum aliqua difficultate quaesita multo gratius inveniri."[10] The utterance that does not deliver the meaning it promises dangles the bait of pleasure before the inquiring intellect.

Chaucer knows the principle, and so, it proves, do his characters. At least Pandarus does. His silence here is designed to pull Criseyde into surmise.

---

9. Carolynn Van Dyke, *Chaucer's Agents: Cause and Representation in Chaucerian Narrative* (Madison, NJ: Fairleigh Dickinson University Press, 2005), 200.
10. Augustine, *De doctrina christiana*, ed. Paul Tombeur (Turnhout: Brepols, 1982), 2.6; translations of this and all works in the essay are mine. See the discussion in D. W. Robertson, Jr., *A Preface to Chaucer: Studies in Medieval Perspectives* (Princeton, NJ: Princeton University Press, 1962), 57–64.

Later in book 2, he will, in a shameless fiction, claim that he was drawn along in the same traction. When she asks how he first learned of Troilus' love, he says that some inconsistent behaviors of Troilus—guilty silences, tears unsuccessfully concealed—provoked a "suspecioun" (2.561) that he was drawn to allay. So he "gan . . . stalke hym softely byhynde" (2.519), eventually overhearing a monologue in which Troilus reveals the source of his sorrow.

There is an element here that adds a wrinkle to Augustine's principle and leads us into a denser, more complex part of the story of how Chaucer came to devise his device. Both these indirections of Pandarus' are advertent actions that pretend to inadvertency: he is not suddenly derailed by distraction to break his discourse, and Troilus does not unwittingly reveal his love; Pandarus feigns the distraction to prompt in her the intense curiosity with which she responds, and lies about Troilus' revelation to keep his visit from seeming a conspiracy. In both cases, inadvertency is something he feigns because it is the warrant of good faith, because it promises that what is revealed has no designs on its audience, indeed has no intention to communicate at all. A man surprised by his own words is unequal to premeditation or insincerity. That is why Pandarus insists on it. He tells Criseyde the story of proxied courtship as a train of things that could not be helped: Troilus could not avoid betraying the fact of his love; Pandarus on discovering it could not resist helping his friend; Pandarus on revealing it to Criseyde cannot but slip into a muse at the thought of her luck. All of this is meant to peel away any suspicion that the courtship is a thing devised and strategized, a suspicion he must avert precisely because it is such a thing. This shows, then, that Chaucer gives his characters an awareness how apparent incompletions and inadvertencies can seem to reveal thoughts unwittingly. It does not show how he uses them to create these characters as characters, or where the technique came from. That story is more tangled.

But the characters' recognition of how they can fake inadvertent gaps and hints does help reveal this longer, more roundabout story of how Chaucer came to contrive his technique of gaps and hints, of clues dropped by characters who do not notice them and would not think them clues if they did. The availability of Augustine's idea does not itself explain why Chaucer should be interested or why his interest would take this form; it is the pose of inadvertency that points to the source that does. For while the inadvertent disclosure by which Chaucer conjures the illusion of subjective depth and presence is a relatively new thing, the advertent pretense of inadvertent disclosure is not; it was codified in a rhetorical figure. Among the tropes introduced in every handbook is that pose of strategically tardy self-censorship called aposiopesis, an almost invariably histrionic figure common in what we might call the operatic mode of antique and medieval literature. Its most famous instance comes in book 2 of the *Aeneid,* as Aeneas narrates how the Trojans, against their interest and all good judgment, took the wooden horse into their city. What tipped their balance was the speech of the Greek Sinon, a speech they trusted because he pretended an unwillingness to speak it. Sinon, "dolis instructus et arte Pelasga" (152), deceives the Trojans. He pretends to have escaped murder at the hands of the Greeks, and affects to be unequal to relating their treachery:

> nec requieuit enim, donec Calchante ministro—
> sed quid ego haec autem nequiquam ingrata reuoluo,
> quidue moror? (2.100–1)[11]

The ablative absolute ("Calchante ministro") suspends grammatical resolution, so that "donec" begins a clause that never achieves either a main verb or a subject; "sed," beginning the next line, audibly aborts the narration in supervening emotion. His suppression of the story near its beginning whets the Trojans' desire to hear its end: *then,* Aeneas says, after Sinon has broken off his telling, the Trojans "burn" ("tum . . . ardemus," 105) with desire to know what he knows but is not saying. Once this tale is done, what had been a curiosity to know the thoughts he was suppressing becomes an unresisting identification with him: "His lacrimis uitam damus et miserescimus ultro" (145). The rhetorical tactic of his bogus awkwardness is obvious to every reader, and should (Aeneas implies) have been obvious to the Trojans: their failure to see it is, now in retrospect, evidence of the mad doom impending. The Trojans help Sinon convince them: their desires connive with his vulgar pretense to obscure its vulgarity and believe what could persuade only the desperate. It is thus that the flames with which they "burn" for him to resume the story become the flames that destroy their city. Virgil portrays Aeneas' retrospective clarity about his people's fatal choice, and borrows the regret to convey the brutal pointlessness of the city's night of destruction; Chaucer, whose *Troilus* makes the city's approaching fall the more haunting for its refusal to narrate it (1.141–44, 5.1765–69), builds his effect from recognizing the chill horror of lines like this.

The figure of aposiopesis might itself have suggested to Chaucer the experiment in characterization. At points Criseyde seems to condense both parties in rhetorical performance—the poser who gulls his audience and the

---

11. Quotations from Virgil, *Opera,* ed. R. A. B. Mynors (Oxford: Clarendon Press, 1969).

audience that chooses to be gulled—in a single subjectivity. In Troilus and in Criseyde, there are gaps apparently invisible to themselves, wobbles of understanding that evoke the presence of a feeling and thinking self with heft and texture. Criseyde's deliberations after Pandarus leaves display a discontinuity not of speech but of affective experience that she both contrives and is shocked at. Thinking about what he has said, she hears a Trojan crowd celebrating Troilus' triumph in the battle from which he is just returning, and from her window sees him pass by:

> Criseyda gan al his chere aspien,
> And leet it so softe in hire herte synke,
> That to hireself she seyde, "Who yaf me drynke?"
> For of hire owen thought she wex al reed,
> Remembryng hire right thus, "Lo, this is he
> Which that myn uncle swerith he moot be deed,
> But I on hym have mercy and pitee." (2.645–51)

The involuntary somatic symptom—the blush that feels like drink gone to the head[12]—looks like an ambush by unexpected feeling, experienced as something that befalls her rather than something she brings forth. Readers have found it easy to take her at her word.[13] Talking to her uncle, she finds it hard to maintain a freedom of response without falling into a tone of bantering premeditation ("Nay, therof spak I nought, ha, ha!" 2.589). Now alone, this rush of feeling seems to reveal a sentimental attachment heretofore unrecognized, deeper than self-interest or self-control. The exclamation "Who gave me drink?" is meant to warrant her guileless authenticity. But the consent implied by the detail that she "leet" his image "in hire herte synke" spoils the impression of surprise: she must in some measure be aware of an effect she chooses to permit. The explanatory backtracking of the next stanza traces her cry to her blush, and the blush to conscious internal discourse: "this is the one my uncle says will die unless I show him mercy." Turn the sequence back around into right order, and this is what happens: she thinks a thought that induces a response she instantly forgets she has induced, pre-

---

12. So I understand the line; but the alternate reading ("love-potion"), proposed by Robert Kilburn Root, ed. *The Book of Troilus and Criseyde* (Princeton, NJ: Princeton University Press, 1926), 445, and endorsed by, e.g., Lee Patterson, *Chaucer and the Subject of History* (Madison: University of Wisconsin Press, 1991), 138, would not alter the point here.

13. E.g., Stephen A. Barney, "Troilus Bound," *Speculum* 47 (1972): 445; Joan G. Haahr, "Criseyde's Inner Debate: The Dialectic of Enamorment in the *Filostrato* and the *Troilus*," *Studies in Philology* 89 (1992): 262. Subtler, more alert readings are adumbrated by, e.g., D. W. Robertson, Jr., "Chaucerian Tragedy," *ELH* 19 (1952): 21–22; and Wetherbee (next note).

meditates what she plans to experience as unforeseen. "Nothing about her reaction is simply spontaneous,"[14] it is true, but the function of the swoon is to convince her that everything about it is. Only by seeming so can the feeling claim to have emerged from depths she had not suspected; indeed, it is the discontinuity of the surprise that produces the effect of psychic depth. The device Chaucer uses to convince us of his characters' interiority is the device Criseyde uses to convince herself of her own. It persuades because it is not seen as a device, because the emotion and the cry seem to come from some part of the self whose response to Troilus is obvious to itself though was not before obvious to her thought.[15]

One stage, then, in Chaucer's deployment of aposiopesis, of rhetorically premeditated discontinuity simulating unpremeditated revelation, is the uncertainty in which he casts his characters' relation to their own avowals. They discover in themselves, and reveal to us, elements of their pasts that land as surprises though the expressions speak as if they are already obvious. In book 3, when Troilus pins Criseyde back on the bed, saying "Now be ye kaught . . . / Now yeldeth yow," she famously answers, "Ne hadde I er now, my swete herte deere, / Ben yolde, ywis, I were now nought heere!" (1208–11). The avowal is neat—it smoothly ducks Troilus' coltish eagerness without ungraciously rejecting it—but it does come as a surprise: since she has so clearly, even when speaking to herself, insisted that she has not yielded, this deflating response creates an uncertainty whether she was pretending before or is pretending now. The work gives us no grounds for deciding; again, just posing the problem does all that the moment needs, inducing the question and with it the assumption that there is evidence *in there* that, if excavated, could explain her. The counterfactual form of her response here implies the range of possibilities that still leaves in place the indefiniteness that implies its own explanation.[16]

But though aposiopesis could alone have been the source of Chaucer's experiment, it probably was not, and Criseyde's counterfactual ("Ne hadde I . . . / Ben yolde") signals what may have brought it to his attention. Counterfactuals and negative conditionals (in forms "if . . . not" and "but if") crowd his poem, as forms of utterance that entertain an indecision that remains formally unresolved.[17] The first words from Troilus's lips after he falls

---

14. Winthrop Wetherbee, III, *Chaucer and the Poets: An Essay on "Troilus and Criseyde"* (Ithaca, NY: Cornell University Press, 1984), 184.

15. Derek Pearsall, "Criseyde's Choices," *Studies in the Age of Chaucer Proceedings* 2 (1986): 17–29.

16. Nicely read in David Aers, *Community, Gender, and Individual Identity: English Writing 1360–1430* (London: Routledge, 1988), 130–31.

17. See, e.g., 1.229; 1.415; 1.746; 1.971; 2.609; 3.578; 3.795; 3.899; 3.1267; 3.1774; 3.794;

in love are the opening words of Petrarch's "S'amor non è"; his translation "If no love is," "abstracting from Petrarch's abstractions,"[18] makes what in Petrarch is the waver of unclarity into a rhetorical counterfactual. The choice of Petrarch neatly suggests the obvious fact about Troilus, that as a lover he is a lyric that can become a narrative only through Pandarus' offices.[19] The love begins to speak with one counterfactual; and the narrator ushers it to its end with another, speaking of the story not told—"if I hadde ytaken for to write / The armes of this ilke worthi man . . . " (5.1765–66). The choice of Petrarch also signals Chaucer's deliberate linking of his characters with the poetic past he chooses for his poem, the tradition into which he inserts it and which he dramatizes within it.[20]

I mean a moment in Dante's *Inferno* when "if not" coincides exactly with an aborted utterance. Before the gates of Dis, Virgil's unflappability briefly lapses. Prevented by the demons from entering the citadel, his attempt to reassure Dante does just the opposite when it falters in mid-sentence: "'Pur a noi converrà vincer la punga,' / cominciò el, 'se non... Tal ne s'offerse.'"[21] The unfinished negative conditional "If not—" functions just like Sinon's unresolved ablative absolute in the *Aeneid:* the interrupted syntax points to meanings the speaker realizes should not be spoken and that the listener must infer. And that is just Dante's source: his Virgil's "if not . . . "—"se non . . . "—in Latin is "si non": *Sinon,* the name of the character to whom Virgil had given poetry's most celebrated interrupted sentence, begins the interrupted sentence Dante gives Virgil, and with the allusion, Dante advertises his novelty: instead of showing a character who pretends inadvertency to look authentic, he shows a character who is authentically inadvertent. Writing the *Aeneid,* everything Virgil did had the rhetorical premeditation of Sinon's uncompleted sentence; but of this poem, Virgil is not the author, and the interrupted conditional shows that, while Dante treats him still as an author, he himself can be blindsided by what transpires. It suggests—only this once, but it only needs this once—that Virgil has an inner life, a series of unpremeditated and unreported thoughts, and that the relative confidence

---

4.98; 4.221; 4.281; 4.437; 4.566–67; 4.637; 4.774; 4.1233; 4.1332; 4.1343; 4.1560; 4.1579; 4.1618; 4.1647; 5.124; 5.897; 5.906; 5.932–33; 5.961; 5.1337; 5.1531; 5.1765.

18. Barney, "Troilus Bound," 447

19. Donaldson, "Elusion of Clarity," 33–34.

20. Ginsberg says that in the *Troilus* he reads Boccaccio through Dante, where elsewhere he reads Dante through Boccaccio. Warren Ginsberg, *Chaucer's Italian Tradition* (Ann Arbor: University of Michigan Press, 2002), 109–11.

21. Quotations are from the Petrocchi edition, as it appears in Dante, *The Divine Comedy,* ed. C. S. Singleton (Princeton, NJ: Princeton University Press, 1970).

with which he negotiates *Inferno* and *Purgatorio* is not the manifestation of a placid interiority but the index to one more complex and obscure.

In *Inferno*, Dante and Virgil both have thoughts. Each guesses at the other's, with unequal results. As they approach Hell, and Dante first reads the inscription on its gate ("Lasciate ogne speranza . . . " [3.9]), he quails: "il senso lor m'è duro" (12). There are several senses in which these words might be "hard," none of which the words or their preceding context is sufficient to specify.[22] Virgil, however, answers "come persona accorta," and enjoins Dante against all *sospetto* and *viltà* (14–15). The knowledge signaled by *accorta* must, accordingly, be Virgil's familiarity not with Hell but with Dante's thoughts. The original complaint, "their sense is hard for me," momentarily bespeaks that uncertainty which projects around it all the possibilities and all the complexities of fallen human subjectivity, which Virgil's words immediately dispel: the words are hard in the sense that they are personally threatening. The unspecifiability *to us* of Dante's thoughts, the limitation that periodically conveys the impression of an affective and intellectual life that surfaces only fitfully into narration, proves to be our limitation; it does not constrain Virgil, who abruptly reduces the enigmas to their insufficiently expressed sense. The situation is asymmetrical: that same participle *accorto* appears, now describing Dante, when at the brink of Limbo Virgil goes pale, and Dante, "del color . . . accorto," asks "Come verrò, se tu paventi / che suoli al mio dubbiare esser conforto?" (4.16–18). That is, Dante confidently interprets an underspecified phenomenon just as Virgil did before, and reaches the same conclusion that Virgil did: that his companion is afraid. But Dante is wrong, as Virgil immediately informs him that his pallor derived from pity, not fear. Virgil is opaque to Dante in a way that Dante is not to Virgil.

These moments of mutual interpretation, both those that succeed and those that do not, assume that there is something to interpret, that the contents of the minds producing those words fix their meaning. Dante also frequently, even iconically, gives his characters moments of unexplained discontinuity and equivocations unresolved, to dangle before the reader evidence of an inner life undescribed and unspecified. During its first very first exchange of dialogue, the narrator has called for help to the figure, "shade or man," who first identifies himself as the singer of Aeneas' story and then immediately poses to Dante questions that Dante unthinkingly bypasses:

---

22. On commentators' difficulties from the beginning regarding these words, see Francesco Mazzoni, *Saggio di un nuovo commento alla "Divina commedia": Inferno canti I–III* (Florence: Sansoni, 1967), 337–42.

"Ma tu perché ritorni a tanta noia?
perché non sali il dilettoso monte
ch'è principio e cagion di tutta gioia?"

"Or se' tu quel Virgilio . . . ?" (76–79)

Strictly described, Dante's response is both a redundancy and a *non sequitur:* it solicits an answer it has already received (Virgil already has said that he is Virgil) and neglects the question just put (it does not explain why he returns to such pain). Those defects serve to convey the affective force channeled through Dante's response: the devotion he expresses in the next lines—"Tu se' lo mio maestro e 'l mio autore" (85)—is communicated first not as a discursive statement but as a prediscursive rush of piety, the very awkwardness of which is meant to give witness to his earnestness. Those failures of coherence and social continuity, the poem implies, are witnesses securer and more eloquent than any declaration of love, and so by burdening his speaker with those failures Dante also gives him the illusion of affective presence that a less cumbersome response would not convey.

In the *Comedy* Chaucer encountered the materials from which he would make the *Troilus'* subjectivity-effect, but that is not its first use for Dante. In the normal course of the *Comedy's* narrative, Dante's narrator is the only character the immensity of whose unexpressed consciousness is suggested by partial and failed and enigmatic suggestions: damned souls are drained of possibility; blessed souls have resolved or are resolving all possibility (in the *Paradiso* and *Purgatorio* respectively) into plenary actuality. This device of characterization, signaling but not displaying the obscurities of a human self still *in via,* is mobilized for a single end, to display the particular darkness in which persons still alive encounter their own selves, which will only be finally displayed and interpreted when they suffer the *contrapasso* of hell or occupy the rose of heaven. But the device of characterization is part of a larger discovery of Dante's, which bears still more importantly on how Chaucer's makes character in the *Troilus.* Something new in the *Comedy,* something unlike anything in the western literature he inherited, is the experience of spatial solidity and coherence, the "continuous presence of a terrain,"[23] it conveys. *Inferno* and *Purgatorio* especially convey not merely the fact of their extension in space, but the experience of their coherence and immensity; *Paradiso* manages to suggest that spatial extension itself is

---

23. Anne Middleton, "Narration and the Invention of Experience: Episodic Form in Piers Plowman," in *The Wisdom of Poetry: Essays in Early English Literature in Honor of Morton W. Bloomfield,* ed. Larry D. Benson and Siegfried Wenzel (Kalamazoo, MI: Medieval Institute Publications, 1982), 103.

insufficiently spacious for completed meaning to inhabit. That the helpful diagrams that nearly every edition and translation of the poem includes can so easily be drawn attests to the mappability of the poem's imaginary space; but that every edition feels the need to include them attests to the exigence of the poem's topographical consistency and continuity. Not only retrospectively can one look back across the landscape traveled, and discover that it fits together; one can prospectively sense that the landscape will be there, without knowing what it is.[24] The immediate scene is felt as, and derives its significance from being, a part of a continuous and consistent whole.

At the start of the *Inferno*, what evokes the presence of this fully elaborated spatial scene is the fact that what is not visible is still sensible, that what is not yet seen makes its imminence felt as sound, seeks out a limit and discovers the space that bounds it. The poem feels its way along its landscape with the same fragmentary suggestion by which it suggests the unspoken and unrealized thoughts of the narrator, a suggestion whose coherence implies what is not disclosed—sounds that establish the presence of a landscape in the darkness before its features can be discerned, prompting a vigilance that wishes to discern them. As soon as Dante passes through the gate of hell into the darkness of the "air without stars," he hears sighs, plaints, cries; four lines cataloguing the sounds, which measure the space that cannot be seen, and the brief simile that catches them up—the sounds "turned about in the perpetually dark air like sand when the wind blows it"—suggests how they imply the bulk of the space they issue from while having no bulk of their own, as the whirlwind of sand outlines a shape that it does not pack with solidity.[25] What they convey provokes the pressure of investigation to fill the implied scene with sight: Dante strains in the next canto to "fix his eyes on the bottom" of a space he can hear but cannot yet see. The famous catechresis describing the darkness of hell—"loco d'ogne luce muto" (5.28)—is more than a striking comparison; it is an expression complementary to the the auditory indications that imply the scene that will become visible,[26] and renders it real by making it sensed before it is viewed.

It is my claim that in Dante Chaucer discovered a principle of literary design and a source of compositional virtuosity: supplying details that imply

---

24. The contrast with the *New Life* suggests how programmatic this was in the *Comedy;* see Mark Musa, "An Essay on the *Vita nuova,*" in *Dante's Vita nuova,* trans. Mark Musa (Bloomington: Indiana University Press, 1973), 100–4.

25. On such devices, see Elaine Scarry, *Dreaming by the Book* (New York: Farrar, Straus and Giroux, 1999), 89–99.

26. In the lines that follow, he says that the sighs come from "turbe . . . / d'infanti e di femmine e di viri," (29–30), which sounds as though he is making the scene out only aurally; but in the next tercet, Virgil wonders why he does not ask what spirits they are that he sees ("che tu vedi," 32).

a coherence they do not disclose—of mental acts, of physical space—can prompt an investigative desire to discern the principles of coherence; the act of seeking it tacitly concedes the reality of the materials supposed to cohere; and it thereby accepts the illusion of its existence. He does play with what Dante learned about implying the coherence of spatial geography: the narration seems to expect us to understand the arrangement of rooms, left undescribed, in Criseyde's and Pandarus' houses: when it has Criseyde descend "the steyre" to "the garden," the definite articles assume the obviousness of their placement.[27] But that is evidently not his chief use for it. Dante is most interested in realizing palpable extension in space embodying the claim that his vision was not "visionary" but simply real.[28] Chaucer retools the device chiefly to represent extension in time, and especially the durable reflexive awareness that constitutes selfhood.

In seeing what Chaucer took from Dante we can see how much he added of his own. What is not to be found in Dante's use of discontinuous dialogue, what is new in Chaucer, is an inadvertency deeper than and different from that which attends mistakes and accidents and surprises. For the inadvertencies he uses include what is unplanned not because it is a mistake or an oversight, but because it is simply presupposed—not the sort of clue people mistakenly leave when they are trying to say something else or nothing at all, but the sort that acts like a clue only because accidents of circumstance obscure to readers what is transparent to the characters. It is dialogue's analogy to Dante's landscape: something obvious to anyone who is present in the scene but unknown to the reader who is not. Chaucer combined the givenness of Dante's landscape, sensed more powerfully in fragmentary evocation than it could be in fuller description, with the suggestive power of the incomplete or fragmentary utterance.

Think again about that laughter that Pandarus and Criseyde share at the start of book 2, whose spontaneity marks the presence of thoughts and meanings that we do not learn because they do not need to be made explicit. I did not observe its most obvious implication: the characters' shared understanding marks not only the presence of minds but their duration together through history, a shared past in which habits of intimacy have settled into second nature.[29] To understand their joke would you would need to relive

---

27. H. M. Smyser, "The Domestic Background of *Troilus and Criseyde*," *Speculum* 31 (1956): 297–315; Saul N. Brody, "Making a Play for Criseyde: The Staging of Pandarus's House in Chaucer's *Troilus and Criseyde*," *Speculum* 73 (1998): 115–40.

28. Charles S. Singleton, *Dante's "Commedia": Elements of Structure* (Baltimore: Johns Hopkins University Press, 1977).

29. Well noted by Wetherbee, *Chaucer and the Poets*, 182.

their lives, to occupy their routine presuppositions. Their easy understanding of what is hazy to the reader conveys that past's presence to them: Criseyde's joke is not clear to us because we have not had the experiences she has had with Pandarus. Their routine teasing performs that intimacy, by signaling how much is shared and can be left unsaid. What can go without saying points to the common experience that relieves communication of the burden of explicitness; but for just that reason, what goes without saying is that which, going unsaid, implies the experience and enables the meanings of what is spoken.

SO THE subjectivity-effect entails and depends upon a history-effect. By it, a past acknowledged but unnarrated gives narrated actions that effect of depth and vividness thoughts acknowledged but unreported give to the characters, and for much the same reason: the past that they can presuppose makes up the thoughts they have. But this history-effect works more broadly too, giving narrative chronology a weirdly backwards relation to readerly expectation, and by that means giving historical sequence itself that illusion of palpability. The *Troilus* imagines the future of its story as a matter closed and fixed; the latitude of possibility that even the most unconvincing constructions of suspense attribute to a story being told is lopped from the *Troilus* before it gets underway. The action begins as Calchas divines the end of the Trojan story (1.67–68), learns what every reader already knows about the city's fate. But the poem has already placed its readers in Calchas' position, informing them, before they have a chance to object, what the whole shape of Troilus' "double sorwe" will be: "in lovynge of Criseyde, / And how that she forsook hym er she deyde" (1.1, 55–56). Knowing this double sorrow has two effects. First, the future immanent to the story presents itself as a constraint, a future built of necessity rather than possibility. We willy-nilly encounter the characters' choices from an ironic superiority: what they claim and plan is measured against our knowledge of their end. The narration itself wiggles impatiently against that knowledge as it moves to its close.[30] The same narrator who at the start of the first book coolly summarizes the story's trajectory resents that trajectory by the start of the fourth: he recoils from the plain statement of "how Criseyde Troilus forsook" with the pointless qualification "or at the leeste, how that she was unkynde": such desperate adjustment of tone is the only freedom the story leaves him. What she

---

30. See Patterson, *Chaucer*, 114–26; Sylvia Federico, *New Troy: Fantasies of Empire in the Late Middle Ages* (Minneapolis: University of Minnesota Press, 2003), 73–83.

did "*moot* hennesforth ben matere of my book, / As writen folk" (4.15–18); constrained to say what she *did,* the only freedom left is imagining what she *meant.* He knows the end of the story because he has read it; that knowledge, like the source that inflicts it on him, feels like bondage once he wants an ending different from the one it offers.

But what yields the narrator some refuge of freedom and yields characters real enough to feel themselves free is, strangely, more of the same. He tells us repeatedly that his poem says only and exactly what he finds in his source, reporting "every word" (1.397) it offers him. This utter fidelity to his source is of course a fiction, but the narrating voice returns to it obsessively. He worries about the details his source does not allow him to fill in (*e.g.,* 1.132–33; 3.501–4; 5.826). This in itself creates some of the solidity of his world and its characters by what it subtracts rather than what it adds: by lacking "facts" it can afford to lack, the poem suggests that its world extends beyond what its narrator knows of it.[31] But it moves further toward the palpability he works hardest at, the seeming presence of his characters as minds and pasts, pressing the bondage of fact so far that it reveals the past as the only source of freedom it can realize. Chaucer seems to achieve this odd homeopathy by taking more seriously than it is meant a claim in one of the sources he thought most about, the *Historia destructionis Troiae.* Guido delle Colonne begins his work precisely by offering to resuscitate his protagonists imaginatively—the "writings of the ancients, faithful custodians of things gone by," offer the image of "things past as if they were present," and to men long dead, "through wakeful acts of reading, pour in the spirit of their strength imagined, as if they were alive."[32] And it offers to evoke their free

---

31. ". . . to create 'truth,' one must be at once precise and insignificant" (Barthes, *S/Z,* 69).

32. "Et antiquorum scripta, fidelia conseruatricia premissorum, preterita uelud presentia representant, et viris strenuis quos longa mundi etas iam dudum per mortem absorbuit per librorum uigiles lectiones, ac si viuerent, spiritu ymaginarie uirtutis infundunt"; Guido delle Colonne, *Historia destructionis Troiae,* ed. Nathaniel E. Griffin (Cambridge: Mediæval Academy of America, 1936), 3. Though there is some difference on how deeply Chaucer used Guido's work, it seems clear that Benson is right to claim its influence on him (C. David Benson, *The History of Troy in Middle English Literature: Guido delle Colonne's "Historia Destructionis Troiae" in Medieval England* [Woodbridge, UK: D. S. Brewer, 1980], 134–43); indeed, he could have relied more on details than he does. It was the *Historia,* for example, that might have suggested to him the utility of the Trojan sewer-system (Troilus, 3.785–91; Guido, p. 48; though on this see Will Robins, "Troilus in the Gutter," in *Sacred and Profane in Chaucer and Middle English Literature: Essays in Honour of John V. Fleming,* ed. Robert Epstein and William Robins [Toronto: University of Toronto Press, 2010], 91–112); when Chaucer tells us that Achilles "despitously" slew Troilus, his word echoes Guido's word (*crudeliter,* p. 204) more closely than Boccaccio's (*miseramente*), and in a single adverb rather than in Benoît de Sainte-Maure's clause conveying the same affective tone ("Grant cruëuté, grant felonie / A fait," 21444–45). See in general George L. Hamilton, *The Indebtedness of Chaucer's "Troilus and Criseyde" to Guido delle Colonne's "Historia trojana"* (New York: Columbia University Press, 1903); and Karl Young, *The Origin*

spacious range of action by severely foreshortening his own: these vivid portraits remain alive for succeeding ages by the *fidelis scriptura* of those who copy them. It is clear enough what Guido means: by leaving transmission of their acts as uncontaminated as possible, the author keeps the record close to the deeds lived and acted; he makes it vivid by keeping it true. Chaucer would have found the source Guido's notion in the source shared with him, Benoît de Sainte-Maur's *Roman de Troie:* "I follow the Latin to the letter; I have not wished to add anything to what I have found written."[33] As a theory of literary effect, this *fidelis scriptura* is wanting; but it poses a claim that Chaucer develops with perversity and flair. Their documentary punctiliousness becomes the psychodrama of Chaucer's narrator, and thus (by a logic this essay has used more than once) both implies that he has a psyche and explains the allure of finding one. For most of his poem, as has been often remarked, the narrator presents himself as a translator hewing to the letter of his single source: "as myn auctour seyde, so sey I" (2.18). Over its course, as is also known, he is snared by the story he tells;[34] as his *fidelis scriptura* lures him into engagement and partisanship, the illusion of his subjective presence comes to rival that of the characters whose story he transcribes. But it is precisely the unrevisability of that story that evokes the investments, measures them, and so evokes a self in the desire to be free of constraint. The moments when he strains to qualify the action ("Men seyn—I not—that she yaf hym hire herte," 5.1050) try to soften or delay the collision with fact. By them he tries to imagine that there is some room for choice in what his source says the story must bring. But two effects, unmistakable though unannounced, are observable in these moments. First, they speak now not of "myn auctour," but of "folk" (4.18), of "men" (5.1050). Somewhere on the way to the story's catastrophe, other sources have silently inserted themselves between the narrator and his Lollius; the implication that he has sought versions of the story alternate to his source insinuates the desire that would make him do that, the desire to find some grounds for denying what it tells him about Criseyde; and he thus comes to have the same unavowed but inferable motives that his characters do.

---

and Development of the Story of Troilus and Criseyde (London: Kegan Paul, Trench, Trübner, 1908).

33. "Le latin sivrai e la lettre, / Nule autre rien n'i voudrai metre, / S'ensi non com jol truis escrit," Benoît de Sainte-Maure, *Le roman de Troie,* ed. Léopold Constans (Paris: Firmin-Didot, 1904), ll 139–41.

34. Most intelligently by Morton W. Bloomfield, "Distance and Predestination in *Troilus and Criseyde,*" *PMLA* 72 (1957): 18–19; E. T. Donaldson, *Speaking of Chaucer* (New York: Norton, 1970), 80; Robert B. Burlin, *Chaucerian Fiction* (Princeton, NJ: Princeton University Press, 1977), 129–31; Carolyn Dinshaw, *Chaucer's Sexual Poetics* (Madison: University of Wisconsin Press, 1989), 39–47.

And second, the hard ineluctability of the story's "facts" is encountered as its known and unyielding future: what *must* ("moot") happen as it advances to its close. At the same time, the possibilities of complexity and freedom are visible in the uncertainties they reveal after the events that cannot be avoided have finally happened. It is not in the facts as they come, because they must come, but in the meanings and purposes of the characters once they have become facts, that the poem can find in its characters of a complexity answering to its investments in them. Once the future slides into the past, its brute facticity mellows into the blur of intentions retrospectively inferred; as intentions, they imply freedom, imply the whole room of psychic possibility that the future event, known only as event, cannot have. Criseyde becomes Diomede's lover, no way around that; but we do not know whether she gave him her heart. Not much, that; but when the future seems frozen into a dead certitude, the past remains rich with possibility.

This is true not only of the characters' empirical past, the store of experience, thought, and purpose that seems to lie behind each action and utterance. It is true also of the world in which they live. Recognition of the *Troilus'* "classicizing" character, a character that constitutes a part of what Chaucer really did to the *Filostrato,* is one of the clearest accomplishments of its recent scholarship.[35] The classicizing project—the actual serious research that underlay it, and the pose of antiquarianism that the narrator adopts— imagines subjective experience as something that has finite historical conditions systematically expressed in period conventions. The poem thus comes to create and then use a sense of historical difference *simpliciter* as a resource for evoking the palpability of its narrative world, through behaviors emerging from codes that we cannot expect ourselves to understand. It is like thoughts thought by another world. In the proem to Book II, Chaucer affects to worry that his characters' love-talk will seem foreign and hapless, and asks pardon if "any word be lame." In his defense, he explains that

> in forme of speche is chaunge
> Withinne a thousand yeer, and wordes tho
> That hadden pris, now wonder nyce and straunge
> Us thinketh hem. (2.22–25)

---

35. See, e.g., Morton W. Bloomfield, "Chaucer's Sense of History," *Journal of English and Germanic Philology* 51 (1952): 308; Alastair J. Minnis, *Chaucer and Pagan Antiquity* (Cambridge: D. S. Brewer, 1982); Barry Windeatt, "Chaucer and the *Filostrato,*" in *Chaucer and the Italian Trecento,* ed. Piero Boitani (Cambridge: Cambridge University Press, 1983), 171; and most magisterially and consequentially, John V. Fleming, *Classical Imitation and Interpretation in Chaucer's "Troilus"* (Lincoln: University of Nebraska Press, 1990).

Behind these lines, obviously, lies the observation of Horace's *Poetic Art:* "multa renascentur quae iam cecidere, cadentque / quae nunc sunt in honore vocabula" (70–71),[36] but the valuation ("pris") of which Chaucer speaks differs a little from Horace's *honor:* he means not what feels elegant but what passes as current, and the variations he plays on Horace's own *vocabula* work systematically in this direction. These lines conceive both language and behavior as produced by normative prescriptions law-like in their systematic character ("Ecch contree hath his lawes"; compare Horace, "*ius . . .* loquendi," 72), so ingrained that they make custom feel like nature. The lines are trying to ward off the charge, not that the Trojan love-talk is unintelligible, but that it is stupid. Their rebuttal supposes that when you understand a word but think it "lame," you have failed to grasp the structure of convention that makes it work. This structure is what he calls "usage" ("in sondry ages, / In sondry londes, sondry ben usages"; compare Horace, "usus," 71) and what we call "culture."[37] In other words, this passage makes language-change the metonym of all that makes the past foreign.

Variability in language has from the poem's beginning been the index of what we know we cannot fully see or grasp: when we are told that Criseyde stands first in beauty despite her widow's black ("natheless"), "Right as oure first lettre in now an A" (170–71), surely the point is not to think of Queen Anne,[38] but to think of those ages, like that narrated in this poem, when the "first letter" had been not *a,* but *alpha* or *aleph.*[39] But a case later in book 2 shows much more dramatically how Chaucer uses the structures of routine philological inference to create the sensation of a past accidentally happened upon, by making readers work at construing a locution unreflectively clear to the characters. Working still to sharpen Criseyde's desire for his news, Pandarus feigns a readiness to leave, as if he has forgotten his promise to reveal it. With literally a word, Criseyde detains him and dismisses everyone else:

---

36. Horace, *Opera,* ed. D. R. Shackleton Bailey (Stuttgart: Teubner, 1985).

37. In book 1, he uses the word to describe the framework of custom within which Trojan paganism goes about its "observances."

38. Originally suggested by John Livingston Lowes, "The Date of Chaucer's *Troilus and Criseyde,*" *PMLA* 23 (1908): 285–306, this understanding has remained uncontroversial in the dating of the poem; see, e.g., Barry Windeatt, *Oxford Guides to Chaucer: Troilus and Criseyde* (Oxford: Clarendon Press, 1992), 4–6; Derek Pearsall, *The Life of Geoffrey Chaucer* (Oxford: Blackwell, 1992), 168.

39. "Litterae Latinae et Graecae ab Hebraeis videntur exortae. Apud illos enim priud citum est aleph, deinde ex simili enuntiatione apud Graecos tractum est alpha, inde apud Latinos A"; Isidore of Seville, *Etymologiae sive originum,* ed. W. M. Lindsay (Oxford: Clarendon Press, 1911), 1.3.4 (not paginated). The biblical declaration "Ego sum alpha et omega" (Rev 1:8, 21:6, 22:13) kept before western eyes the first letter of the Greek alphabet; in the unlikely event that Chaucer forgot this circumstance, he would have been reminded by *Paradiso* 26: "Lo ben che fa contenta questa corte / Alfa e O è di quanta scrittura / mi legge Amore" (16–18).

"I have to doone
With yow, to speke of wisdom er ye go."
And everi wight that was aboute hem tho,
That herde that, gan fer awey to stonde (2.213–17)

"Wisdom" here clearly has specific illocutionary force, a delicate and inexplicit request for privacy; the quick unanimity of her retinue's withdrawal ("everi wight" "gan") shows that it is a conventional euphemism readily understood by all—that it is (in the sense just discussed) *usage*. But it is not Middle English usage. As far as I can find, "wisdom" appears nowhere else that with such euphemistic sense or illocutionary force, nor does the sense seem to be borrowed from any other language.[40] Chaucer invents an alien colloquialism, jargon of a past that never was, and leaves his readers to infer it from use and effect—and, if seized by a reflective mood, to notice that that meaning becomes inferentially available to them only by the accident of narrated detail: Criseyde's sentence alone—"I have to doone / With yow, to speke of wisdom" would, without the report of her household's reaction, have seemed merely to say what the English words convey—and only the report of its effect on Criseyde's retinue conveys the meaning that its use alone would not have done.

This conveys just how much can "change" when form of "speche" changes, just what difference the proem to book 2 describes. Things spoken differently feel different: "in som lond were al the game shent, / If that they ferde in love as men don here." The past is communicated *as* a past to the extent that it fails to communicate; the ignorance that keeps us from sharing its structures of feeling makes the importance of those structures felt through their absence.[41] But just when this passage in the proem to book 2

---

40. Neither OED nor MED, both *s.v.* "wisdom (n.)," shows any trace of the sense; nor does any passage cited in either show an undetected usage in this sense. Only MED's sense 4(c), uncertainly offered—"? a clever plan, an agreed-upon counsel"—comes at all close; its only instance is from the *Ludus Coventriae* and thus much later than Chaucer. Similarly, Lewis and Short, Forcellini, and Niermeyer offer no use of *prudentia, sapientia,* or *philosophia* as a concrete noun in any sense close to this one, or any passage using it as such; and the same is true in French for *prudence, sapience* or *science*. I might have missed something; but even if Chaucer created it off another language's usage, my point here stands. Similarly, the sense that Chaucer seems to construct is easy enough to derive—it relates most directly to those established senses that deal with practical reason and judgment (MED sense 3) and with counsel (MED sense 4)—but this is no objection, since the reader's ability to infer Criseyde's insinuation must depend on established Middle English senses of the word.

41. Chaucer would later find in the tale of Griselda a story as if designed to create for all readers a "modernity" that isolates them from the thought world of the story; see Anne Middleton, "The Clerk and His Tale: Some Literary Contexts," *Studies in the Age of Chaucer* 2 (1980): 121–22, and chapter 7 above.

gets most thoughtful about the baffling self-identity of the past, it takes a final step that undoes the whole effect by proving too much. What finally is most mysterious about the cultural past is how little mystery, after all the worry and bother, it actually presents:

> Ek scarsly ben ther in this place thre
> That have in love seid lik, and don, in al;
> For to thi purpos this may liken the,
> And the right nought. (42–46)

This would seem to demolish everything that went before, to make cultural difference nothing more than idiosyncrasy writ large, and the radical historical discontinuity on which this proem seemed to insist nothing more than the difference between how you ask a girl out and how your best friend does. But then history and selfhood define each other. One might say that the difference between the Trojan past and the English present is no more than the difference between *you* and *you;* but then one has also said that the difference between *you* and *you* is as vast as the difference between two historical worlds. The subjectivity-effect and the history-effect are indistinguishable.

The trick by which Chaucer flourishes a historical "alterity" and then whips it away again suggests how it is simply the desire for a mystery, to feel what would be needed to understand sympathetically, that constructs the fascination both of the past and of other people as literary narrative constructs it, even while acknowledging that the construction of character is as much a device as the construction of the pagan past. Chaucer flaunts this; and he flaunts at the same time its endlessly renewable character. Even as book 2's proem first promises us the touch of a world not ours and then stumbles into conceding that it's our world after all, it substitutes another past that can serve as object of the reader's desire. The deictic features in the lines just quoted—"scarsly ben ther in this place"; "this may liken the, / And the right nought"—imply a context of performance that has nowhere clearly been signaled up to this point. Readers of the *Troilus* could assume that they are the addressees to whom the poem has repeatedly spoken *until* they reach this address in book 2, which implies an audience present to the speaker and object of his physical gestures—required for the distinction between "the" and "the" in lines 45–46 to be meaningful—they discover that in fact they have not been hearing the author's address to themselves but overhearing an address never meant for them, an address implying that the poem was made for an audience whose immediacy to the occasion was so obvious as ordinarily to escape remark. This, in its turn, proves to be a feint. The poem does not try to sustain the fiction that it is script or transcript of some past performance whose occasion has vanished. It erects that fiction just long enough to trigger the sensation that readers with the book in their hands are adventitious witnesses of a vanished performance—that they cannot share in the immediacy of Chaucer's own presence and the shared privacies that familiarity encoded, that the book is only the mute image of an event now irrecoverable—and then drops it, training the sensibility in a particular kind of poetic effect, the investigative impulse whose literary use is to fill out the imagined reality of what at the same time it can still know to be unreal. At the end, Chaucer launches the poem into the world as a writen object ("Go, litel bok" 5.1786), a text that Gower or Strode might read and revise (5.1856–59).

These games enact a demonstration of an authrial power, the power to create a past just by creating the desire for it. But even within them there arises yet another notation of loss, in which a future paradoxically too well known not only accompanies but produces the effect of a lost past. In this case, it is not some element of the narrative the book proffers nor of the performance in which it might originally have proffered it, but of the book itself, the artifact that is the object of reading. After bidding the work farewell, the speaker's *congé* turns in the next stanza to the anxious contemplation of its future:

> for ther is so gret diversite
> In Englissh and in writyng of oure tonge,
> So prey I God that non myswrite the,
> Ne the mysmetre for defaute of tonge. (1793–96)

We have collectively loved these lines for what they have said about the textual entropy of manuscript culture and the formal instability of Middle English.[42] But their pedagogical utility does not explain why Chaucer wrote them. Textual entropy was a fact everyone knew. The difficulty of maintaining a correct copy of the Bible brought it early and often to visibility: there are "almost as many versions as there are copies," as St. Jerome had said in his *praefatio* to the four Gospels.[43] The very power of *mouvance* and variation

---

42. Compendiously and brilliantly expressed in Ralph Hanna, "Presenting Chaucer as Author," in *Medieval Literature: Texts and Interpretation*, ed. Tim William Machan (Binghamton, NY: Medieval and Renaissance Texts and Studies, 1991), 17–39.

43. "tot . . . exemplaria pene quot codices"; Jerome, *Praefatio in quattuor evangelia*, PL 29.526. The problem was visible merely upon informed reading of sources: "tot iam saeculis aliud legit Hieronymus, aliud Cyprianus, aliud Hilarius, aliud Ambrosius, aliud Augustinus"; Erasmus, *Apologia in Novum Testamentum*, in Desiderius Erasmus, *Ausgewählte Werke*, ed. Annemarie Holborn and Hajo Holborn (Munich: Beck, 1933), 166.

to explain the ordinary premises of medieval poetry shows that it needed no emphasis. Certainly the uncodified status of written English and its dialects—the "diversite / In Englissh and in writyng of oure tonge"—increased the probability of scribal error, especially of the sort that would incommode the music of verse-rhythm. Certainly, too, Chaucer's prayer acknowledges that the more successful his work proves, the more quickly and disastrously it will devolve from what he wrote. But this explains the reference of the lines, not the point of explaining what needed no explanation. That is their virtuosity: by recording common knowledge as if it were a pathos peculiar to himself, he sublimates that knowledge into a recognition that even the work you think you are reading is itself not quite available to you. Readers, holding in their hands a manuscript of the *Troilus*, could not know how far down the line of its dissemination their own copies are; could not know how much miswriting had disrupted the text being read, how often or how badly mismetering had smudged the verse.

THAT IS, the *Troilus and Criseyde* itself becomes a past unavailable to confident apprehension though witnessed by its fragmentary survivals. After teasing its audience with the thought that the minds of its characters, their histories severally and together, and the affective texture of the Trojan world are all objects beyond their ken—and the more to be desired for that—the poem concludes by translating *itself* beyond their ken, recalling that the book is not what Chaucer wrote but an imperfect record of it. Chaucer's integral *Troilus* is the lost past that remains lost, an object of investigative desire instead of an object of experience.

And this gives us the author, Chaucer, the putative real felt *as* real (just as the past is felt *as* past) by being encountered as the missing explanation of its apparent effects. This poem evokes its author not as the speaker and guarantor of the words on the page but as a biographical entity of uncertain relation with them. The stanza before his hopeless prayer for the continuing integrity of his work, he has hoped that, after this "tragedye" of *Troilus and Criseyde*, he will be given to "make in som comedye." This hope is easily read as looking forward to the *Canterbury Tales*[44]; whether it does, the line is designed to prompt just such speculations, to place the author as a historical datum insufficiently apprehended. Chaucer makes his own career a fact only partly explicable, like the thoughts of Criseyde and Pandarus, a fact that stays just

---

44. Donald R. Howard, *The Idea of the "Canterbury Tales"* (Berkeley and Los Angeles: University of California Press, 1976), 30–45; John M. Fyler, *Language and the Declining World in Chaucer, Dante, and Jean de Meun* (Cambridge: Cambridge University Press, 2007), 139.

out of sight behind the work's gaps and enigmas and so is to be sought with the greater energy. The history that produces the poem is produced as an effect by that poem, just as are the history that the poem portrays and the characters that people it. The history-effect devises the erotic intrigue in the story it tells, but also develops an authorial intrigue in the telling of it, and the latter is as much a part of its literary performance as is the former. Certainly there are things we can know about the *Troilus* that it does not know about itself; but it does not allow us to know which things these are.

nine

Seigneurial Poetics, or The Poacher, the Prikasour, The Hunt, and Its Oeuvre

FRANK GRADY

I F "THE REFOCUSING of literary studies on textuality itself as central to any possible adequate literary history of the Middle Ages appears to be the chief contribution that studies in medieval literature might offer to literary studies generally in the coming generation," then we have evidently still got a lot of work to do. That sentence is from Anne Middleton's contribution to the critical anthology *Redrawing the Boundaries*, published in 1992.[1] The essay is typically prescient—it predicted, for example, a productive dialogue between medieval and postcolonial studies almost a decade before a wave of publication in that area—but also a bit optimistic about the capacity of "literary studies generally" to receive its gift. In 2007, *PMLA* published an essay by Marjorie Levinson called "What Is New Formalism?" which took up specifically the "form after historicism" issue that serves as one of the organizing principles for this volume; that piece includes in its bibliography—that is, the extended bibliography of the on-line version, the one that includes three bibliographical appendices—the name of exactly one medievalist, Katherine O'Brien O'Keeffe, cited as editor of a collection about electronic editing, in a section entitled "Alternative Solutions to Problems Raised by New

---

1. Anne Middleton, "Medieval Studies," in *Redrawing the Boundaries: The Transformation of English and American Literary Studies*, ed. Stephen Greenblatt and Giles B. Gunn (New York: Modern Language Association of America, 1992), 26.

Formalism."[2] The optimism of Middleton's 1992 essay is not hard to understand, since its author has certainly done her part; reading Middleton's work has always meant attending to form and its histories, and to exploring in the fullest possible manner instances of formal innovation discovered in places where the rest of us would seldom think to look. It is a modest example of such practice that I offer in this essay.

I will advance the proposition that when Middle English writers juxtapose representations of hunting, that aristocratic amusement turned literary topos, with tales of tragedy (a term that here comprehends both stylized *de casibus* falls of fortune and a more general *ubi sunt* moralizing about the inevitable conclusion death brings to all earthly endeavor)—tales that are themselves compiled from Latin and French sources, or that are in other words translations—they are doing something more than just appealing to aristocratic tastes for recreative venery and Fortune-based historicizing. Rather, the depiction of hunting, the writing of tragedy, and the practice of translation are mutually implicated literary activities that, through their analogous imposition of form on contingent phenomena, contribute to the reproduction of what I would call the seigneurial poetics of later Middle English writing. The juxtaposition of these elements is surprisingly common in the period; in this essay I will confine myself to just two examples: the alliterative *Parlement of the Thre Ages* and Chaucer's *Monk's Tale*.

Textual Poaching in *The Parlement of the Thre Ages*

The Parlement is a dream-vision/debate-poem hybrid. In the prologue, the narrator strikes out on a solitary hunting expedition one May morning, and the first hundred lines describe in fine detail his successful stalking of a hart; once he has dressed his kill, he falls asleep and dreams of a debate between three allegorical personifications, Youthe (who extols the manifold pleasures of the aristocratic life), Medill Elde or Middle Age (who is most concerned with developing a healthy real-estate-based financial portfolio), and Elde, who harangues them both for their misguided priorities and takes up the bulk of the dream—indeed, almost half the poem—with an account of the Nine Worthies, all of whom were once great but all of whom are now dead. "Ne noghte es sekire to ȝoureself in certayne bot dethe" (635), he somewhat redundantly opines: "*Vanitas vanitatum & omnia vanitas*" (639).[3] In a short

---

2. *PMLA* 122 (2007): 558–69; the bibliographical appendices can be found at sitemaker.umich.edu/pmla_article.

3. Quotations are drawn from *The Parlement of the Thre Ages*, ed. M. Y. Offord, EETS 246 (London: Oxford University Press, 1959), hereafter cited parenthetically by line number.

eleven-line conclusion, the dreamer wakes at the sound of a bugle and heads back to town, presumably—though this is not made explicit—chastened by his experience.

The poem's first modern editor, Sir Israel Gollancz, described the *Parlement* long ago as a summary or epitome of familiar alliterative scenes and devices, a reputation it has suffered under ever since; forty years later, Dorothy Everett called it "a mosaic of conventions."[4] Obviously—speaking of conventions—I wish to disagree. Certainly we have been correctly taught to count among the more reliable elements of alliterative practice the *chanson d'aventure* countryside prologue, the morally dubious narrator, the debate of ostensibly irresolvable issues by allegorical personifications, the hunting and hawking topos, and even the macaronic conclusion to Elde's speech, in which he quotes, in addition to Ecclesiastes, the Office of the Dead and Luke's gospel. But to leap from that observation to regarding the *Parlement* as largely a collection of alliterative poetry's greatest hits begs a number of questions, most prominently the issue of just when invention hardens into convention. For example, while the yoking of the Nine Worthies to the *ubi sunt* theme is certainly underwritten by a familiar medieval moral logic, the *memento mori* motif and its penitential reflex, the connection is hardly an inevitable one; there are numerous examples of the Worthies being used uncritically to celebrate rather than undermine aristocratic ideologies. In fact, the chief source of the Worthies passage in the *Parlement* does exactly that. In Jacques de Longuyon's French romance *Les Voeux du Paon*, "The Vows of the Peacock," a 1312 addition to the large body of medieval French Alexander literature—typically considered to be the first literary appearance of the Worthies on the same billing anywhere—the Nine are introduced only to enhance the poet's praise of Porrus, son of Clarus, king of India and Alexander the Great's antagonist. Their purpose is comparative, purely secular and purely courtly. Thus the *Parlement*-author's use of the Nine might best be regarded as a formal experiment—a fairly safe and controlled experiment, perhaps, and in the eyes of some critics a failed one—but an experiment nonetheless.[5]

---

4. Quoted in Anne Kernan, "Theme and Structure in *The Parlement of the Thre Ages*," *Neuphilologische Mitteilungen* 75 (1974): 254.

5. William Kuskin discusses the flexibility of the Worthies topos in "Caxton's Worthies Series: The Production of Literary Culture," *ELH* 66 (1999): 511–51. The creation of a rhetorical *topos* that subordinates the earthly accomplishments of the Nine to the penitential imperative of Christian eschatology is in keeping with what seems to be a general rise in vernacular *de casibus* writing in the later Middle Ages, but even if we posit, as many critics do, some intermediate tradition of wholehearted moralization, there is a clear sense in which the author of the *Parlement* reinvents this particular wheel. Nor is the connection once made an inevitable one; in the Middle English tail-rhyme romance *Sir Degrevant*, a poem roughly contemporary with the *Parlement*, the three Christian Worthies appear in

In this context of formal literary experimentation I want to consider the juxtaposition of the poem's hunting scene and its Worthies series, and the way in which they produce mutually implicated organizational strategies for a literary undertaking like the *Parlement*. Such a move cannot help but call up *Piers Plowman* and the rich accounts of its formal intelligibility that Anne Middleton has provided; one thing that the *Parlement* shares with *Piers* is that *chanson d'avanture* prologue, something that Middleton long ago taught us to recognize as "the essential paradigm of literary fictive narration in this period."[6] The dense presence of conventions like this in a text organized according one of the central dynamics of the "formal" corpus of alliterative poetry—that is, the tension between the necessity of penitential action and the celebration of aristocratic ideology—makes *The Parlement of the Thre Ages* into, as it were, a rich man's *Piers Plowman*.

When the narrator sets out "In the monethe of Maye when mirthes bene fele," he describes himself as going out to try his luck ("my werdes to dreghe") at getting a shot at a deer, "happen as it myghte"—phrases that point to both the unbound and unpredictable character of these literary springtime outings, and to the contingent nature of this particular expedition, the hunting enterprise itself. The formal aspects of hunting—both the tactics of stalking and shooting and the rituals of brittling or butchering—

---

a mural decorating the chamber of Melidor, Degrevant's beloved, where they are not moralized but simply offered as one sign of Melidor's aristocratic taste and her refined sense of interior decoration. Another example would be Deschamps's 1386 *balade* "Against the Vices of the Times," which contrasts the debased state of contemporary chivalry with the lordly perfection represented by the Worthies. Finally, we can point to the entertainment presented to Queen Margaret in Coventry in 1455, in which each of the Worthies delivered a speech of praise and fealty to the Queen—hardly an occasion for *ubi sunt* moralizing. Given the difficulty of dating the *Parlement*, we could add Caxton's use of the Worthies in his 1485 preface to *Le Morte Darthur* to the "roughly contemporary" category as well. I owe the *Degrevant* citation to William Marvin, "Slaughter and Romance: Hunting Reserves in Late Medieval England," in *Medieval Crime and Social Control*, ed. Barbara Hanawalt and David Wallace (Minneapolis: University of Minnesota Press, 1999), 224–52; see also Roger Sherman Loomis, "Verses on the Nine Worthies," *Modern Philology* 15 (1917): 211–20, and Dennis V. Moran, "*The Parlement of the Thre Ages:* Meaning and Design," *Neophilologus* 62 (1978): 620–33.

6. Anne Middleton, "The Audience and Public of *Piers Plowman*," in *Middle English Alliterative Poetry and Its Literary Background: Seven Essays*, ed. David Lawton (Cambridge: D. S. Brewer, 1982), 114. She continues: "In presenting a speaker intent on something else—usually solitary diversion and pleasure, though sometimes a routine form of devotion—who happens upon truth or transformation unawares, in a place, time, and state of mind where it was least looked for, this formula thematizes the role of the fictive and the nugatory as a method of a specifically literary didacticism. In literary fiction, it implicitly argues, truth presents itself first to peripheral vision, as it were, and remains active and visible only so long as the adventurer defers uttering a correct verdict on its nature. This mode of fictive presentation disclaims the literal historical truth, or divine or genuinely mystical origin, for the marvel disclosed, even while it appropriates the familiar narrative details of reports which do make such claims . . . the 'truth' of its discourse is purely contingent. In playing upon a wide range of discourses which command belief, it offers an exercise of affective memory and recognition for *salus anime*."

seek to make a basically contingent undertaking into an expression of lordly ceremonial control. Hunting in the medieval aristocratic manner is always a form of organizing the world, first into groupings of predator and prey and then, with increasingly fine distinctions, into increasingly precise categories: which is the noblest beast of the chase? what is the appropriate hawk for an earl? how should the spoils be apportioned? Moreover, hunting as it is represented in English texts also involves the ongoing invention and renewal of an appropriate and specific language, a vocabulary of the chase, a phenomenon that will be familiar to anyone who can recall working through the third fitt of *Sir Gawain and the Green Knight* for the first time. The vernacular hunting manuals of the era, like the *Master of Game* or the *Boke of St. Albans*, are as much taxonomies as they are practical guides, and the author of the *Parlement*, who describes with technical precision both the brittling and the hawking enjoyed by Youthe, is clearly a close reader of this language too, someone who recognizes that it is the formal description of the hunt that truly establishes its capacity to bring order to the enterprise, and to the part it plays in aristocratic life.[7]

Critical attempts to explain the relevance of the hunting prologue to the body of the poem tend to hew to the moral/allegorical line, arguing that the hunt is a pride-of-life episode that looks forward to the penitential correction of the dream vision, or that it introduces the mortality theme that, according to Russell Peck, unifies the poem. "Death," writes Peck, "is the masterhunter whom none can escape,"[8] and the poem's lesson is that the hunter, too, is being stalked. Thus the portion of the poem frequently celebrated for its wealth of realistic detail, right down to the gnats pestering the narrator as he stands motionless waiting for a shot, is at the same time seen as being allegorically freighted—particularly the cutting out of the "corbyns bone," that piece of gristle from the breastbone traditionally thrown to the ravens during the brittling. To paraphrase Elde, there's nothing so certain, in accounts of the prologue, as the critics' morbid reflection on the significance of the "corbyns bone."[9]

---

7. I do not put any stock in the notion that the author was somehow writing entirely from personal experience; the *Parlement* is a fully bookish poem in all respects. That does not mean he was unacquainted with hunting, just that the poem is not some sort of transcription of the experience. For recent discussions of the linguistic and pedagogical work of aristocratic hunting literature, see Trevor Dodman, "Hunting to Teach: Class, Pedagogy, and Maleness in *The Master of Game* and *Sir Gawain and the Green Knight*," *Exemplaria* 17 (Fall 2005): 413–44; and Ad Putter, "The Ways and Words of the Hunt: Notes on *Sir Gawain and the Green Knight*, *The Master of Game*, *Sir Tristrem*, *Pearl*, and *Saint Erkenwald*," *Chaucer Review* 40 (2006): 354–85.

8. Russell Peck, "The Careful Hunter in *The Parlement of the Thre Ages*," *ELH* 39 (1972): 334.

9. A survey of the criticism concerning *The Parlement* quickly reveals two recurrent preoccupations that to a great extent frame, and constrain, many accounts of the poem. The first is this question

Some readers will remember that the hunting narrator of the *Parlement* is in fact a poacher, a revelation made 95 lines into the poem when he describes hiding his spoils from the "fostere [forester] of the fee." Now, poaching was an aristocratic pastime too; records of the forest eyre show that offenses against the venison—that is, the illegal taking of deer on the royal forests—were regularly committed by knights, barons, lords, abbots, and even the occasional archbishop. Such accounts help to explain why an episode of poaching might appeal to and even titillate an aristocratic audience. It also suggests why the poaching prologue is appropriate for the *Parlement*, a poem that both celebrates and condemns the aristocratic "lifestyle": poaching is both illegal and widespread, a transgressive activity that is subject to laws that were both specific in their strictures and, according to Barbara Hanawalt, laxly enforced in practice[10]—specifically designed, one might say, to advertise the license enjoyed by aristocrats who get to flout the very rules that establish and protect their privileges. The *Parlement* implies an analogy

---

of relevance, and the second is the question of proportion: if the plainly penitential moral delivered by Elde at line 635 is in fact the poem's chief message, why does its chief messenger spend 283 lines—three-quarters of his speech, and almost half the poem—extolling the matchless virtues of the Nine Worthies, in language that is long on praise and surprisingly short on rhetoric of the *memento mori, contemptus mundi, de casibus,* or *ubi sunt* variety?

Typically, a successful (or at least plausible) answer to one of these questions precludes an equally successful answer to the other. An argument like Peck's must underplay the poem's efforts at a realistic representation of hunting in favor of a moral reading, while attempts to account for Elde's "diffuse," "rambling," and "allusive" speech typically have to adopt the opposite presumption—that is, that the poem is not so thoroughly saturated with prevenient penitential feeling as moral readings of the prologue suggest. Either Elde himself is a flawed and ineffective spokesman for the poem's *moralitee* (that is, because he is a realistic representation of a rambling old crank), or the digressive account of the Worthies is meant to be enjoyed for its own sake, as an indulgence of the aristocratic taste for romance heroism. This brief reverie is nevertheless recuperated by the rhetorical bracketing of Elde's succinct *memento mori* pointing—a line here, a line there, a dozen or so lines at the end. Thus this argument explains away the problem of proportion by inversion, suggesting that the solution lies in giving greater weight to fewer lines, the lines that directly articulate the penitential theme—a plausible position whose only flaw is that it is really no more plausible than its opposite. Representative examples of both approaches, largely established in the 1970s, include R. A. Waldron, "The Prologue to 'The Parlement of the Thre Ages,'" *Neuphilologische Mitteilungen* 73 (1972): 786–94; Beryl Rowland, "The Three Ages of *The Parlement of the Thre Ages,*" *Chaucer Review* 9 (1975): 342–52; Thorlac Turville-Petre, "The Ages of Man in the *Parlement of the Thre Ages,*" *Medium Ævum* 46 (1977): 66–76; Moran, "*The Parlement of the Thre Ages*: Meaning and Design"; Turville-Petre, "The Nine Worthies in *The Parlement of the Thre Ages,*" *Poetica* 11 (1979): 28–45; David V. Harrington, "Indeterminacy in *Winner and Waster* and *The Parliament of the Three Ages,*" *Chaucer Review* 20 (1986): 246–57; and Lisa Kiser, "Elde and His Teaching in *The Parlement of the Thre Ages,*" *Philological Quarterly* 66 (1987): 303–14. There is a brief but characteristically incisive account of the poem in A. C. Spearing's *Medieval Dream Poetry* (Cambridge: Cambridge University Press, 1976), 134–37.

10. Barbara Hanawalt, "*Men's Games,* King's Deer: Poaching in Medieval England," *Journal of Medieval and Renaissance Studies* 18 (1988): 175–83. See more generally William Perry Marvin, *Hunting Law and Ritual in Medieval English Literature* (Cambridge: D. S. Brewer, 2006).

between that activity, morally suspect but enthusiastically pursued, and its larger analysis of the aristocratic life in general, which Elde finds full of spiritually useless practices that are nevertheless minutely and lovingly described by Ʒouthe.

In fact there's yet another analogy operating here, one that connects poaching with the consumption and composition of poetry itself. In making this claim I follow Michel de Certeau, who himself borrows the term "poaching" to describe the kind of "playful, protesting, fugitive" (175) reading practice that can appropriate a given or authoritative text for its own contradictory or alternative or transgressive purposes. In the Worthies passage the author of *The Parlement of the Thre Ages* is doing something similar with his received sources, adapting—poaching—a series of authoritative French (and sometimes Latin) texts to fit the needs of his own vernacular exercise. Jacques de Longuyon disposes of the Worthies in an economical ninety-five lines, while the *Parlement*-poet's various additions, omissions, and dilations triples that length. Hector's portrait, for example, is supplemented by material drawn from Guido delle Collonne's Latin *Historia destructionis Troiae*—a text, as James Simpson has pointed out, with a very significant presence in English literary culture in the fourteenth and fifteenth centuries,[11] and in this case a source that is itself obscured by the *Parlement*-poet's very Chaucerian citation of "Dittes and Dares," Dictys Cretensis and Dares Phrygius, at the end the passage. The poet's account of Alexander is a pastiche of the ancillary Alexander romance the *Fuerre de Gadres* and the *Voeux du Paon* itself—that is, the events that frame Jacques' account of the Nine Worthies are in the *Parlement* incorporated into the Worthies passage itself. The *Voeux* material on Julius Caesar and Arthur is similarly supplemented with British legends and histories, and finally Charlemagne, who merits a summary nine lines in the French poem, receives more than sixty in the *Parlement* that merge the story of *Sir Ferumbras*—perhaps I should say some version of the Ferumbras story—with the events of the *Song of Roland*. In the course of violating the integrity of his source-texts by translating, "in-eching," and (as already noted) remoralizing their words, he obviously manifests his own poetic stealth and cunning and patience; in this sense, the reconstruction of a new poem out of disparate parts mirrors inversely the deft dismembering of the deer that is one measure of the poacher's expertise. The poet is perhaps not as successful as his poacher in hiding his handiwork—at one point he has Joshua parting the Red Sea—but the analogy is hard to ignore. It's a

---

11. James Simpson, "The Other Book of Troy: Guido delle Colonne's *Historia destructionis Troiae* in Fourteenth- and Fifteenth-Century England," *Speculum* 73 (1998): 397–423; Michel de Certeau, *The Practice of Everyday Life,* trans. Steven Rendall (Berkeley: University of California Press, 1984).

potentially productive one, considering the degree to which Middle English alliterative poetry—indeed, Middle English poetry generally—comprises an extended exercise in the translation and adaptation of texts from other literary traditions, though I admit that in trying to recruit "poachers" who serve aristocratic tastes into de Certeau's realm of the playful, the protesting, and the fugitive, I make a somewhat counterintuitive claim.[12]

Let me offer another one, which will help move the discussion toward Chaucer's Monk: Elde's attempt to shoehorn all earthly events into one master narrative in the *Parlement*[13] is a gesture that paradoxically calls into question the power of this sort of formalism to produce meaning. It is typically the case that tragedies of Fortune or *ubi sunt* narratives also always *pose* the problem of form; by compelling all events to conform to the same narrative, such strategies actually call that problem to our attention, by highlighting the various mismatches of story and moralization, our divided emotional responses, and the divergence of source and text. The work of organization is inevitably foregrounded, though the text might try to obscure the problematic nature of that work by piling up instances—as indeed Elde does, by following up his account of the Worthies with a list of wise men and famous lovers who were also laid low by death. Maura Nolan would perhaps call this a species of "virtuous prolongation," and my thinking here has been strongly influenced by her recent work on Fortune in Lydgate and Langland, particularly the idea that "thinking about Fortune poses the problem of poetic function."[14] To put it another way, there is an additional operation of translation and adaption at stake in Elde's harangue: the problem of translating moralizing discourse into moral action, of deriving practical spiritual guidance from what Ralph Hanna calls, in his contribution to this volume, a rhetoric of catechesis based on iterative structure (all those Worthies, all now dead and buried).[15] The *Parlement* leaves that problem to us individual poachers, as it were—a standard maneuver, really, for the dream-vision form.

---

12. For recent reflections on Middle English as "a translated and actively translating language," see Michelle R. Warren, "Translation," in *Oxford Twenty-First Century Approaches to Literature: Middle English*, ed. Paul Strohm (Oxford: Oxford University Press, 2007), 58.

13. Even Elde's switch from the personal to the exemplary mode is striking; after starting with a chillingly effective reminder to his interlocutors that what they are, he once was, and what he is they will be ("Makes ȝour mirours bi me, men, bi ȝoure trouthe")—lines that reveal the poem's affinity with the "Three Living and the Three Dead" tradition—he suddenly turns to the exemplary mode with the Worthies, as if his own example, or the personal mode itself, is insufficient.

14. Maura Nolan, "Lydgate's Literary History: Chaucer, Gower, and Canacee," *Studies in the Age of Chaucer* 27 (2005): 87. By "function" Nolan here means "role": "What, in a world governed by Fortune, is poetry *for?*" she asks. In this essay I'm more interested in how poetry works—how the motif of Fortune or the *ubi sunt* contributes to its function as poetry.

15. See chapter 6.

The *Monk's Tale*, on the other hand, is more specific in locating the resistance to its prescriptions.

Hunting, Holy Men, and *homo grammaticus*

The broad similarities between the *Parlement* and Chaucer's *Monk's Tale* should be evident; they are each ostensibly collections of lugubrious exempla, designed to convey a conventional medieval moral about the instability of earthly joys: "Lat no man truste on blynd prosperitee," as the Monk puts it.[16] Their rhetoric is slightly different; the *Parlement* applies the *ubi sunt* motif to the template of the Nine Worthies, while the *Monk's Tale*, following the model of Boccaccio's *De casibus virorum illustrium*, tells tragedies of Fortune, in which the unanticipated but simultaneously inevitable interventions of that goddess cast those who once stood in high prosperity into misery, such that they endeth wretchedly. Because Fortune, like death, cannot be propitiated or avoided—"ther nas no remedie / To bring hem out of hir adversitee," laments the Monk—one is tempted to say "nine of one, seventeen of the other," and lump these poems together. Moreover, criticism of both poems has produced a similar dissensus of opinion. Just as the *Parlement* is either a poem that relentlessly drives home its straightforward *memento mori* message through its repeated exposure of worldly achievement's inevitable submission to death or a poem that undermines its own moral clarity and its penitential spokesman Elde by virtue of its indulgent celebration of the pleasures and accomplishments it is trying to disavow, so the *Monk's Tale* is either a turgid, repetitive, and reductive collection of moralizing tales that reveals its narrator's lack of philosophical sophistication, or a tale that satirizes its teller's inability to bring his stories to heel, exemplified on the one hand by his indulgent treatment of, say, the "myghty queene" Zenobia or "worthy, gentil Alisandre," and on the other by his inability to distinguish adequately between the consequences of human betrayal and the effects of divine intervention. It should be clear by now that such a difference of opinion—in fact, this exact difference of opinion—is inevitable: not only does it reproduce the great divide in twentieth-century criticism of medieval poetry between those who argue for the inescapable immanence of the penitential theme and those who want to attribute some substantive value to the celebration and representation of the secular world and its various

---

16. All quotations from Chaucer are drawn from *The Riverside Chaucer*, gen. ed. Larry D. Benson, 3rd ed. (Boston: Houghton Mifflin, 1987), here VII.1997.

inhabitants, but it also reproduces contemporary medieval anxieties about the conflict between aristocratic accomplishment in the world and penitential withdrawal from it, the seigneurial bind that routinely expresses itself textually in *de casibus* writing.[17]

The *Parlement* and the *Monk's Tale* have another thing in common: they both have hunting narrators, and hunting narrators whose pursuit of the sport is equally transgressive. The *Parlement's* dreamer is a poacher, whereas the Monk hunts—"Of prikying and of huntyng for the hare / Was al his lust, for no cost wold he spare" (I.191–92)—despite the fact that such pursuits were formally forbidden to clerics.[18] The Monk, however, "yaf nat of that text a pulled hen, / That seith that hunters ben nat hooly men."[19] It's a commonplace that the Monk's *General Prologue* portrait is heavily ironized by virtue of this pithy resistance to clerical and, elsewhere in the portrait, specifically monastic ideals. But it's worth noting that both Jill Mann's survey of the estates literature and David Knowles's review of monastic visitation records turn up a surprising small number of hunting monks[20]; what

---

17. Relevant here is David Wallace's reading of the *Monk's Tale* as expressing Chaucer's response to a dual (and dueling) literary inheritance: the praise of great men's lives modeled in Petrarch's *De viris illustribus,* and the focus on the fall of princes as found in Boccaccio's *De casibus virorum illustrium.* Wallace argues that Chaucer aligns himself with Boccaccio's critical focus on the falls of antisocial, tyrannical great men and against the model of Petrarchan absolutism, while characteristically mentioning Petrarch in the text (at 2326) but obscuring any indebtedness to Boccaccio. For Wallace, the tale is "energized chiefly by pressures external to its own formal constitution" (ultimately Chaucer's own Ricardian moment, which would produce its own discourse of tyranny); my argument here is that the potential for both the celebration of secular achievement and the anatomizing of a tragic fall is inherent in the *de casibus* form, available for activation in any particular literary tradition, vernacular or Humanist, medieval or modern. See David Wallace, *Chaucerian Polity: Absolutist Lineages and Associational Forms in England and Italy* (Stanford, CA: Stanford University Press, 1997), 299–336 (quotation from 299).

18. By the Council of Vienne in 1312; David Knowles, *The Religious Orders in England,* vol. 2: *The End of the Middle Ages* (Cambridge: Cambridge University Press, 1955), 246–47. Coincidentally, the date of *Les Voeux du Paon is 1312.*

19. Probably a reference to Gratian, says the Riverside (807).

20. Jill Mann has traced the contribution that the "hunting cleric" stereotype makes to the *General Prologue's* irony, and it is true that in the satiric tradition there are plenty of such accusations; close at hand we have the example of Langland's Sloth, who is better at hare-hunting than understanding the Psalms:

"I have be preest and person passynge thritty wynter,
Yet kan I neyther solve ne synge ne seintes lyves rede,
But I kan fynden in a feld or in a furlang an hare
Bettre than in *Beatus vir* or in *Beati omnes*
Construe clausemele and kenne it to my parisshens."
(*The Vision of Piers Plowman* B 5.416–20; ed. A. V. C. Schmidt, 2nd ed. [London: Dent, 1995])

But it turns out that among the ranks of the hunting clerics there really *aren't* that many monks, something that Mann admits when she suggests that Chaucer "derives this feature from the general

we see in the Monk's portrait may be not so much the deployment of a stereotype as the invention or at least stabilization of one. If we think of the Monk's hunting habit as not so much enjoined upon Chaucer by satiric tradition as bequeathed by him to subsequent generations of poets and critics, then perhaps we are freed to look again at his opinion of the text "That seith that hunters ben nat hooly men," and to find in it not just the perspective of a newfangled "outridere" but a pithy expression of Youthe's take on Elde's moralizing. That is, the Monk's comment suggests that hunting should be treated contingently rather than morally, as a seigneurial pastime rather than as an eschatologically freighted undertaking. It's not just a rejection of a monastic rule, but also a rejection of a moralizing perspective on worldly activity as such.

Of course that moralizing perspective is exactly the one embodied in his tale, a fact that is often seen as something of a surprise. The Monk may be an "outridere," but his *Tale* comes straight out of the scriptorium, and we learn in the prologue to his tale why it is that he doesn't spend too much time in his cell—it's apparently crammed floor-to-ceiling with tragedies. In addressing the question of why Chaucer saddles his hunting monk with a series of *de casibus* anecdotes, though, I am going to suppress the impulse to discover some irrefutable psychological continuity between portrait and tale, and instead champion the Monk's formalism as a token of a thoroughgoing if not entirely consistent attention to problems of literary form. This formalism inheres in all aspects of his appearances in the *Canterbury Tales*,[21] not only the formally constraining narrative pattern of *de casibus* tragedy, and in the Monk's devotion to hunting, which seeks to make a entirely contingent

---

stereotype of the cleric" (*Chaucer and Medieval Estates Satire* [Cambridge: Cambridge University Press, 1973], 24). There is certainly one well-known monk, the Leicester abbot William de Cloune (d. 1378), "the most famous and notable hunter of hares among all the lords of the realm," according to Knighton's *Chronicon* and subject of a 1939 essay by Ramona Bressie that is now memorialized in the notes to the *Riverside Chaucer*, and in which she suggests that Cloune might have been a model for the Monk. What's most interesting about Bressie's essay is the way in which its opening assertion—"Hunting monks seem to have been common in Chaucer's time" ("A Governour Wily and Wys," *Modern Language Notes* 54 [1939]: 477)—cites as evidence the work of Chaucer, Langland, and Gower, drawing what seems to me a rather tightly knit hermeneutic circle. Knowles, writing in the second volume of his survey of the religious orders in England, makes a similar observation: "Hunting has often been regarded as a common monastic diversion of the Middle Ages. Chaucer and Langland are no doubt primarily responsible for this impression, but it must be acknowledged that neither in visitation records nor in the decrees of chapter does it appear as one of the most formidable causes of laxity" (*The Religious Orders in England*, 2:246–47). See also Nicholas Orme, "Medieval Hunting: Fact and Fancy," in *Chaucer's England: Literature in Historical Context*, ed. Barbara Hanawalt (Minneapolis: University of Minnesota Press, 1992), esp. 134–36.

21. And it is often derided as a character flaw, a sign of his "failed sociality or failed participation in the spiritual body," as Aranye Fradenburg puts it: Fradenburg, *Sacrifice Your Love: Psychoanalysis, Historicism, Chaucer* (Minneapolis: University of Minnesota Press, 2003), 139.

undertaking into a routinized expression of lordly privilege, but also in the strict requirements of translation and versification, to which he pays unusually close attention.²²

The *Prologue* to the *Monk's Tale* is in fact rich in the language and gestures of the academic prologues or *accessus ad auctores* characteristic of scholastic and university texts, as they have been described by Alastair Minnis and Rita Copeland, a fact that perhaps deserves more attention than it has received. Indeed, it takes the general form of an accessus, complete with a *nomen auctoris* provided by the Host: "But, by my trouthe, I knowe nat youre name. / Wher shal I calle yow my lord daun John, / Or daun Thomas, or elles daun Albon?" (VII.3119–20). There is also an implicit *vita auctoris* embedded here, as the Host goes on to speculate that "Upon my feith, thou art some officer, / Som worthy sexteyn, or some celerer, / For by my fader soule, as to my doom, / Thou art a maister whan thou art at hoom; / No pover cloysterer, ne no novys, / But a governour, wily and wys . . ." (VII.3125–30). Additionally, we find in the Monk's own words not only an account of his other *opera auctoris* ("I wol doon al my diligence, / As fer as sowneth into honestee, / To telle yow a tale, or two, or three. / And if you list to herkne hyderward, / I wol yow seyn the lyf of Seint Edward; / Or ellis, first, tragedies wol I telle, / Of which I have an hundred in my celle"; VII.3159–62), but also a vocabulary that draws upon Latinate aca-

---

22. What do we gain by thinking of the *Monk's Tale* as an exercise in translation? That it is one is beyond question, as it draws on a number of sources: Boccaccio's *De casibus virorum illustrium* and *De claris mulieribus*, Boethius's *Consolation*, Dante's *Comedy*, Ovid, possibly Vincent of Beauvais's *Speculum historiale*, and—cited within the tale—Lucan, Suetonius, Valerius Maximus, and the Vulgate Old Testament. Despite this range of sources, though, we have not been accustomed to think of the tale in terms of translation. One reason for this is the fact that the *Monk's Tale* is narrated in the shadow of a tale that we *do* think of in that way—indeed, almost exclusively as a translation—the *Tale of Melibee*. Moreover, given that Melibee is a close rendering of a single source, Renaud de Louens's *Livre de Melibee et de Dame Prudence*, and thanks to the fact that it is assigned in the *Canterbury Tales* to the pilgrim Chaucer, we have been encouraged to think of it as an exemplary instance of Chaucer's practice of translation, the rendering of a single text in whatever language into Middle English: the *Boece* from Latin, *Melibee* or the *Roman* from French, *Troilus* or the *Knight's Tale* from Italian. Finally, the correspondence of modes—Renaud's prose translated into Chaucer's—tends oddly enough to obscure the considerably more impressive feat of translation in the *Monk's Tale*, where a variety of different sources (for the most part prose) are reduced (an advisedly chosen word) to the eight-line ababbcbc stanza that Chaucer uses in only two other places, in "An ABC" (a translation from Guillaume de Deguileville's *Pèlerinage de vie humaine*) and in the short poem "The Former Age" (in large part a translation of *Consolation* 2m5). The appearance of this "early" stanza form can foreground for us the fact of translation, paradoxically through the way it obscures the differences among the *Tale*'s sources. Wallace, commenting on the stylistic aims of this translation project, observes that "The *Monk's Tale* falls, or moves uncertainly, between its attempt to develop and sustain an elevated 'heigh style' that approximates humanist Latin and the pull of a native vernacular" (*Chaucerian Polity*, 313).

demic discourse and that is most expressive and connotative in that context: "declaryng" (3172), "mateere" (3174), and "manere" (3181).[23]

Taking the *Monk's Tale* as an example of what Copeland calls "secondary translation"[24] provides the Monk's opening definition of tragedy with a new intelligibility, as insofar as it prospectively seeks to govern the import of his little tales it represents the imposition of an *intentio auctoris* through which the vernacular translator becomes vernacular *auctor*. "Tragedie is to seyn a certeyn storie, / As olde bookes maken us memorie, / Of hym that stood in greet prosperitee, / And is yfallen out of heigh degree / Into myserie, and endeth wrecchedly. / And they ben versified communely / Of six feet, which men

---

23. Kurt Olsson has made a similar suggestion in "Grammar, Manhood, and Tears: The Curiosity of Chaucer's Monk," *Modern Philology* 76 (1978): 1–17. For the academic vocabulary see Rita Copeland, *Rhetoric, Hermeneutics, and Translation in the Middle Ages: Academic Traditions and Vernacular Texts* (Cambridge: Cambridge University Press, 1991), 189ff.

24. "Secondary translation" is the process through which a vernacular writer uses "the techniques of exegetical translation to produce, not a supplement to the original, but a vernacular substitute for that original" (Copeland, *Rhetoric, Hermeneutics, and Translation,* 179). In secondary translation—and here I oversimplify Copeland's work—the vernacular author borrows from the scholarly *accessus* (especially the *accessus Ovidiani*) the hermeneutical procedure by which a later academic reader of, say, Ovid's *Heroides* would try to establish a unifying *intentio auctoris* to make sense of a heterogeneous collection of tales, and uses this method, as Copeland says, "as the point of invention for his own text" (190). It's akin to—and here I *really* oversimplify Copeland's claims—that moment when students ask if maybe we could just tell them what they should be looking for in the new poem or novel we've just assigned. One of Copeland's examples is the Prologue to the *Legend of Good Women,* and perhaps it would be most useful to observe how she describes it: "But in Chaucer's Prologue, that single, unifying *intentio* . . . constitutes a *prospectus* to the *Legend;* it represents the *prospective* reasoning of the poet himself that brought the collection into being. But Chaucer's prospective stance is also curiously akin to the stance of the exegetes: in identifying Ovid's *intentio* from their own historically belated position, the exegetes arrogated to their perceptions a certain prospective power" (189). Though Copeland's argument insofar as it attends to Chaucer is largely confined to the *Legend,* we can substitute "Monk's Prologue" for "Legend of Good Women Prologue" here without producing any significant misrepresentation of what's going on in the former, as the *Legend* and *Monk's Tale* have a lot in common—both are univocal, inorganic tale collections that hew to a single reiterated narrative line, and both are offered in some kind of spirit of resistance to an external demand: it may be a bit counterintuitive to suggest that the *Legend's* God of Love, who demands stories of good women, and the *Tales'* Harry Bailly, who inadvertently tells us more than he wants to about a woman named Goodelief, are similar kinds of readers (and certainly they have different degrees of influence over the tellers whose tales they solicit), but I think that on one level they are; they are both confined within a fairly narrow horizon of expectation, however much their individual horizons may differ. Moreover, both poems are highly rhetorical; Copeland cites the use of *occupatio* and *abbreviatio* that characterize the narration of the *Legend's* various chapters, while the *Monk's Tale,* full of *repetitio, exclamatio, apostrophatio, superlatio, oppositio,* and other figures, was long ago judged by Manly to be the most rhetorical of the *Tales,* "with nearly 100 percent. of rhetoric" (in second place is the *Manciple's Tale,* with a measly 61 percent). Jahan Ramazani, "Chaucer's Monk: The Poetics of Abbreviation, Aggression, and Tragedy," *Chaucer Review* 27 (1993): 263, quoting J. M. Manly, "Chaucer and the Rhetoricians," repr. in *Chaucer Criticism: The Canterbury Tales, ed.* Richard J. Schoeck and Jerome Taylor (Notre Dame, IN: University of Notre Dame Press, 1960), 268–90.

clepen exametrron. / In prose eek been endited many oon, / And eek in mee-
tre, in many a sondry wyse. / Lo, this declaryng oghte ynogh suffise"—these
lines have often occasioned critical comment due to the Monk's unusually
close attention to matters of prosody as well as content, and if we think
about this attention in the context of academic translation as described by
Copeland, we can see how the prospective application of *intentio* is, from
the perspective of medieval rhetorical practice, what we have come to (mis)
recognize as the "reductiveness" of the Monk's formulaic tragedies.

Modern critics are not the only ones to have found the iterative structure
of the tale more than they could bear; in a sense the history of its reception
begins even before the tale can come to a proper end. In the *Parlement of the
Thre Ages*, the debate about the best way to characterize the exigencies of the
aristocratic life concludes, if imperfectly, with Elde's *ubi sunt* series; in the
Monk's Tale this order is reversed, and his series of tragedies is what prompts
the dispute. It is disguised as an interruption:

"Hoo!" quod the Knyght, "good sire, namoore of this!
That ye han seyd is right ynough, ywis,
And muchel moore; for litel hevynesse
Is right ynough to muche folk, I gesse.
I seye for me, it is a greet disese,
Whereas men han been in greet welthe and ese,
To heeren of hire sodeyn fal, allas!
And the contrarie is joye and greet solas,
As whan a man hath been in povre estaat,
And clymbeth up and wexeth fortunat,
And there abideth in prosperitee.
Swich thyng is gladsom, as it thynketh me,
And of swich thyng were goodly for to telle."
"Ye," quod oure hooste, "by seint poules belle!
Ye seye right sooth; this Monk he clappeth lowde.
He spak how Fortune covered with a clowde
I noot nevere what; and als of a tragedie
Right now ye herde, and, pardee, no remedie
It is for to biwaille ne compleyne
That that is doon, and als it is a peyne,
As ye han seyd, to heere of hevynesse.
Sire Monk, namoore of this, so God yow blesse!
Youre tale anoyeth al this compaignye."
(2767–89)

This outburst expresses in narrative form exactly the philosophical stand-off captured in the *Parlement*, and indeed expresses it as a problem of the form of narrative: which way do you want your story arc to go? In one sense it is as if Youth and Medill Elde, rather than letting Elde have the last word, get to speak again at the end of the *Parlement*'s dream, the one praising once more the attraction of tales of aristocratic accomplishment and the other decrying the irrelevancy of *ubi sunt* episodes to the bourgeois values he would presumably share with that fair burgess, the Host. The Knight, in fact, seems to belong to exactly the same interpretive community as Youthe, as both extol the recreative payoff of a happy ending; at the end of a hard day's hawking, Youthe likes to retire "Riche romance to rede and rekken the soothe / Of kempes and of conquerours, of kynges full noblee, / How thay wirchipe and welthe wanne in thaire lyves" (250–52).

It is of course conventional to see in this incident an expression of estate antagonism; we don't have to subscribe to R. E. Kaske's characterization of the Monk as a parody of the Knight, here receiving his comeuppance,[25] to appreciate the animus unleashed when a Knight speaks directly (if politely) to a Monk about the content of a clerical discourse that he assumes is directed at him, or at least at his class. For all that's conventional about the Monk's *de casibus* moralizing, it's still a rather pointed reminder of the "brotelnesse" of aristocratic privilege, and we could certainly see Chaucer—by having the Knight's interruption precede the more prosaic objections of the Host—as engaged in restoring some life to a conflict that the Monk's performance has rather drained of its vitality.

But in fact what is chiefly represented here is an intramural conflict of the seigneurial classes, one from which the bourgeois host is excluded in a fundamental way (just as Medill Elde gets the fewest lines in the *Parlement*).[26] The Monk is, indeed, an antitype of the Knight, both in the *General Prologue* and in the epilogue to his tale, but the Knight is also an avatar of the Monk, because they both face, from different angles, the same choice between worldliness and withdrawal. Larry Scanlon expresses the Monk's choice in these useful terms:

> When Chaucer makes his Monk both moralist and outrider, he articulates the Church's dilemma in its broadest terms. The Monk combines in one

---

25. Robert E. Kaske, "The Knight's Interruption of the Monk's Tale," *ELH* 24 (1957): 249–68.

26. Note that his objection to the *Tale* derives from ignorance rather than class anxiety—"He spak how Fortune covered with a clowde / I noot nevere what"—and of course both Knight and Monk are lords from the perspective of the Host, the former "Sire Knyght . . . my mayster and my lord" (*GP* 837) and the latter "My lord, the Monk" (VII.1924).

character two forms of confrontation between the Church and the world: the legitimate role of moral correction, and the less legitimate role of self-interested proprietor that inevitably accompanies it. If the Church stays cloistered it remains morally pure, but fails in its obligation to correct society at large. And yet spiritual authority differs so radically from the secular political power it must correct, that as soon as the Church moves into the world, chances are it will be contaminated.[27]

But this formulation, seen once again in the context of the *Parlement of the Thre Ages* and the Knight's "Hoo! . . . Good sire, namoore of this!," invites us I think to reverse the terms for a moment, and to consider the two forms of confrontation between the world and the Church: between, that is, the imperative of the noble life in which defense of Christendom—one of the abiding ideological justifications for aristocratic privilege—is inevitably accompanied by various threats to the soul of the individual defender (e.g., *surquidrie,* as Malory might put it), and on the other hand a penitential withdrawal from such activity that, for all the good it can do for the soul, would necessarily abrogate the individual knight's obligation to fight "in his lordes were" and "for oure feith."[28]

Rather than seeing the Knight and the Monk purely as antagonists at this moment, then, we would do better to see them as mutually implicated in and dialectically articulating an *agon* characteristic of the lordly class to which they both belong (and to which the Host stands in a kind of double, or better, parallel subordination): "How shall the Church in the World be served by its *gouvernours?*," that is, by that class of actors who are always both "outridere" and *viator?* This is the question, I think, that *de casibus* texts not

---

27. Scanlon, *Narrative, Authority, and Power: The Medieval Exemplum and the Chaucerian Tradition* (Cambridge: Cambridge University Press, 1994), 221. We can find confirmation of this latter point in the work of Gower and Langland, who in the *Confessio* and *Piers Plowman,* respectively, decry the Donation of Constantine as "venym schad / In holy cherche of temporal/ Which medleth with the spirital" (Gower, *Confessio Amantis,* in *The Complete Works of John Gower: The English Works,* ed. G. C. Macaulay [Oxford: Clarendon Press, 1899–1901], 2.3490–92); for them the Donation is the typological, foundational instance of clerical worldliness, imagined not in individual terms—a worldly monk, a venal friar, a courtly prioress—but institutionally. Moreover, in England the last quarter of the fourteenth century witnessed an ongoing debate about the participation of clerics and specifically monks in secular administration, with the Benedictine Uthred de Boldon arguing in favor and both the friars and the Lollards condemning the practice. See Alan Fletcher, "Chaucer the Heretic," *Studies in the Age of Chaucer* 25 (2003): 97–98.

28. And as Scanlon goes on to observe, in this particular exchange it is the Knight who is much more the fantasist in his taste for upward rather than downward story arcs: "The accession of a poor man to rich estate only further confirms the essential instability that the Monk has argued defines human history. On this point, the cultural authorities, medieval and humanist alike, are on the Monk's side, and not the Knight's" (*Narrative, Authority, and Power,* 226).

only pose, but in fact only *ever* pose, or only ever *pose* and can never answer, because of the form of lamentable exemplarity (or exemplary lamentation) in which they are bound to pose it: "O worthy, gentil Alisandre, allas, / That evere sholde fallen swich a cas!"

This observation about the "common social location" of Knight and Monk harks back appropriately enough to "The Audience and Public of *Piers Plowman*"; for Anne Middleton the lay and clerical readers of *Piers* also formed a single audience, one devoted to the pursuit of "those tasks and offices where spiritual and temporal governance meet."[29] *Piers* addresses the needs of that audience in a form that, whatever its own dead ends and *aporias,* manages largely to avoid the double bind of *de casibus* writing. Not so the Monk and the Knight, who are caught in the snare and are inevitably of two minds about it. The *Monk's Tale* may say "no no" to the value of earthly activity, but his portrait says "yes yes," and tells a story of attachment rather than ascesis: "of hunting for the hare / Was al his lust." And when the Knight expresses a dislike of stories that end with a *sodeyn* fall, he's implicitly disavowing his own tale, which, while it contains within itself multiple iterations of his preferred plot—the wretched Arcite certainly waxes fortunate, and his cousin Palamon ultimately abides in prosperity—also features the sudden, mortal fall of someone who had risen from a certain kind of misery up to *solas*. One need not fully subscribe to the "crisis of chivalry" reading of the *Knight's Tale* (though I do) to admit that the Knight here resembles not the Neoplatonist Theseus of the end of his tale, making virtue of necessity, but the devastated Theseus of a few dozen lines earlier, who can only be consoled by his elderly father Egeus, and his sunny observation that "This world nis but a thurghfare ful of wo." Indeed, at the end of the *Monk's Tale* the Knight seems to reject the philosophical perspective altogether, articulating instead an affective preference for one genre over another. This is characteristically Chaucerian; as the Miller's *Prologue* indicates, questions of genre and form are where questions of class typically go to hide in the *Canterbury Tales.*

In fact the epilogue to the *Monk's Tale* is not the first place we have witnessed the Knight interrupting some conventional activity with a "Hoo! Namoore of this." This is exactly the phrase that Theseus uses when he comes across Palamon and Arcite fighting in the grove, up to their ankles in blood:

This duc his courser with his spores smoot,
And at a stert he was bitwix hem two,

---

29. Middleton, "Audience and Public," 104.

And pulled out a swerd and cride, "Hoo!
Namoore, up peyne of lesynge of youre heed!
By myghty Mars, he shal anon be deed
That smyteth any strook that I may seen.
But telleth me what myster men ye been,
That been so hardy for to fighten heere
Withouten juge or oother officere,
As it were in a lystes roially."
(1704–13)

It's at this point that Theseus learns of the cousins' feud, and conceives of his plan to give it some order, to channel its volatile energies into the proper chivalric forms—a plan that ends with Arcite suffering his fatal fall. What is it that explains his coincidental arrival, the kind of unlikely event that, as the Knight says, might not happen once in a thousand years? What was Theseus doing in the grove at that particular time? Why, he was hunting, of course; mighty Theseus

. . . for to hunten is so desirus,
And namely at the grete hert in May,
That in his bed ther daweth hym no day
That he nys clad, and redy for to ryde
With hunte and horn and houndes hym bisyde.
For in his huntyng hath he swich delit
That it is al his joye and appetit
To been hymself the grete hertes bane,
For after Mars he serveth now Dyane.
(1673–82)

Like the poacher of the *Parlement*, Theseus is up and out early to seek his *avanture;* like the author of the *Parlement*, the Knight links this aristocratic recreation by analogy (but not by allegory) with a larger project of trying to address through a carefully constructed narrative the unresolved problems of the lordly life in this world, what has been famously described as "the struggle between noble designs and chaos."[30]

Literary representations of the hunt can certainly provide diverting episodes in the midst of siegneurial fictions that have, ultimately, more serious

---

30. The phrase is Charles Muscatine's, from "Form, Texture, and Meaning in Chaucer's Knight's Tale," *PMLA* 65 (1950): 929.

designs. But the constructed nature of the literary hunt—its formal elaboration in terms of process, ritual, and diction—also makes it a useful and flexible mechanism for the redirection of anxieties about the contingency and precariousness of lordly advantage in a world that sometimes seems to be ruled by Fortune, and about the construction of vernacular fictions in the shadow of more authoritative traditions. The *Parlement of the Thre Ages* and the *Monk's Tale* are particularly rich examples of the collocation of venery, tragedy, and translation, but we also find it in Chaucer's *Book of the Duchess* and *Sir Gawain and the Green Knight,* both of which advertise their indebtedness to "olde bookes" and use hunting scenes as oblique preludes to episodes of aristocratic loss; in *The Awyntrs off Arthur,* where the hunt is literally haunted by the spectre of the end of noble privilege, a queen (Guenevere's mother) now "couched in clay" and advertising herself as a mirror for princesses; and in the *Siege of Jerusalem,* which raises the stakes to the cultural level by adding a recreational hunting and hawking expedition to its ambitiously violent *translatio imperii* narrative.[31] The fictional hunt, at least, can succeed, and can bring a formally satisfying if temporary sense of order and control to parallel narratives in which history, though also represented in conventional forms, tends not to cooperate with the aims of seigneurial self-regard.

---

31. On this theme in the *Siege,* see, e.g., David Lawton, "Titus Goes Hunting and Hawking: The Poetics of Recreation and Revenge in *The Siege of Jerusalem,*" in *Individuality and Achievement in Middle English Poetry,* ed. O. S. Pickering (Cambridge: D. S. Brewer, 1997), 105–17. An additional if somewhat contrary example of the phenomenon can be found in the alliterative *Morte Arthure,* where Arthur's dream of Fortune's wheel begins in a wood full of "wolves and wild swine and wicked bestes" (3232) that instead of submitting to the chase are doing the chasing.

ten

Agency and the Poetics of Sensation in Gower's *Mirour de l'Omme*[*]

MAURA NOLAN

PERHAPS the most consistent theme over the course of Gower's writing career is his resistance to the idea of Fortune. In the *Vox Clamantis* and the *Confessio Amantis*, he repeatedly argues that the notion of Fortune is a fraud, a way of dodging responsibility; as he tells us in the Prologue to the *Confessio*, "man is overal / His oghne cause of wel and wo. / That we fortune clepe so / Out of the man himself it groweth."[1] These negations enable Gower to put forth a distinctive vision of human agency and its relation to sin and punishment: because the sorrows of the world are directly caused by the actions of sinners (who have free will), uncovering the causes for worldly sorrow reveals agency, manifested by the free acts of autonomous individuals. But neither the figure of Fortune nor the theology of free will is as simple as that definition of agency implies. This essay focuses on the *Mirour de l'Omme*, one of Gower's earliest attempts to grapple with the complexities of

---

[*] I am grateful to Dan Blanton, Andrew Cole, Matt Giancarlo, Steve Justice, and, as always, Jill Mann. Anne Middleton's influence is everywhere apparent in my thinking about Gower, a "new man" whose place in literary history was first clarified for me by her remarkable accounts of fourteenth-century literature. Anne makes it possible to think both formally and historically, and I am indebted to her, in print and in person, for showing me the way.

1. *Confessio Amantis*, Prologue, lines 546–49, in *The Complete Works of John Gower: The English Works*, ed. G. C. Macaulay (Oxford: Clarendon Press, 1899–1901), 2:19–20. Subsequent references will be in the text by book and line number.

214

Fortune, free will, and the human relationship to the divine. In particular, it examines a mode of expression that might be termed a "poetics of sensation," a mode that allows Gower to experiment formally with questions of agency, contingency, and free will. As I will show, he carries out these experiments while testing the limits of the discourses he has inherited, discourses ranging from the didactic to the sublime to the beautiful.

The *Mirour* is thirty thousand lines long and written in twelve-line stanzas of octosyllabic Anglo-Norman verse; it exists in a single manuscript, Cambridge, University Library Additional MS 3035.[2] It appears as the *Speculum Meditantis* on Gower's tomb at Southwark Cathedral, where an effigy of Gower lies with its head on three books that represent his three major works. The *Mirour* has an important role to play in assessing the emergence of late 14th-century literary culture, not only because it was written quite early—during the waning years of Edward III's reign—but also because it was written in Anglo-Norman rather than English, thus narrowing its readership to those social groups most likely to read French: the aristocracy, these gentry and the clergy. The *Mirour* reveals a tentative poet seeking to forge an authorial identity out of various cultural materials, including genres, images, discourses, and figures, and doing so in a fairly conventional way; the text comprises three successive genres: a didactic sermon on virtues and vices, an estates satire, and a Marian *vita*, or "Life of the Virgin." What exceeds the conventions, however, is the way in which Gower's identity is riven between two discursive modes, the didactic and the sensual. These modes play significant roles in all three of Gower's major works, but they are made particularly explicit in the *Mirour,* where didactic genres are juxtaposed to a descriptive mode that mimics the human experience of contingency and divinity, in the figures of Fortune and the Blessed Virgin. As I will show, even this opposition between didactic and descriptive modes breaks down; both figures themselves are constituted by a tension between their didactic function and the sensual materiality of the language with which they are described.

---

2. Introduction to *Mirour de l'Omme,* trans. William Burton Wilson (East Lansing, MI: Colleagues Press, 1992), xv–xvi; xxii–xxiii. See also Macaulay, *Complete Works,* 4: vii–xxx; and John Fisher, *John Gower: Moral Philosopher and Friend of Chaucer* (New York: New York University Press, 1964), 37–69. Quite by chance, the *Mirour* is an unfinished literary work; its single manuscript breaks off suddenly near the end, making any conclusions about its overarching goals difficult to sustain. But perhaps the loss is not really a loss, in that Gower's larger literary project has barely begun when the *Mirour* ends; even if the text were finished, it would still represent only Gower's preliminary thoughts about Fortune and agency, chance and fate. At the same time, however, the combination of conceptual work, formal experimentation, and a mixture of genres calls to mind similar fourteenth-century works, such as Chaucer's *Canterbury Tales* and Langland's *Piers Plowman* (not to mention Gower's own *Confessio Amantis*). I discuss the role of Fortune in *Piers Plowman* in my essay, "The Fortunes of *Piers Plowman* and Its Readers," *Yearbook of Langland Studies* 20 (2006): 1–41.

Because the figure of Fortune is primarily a literary or aesthetic device—an image that functions symbolically by clothing an abstraction in a concrete and tangible physical form—it also brings to the fore questions about the relationship between the aesthetic (as a mode of expression, a set of techniques, that calls upon bodily sensation) and human agency. This essay seeks to disentangle the knotty relationship between the didactic and the sensual in the *Mirour* by exploring the way in which the abstract qualities evoked by Fortune (contingency, change, and agency) and by the Blessed Virgin (divinity, the sacred) are manifested in language via specific aesthetic techniques that depend upon sensory, material, and physical perceptions of the sublime and the beautiful. Parsing the relationship between didactic and sensual modes of writing is a first step toward an anatomy of Gower's vision of poetics over the course of his career, one that takes into account both his obsessive concern with agency and his turn to a poetics of sensation.

Classical, Boethian, Aristocratic Fortunes

In his major works, Gower mines the Fortune tradition that begins with Boethius' *Consolation of Philosophy* in order to exploit—even as he alters—its representation of human agency and temporal contingency. In the *Vox Clamantis* and *Confessio Amantis,* he repeatedly negates the idea that chance plays a role in human history. Instead of using Fortune as a shorthand for "contingency" or "chance," Gower invokes the figure as an example of false consciousness or deliberate self-deception by constructing a straw man, an amorphous "everyone," whom he blames for using Fortune to evade responsibility for sin. An intertextual network of writing about Fortune lends verisimilitude (though not philosophical content) to his claims, particularly the French poetry of figures like Jean de Meun and Guillaume Machaut, as well as Latin texts like Alan of Lille's *Anticlaudianus.*[3] Having established the

---

3. For examples, see Reason's description of Fortune in *Le roman de la rose,* ed. Armand Strubel (Paris: Librairie Générale Française, 1992), lines 5897–6173; Guillaume de Machaut, *Le livre du voir dit,* ed. Paul Imbs, Jacqueline Cerquiglini-Toulet, and Noël Musso (Paris: Librairie Générale Française, 1999), lines 8606–717. An important source for Gower in the *Confessio Amantis* and for the Fortune tradition in general was Alan of Lille's *Anticlaudianus,* especially book 8; see Alain de Lille, *Anticlaudianus,* ed. R. Bossuat (Paris: Librairie Philosophique J. Vrin, 1955), 173–83. In general, Gower draws on the popularity of Fortune in the later Middle Ages, made manifest in the many visual representations of the figure that have survived; see Yoshiaki Todoroki, *An Addition to Miniatures of the Goddess Fortune in Medieval Manuscripts* (Tokyo: Seibido, 2000), which is a sequel to the very-difficult-to-obtain volume by Tamotsu Kurose, *Miniatures of the Goddess Fortune in Medieval Manuscripts* (Tokyo: Sanseido, 1977). A large proportion of these illustrations are found in manuscripts of Boccaccio's *De casibus virorum illustrium* (vol. 9 of *Tutte le opere di Giovanni Boccaccio,* ed. Vittore Branca [Milan: Arnoldo

premise in both the *Vox* and the *Confessio* that citing Fortune is a way of shirking responsibility, Gower proceeds to mount sustained and careful arguments against using Fortune in either a factual or a fictional way, arguments that have at their core a notion of individual responsibility and agency that ascribes to human beings the capacity to control their own destinies as well as the fate of the world.[4]

This interest in agency plays an important role in the *Mirour* as well, though Fortune does not appear until midway through the second genre in the compilation, the estates satire, when Gower describes the place of sovereigns and the role of the nobility in society. Having described the estate of Holy Church, he tells readers that he will now turn to "l'estat de cex qui ont le siecle en governance" [the estate of those who have the world in their governance].[5] Ironically enough, because of the vagaries of Fortune, a leaf of the manuscript has been lost at this point, leaving a gap of 192 lines just after Gower introduces his theme and immediately before readers encounter Fortune for the first time, in the story of Nebuchadnezzar, whom Fortune placed atop her wheel: "Fortune estoit de son assent / Et sur sa roe en halt l'assist" [Fortune was on his side and seated him in the high place on her wheel] (lines 21983–83, Wilson, 291). By introducing Fortune in the section of his estates satire devoted to the nobility, Gower asserts her class-specific rhetorical status and emphasizes her function as a specialized mode of aristocratic self-understanding, one he contrasts with other modes in the *Mirour*, such as the clerical discourse of the treatise on the vices and virtues and the hagiographical language of the Marian *vita*. The Fortune passage consists of seventy lines of conventional language and images:

Mondadoro, 1983]). For an account of these manuscripts and images of Fortune, see Phyllis Anina Nitze Thompson, "The Triumph of Poverty over Fortune: Illuminations from Boccaccio's *De Casibus Virorum Illustrium*" (PhD diss., Boston University, 1994). Alan Nelson gives a series of examples of mechanical wheels of Fortune that appeared in pageants and performances in his "Mechanical Wheels of Fortune, 1100–1547," *Journal of the Warburg and Courtauld Institutes* 43 (1980): 227–33, with illustrations on pp. 28–29. The Wheel of Fortune was also the subject of wall paintings, both at royal residences and at Rochester Cathedral; Henry III had the image painted above the king's seat in the hall at Winchester and on the fireplace in the chamber of the king at Clarendon. See Tancred Borenius, "The Cycle of Images in the Palaces and Castles of Henry III," *Journal of the Warburg and Courtauld Institutes* 6 (1943): 40–50, 44 (plate 10a shows the Wheel of Fortune at Rochester Cathedral).

4. In these texts, Gower repeatedly comments on figures who try to account for history by invoking Fortune; in the *Vox,* Gower tells us "Fortunam reprobat nunc omnis homo" [Every man now reproves Fortune] (*Vox Clamantis,* book 2, chapt. 1, line 47, in Macaulay, *Complete Works,* 4:85), and in the *Confessio,* he explains that: "For man is cause of that schal falle./Natheles yet som men wryte/ And sein that fortune is to wyte" (*Prologue,* lines 528–30).

5. Macaulay, *Complete Works,* 1:246, heading; the translation is from Wilson, *Mirour,* 291. All subsequent references will be given in the text by line number and page number. I have occasionally modified Wilson's translations for clarity.

218   PART II, CHAPTER 10

> O tu Fortune l'inconstante,
> Du double face es variante,
> L'une est en plour, l'autre est en ris; . . .
> O tu Fortune la nounstable,
> En tous tes faitz es deceivable . . .
> Trop est ta roe ades muable,
> Le dée du quell tu jueras
> Ore est en sisz, or est en as. . . .
> O tu Fortune la marage,
> Ore es tout coye au sigle et nage,
> Menable et du paisible port;
> Ore es ventouse, plein du rage,
> Des haltes ondes tant salvage,
> Que l'en ne puet nager au port . . .
> Fortune, endroit du courtoisie
> Tu ne scies point, ainz malnorrie
> Par droit l'en te porra prover:
> Car qui plus quiert ta compainie
> Et plus te loe et magnifie,
> Tu plus celluy fais laidenger,
> Et qui fuïr et aviler
> Te quiert, celluy fais honourer.
> (lines 22081–83; 22093–94; 22101–3; 22105–10; 22117–24)

[O inconstant Fortune, you are variable with your double face. One face is in tears, the other in smiles . . . O unstable Fortune, you are deceptive in all your doings. . . . Your wheel is very changeable; the die with which you play is sometimes a six, sometimes an ace . . . O vexatious Fortune, now you are quiet for sailing and voyaging, pleasant and of peaceful demeanor, now you are windy and full of such savage storm with high waves that one cannot sail to port. . . . Fortune, you can do nothing by right of courtesy, for you can be rightly proven to be badly brought up. He who most seeks your company and most lauds and exalts you is the one whom you abuse the most. And he who seeks to flee and revile you is the one whom you honor.] (Wilson, 293; lines 22081–117)

Gower's description of Fortune is clearly drawn from a variety of Boethian accounts, including the long discussion of Fortune in the *Roman de la Rose*; he includes a very similar account in Book 2 of the *Vox Clamantis*.[6] The dif-

---

6. See *Vox Clamantis*, book 2, lines 145–216; Gower also describes Fortune as having two hand-

ference between the account of Fortune in the *Mirour* and those in the *Vox* and the *Confessio* does not lie in their representations of the goddess herself, but rather in the contexts in which those depictions are embedded. In the *Vox* and the *Confessio*, Gower explicitly rejects Fortune from the very beginning; readers are never allowed to rest comfortably within the aristocratic discourse of random Fortune and her arbitrary wheel. But in the *Mirour*, Gower's description of Fortune is not accompanied by claims like "That we fortune clepe so / Out of the man himself it groweth" (*Confessio*, Prol. lines 548–49); it stands alone, just as the other genres in the *Mirour* stand separately, and is modified only by its juxtaposition with other models of causality and other ways of determining what is wrong with the world.

Taken by itself, Gower's representation of Fortune in this early text gives the impression that the image of the goddess functions as a reasonable shorthand for the operation of chance in the lives of people and realms. Gower is still parsing the grammar of historical causation here, reproducing the models he has inherited (the didactic and devotional genres that make up the *Mirour*) rather than reshaping and rewriting them in order to forge his own poetic mode. This method of juxtaposing genres has both formal and thematic implications. Because Gower keeps each genre intact formally, he also retains the vision of causation that each implies, moving from one to another without explicitly challenging their generic worldviews. Readers inevitably compare the genres as the text progresses, but Gower never authoritatively articulates a single vision of the world. Instead, he forces readers to recognize the capacity of form to shape experience and perspective by aligning genres and discourses under the loose rubric of the narrative "I"—a figure so vaguely defined that only the first-person pronoun provides the illusion of a consistent voice.

As I have suggested, Gower's understanding of Fortune in his later work is based on his insistence on human agency: human beings have the power to make and remake the world, but they are anxious to disavow that power by invoking Fortune in order to escape responsibility for their own sins. The Fortune thus invoked, however, is not quite the same as the figure that appears in the Boethian model, in which Fortune represents an aspect of God's providence—providence as seen through human, fallible eyes. Instead, when members of the aristocracy gesture to Fortune, they are using the term as a shorthand for chance or fate. That is, either Fortune is random and

---

maidens, "Renomée" and "Desfame," which recall Chaucer's description of Fortune in the *House of Fame* as commanding Eolus' two "clariouns"—"Clere Laude" and "Sclaundre" (lines 1573–82). J. S. Tatlock also points out this link in his *Development and Chronology of Chaucer's Works* (London: Kegan Paul, Trench, Trübner, 1907), 38–40.

contingent—her wheel spins arbitrarily—or, in the classical sense, Fortune represents destiny, the fate that human beings cannot escape and for which they bear no responsibility. Neither of these vernacular uses of the concept reflects the sophistication of the Boethian relationship between providence and fate, which accounts for the problems posed by suffering innocents and prosperous sinners by suggesting that God's providence is a mystery to human beings. For Boethius, all that humans can see is the working of fate, which is providence as it unfolds in time.[7] Were humans able to comprehend God's providence, they would understand how all things, even punishment for the innocent and reward for the guilty, work together to produce an ultimate good. When Gower critiques the ideas about Fortune that are deployed in the world around him—Fortune as contingency and Fortune as destiny—he is in part critiquing the failure of those ideas to encompass a notion of providence. At the same time, Gower suggests that such failed models of Fortune constitute refusals of agency and culpability, to which he responds by insisting upon human responsibility for the condition of the world. Unlike Boethius, who emphasizes the mystery of providence, Gower imagines a world of direct causation in which human beings are specifically punished or rewarded for bad or good acts. Within this structure of causation, it is human sinfulness that accounts for the degradation of the world, its sorrow and misery, its horror and despair. At the start of the *Mirour*, Gower has not yet reached this conclusion. But as the text progresses, the idea of direct causation begins to take shape, emerging from his meditation on the problem of agency—only to be superseded by a set of formal and

---

7. See the *Consolation of Philosophy*, Book IV, pr. 6: "Nam providentia est ipsa illa divina ratio in summo omnium principe constituta quae cuncta disponit; fatum vero inhaerens rebus mobilibus dispositio per quam providentia suis quaeque nectit ordinibus. Providentia namque cuncta pariter quamvis diversa quamvis infinita complectitur; fatum vero singula digerit in motum locis formis ac temporibus distributa, ut haec temporalis ordinis explicatio in divinae mentis adunata prospectum providentia sit, eadem vero adunatio digesta atque explicata temporibus fatum vocetur.... illud certe manifestum est immobilem simplicemque gerendarum formam rerum esse providentiam, fatum vero eorum quae divina simplicitas gerenda disposuit mobilem nexum atque ordinem temporalem" [For providence is the divine reason itself, established in the highest ruler of all things, the reason which disposes all things that exist; but fate is a disposition inherent in movable things, through which providence binds all things together, each in its own proper ordering. For providence embraces all things together, though they are different, though they are infinite; but fate arranges as to their motion separate things, distributed in place, form and time; so that this unfolding of temporal order being united in the foresight of the divine mind is providence, and the same unity when distributed and unfolded in time is called fate . . . this surely is clear, that the unmoving in simple form of the things that are to be enacted is providence, and fate is the movable interlacing and temporal ordering of those things which the divine simplicity has disposed to be done]. See Boethius, *Consolation of Philosophy*, in *The Theological Tractates and the "Consolation of Philosophy,"* ed. and trans. H. F. Tester, E. K. Rand, and S. J. Tester (Cambridge, MA: Harvard University Press, 1973), book II, prose 2 and prose 1; subsequent references will be in the text by book and meter or prose number. I have modified this translation slightly.

aesthetic questions attending Gower's representations of Fortune and the Blessed Virgin.

Fortune and Narrative; Lyric and the Blessed Virgin

In the *Mirour,* exploring the causes for sin and for worldly troubles in the genres of the treatise and the estates satire leads Gower closer to the conclusion that human sin causes the evils that afflict the world. In the *Vox* and the *Confessio,* this idea produces a particular kind of narrative voice. In the former, Gower's narrator takes up a persona of public authority, a "voice crying in the wilderness" as he deploys the genre of the estates satire; in the latter, the narrator of the Prologue and its estates satire speaks with a similarly uncompromising force. But the *Mirour* presents a very different narrator and thus a very different mode of representation for problems of agency. After giving voice to his Anglo-Norman estates satire, this narrator behaves more like Amans than Genius:

> Jadis trestout m'abandonoie
> Au foldelit et veine joye,
> Dont ma vesture desguisay
> Et les fols ditz d'amours fesoie,
> Dont en chantant je carolloie:
> Mais ore je m'aviseray
> Et tout cela je changeray,
> Envers dieu je supplieray
> Q'il de sa grace me convoie;
> Ma conscience accuseray,
> Un autre chançon chanteray
> Que jadys chanter ne soloie.
> (lines 27337–48)

In olden days I gave myself freely to wantonness and vain joy. I decked myself out in fancy clothes and composed foolish love ditties, which I danced about singing. But now I will take thought, and I will change all that. I will beg God to accompany me with His favor. I will accuse my conscience, and I will sing a different song from the one I used to sing. (Wilson, 358)

Gower uses his narrator to demonstrate the effect of his sententious text by showing us a speaker who has absorbed the lessons of the treatise on virtues and vices and the estates satire. This speaker has applied those lessons to his own life and claims to have been profoundly transformed. He asserts that he has left love poetry—"ditz d'amours"—and its performance behind in order to sing a new song, one that will transform listeners by making them feel sorrow at the beginning and spiritual joy at the end, "Au commencer dolour avras / Et au fin joye espirital" (lines 27353–54). This new song is a song of the heart, "un chançon cordial" (line 27351), and it describes the reform of a single person—the narrator—as he prays to the Blessed Virgin for help. The introduction of this confessional mode retrospectively frames the entire project, making the three genres that comprise the *Mirour* part of a highly personalized narrative of sin and forgiveness.

Despite his confident assertion that "Un autre chançon chanteray" [I will sing a different song], the narrator comes close to despair; he is so overcome with shame that he fears God—"Comment vendray mon dieu devant?" [How shall I come before my God?] (line 27403)—and turns to the Virgin Mary for help: "je supplie nepourqant / Ma dame plaine du pité" [nevertheless I pray to my Lady full of pity] (lines 27407–27408). The account of the Virgin's life that follows is intimate and subjective; the narrator interjects his own pleas for mercy and assistance into the story, repeatedly reminding readers of his anxieties about his own sinfulness and inadequacy.[8] In contrast, the didactic and satirical modes of the first two-thirds of the *Mirour* are typically rationalistic, with distanced or highly conventional narrators, and objective rather than affective sensibilities; these modes are designed to convince readers through reason and logic rather than emotional identification. Gower's introduction of the first-person complaint, in which the speaker solicits the affective identification of listeners or readers, occurs just as his exploration of the problems of blame and causation—initiated by his discussion of Fortune—becomes urgent. The narrator's profound shame at his own culpability for the condition of the world disrupts the forward progress of the *Mirour*, making it essential that he assuage his guilt for the text to continue. The remedy for disabling guilt is, unsurprisingly, prayer and repentance; the "Life of the Virgin" offers the narrator the chance to engage in both, particularly as it reaches its conclusion.

This emergent tension in Gower's conception of poetics, between its didactic function and its sensuality, becomes most pronounced as the narrator engages in prayer, a mode both exemplary (designed to model the proper attitude to divinity) and mimetic (as it strives to reproduce the experience of

---

8. See, for example, lines 27901–12 and lines 28585–96.

encountering the divine). As a result, I have chosen to focus here on the lyrical prayer with which Gower concludes the *vita*. Although the larger narrative of the Virgin's life—especially its representation of the Annunciation, in which Mary is asked to submit to the will of God—persistently engages the problems of agency and consent, the concluding prayer forges a striking link between the discourse of agency and the discourse of sensibility, one that makes it possible to specify the relation of poetry to Fortune.[9] In so doing, it anticipates the aesthetic concerns of the *Vox* and the *Confessio*, and makes an important claim for the domain of the sensual as the proper domain of poetics.

As Gower's narrator tells us, for the Virgin's "remembrance / De ton honour et ta plesance" [remembrance of [her] honour and [her] pleasure] (line 29905), he will write down her various names. He then constructs an elaborate apostrophe, comprising a series of names and metaphors without any narrative or commentary:

O dame, pour la remembrance
De ton honour et ta plesance
Tes nouns escrivre je voldrai;
Car j'ay en toy tiele esperance,
Que tu m'en fretz bonne alleggance,
Si humblement te nomerai.
Pour ce ma langue enfilerai,
Et tout mon cuer obeierai,
Solonc ma povre sufficance,
Tes nouns benoitz j'escriveray,
Au fin que je par ce porray,
Ma dame, avoir ta bienvuillance.

O mere et vierge sanz lesure,
O la treshumble creature,

---

9. I discuss the Virgin's life in a longer version of this article. Gower turns to the Marian *vita* because it is a narrative that highlights a distinct moment of human choice: Mary's acquiescence to God's will when she agrees to bear his son. Significantly, that positive choice is in fact a decision to become the passive object of God's action; the Virgin accepts God's wishes by saying "thy will be done," thus placing herself in divine hands and allowing herself to be impregnated. For Gower, it is essential that the Virgin consent to the use of her body as a staging ground for the redemption of humankind, because Christianity itself is thus founded upon an initial act of free will. This display of free choice enables Gower not only to explore the nature of positive action, but also to meditate on the relationship between poetry and the theology of free will.

Joye des angles gloriouse,
O merciable par droiture,
Restor de nostre forsfaiture,
Fontaine en grace plentevouse,
O belle Olive fructuouse,
Palme et Cipresse preciouse,
O de la mer estoille pure,
O cliere lune esluminouse,
O amiable, o amourouse
Du bon amour qui toutdis dure.

O rose sanz espine dite,
Odour de balsme, o mirre eslite,
O fleur du lys, o turturelle,
O vierge de Jesse confite,
Commencement de no merite,
O dieu espouse, amye, ancelle,
O debonaire columbelle,
Sur toutes belles la plus belle,
O gemme, o fine Margarite,
Mere de mercy l'en t'appelle,
Tu es de ciel la fenestrelle
Et porte a paradis parfite.

O gloriouse mere dée,
Vierge des vierges renommée,
De toy le fils dieu deigna nestre;
O temple de la deité,
Essample auci de chastité,
(lines 29905–45 [end])

[O Lady, for the remembrance of your honor and your pleasure, I should like to write your names. For I have such hope in you that if I thus name you humbly, you will alleviate my burdens. Therefore, I will prepare my tongue, and I will completely obey my heart; I will write your blessed names as best I can, according to my poor ability, to the end that I may have, my Lady, your good will.

O Mother and unblemished Virgin, O very humble creature, glorious joy of the angels, O justly merciful restorer of what we forfeited, fountain plentiful in grace, O beautiful fruitful olive tree, palm and precious cypress, O pure star of the sea, O bright luminous moon, O lovable, O loving with the good love that lasts forever!

O rose named without thorns, fragrance of balsam, O finest myrrh, O flower of the lily, O turtledove, O Virgin of Jesse's line, beginning of our merit, O spouse of God, beloved, handmaiden of God, O gentle dove, the most beautiful above all the beautiful, O gem, O fine pearl, mother of mercy you are called; you are the window of heaven and gate to perfect Paradise.

O glorious Mother of God, famed Virgin of virgins, the Son of God deigned to be born of you; O temple of the Deity, and example also of chastity . . .] (Wilson, 395)

The apostrophe is purposeful: as the narrator tells us, "Que tu m'en fretz bonne alleggance, / Si humblement te nomerai" (lines 29900–10) [if I thus name you humbly, you will alleviate my burdens] (Wilson, 395). These names function as praise: they are metaphors drawn from the natural world that honor the virgin by suggesting that she resembles the items catalogued: flowers, trees, fragrances, birds, gems, and the sea. Each of these items is characterized by stasis; the olive tree is ever in fruit, the rose blooms perpetually, the pearls glow and the ocean shines forever. This stasis contrasts markedly with the natural images from the apostrophe to Fortune earlier in the *Mirour:*

O tu Fortune la marage,
Ore es tout coye au sigle et nage,
Menable et du paisible port;
Ore es ventouse, plein du rage,
Des haltes ondes tant salvage,
Que l'en ne puet nager au port:
Tu es d'estée le bell desport
Flairant, mais plus sodain que mort
Deviens utouse et yvernage;
Tu es le songe qant l'en dort,
Qe tous biens par semblante apport,
Mais riens y laist de l'avantage.
(lines 22105–16)

[O vexatious Fortune, now you are quiet for sailing and voyaging, pleasant and of peaceful demeanor, now you are windy and full of such savage storm with high waves that one cannot sail to port. You are the fine fragrant entertainment of summer, but, more sudden than death, you become turbid and wintry. You are the dream when one sleeps that brings the appearance of all good things but leaves nothing of value.] (Wilson, 293)

Fortune's sea is windy and changeable; her fragrance fades and her flowers are covered with snow. Unlike the metaphors describing the Blessed Virgin, these images embody variation and alteration; they are active predicates that create change and motion. All of the action, in fact, resides in the goddess and her wheel: Gower's narrator can do no more than represent her, not in the hope of creating a changed world, but rather as a way of illustrating the perils of attributing causes to Fortune rather than to human agency. Fortune's variability is the source of her danger, and the representation of that variability requires an aesthetic mode that is adequate to its magnitude, a magnitude that seems to be beyond human measurement and comprehension. That mode is the sublime. Immanuel Kant describes the sublime as having "a magnitude that is equal only to itself," by which he means that the greatness of the sublime consists not in the measurement of something very large, but rather in a "striving to advance to the infinite" that originates in the human mind.[10] In other words, Fortune represents an attempt to come to terms with the sublimity of contingency, the degree to which chance *seems* infinitely variable and overwhelmingly powerful—though of course, in Boethian and providential terms, nothing about chance is random. The fact that human beings experience chance in that way is a measure of their distance from God and their inability to grasp his larger plan.

The metaphors through which Gower describes Fortune are all illustrations of nature's power and changeability—the storm at sea, the dying flowers—and they arouse sensations in the reader that mimic the experience of the sublime, the human encounter with radical contingency and uncertainty. As Edmund Burke explains, "Whatever is fitted in any sort to excite the ideas of pain, and danger, that is to say, whatever is in any sort terrible, or is conversant about terrible objects, or operates in a manner analogous to terror, is a source of the sublime."[11] Fortune's description—the way in which she is likened to a "savage storm with high waves," so violent that she traps sailors at sea, "more sudden than death" and "turbid and wintry"—exploits the sensations of pain and danger brought about by uncontrolled natural

---

10. Immanuel Kant, *Critique of the Power of Judgment*, ed. Paul Guyer and trans. Paul Guyer and Eric Matthews (Cambridge: Cambridge University Press, 2000), Book II.25, p. 134.
11. Edmund Burke, *A Philosophical Enquiry into the Origin of Our Ideas of the Sublime and Beautiful* (London: J. Dodsley, 1767), Part I, section 7, page 58.

forces in order to create in the reader the feeling of the sublime—the feeling of being faced with the arbitrariness of life in the world. The aesthetic of the sublime, the metaphors for Fortune, mediate between the sensuous experience of "pain and danger" and the mental experience of the sublime, the human confrontation with the idea of a contingency beyond comprehension. Fortune stands in for this idea, lending it a human shape and a form made legible by the aesthetic of pain and danger, the mode of the sublime. It is a mode mistakenly associated with Fortune, whose infinity—her infinite variability, her inhuman power—is fundamentally deceptive; she may seem like a goddess, but she is at root a metaphor, firmly yoked to a providential understanding of human history. But as Gower recognizes, the expressive mode of the sublime is essential to representing the human *perception* of contingency, even if that perception is a false one.

In Gower's description of Fortune in the *Mirour,* the sublime functions descriptively but does not incite action; it evokes emotion as a warning, but never implies that it can produce change in the world. In contrast, the prayer to the Virgin has a purpose; it is designed to convince Mary to act in favor of the supplicant. Paradoxically, it is the purposefulness of the "naming" of the Virgin that explains why the list of names—unlike the predicate-laden apostrophe to Fortune—is unchanging and still. The act of nominalizing the Virgin transfers energy from Fortune's apostrophe to the exchange between supplicant and divinity. The narrator creates a lyrical object in order to give it to the Virgin as a gift, an act of piety that engages the recipient in a process of give and take. Though Fortune is described in active and forceful images, the genre of complaints to Fortune is sterile; there can be no exchange, because Fortune does not engage in bargaining. She is either relentlessly arbitrary or subordinate to God's will, in which case she lacks the power to act.[12] As a result, complaints to Fortune, no matter how forceful, lack efficacy; the complainant is powerless to effect change because Fortune herself is unchanging in her changeability. In contrast, the Virgin's names, layered atop one another in elegant and pleasing fashion, offer the devotion and praise that can compel her to act in favor of the narrator.

As a formal matter, the contrast between Fortune and the Virgin represents a clash of discursive modes. It is a clash concealed by the sheer size

---

12. Indeed, when Boethius' Lady Philosophy ventriloquizes Fortune in book 2 of the *Consolation,* the first thing she says is "Quid tu homo ream me cotidianis agis querelis?" [Why, man, do you daily complain against me?]; Philosophy herself explains: "Fortunae te regendum dedisti; dominae moribus oportet obtemperes. Tu vero volventis rotae impetum retinere conaris? At, omnium mortalium stolidissime, si manere incipit, fors esse desistit." [You have given yourself over to fortune's rule: you must accommodate yourself to your mistress's ways. Will you really try to stop the whirl of her turning wheel? Why, you are the biggest fool alive—if it once stop, it ceases to be the wheel of fortune].

of the *Mirour* as a whole, which surrounds these two female figures with literary and religious conventions and obscures their significance. In large part, the *Mirour* describes effects rather than causes—responses to events in the world (vices and virtues) and the degraded condition of social groups (estates satire). Even the Virgin's "Life" is a narrative of effects, the consequences of God's decision to save humanity. The descriptions of Fortune and the Virgin stand in stark relief against this background, highlighted as attempts to account for the *causes* of events and conditions in the world. Fortune demands the mode of the sublime; the Virgin requires a poetics of beauty. Fortune wreaks havoc; the Virgin answers prayers. In so doing, the two figures function in diametrically opposed ways. Fortune enables a poetry of action and motion; the very act of representation requires the poet to mimic her variability, changeability, and force. The Virgin, in contrast, demands a poetry of images and names; representing her requires a poetics that resists temporality and embraces stasis *even though* (or perhaps *because*) it is designed to elicit a response. These are two very different poetic modes, particularly when considered in relation to the tension between didacticism and sensibility that structures the *Mirour* throughout. The overall shape of the work, which leads up to the apostrophe to the Virgin, seems at first glance designed to illustrate the foolishness of trusting Fortune and the virtue of praying to Mary, showing how human beings are paralyzed by a model of causation that is subject to Fortune, but enabled by a model that includes an intermediary and rewards supplication.

But this conclusion is not, in formal terms, really a conclusion; the text simply breaks off part way through the list of names, making it difficult to interpret the *Mirour* in this progressive, linear way. The sudden ending leaves intact the two modes that are embodied by the apostrophes to Fortune and to the Virgin, which might usefully be labeled "narrative" and "lyric" (one signifying action, the other temporal stillness). The *Mirour* is suspended rather than concluded; Fortune is never completely abjured and the Virgin never takes action as a mediator or intercessor. Instead, several of the manuscript's final leaves are missing, making it impossible to determine how Gower would have ended the text, or what he would have concluded after his prayer to the Virgin. Despite this accident of textual history, the opposition the *Mirour* creates between narrative and lyric remains critical to understanding Gower's attempts to juggle the competing elements of his poetic identity. The fact that the two modes remain in suspension at the end of the *Mirour* may be an accident, but it is a prescient one; as the *Confessio Amantis* will show, Gower discovers that he cannot accomplish his poetic tasks without narrative—and it is narrative that is Fortune's province, her special discursive form. The final book of the *Confessio*, which tells the story of Apollonius of Tyre, illustrates the dependence of the romance genre on the twists and turns of Fortune; romance requires unexpected events, unpredictable disasters, and chance encounters in order to function. Even though individual stories within the romance genre might be told and re-told, becoming familiar to their audiences, events within the narrative are still described as sudden, random, and surprising for the characters, who are subject to the vicissitudes of Fortune. The romance genre thus relies on Fortune to create narratives of suspense and fulfillment, and functions very differently from the kind of narrative found in genres like the saint's life or the Marian *vita*, particularly when the story being told is familiar to every Christian.

The "Life of the Virgin" has no room for Fortune; all of its events are familiar and all were accomplished according to the will of God. The narrative mode I have linked to Fortune is inimical to such stories; even though Marian lives consist of a sequence of events, those events are never presented as the shocking or surprising interventions of Fortune that characterize the romance. Instead, readers experience the story as the unfolding of God's plan; even Mary's response to the Annunciation—certainly a surprising moment, from her perspective—firmly emphasizes the intention at work in the Angel's announcement by invoking God's will: "thy will be done." Because the "Life of the Virgin" is so permeated by this sense of intention, its narrative sequence has a ritualized quality, made even more pressing by the repetition of the story in a variety of media in medieval culture—in the liturgy, in multiple Marian *vitae*, in cycle plays, and elsewhere. It is this predictability that produces Gower's turn to the lyrical list of names at the end of the *Mirour*. The lyrical mode allows him to experiment with the sensuality of devotional language and to push the voice of the moral poet to its aesthetic limits. It also, retrospectively, reveals that the opposition between Fortune and the Virgin—narrative and lyric, motion and stasis—is merely part of a larger poetic division in the *Mirour* between the didactic and the sensual or mimetic. This division lies at the heart of Gower's efforts to forge a poetic identity out of the materials available to him, materials ranged along a spectrum from what Chaucer would later call "sentence" to "solaas," the Horatian model of "use and delight."[13]

---

13. *Riverside Chaucer*, ed. Larry D. Benson (Boston: Houghton Mifflin, 1987), *General Prologue*, I:798. Subsequent references will be in the text by fragment and line number.

Use and Delight, Didacticism and Mimesis

Throughout the *Mirour*, Gower juxtaposes genres of "useful" writing—the treatise on vices and virtues, the estates satire, and the Marian *vita*—and raises the question of their relationship to the public and to the individual. The narrator moves from the opening treatise, which focuses on individual sin, to an indictment of the realm and the estates that comprise it, before breaking down and lamenting his sinful condition. This movement allows Gower to demonstrate his thesis that man is a microcosm, responsible for all of the ills that afflict the world; in the narrator, he shows readers the proper response of individuals to sinfulness: they must accept responsibility for the effects of their actions on the world, and attempt to remedy sin through prayer. The three genres that make up the work are each characterized by their use of the first person, but it is not until Gower introduces the confessional mode as he turns to the "Life of the Virgin" that those speaking subjects retroactively become one voice. This narratorial voice makes it clear that the individual is the key to changing the world, thereby producing the impression that the function of writing is to create reform; as long as a text can inspire individual change, it has fulfilled its task.

There are three crucial moments in the *Mirour*, however, at which this purely functional model breaks down. These moments of breakdown suggest that Gower has begun to envision a poetics capable of doing more than advising and admonishing its readers. The first of these, Gower's apostrophe to Fortune, suggests that representing difficult and ambiguous concepts demands a special kind of language. Without poetic images like Fortune's double face, her wheel, her dice, and metaphors like "bad weather" or "calm seas" for her actions, ideas like contingency, arbitrariness, and chance would have to be explained to readers using a conceptual—and thus difficult—vocabulary. Gower's goal of writing for lay people makes it clear that he plans to write in nontechnical, nonphilosophical language; like Boethius' Lady Philosophy, he offers "gentle and pleasant" ["molle et iucundum"] medicine, the "sweet persuasiveness of rhetoric" ["Rhetoricae suadella dulcedinis"] (book 2, prose 1)—and like Philosophy, Gower's rhetoric concerns Fortune. The danger of such sweet rhetoric is that it can be directed at the wrong object, as when a man "loe et magnifie" [lauds and exalts] Fortune (line 22121; Wilson, 293)—a foolish kind of praise that results in abuse and suffering at Fortune's hands (not because Fortune responds specifically to individuals, but because all individuals dependent on Fortune must endure eventual suffering). In contrast, Gower's apostrophe, like Lady Philosophy's description of Fortune, functions as a way of countering that praise—not as its opposite, which would be denigration, but as an instructive and descriptive mode of discourse that negates Fortune by exposing her true nature with the help of the "sweet persuasiveness of rhetoric." Boethius explains why Fortune must be described in this way by using the metaphor of medicine; similarly, the poetically pleasing qualities of Gower's description are designed to prepare the reader for the strong medicine—i.e., the instructions for reform—to follow. This combination of the sensual and the didactic, in which aesthetics are subject to instrumental ends, is familiar to readers of Gower as the presumptive poetic model on which he relies (or seems to rely) throughout his career.

However, when Gower warns against praising Fortune—against using rhetoric for delight, as when a man "loe et magnifie" Fortune (line 22121; Wilson, 293)—he opens the door for the idea that poetic language exceeds instrumentality. This latter suggestion comes to the fore in two subsequent passages, one from the beginning and one from the end of the "Life of the Virgin," which make explicit the metapoetic subtext introduced by the apostrophe to Fortune. These passages deploy a language that specifically conceptualizes what I have called the "poetics of sensation," the appeal to the senses with which a poet can mimetically re-create certain forms of experience for readers. It is from this language that Gower derives a definition of the poet as supplicant, agent, and creator all at once—a definition not limited to usefulness or to the poet's capacity to reform his audience. In the first of these passages, the narrator describes his own sinfulness and seeks a remedy for his spiritual ill-health:

> Pour ce, ma dame, a ta *plesance*
> Solonc ma *povre sufficance*
> *Vuill conter* ta concepcioun,
> Et puis, ma dame, ta naiscance;
> Sique l'en sache ta puissance,
> Qui sont du nostre nacioun:
> Les clerc en scievont la leçoun
> De leur latin, mais autres noun,
> Par quoy en langue de romance
> J'en fray la declaracioun,
> As lays pour enformacioun,
> Et a les clercs pour *remembrance*.
> (lines 27469–80; emphasis added)

[Therefore, Lady, at your pleasure, according to my poor gifts, I want to tell of your conception, and then, Lady, of your birth, so that the people of our nation may know your power. The clerics know about it from their Latin, but others do not know. Therefore I will make the declaration of it in the French tongue for the information of the lay folk and as a reminder to the clerics.] (Wilson, 360)

I have already mentioned the significance of Gower's choice of Anglo-Norman, which is effectively a choice of audience—the people of "nostre nacioun" who read French but perhaps not Latin, the gentry and aristocracy. Gower makes it clear here that he is writing for readers both secular and elite, a group for whom the text functions as an exemplar of right action. This passage sets in place crucial terms for understanding Gower's poetic vision by highlighting the relationship between the Virgin and the self-conception of the narrator. First, the speaker addresses the Virgin directly, indicating conditionally that he "would like to tell" ["vuill conter"] about her conception and her birth. The uncertainty he expresses by using the conditional phrase rests on two aspects of the implicit dialogue between the narrator and the Virgin: first, Mary's "pleasure" ["plesance"] and second, the inadequacy of the narrator, his "povre sufficance," meaning his "poor intellectual capacity," his "poor gifts." These two terms, "plesance" and "sufficance," seem at first to be part of a conventional humility topos, a means for the narrator to emphasize his inadequacy in the face of the Virgin's great power, her "puissance." However, they also suggest that "pleasure" and "sufficiency" are crucial notions for Gower's poetics, dedicated here to efficacious praise.

Unlike the apostrophe to Fortune, the "Life of the Virgin" includes exaltation, properly directed praise to a divinity with the power to act. Where Fortune is arbitrary, the Blessed Virgin responds to prayer; while Fortune rejects those who praise her, Mary intercedes for her supplicants with great authority. The narrator must have "sufficance," a word that refers to both "intellectual capacity" and "satisfaction" or "sufficiency"—in other words, *enough*.[14] This quality of sufficiency markedly contrasts with the victims of Fortune, who are either excessively wealthy and powerful or utterly abject, at the top or bottom of her wheel. It suggests that Gower understands the role of the poet as a moderating figure, a figure able to mediate between the divine and human as well as between the clergy and laymen. Even if it is

---

14. *Dictionnaire du Moyen Français* (1330–1500) <http://www.atilf.fr/dmf> (last accessed September 14, 2012), s. v. "suffisance," article 3/12, B ("contentement, satisfaction") and C ("aptitude, capacité intellectuelle").

"povre," the narrator's "sufficance" is still *enough;* despite labeling himself in a humble way, he is able to recount the Virgin's life with authority.

"Plesance" functions in a similar way to define the role of poetics in relation to both divine and human enterprises. It means, very simply, "pleasure," but Gower's use of the word is not simple. "Plesance" carries with it the connotation of "approval," rendering "a ta plesance" something like "with your approval"—an appropriate phrase for a poet to use when embarking upon praise for a figure of great power like the Virgin. It also suggests "will" or "desire" and thereby implies that the will of the Virgin controls the "Life"; the narrator abdicates his own will by using the phrase "a ta plesance" [at your will], performing his submission to the Virgin even as he repeatedly engages in the powerful practice of naming.[15] It is a practice that comes to fruition in the second metapoetic passage from the "Life," a companion to the first, which appears near the end of the *Mirour:*

> O dame, pour la *remembrance*
> De ton honour et ta *plesance*
> Tes nouns *escrivre* je voldrai;
> Car j'ay en toy tiele esperance,
> Que tu m'en fretz bonne alleggance,
> Si humblement te nomerai.
> Pour ce ma langue enfilerai,
> Et tout mon cuer obeierai,
> Solonc ma *povre sufficance,*
> Tes nouns benoitz *j'escriveray,*
> Au fin que je par ce porray,
> Ma dame, avoir ta bienvuillance.
> (lines 29905–16; emphasis added)

[O Lady, for the remembrance of your honor and your pleasure, I want to write your names. For I have such hope in you that if I thus name you humbly, you will alleviate my burdens. Therefore, I will prepare my tongue, and I will completely obey my heart; I will write your blessed names as best I can, according to my poor ability, to the end that I may have, my Lady, your good will.] (Wilson, 395)

In this second passage, Gower once again makes explicit the bargain between the Virgin and the narrator; he names her, and she takes away his suffer-

---

15. *Dictionnaire du Moyen Français,* s. v. "plaisance," A ("agrément, plaisir") and B ("gré, volunté")

ing. But this simple notion of exchange does not account for the emergent discourse of poetics that characterizes the opening and concluding portions of the *vita*. The key terms—"plesance," "povre sufficance," and "remembrance"—appear in both passages, creating a frame around the "Life" that gestures beyond an exchange-based model of prayer by introducing an interpretive vocabulary at the end of the *Mirour* that defines the sensual effects, the writerly qualities, and the narrative function of Gower's poetics. To start with the final term on the list, "remembrance" refers in the first passage to the narrator's original plan for writing the *vita*—as information for lay people and as a "remembrance," or "reminder" to clerics. In the second passage, the narrator once again claims that he is writing for "remembrance," in order to memorialize the "honour" and "plesance"—honor and pleasure—of the Virgin. These uses of "remembrance" point to Gower's investment in history; although the *Mirour* is not a particularly historical poem, Gower understands his writing to have an historical purpose, to be part of the record of the past—and he uses poetry to bring the past to a wider audience of both lay persons and clerics. But "remembrance" is more than the recapitulation of past events, more than simply the memorialization of what has been lost to time. The word itself comes from the Latin *memor*, "mindful, remembering."[16] A close analogue can be found in another Latin word, one which Gower would certainly have known: the verb *membro*, "to form limb by limb" and by extension, *re-membro*, "to form again."[17] Gower's "remembrance" revivifies and reanimates, making the dead live once again; it extends beyond the efficacy of the moral poet to reveal the author as creator, a notion that Gower has repeatedly put forward over the course of the *Mirour*.

Poets can create representations of absent persons, objects, and gods; they can produce imitations that both recall the past and inspire the emotions associated with it. This latter use of the word suggests that the list of names the narrator plans to compile will function like a painting or a statue, as a substitute for the presence of the saint; the Virgin's blessedness will be illustrated mimetically in both its content and its form. The literary devices used to structure the list of names, as well as the referents of those names—flowers, fragrance, stars, trees, gems—imitate the beauty and virtue of the Virgin by embodying her aesthetic values and arousing in readers feelings of admiration and devotion. Gower remakes the Virgin through remembrance, creating a literary object that mimics an encounter with her divinity through sensual experience. This mimesis is not a mode of instruction or reform. It

---

16. C. T. Lewis and C. Short, eds., *A Latin Dictionary* (http://www.perseus.tufts.edu/hopper/resolveform?redirect=true&lang=Latin; accessed April 5, 2011), s. v. "memor, memoris," I.
17. Lewis and Short, *A Latin Dictionary*, s. v. "membro, membrare," I.

is, rather, an invitation to an experience of sensual excess that articulates the purpose of poetry in a new way. The reader is not asked to change, but rather to remember her own sensory experiences as the poem calls them up and allies them to the divine. She sees again the beauty of a flower and scents its fragrance; the poem disciplines that sensation and its pleasure by transforming them into symbols of divinity, names for the Blessed Virgin.

Coupled with this notion of "remembrance" as a form of experiencing the divine is Gower's concept of writerly adequacy, which he highlights by repeating the phrase "ma povre sufficance" at the beginning and end of the *vita*. This gesture of humility posits the notion of *sufficiency* as a human quality essential to poetics. In the first passage, "ma povre sufficance" appears at the beginning of the stanza in which Gower describes his project; it governs his narration of the Virgin's conception and birth. This posture of inadequacy carries with it the notion of the poet as a mediator, a humble figure who stands between the Latinate world of clerical knowledge and the lay audience. By the time Gower turns to the list of names for the Virgin that concludes the *vita,* his repetition of the phrase "ma povre sufficance" has moved from its governing position at the start of a stanza to its end, following a series of assertions by the narrator that he will take specific actions, summed up in a sequence of four verbs: "escrivre" [to write], "nomer" [to name], "enfiler" [to prepare; literally, to file], and "obeir" [to obey].[18] This sequence of verbs delays the humility topos, "ma povre sufficance," until after the work of poetic creation has been broken down into a series of steps, with two primary effects. First, and most obviously, the delay implies that the narrator has become much more assertive over the course of recounting the Virgin's life; he no longer needs the protective cloak provided by his gesture of humility. Second, the list of poetic actions—obeying, preparing, naming, and writing—functions as an implicit definition of "sufficance" itself. To have a sufficiency, for a poet, is to be capable of performing a series of poetic acts, here carefully set out one by one as a graduated map of the process of writing poetry. Part of what Gower wishes to accomplish in the "Life," it becomes clear, is to disambiguate poetry as a practice, producing a series of predicates that locates the poet's role in the performance of various discrete and identifiable actions. This focus on the poet as an active and forceful figure not only sets in place Gower's vision of the artist, but it also

---

18. The expression "ma langue enfilerai"—"I will file my tongue"—is familiar from Chaucer's uses of it in *Troilus and Criseyde* (2:1681), referring to Pandarus ("This Pandarus gan newe his tong affile"), and in the *General Prologue* (I:712), referring to the Pardoner ("He moste preche and wel affile his tonge"). The *Riverside* notes to *Troilus and Criseyde* suggest that the expression refers to smoothing the tongue, rather than sharpening it, but it clearly means "preparing to speak" in either case.

seamlessly corresponds to the themes with which he has been concerned throughout the *Mirour:* the themes of agency, will, consent, and Fortune. The poet, like every other human being in Gower's model, must embrace agency and align his will properly—he must obey, as well as prepare, name, and write.

This nexus of agency and will is intimately connected to the final—and most significant—poetic term framing the *vita:* "plesance." In my discussion of Gower's first use of the term, I suggested that "plesance" implies both "pleasure" and "will" or "approval" in reference to the Virgin and her response to the narration of her life. Within the broader structure of the "use and delight" model of literature, the introduction of "plesance" marks one of the first times in the *Mirour* that Gower explicitly suggests that pleasure has a place in the text. Indeed, at the very beginning of the larger work, Gower addresses his audience as "amourouse sote gent" [foolish, loving people] (line 19; Wilson 3), and warns that:

> Car s'un soul homme avoir porroit
> Quanq' en son coer souhaideroit
> Du siecle, pour soy deliter,
> Trestout *come songe* passeroit
> En nient, et quant l'en meinz quidoit,
> Par grant dolour doit terminer:
> Et puisque l'amour seculer
> En nient au fin doit retorner,
> Pour ce, *si bon vous sembleroit,*
> Un poy du nient *je vuill conter;*
> Dont quant l'en quide avoir plenier
> La main, tout vuide passer doit.
> (lines 20–32; emphasis added)

[For if any man could have whatever his heart desired of the world, for his delight, it would all pass away like a dream into nothing and, when he least expected it, end in great sorrow. And because love of the world must turn again to nothing in the end, I want therefore (if it seems good to you) to tell you a little about nothing. When one imagines he has a handful of it, he must go away completely empty.] (Wilson, 3).

In these very first lines of the *Mirour,* the logic of sin that pervades the text is already very clear: those who love the world and who take delight in the world are doomed to lose everything and to end in great sorrow. In this model, the poet describes the sinfulness of the world in order to expose the foolishness of worldly desires to "whoever wishes to flee evils" ["quiq' en voet fuïr les mals"] (line 10). The *Mirour* thus begins by establishing the narrator as an arbiter of morals, firmly placing pleasure on the side of sin and insisting that delight is "come songe" [like a dream] (line 23); the individual imagines ["quide"] that his hand is full ["plenier / La main"] (lines 31–32) of whatever he desires in the world. The human imagination, according to this logic, is a treacherous thing; it deceives human beings by convincing them that delight in the world is satisfying—that their hands are full—when in fact they are bereft, completely empty, with no real goodness (the goodness of God) to give them lasting satisfaction. The narrator offers his text as a demystification of the imaginary plenitude offered by worldly delight, saying to readers, "I want to tell you a little about nothing" ["Un poy du nient *je vuill conter*"] (line 30).

This process of demystification seems to promise a negation of pleasure and delight, a demonstration that the imagination and its fruits are fundamentally unreal: "nient" [nothing], "vuide" [empty]. However, one clause hints at the metapoetic discourse that will emerge as the frame for the "Life of the Virgin": "je vuill conter" [I want to tell] (line 30). Here, the narrator addresses the audience using the same construction he will later use to address the Virgin, "je vuill conter," a phrase that appears at the start of the *vita*: "*Vuill conter* ta concepcioun, / Et puis, ma dame, ta naiscance (lines 27471–72). The narrator's use of the phrase at the beginning of the *Mirour* is part of a gentle address to his readers, which solicits their consent for the sermon to follow and asks them to judge the quality of his wish—whether it "sembleroit bon" [seems good] (line 29) or not. This gesture to the critical faculties of his readers is echoed at the start of the *vita*, when the narrator addresses the Virgin by saying "a ta plesance" [at your pleasure] (line 27469), "vuill conter" [I want to tell] (line 27471). In both cases, the act of telling depends on the assent of the audience; either human readers find the narrator's plan "bon," or the Blessed Virgin finds "plesance" in the prospect of hearing the narration of her own life. The difference between "bon" [good] and "plesance" [pleasure] lies in the relationship of human beings to the category of pleasure, which is inextricably bound up with the body and thus with sin. When Gower chooses the term "bon," he deliberately selects a word that suggests spiritual good rather than pleasure. He proleptically informs readers that what he has written is designed to be judged by the higher faculties of human beings, those faculties that assess the virtue of the text by evaluating what "seems good" in it. In contrast, although delight and pleasure, enjoyment and "solaas," are poetic qualities, they are also dangerously linked to lechery, overindulgence, and physical excessiveness of all kinds, as Gower's lengthy treatise on the vices repeatedly reminds his audience. That is why, when "plesance" appears in the text, it is firmly linked to the Virgin; the dangers of pleasure do not afflict her as they afflict human beings, who must be reminded to seek out the good.

"If it seems good to you" ["si bon vous sembleroit"] is one of two references in this passage to "seeming," to the deceptiveness of the world and to the uncertainty of human perception. In the second reference, Gower explains that if man could have all that he desired, "Trestout *come songe* passeroit / En nient" [it would all pass away *like a dream* into nothing] (lines 23–24). The anxiety expressed here about the human capacity to judge reality, to know when dreams are real and when they are false or to assess the virtue of a text, is assuaged at the end of the *Mirour* by the narrator's request for the Virgin's approval before writing the *vita*. For Gower, this request is a poetic device, designed to authorize his text and to introduce the notion of "plesance" without the implication of licentious desire or worldly delight. In neither of the framing passages from the "Life" quoted above is "plesance" associated with any being but the Virgin herself. It is "at her pleasure" that the *vita* begins, and when the narrator turns to the list of names at the end, he claims that it is "pour la remembrance / De ton honour et ta plesance" [for the remembrance of your honor and your pleasure] (lines 29905–6). This syntax offers more than one potential meaning for the line. While it is possible to see "ta plesance" as subject to "remembrance" (so that what is remembered is the Virgin's "honor and plesance"), it is also possible to read "remembrance" and "plesance" as a pair, coupled inside the prepositional phrase begun by "pour" (so that the line might be translated as "for the remembrance of your honor and for your pleasure"). In the first case, what is remembered is the Virgin's honor and her pleasure, meaning either her approval of the *vita* or her pleasure at bearing Christ. In the second case, it is the narrator's recitation of her names that is associated with the Virgin's pleasure; "pour . . . ta plesance, tes nouns escrivre je voldrai" [for your pleasure, I would like to write your names] (lines 29905–7). This latter interpretation suggests that the purpose of writing is to give delight, to create pleasure for the listener or reader, who is represented here by the Blessed Virgin. In some ways, the *Mirour* has traveled a great distance from the anxious "si bon vous sembleroit" [if it seems good to you] with which it began. But Gower's solution to this original anxiety about the delights of the world, "l'amour seculer" [love of the world] (line 31), is not a human solution. He can make room for "plesance" only by projecting it onto a divine creature, one whose identity is premised on her freedom from the desires of the flesh, the Virgin Mary.

There is a great gulf between this "plesance" and the "moost solaas" (I:798) of Chaucer's ebullient Host in the *Canterbury Tales*. At the same time, however, the emergence of "plesance" at the end of the *Mirour* represents Gower's recognition that the aesthetic value of poetry is in part dictated by its sensuality, by the ways in which it uses language mimetically to arouse emotions and feelings and to reproduce beauty and sublimity, here, in the figures of the Virgin and Fortune. This recognition makes explicit a change in the *Mirour's* understanding of poetics that gradually emerges over the course of the poem, a shift made manifest by a difference in Gower's use of self-referential language between the poem's opening verses and the concluding list of names for the Virgin. Until the final passage from the *vita*, Gower primarily uses the verb "conter," "to tell," to refer to his literary practice; as I have noted above, he deploys the phrase "je vuill conter" [I want to tell] to introduce both the Virgin's life and the *Mirour* as a whole. At the very end of the text, however, Gower twice describes his naming of the Virgin using the verb "escrivre," "to write." This movement from "conter" to "escrivre" alters the discursive mode that has dominated the *Mirour*. No longer is Gower instructing, teaching, or preaching; no longer is the text didactic. Instead, moralizing poetry—telling—is replaced by writing, a particular way of using language to create a site for contemplation and reflection.

Gower's emphasis on writing evokes the materiality of the text, the way in which something written is an object as well as a sequence of words. In writing, language acquires a solidity that it lacks in telling. As the spoken word is transformed into marks on paper, the temporality of language is altered; what is ephemeral is captured and preserved, the fleeting utterance becomes the long-lasting page. In contrast, Gower's use of "conter" aligns his text with the exemplary tradition, a kind of writing that perpetually recalls its relationship to spoken forms like the sermon, in which the exemplum is recounted in the service of a moral. How the exemplum is told hardly matters; the audience listens for its *sentence* and extracts the lesson from its form. But when Gower highlights the writtenness of the naming passage, he explicitly invites readers to linger over it, to attend to the profusion of names without being goaded to a conclusion by the forward-driving force of narrative. Indeed, the naming passage goes in no direction and proceeds to no end; it repeats the same gesture over and over as the list of names grows, all with the same referent. It is as if Gower engraves a memorial with a series of epitaphs, covering the top and bottom and front and back of the stone in order to instantiate divinity from every angle and perspective.

Readers experience this writtenness as an exercise in transforming the many into the one, as the incantatory sequence of names arouses a variety of sense perceptions, each of which substitutes for direct experience of the divine. Readers see the "cliere lune esluminouse" [bright luminous moon] (line 22926, Wilson, 395), they smell the "odour de balsme" [fragrance of balsam] (line 22930), they feel the "rose sanz epine" [rose without thorns], and they hear the sonorous assonance and consonance of Gower's verse, "O amiable, o amourouse / Du bon amour qui toutdis dure" (lines 29927–28). The Blessed Virgin is thus made somatically real as she is translated into a series of bodily sensations that focus and intensify contemplation. The naming passage invites readers to read again, to let time stand still as they experience those sensations and thereby experience, through language, divinity itself. That experience is mimetic in a specific way: Gower's list of names does not itself imitate the Blessed Virgin, but rather mimics the human experience of the ineffable, that which is beyond language and rational understanding. This mimesis is an artifact of writing, as opposed to telling, and it represents a special kind of aesthetic practice. It is a practice unburdened by temporality or by contingency; it is instead ornamented, layered, and beautiful. It is designed to appeal to the senses. Gower may have displaced "plesance" from humans to the Virgin, substituting divine for worldly delight, but the naming passage belies this displacement by repeatedly calling upon sensory pleasure to represent the Blessed Mother. The list of names binds "plesance" to the discourse of devotion, producing a vision of poetics that can include both the moralizing narratives of the *Mirour* and its lyrical passages of praise. Indeed, "plesance" enables remembrance—the other function of poetry defined by the *vita*—by appealing to the sensual, embodied nature of human beings, fixing the Virgin in their minds by linking her to feelings of pleasure and enjoyment.

When the *Mirour* ends, it does so suddenly and reluctantly; the loss of its final leaves deprives readers of Gower's conclusion, which might have resolved some of the questions raised by the metapoetic gestures with which he frames his "Life of the Virgin." At the same time, however, it is clear that Gower seeks, at the very end of his text, to find a way to synthesize the concern for agency provoked by Fortune and the aesthetic values he finds essential to the production of verse. As I have suggested, Fortune can signify in multiple ways, as a principle of contingency, an artifact of providence, and as an excuse for human failings. In all of these cases, the remedy for Fortune is agency, the assertion of the human will and the refusal of bodily desire. Gower knows full well, however, the limits of agency within the Christian model of freedom derived from St. Augustine: acts of free will require the grace of God; such acts depend upon an acquiescence to God's will; and "freedom" does not mean *freedom to* act but rather *freedom from* the desires of the flesh.[19] Because the Augustinian model understands agency to be derived from submission to God's will, not from the overt acts—good or evil—of human beings, it exerts an implicit pressure on Gower's vision of human sin as the source of the world's ills. This pressure accounts for the complexity of Gower's representations of agency in the *Mirour* and elsewhere; though he explicitly embraces an agency founded on action rather than on submission, he also repeatedly undermines that notion, either by exploring the relationship of human beings to the divine or by depicting Fortune as irresistible contingency, as a force of changeability that agency cannot remedy.

The contradictory and troublesome status of agency has an important bearing on Gower's attempts to craft a poetic identity and to negotiate his own understanding of the value and purpose of creative work. His embrace of an agency of acts seems to correspond with a vision of poetics that is didactic and functional; just as human actions have effects in the world, so too does moralizing poetry reform its readers. But Gower's turn to praise at the end of the *Mirour* belies the apparent functionalism of his philosophical statements. The sensory appeal of his praise for the Virgin, its determined engagement with embodied pleasure, divulges Gower's fascination with the capacity of the aesthetic to mirror and to evoke the divine. In contrast, Fortune represents an inverse aesthetic; whether she stands for contingency, for providence, or for fate, Fortune is herself an aesthetic device designed to communicate difficult concepts to people unfamiliar with abstraction. That is why allusions to Fortune are often accompanied by elaborate and vivid descriptions, much like the one that Gower includes in the estates satire portion of the *Mirour*. But the aesthetic qualities associated with praise or exaltation are turned upside-down by Fortune, whose image always includes oppositions like crying and laughing, high and low, stormy and calm, and so forth. Hers is an aesthetic of contradiction, one that is thoroughly committed to the body and to the variability of emotion and desire.

In the *Mirour*, this discourse of Fortune stands in tension with the language of praise for the Virgin. At the same time, both modes of expression

---

19. See St. Augustine, *De civitate Dei*, ed. William Green (Cambridge, MA: Harvard University Press, 1978), volume IV, Book XIV, for extensive discussion of free will. I use Henry Bettenson's translation: *Concerning the City of God against the Pagans* (London: Penguin Books, 1972). Augustine states that "the choice of the will, then, is genuinely free only when it is not subservient to faults and sins" (569), and later argues that "the retribution for disobedience is simply disobedience itself. For man's wretchedness is nothing but his own disobedience to himself, so that because he would not do what he could, he now wills to do what he cannot.... Even against his volition his mind is often troubled; and his flesh experiences pain, grows old, and dies, endures all manner of suffering. We should not endure all this against our volition if our natural being were in every way and in every part of obedience to our will" (575–76).

constitute aspects of the aesthetic that exceed the didactic (sublimity in the case of Fortune, beauty in the figure of the Virgin) and thereby produce a mimesis that goes beyond instrumentality to reproduce the human experience of the ineffable—of radical contingency or of divinity. This mimesis is not goal-directed; it does not recreate experience in order to compel readers to act in a particular way. Indeed, readers are not necessary to it. Rather, the poet's production of experience has significance in and of itself, because it creates an object in which the potential energies of contradiction, sublimity, beauty, and delight are stored—a kind of cultural battery that captures some of the power exerted by those forces to which human beings are subject, forces like contingency, unpredictability, God himself.

These forces are threats to human agency, reminders that human beings are surrounded by powers far greater than themselves. Gower's description of Fortune and his list of names for the Virgin represent two attempts to negotiate the relationship between that subjection and the desire for agency implicit in all of his work. In both cases, he turns to aesthetic modes of expression as a way of exerting control over the powerlessness endemic to human life. Such modes function by mimetically reproducing the human experience of contingency or the divine, sublimity or the beautiful. By establishing himself as the author of this mimesis, Gower begins to articulate a notion of literary authority that allows the poet to have agency while remaining committed to the ideals of didactic work. His representation of Fortune catches hold of contingency by deploying contradictory predicates, substituting mimesis for the kind of overt and didactic warning he deploys in the *Vox* and *Confessio*. In the list of names that concludes the *Mirour*, Gower produces a sensory aesthetic that mimetically reproduces an experience of beauty, which proclaims its subordination to divinity while also enabling him to take up the powerful position of the names. Just as the Virgin hails God in her answer to the angel Gabriel, so too does Gower hail the Virgin, defining her—indeed, creating her—in poetry. Though the Virgin inevitably supersedes Fortune, since it is through her intercession that human flaws can be overcome, the two figures remain bound together in the *Mirour* by the poetics of sensation through which they are represented. In his later work, Gower will confront Fortune, agency, and divinity many more times, and he will negotiate their demands in different ways. The solution he finds in the *Mirour* to the problems of poetic agency and poetic sensuality—its "plesance"—lies in his turn to lyric naming, but it is only a stopgap; he must still address his role as a public poet, negotiate the relationship of Latin and vernacular languages, and, finally, grapple with narrative and its relation to contingency.

What the *Mirour* demonstrates, however, is how Gower creates a space for sensation within the didactic poetic structure that he feels compelled to reproduce. It is a space that opens up in his later work in innovative and often surprising ways. Gower's use of the expressive modes of the sublime and the beautiful, transmitted through the poetics of sensation, reveals to us a poet far more complex than he seems at first glance, when his penchant for moral poetry tends to override the formal subtleties of his verse. Perhaps the word that best describes the *Mirour de l'Omme*—a word that captures the sense in which it is both didactic and sensual—is "experimental." It is a word that reminds us that Gower was surrounded by competing literary traditions in multiple languages, genres, registers, and styles, and that he understood his role as a poet to be a form of negotiation that could both reconcile and exploit those traditions' clashes and contradictions.

Identifying the experimental quality of the *Mirour* is a first step toward accounting for Gower's multilingualism, because it allows us to see that he was not simply imitating his literary predecessors. Gower sought, throughout his career, to build a body of work that persistently experimented with tradition—literary tradition, philosophical tradition, discursive tradition—by exploring the ways in which sensory data allow human beings to apprehend ideas and realities in language. This exploration, carried on in French, Latin, and English, repeatedly asks what poetry is *for*. As the *Mirour* shows, the answer to that question must be sought at the juncture of experience and ideation—the point at which the particular and the abstract make contact—and that juncture is only visible in modes of representation, such as poetry or other kinds of art. For Gower, the poetics of sensation I have described in the *Mirour* provides a means by which the fusion of sense data and abstraction can be mimetically reproduced. This mimesis is not an imitation of reality or of a past text, but a means by which experience can be reproduced again and again. Recreating the experience of the sublime or the beautiful, radical contingency or divinity, lies at the heart of Gower's aesthetic enterprise, beginning with the *Mirour* and persisting throughout his career, and always in tension with (but never subordinate to) his identity as "moral Gower."

eleven

Troilus and Criseyde
Genre and Source

LEE PATTERSON

AT THE END of *Troilus and Criseyde*, as everybody knows, Chaucer addresses his poem as "litel myn tragedie" (5.1786). And as virtually everybody also knows—or at least thinks they know—Chaucer derived this generic term from a sentence in Boethius's *Consolation of Philosophy* and its attendant gloss.[1]

> What other thynge bywaylen the cryinges of tragedyes but oonly the dedes of Fortune, that with an unwar strook overturneth the realmes of greet nobleye? (*Glose.* Tragedye is to seyn a dite of a prosperite for a tyme, that endeth in wrecchidnesse.)[2]

---

* This essay appeared in Lee Patterson, *Acts of Recognition: Essays on Medieval Culture* (Notre Dame, IN: University of Notre Dame Press, 2009).

1. Henry Ansgar Kelly, *Ideas and Forms of Tragedy from Aristotle to the Middle Ages* (Cambridge: Cambridge University Press, 1993), shows the range of meanings that were attached to the word *tragedy* in the Middle Ages. Nonetheless, he is confident that "Chaucer's primary source for his understanding of tragedy was Fortune's rhetorical question in Boethius' *Consolation of Philosophy*" (Kelly, *Chaucerian Tragedy* [Cambridge: D. S. Brewer, 1997], 50).

2. *Boece*, Book 2, prosa 2, lines 67–72; all citations from Chaucer, except those from *Troilus and Criseyde*, are from *The Riverside Chaucer*, gen. ed. Larry Benson, 3rd ed. (Boston: Houghton Mifflin, 1987). Citations from *Troilus and Criseyde* are from *Troilus & Criseyde: A New Edition of "The Book of Troilus,"* ed. B. A. Windeatt (London: Longman, 1984). The gloss derives from the *Commentary* on the

Most scholars have assumed that the challenge for the reader of the *Troilus* is to accommodate its complex narrative to this simplistic generic model.[3] One problem with this strategy is that Boethius makes it clear that tragedy as thus defined is a debased form that should be avoided by the philosophically sophisticated. Lady Philosophy's pedagogy aims to raise the prisoner's intellectual capacity from *imaginatio* to *ratio*. In the first two books of the *Consolation* Philosophy operates at the level of imagination, most pointedly by the *prosopopeia* by which Philosophy speaks as if she were Fortune, "usynge the woordes of Fortune" (2, pr. 2, 2). Before she begins, Philosophy makes it clear that this account of the workings of Fortune is preliminary and philosophically facile. Here Philosophy is instructing her "nory" with "softe and delitable thynges," using "the suasyoun of swetnesse rethorien" (2, pr. 1, 37, 40–41). At the end of "Fortune's" self-description, the prisoner says: "thise ben faire thynges and enoyted with hony swetnesse of Rethorik and Musike; and oonly whil thei ben herd thei ben delycious, but to wrecches it is a deppere felynge of harm" (2, pr. 3, 8–12). Lady Philosophy agrees with him: "For thise ne ben yet none remedies of thy maladye, but they ben a maner norisschynges of thi sorwe, yit rebel ayen thi curacioun" (2, pr. 3, 19-20). The point for our purposes is that among these preliminary and philosophically inadequate teachings are tragedies. They are part of the dangerous poetry purveyed by the Muses rather than the healing wisdom purveyed by Lady Philosophy (see 1, pr. 1, 44–77). They do not instruct the reason but, through the imagination, move the emotions. That is why they are described as "cryinges" that can only "bywaylen" Fortune, as if her workings were by definition harmful, while later the prisoner will earn that *all* Fortune is good, especially that which the unenlightened think is bad—i.e., that which deprives its "victim" of a good that he thinks is valuable, although the only truly valuable possession is a wisdom that once learned can never be lost. In sum, then, for Boethius tragedy is suspect because by appealing to the imagination rather than reason, it arouses emotions rather than imparting knowledge, and the information it does provide is philosophically wrong.

Consolation by Nicholas Trevet: "Tragedia est carmen de magnis iniquitatibus a prosperitate incipiens et in adversitate terminens."

3. The most egregious example of Procrustean torture is D. W. Robertson's influential "Chaucerian Tragedy," *ELH* 19 (1952): 1–37, but there are literally dozens of interpretations that take as given that the Boethian definition of tragedy is central to the meaning of the poem. A brief listing of some of them can be found in Karla Taylor, *Chaucer Reads the "Divine Comedy"* (Stanford, CA: Stanford University Press, 1989), 214 n. 6. To that list one can add Derek Brewer, "Comedy and Tragedy in *Troilus*," in *The European Tragedy of Troilus*, ed. Piero Boitani (Oxford: Clarendon Press, 1989), 95–109; Kelly, *Chaucerian Tragedy;* and Christine Herold, *Chaucer's Tragic Muse: The Paganization of Christian Tragedy* (Lewiston, NY: Edwin Mellen Press, 2003).

The Monk's Tale shows that Chaucer was entirely aware of Boethius's condemnation of tragedy. As almost every reader has pointed out, his tragedies are philosophically incoherent.[4] More to my point, they appeal to the emotions through what the Monk evidently thinks are powerful images rather than to the reason through rational instruction: hence he begins his *Tale* by saying that he "wol *biwaille* in manere of tragedie / The harm of hem that stoode in heigh degree" (1991–92); later he expresses Lady Philosophy's argument about the limitations of tragedy as philosophically useful more exactly:

> Tragedies in noon oother maner thyng,
> Ne kan in syngyng *crye ne biwaille*,
> But for that Fortune alwey wole assaille
> With unwar strook the regnes that been proude. (2760–63)

The best example of tragedy's incapacity to move beyond emotionalism is the story of Ugolino with which the modern instances (and in all likelihood the *Tale* itself) closes.[5] Dante presented Ugolino in the *Inferno* as the final demonstration of the way the sinner can manipulate language to misrepresent the most violent sins, and the Monk surpasses Dante's exculpation with exactly the version of his story, larded with scriptural allusions, that Ugolino would have wished.[6] That Chaucer does not want us to miss the fact that the *Tale* is directed against the Monk's gross misreading of Boethius is accomplished by having him refer to the dismissive definition of tragedy given by Lady Philosophy not once but three times (VII.1973–79, 1991–98, 2760–65)—a sign of his pride in a learning that is all too shallow.

So if we are to dismiss the definition of tragedy that Philosophy gives in the *Consolation* as defining a form that Chaucer would have taken seriously, what else could he have meant by calling his poem a tragedy? There is another definition of tragedy available to Chaucer, which we may call, in shorthand, the Dantean. Not that Dante invented this definition, but in having Virgil call his *Aeneid* "alta mia tragedìa" (20, 113) he was referring to a long medieval tradition that defined classical epic as tragedy. The connection in fact goes back to Aristotle's *Poetics*, who describes the differences

---

4. An early analysis along these lines is R. E. Kaske, "The Knight's Interruption of the Monk's Tale," *ELH* 24 (1957): 249–68.

5. I agree with Ralph Hanna that Hengwrt's location of these instances at the end of the tale is more likely to represent Chaucer's intention than the order in Ellesmere, where they are located midtale: Ralph Hanna, *Pursuing History: Middle English Manuscripts and Their Texts* (Stanford, CA: Stanford University Press, 1996), 151.

6. Piero Boitani, "The 'Monk's Tale': Dante and Boccaccio," *Medium Ævum* 45 (1976): 50–69.

of form and mode between drama and narrative, but who notes a similarity of content: "Epic poetry agrees with tragedy in so far as it is an imitation in verse of characters of a higher type."[7] While the Middle Ages soon lost any sense of the what the classical theater was, the connection between elevated characters and tragedy remained. For Isidore of Seville, tragedies are not dramas but poems (*carmina*) that treat "public matters and the history of kingdoms" (*tragici vero res publicas et regum historias [praedicant]*) or, in a later discussion "the ancient deeds and sorrowful crimes of wicked kings" (*antiqua gesta atque facinora sceleratorum regum luctuosa*).[8] In a culture which lacked any clear generic category in which to locate what in antiquity was known as an *epos* or *carmen heroicum*, the works that we now call epics were instead designated as tragedies. This shift in nomenclature was complete by the end of the twelfth century. In an *accessus* to Ovid's *Amores*, the student is told that "tragedy is . . . poetry about the deeds of nobles and kings,"[9] and by the early fourteenth century Albertino Mussato defined a tragedy as a poem written in heroic meter—hexameters—and dealing with the "open wars in the field waged by sublime kings and dukes." For Albertino, tragedians include Ennius, Lucan, Virgil and Statius.[10]

The point, then, is that our epic equals the medievals' tragedy. Moreover, and equally important, is the fact that for them tragedy is an account of historical deeds. Medieval writers understood the *Aeneid*, the *Thebaid* and the *Pharsalia* as accounts of things that really happened, as histories. After recounting the plot of the *Aeneid*, Conrad of Hirsau says that "Virgil has taken both the subject-matter and his intention from this history." And speaking of the *Thebaid*, he says that "Statius . . . took the subject-matter of his work from the beginning or the end of the actual war."[11] Indeed, Servius—followed by Isidore—complained that "Lucan did not deserve to be reckoned among the poets, for he seems to have written a history, not a poem" and Arnulf of Orléans said bluntly that Lucan's "intention is to deal

---

7. S. H. Butcher, trans., *Aristotle's Theory of Poetry and Fine Art*, 4th ed. (New York: Dover, 1955), sec. 5.

8. *Etymologiae* 8.7.6 (*PL* 82.308) and 18.45.1 (*PL* 82.658). Isidore does add, in a gesture toward the drama, that tragedies were sung "while the people looked on" (*spectante populo concinebant*).

9. A. J. Minnis and A. B. Scott, eds., *Medieval Literary Theory and Criticism c. 1100–c. 1375: The Commentary Tradition*, rev. ed. (Oxford: Clarendon Press, 1991), 23.

10. Kelly, *Ideas and Forms of Tragedy*, 138. For other examples of medieval writers who define tragedy as describing historical events, see 131 (Nicholas Trevet), 151 (Jacopo Alighieri), 153 (Pietro Alighieri), 155 (Benvenuto da Imola), 161 (an anonymous French translation of the *Consolation*, made in the early fourteenth century, which illustrates Boethius's comment about tragedies by reference to the *chansons de geste*), and 162 (Renaut de Louhans, who also gives as examples of tragedies *chansons de geste*).

11. Minnis and Scott, *Medieval Literary Theory*, 63, 61.

with the *historia*" of the civil war between Caesar and Pompey.¹² Bernard Silvestris included Virgil among the *historici* and Alexander Neckham told his students to read the "historians" (*ystoriographi*) Virgil, Statius and Lucan.¹³ And of course when Petrarch came to write his own *carmen heroicum*, the *Africa*, he chose as his topic the deeds of Scipio Africanus.¹⁴ Indeed, even the Monk seems to know that his miserable little narratives are in fact histories: as he says in the first line of his definition: "Tragedie is to seyn, a certeyn *storie*" (1973)—that is, a history.

Chaucer could have derived this non-Boethian and much more capacious understanding of tragedy from many sources, but he almost certainly learned it from Dante. In Canto 20 of the *Inferno*, we remember, Virgil refers to *l'alta mia tragedia* (20.113). Virgil calls his poem a *high* tragedy because it is written in an elevated style (in the *De vulgari eloquentiae* [2.6.5] Dante says that tragedy is written in a *stilus superior*) and because it deals with important matters. As the commentary known as the *Anonimo Fiorentino* (c. 1400) says, tragedy treats "the magnificent deeds and the crimes of powerful men, as did Virgil, Lucan and Statius."¹⁵ Shortly after this identification of the *Aeneid* as a tragedy, Virgil and Dante meet the Malebranche, a squadron of devils with vulgar names and the manners of Neapolitan street urchins. Taunting each other and Virgil, they are nonetheless unable to shake the ancient poet's severe and even haughty demeanor. But Dante is also unable to persuade him that the devils do in fact represent a real threat. Hence the travelers soon discover that Virgil has been tricked by them into thinking that there is a bridge over the sixth *bolgia* (whereas in fact it had been destroyed by the earthquake that occurred at the moment of Christ's death), and they are forced to escape the pursuing devils by a hasty and undignified slide down the side of the sixth *bolgia*. There they are met by the hypocrites, one of whom replies to Virgil's complaint that the devils lied to him with a laconic comment:

---

12. For Servius and Isidore, see Kelly, *Ideas and Forms of Tragedy*, 83 and 115; for Arnulf, see Minnis and Scott, *Medieval Literary Theory*, 155. For a full account of Servius' understanding of *historia*, see David B. Dietz, "*Historia* in the Commentary of Servius," *Transactions of the American Philosophical Association* 125 (1995): 61–97.

13. For Bernard Silvestris, see Maura K. Lafferty, *Walter of Châtillon's Alexandreis: Epic and the Problem of Historical Understanding* ([Turnhout]: Brepols, 1998), 45; for Alexander Neckham, see David Anderson, *Before the Knight's Tale: Imitation of Classical Epic in Boccaccio's "Teseida"* (Philadelphia: University of Pennsylvania Press, 1988), 148.

14. See *Seniles* 18.1, in *Letters of Old Age X–XVIII*, trans. Aldo S. Bernardo, Saul Levin, and Reta A Bernardo (New York: Italica Press, 2005), 672–79.

15. Almost all the early commentaries and many later ones can be accessed on the Internet at the Dartmouth Dante Project. For this specific citation, see http://dante.dartmouth.edu/search_view.php?doc'140051010000&cmd'gotoresult&arg1'11.

Once in Bologna, I heard discussed
the devil's many vices; one of them is
That he tells lies and is the father of lies. (23.142–44)

The most important point for my argument here is that it is also within these cantos—just a few lines after Virgil's identification of the *Aeneid* as a *tragedìa*—that Dante first designates the genre of the very poem he is writing: *la mia comedìa* (21.2). Dante thus indicates the way in which his *Commedia* can include elements that a *tragedìa* cannot, specifically the cheerfully vulgar devils who take such pleasure in mocking Virgil. To be sure, the curve of the action from "wo to wele" (as Egeus says in *The Knight's Tale*) is central to Dante's definition, but so too is the stylistic variation that characterizes comedy. As Pietro Alighieri says in his commentary, comedy is written "in a style that is, in the main, lowly . . . [yet also] in the high and elevated style."[16] The mixed style of comedy can accommodate elements that the uniformly high style of tragedy cannot. But equally important as these two criteria—the shape of the action, the level of the style—is subject matter. Tragedy deals with the world of public events, of history: according to Donatus, "tragedy aspires to historical truth."[17] But comedy describes not events but, as one medieval description of Terence puts it, "the habits of men, both young and old"—*mores hominum, iuvenumque senumque.*[18] According to the schoolbook definitions, it concerns itself with *privatae personae, privati homines, res privatorum et humilium personarum.*[19] The subject matter of comedy is what we would call the character: it represents men and women not in terms of their social existence but as individuals, as the unique and individualized personalities—or souls—whom we meet throughout the *Commedia*. Two lines after designating the *Troilus* a "tragedye," and just before telling it to kiss the footprints of the great classical tragedians—"Virgile, Ovide, Omer, Lucan and Stace" (an invocation itself taken from the end of the *Thebaid*)—Chaucer prays God for the "myght to make in some comedye" (5.1788). In other words, just as Dante contrasts Virgil's *tragedìa* with his own *comedìa* so does Chaucer contrast the tragedy of *Troilus* with an unnamed future work. That this "comedye" is indeed the *Canterbury Tales* seems to me not merely plausible but virtually self-evident.[20]

---

16. Minnis and Scott, *Medieval Literary Theory*, 481.
17. Cited by Wilhelm Cloetta, *Beiträge zur Literaturgeschichte des Mittelalters und der Renaissance*, vol. 1: *Komödie and Tragödie im Mittelalter* (Halle: Niemeyer, 1890), 28.
18. Cited by Cloetta, *Beiträge zur Literaturgeschichte*, 34.
19. These definitions come, respectively, from Donatus, Isidore, and Lactantius Placidus; all are cited from Cloetta, *Beiträge zur Literaturgeschichte*, 28, 19, and 21.
20. For the ways in which the *Canterbury Tales* fit medieval definitions of comedy, see Patterson,

If we grant, then, that Chaucer called *Troilus and Criseyde* a tragedy because he thought of it as analogous to the great classical epics, what are the consequences for interpretation?[21] An obvious one is that we should stop trying to fit the *Troilus* into the Boethian definition of tragedy—a futile task, as criticism has persistently if inadvertently demonstrated—and realize that Chaucer thought of his poem as a history, as (to quote Isidore of Seville again) a *narratio rerum gestae*, an account of things done. Whatever else it may be, *Troilus and Criseyde* is a poem about Troy, the founding moment of European secular history. In 1355, the Northumbrian knight Sir Thomas Gray began his history, the *Scalacronica* with a vision of the ladder of history resting upon two books, the Bible and "la gest de Troy."[22] Virtually every European kingdom ascribed its founding to a Trojan exile, Brutus for Britain, Francus for France, and so on. Furthermore, Trojan history was a topic of significant concern in the English cultural and political world of the late fourteenth and early fifteenth centuries. More or less contemporaneous with Chaucer are two Middle English versions of Guido, the alliterative *Destruction of Troy* and the so-called *Laud Troy Book*, and an abridgement of Benoît, the *Seege of Troye*. Also relevant to this body of writing is the vernacular chronicle, the *Brut*, which promoted London's Trojan origins and its unofficial name of Troynovaunt. Then in the early fifteenth century Lydgate produced his massive *Troy Book* at the behest of Henry V, a very brief prose *Sege of Troy* was composed at the same time, and about 1475 Caxton printed as his first book an English translation of Raoul Lefevre's French translation of Guido delle Colonne's *Historia destructionis Troiae*, itself a translation into the sober Latin prose of the historian of Benoît de Saint-Maure's verse *Roman de Troie*.

A second consequence of recognizing the *Troilus* as a history, despite the narrator's disingenuous dismissal of Dares and Dictys, is to avoid designating the poem, as so many modern readers have done, a romance. Seventy-five years ago Karl Young entitled an article "Chaucer's *Troilus and Criseyde* as Romance"; fifty-five years ago Charles Muscatine saw elements of both

---

Chaucer and the Subject of History (Madison: University of Wisconsin Press, 1991), 242–43.

21. Inevitably, after working out this interpretation of Chaucer's "tragedye" I discovered that I was not the first to make such a suggestion: see Richard Neuse, *Chaucer's Dante: Allegory and Epic Theater in the "Canterbury Tales"* (Berkeley: University of California Press, 1991), 25; and Vincent Gillespie, "From the Twelfth Century to c. 1450," in *The Cambridge History of Literary Criticism*, vol. 2: *The Middle Ages*, ed. Alastair Minnis and Ian Johnson (Cambridge: Cambridge University Press, 2005), 207. This definition of tragedy as epic as applied to the *Troilus* is consistent with the reading of the poem given by Winthrop Wetherbee, *Chaucer and the Poets: An Essay on "Troilus and Criseyde"* (Ithaca, NY: Cornell University Press, 1984).

22. Sir Thomas Gray, *Scalacronica*, ed. Joseph Stevenson (Edinburgh: Maitland Club, 1836), 2.

romance and the psychological novel in the poem, but admitted that it was "a genre unto itself"; twenty years ago, Barry Windeatt applied the terms epic, history, tragedy, drama, lyric, fabliau, allegory and (of course) romance to the poem, and ended by saying that "through its very inclusiveness of genres it becomes distinctively and essentially *sui generis*"; and ten years ago Roy Pearcy described the poem under the rubric of tragedy and romance while Corinne Saunders coined the term "epic romance" to try to capture its generic lability.[23] The problem with using the term *romance* to describe the poem is not only that it ignores Chaucer's own generic identification of "tragedye" but that *romance* was one of the few generic terms that had a distinctive meaning for medieval readers. Although the term covered a broad lexical field, and never (so far as I know) received any sustained theoretical attention, most readers and writers had a pretty clear idea of what it meant. In England it originally signified French as opposed to Latin: in his *Story of England* (completed in 1338), Robert Mannyng of Brunne wrote that "Frankysche speche ys cald Romaunce," and he described one of his main sources, Pierre Langtoft's *Le regne d'Edouard Ier*, as written "in romance."[24] But the primary medieval meaning—romance as a narrative—had already developed in the twelfth-century, when Chrétien de Troyes used the term *roman* to designate his work. "Cest romanz fist Crestïens" he says in the Prologue to *Cligés*.[25] Occasionally, to be sure, the term was applied to works that we would hardly consider romances. The English translation of Robert Grosseteste's *Chateau d'amour,* a personification allegory about the battle between the vices and virtues, opens with a firm generic marker: "Here begynnes a romance of Englische of the beginning of the world." Other works that call themselves romances include the *Myrour of Lewed Men*, the *Trental of St. Gregory* and *Meditations on the Life and Passion of Christ*.[26] But on the whole the term was restricted to the narratives that fit the primary definition now offered by the Middle English Dictionary: "A written narrative of the adventures of a knight, nobleman, king, or an important ecclesiastic, a chivalric romance." Two presuppositions are important here: the focus on an

---

23. Karl Young, "Chaucer's *Troilus and Criseyde* as Romance," *PMLA* 53 (1938): 38–63; Charles Muscatine, *Chaucer and the French Tradition* (Berkeley: University of California Press, 1957), 132; Barry Windeatt, *Oxford Guides to Chaucer: Troilus and Criseyde* (Oxford: Clarendon Press, 1992), 138–79; Corinne Saunders, "*Troilus and Criseyde:* An Overview," in *Chaucer,* ed. Corinne Saunders, Blackwell Guides to Criticism (Oxford and Malden, MA: Blackwell, 2001), 129.

24. See the *MED*, *s.v.,* 3.

25. See Rita Copeland, "Between Romans and Romantics," *Texas Studies in Literature and Language* 33 (1991): 215–24.

26. Paul Strohm, "*Storie, Spelle, Geste, Romaunce, Tragedie:* Generic Distinctions in the Middle English Troy Narratives," *Speculum* 46 (1971): 348–59.

individual hero[27] and the absence of any requirement that the adventures be amorous.[28] Indeed, the contemporary meaning of romance as a love affair, or as designating specifically the erotic rather than the fanciful or exotic, did not emerge at all—surprisingly—until the second half of the nineteenth century.[29] Yet this is certainly the dominant meaning of the word now: if you Google *romance* the first website that pops up is "Lovingyou.com: Love, Romance and Relationship Resources" and all of the ads on the Google webpage are of a similar nature, ranging from "Find Romance Online" to "In Home Sex Toy Parties."

Yet if Chaucer thought of himself as writing a poem about history, why then is his poem dominated by a love affair? Or to put the question in another and more useful way, given the vast amount of Trojan material available to him, why did Chaucer choose as his source Boccaccio's *Il Filostrato*? Boccaccio's poem is after all not a history (or "tragedye") at all but a *cantare*, a genre that deals almost entirely with the amorous doings of the courtly world.[30] The changes Chaucer made to his source have spawned an academic cottage industry, one to which I shall myself make a small contribution here. But the prior question—why this source rather than some other?—seems

---

27. Strohm shows that medieval discussions of romances bear witness to the assumption that they "deal with the deeds of a notable hero" ("*Storie, Spelle, Geste,*" 355).

28. As Jennifer Fellowes points out, "The modern connotations of the term 'romantic' might lead us to expect that love between the sexes is the primary focus of these narratives, but this is not normally the case. . . . This is not to say that love and marriage do not play an important part in most romances, but usually they subserve other themes such as the hero's growth to maturity . . . or are seen in relation to knightly prowess, honour . . . and loyalty" (introduction to *Of Love and Chivalry: An Anthology of Middle English Romance*, ed. Jennifer Fellowes [London: J. M. Dent, 1993], vi).

29. The first use of romance as signifying either an erotic event or—as an adjective—an erotic emotion that I have found occurs in George Meredith's *Diana of the Crossways* (1885), where Diana rather unkindly compares Thomas Redworth, the good man who has always loved her, to Lord Dannisburgh, the wicked but oh-so-exciting man who has nearly ruined her:

> her hope of some last romance in life was going; for in him [Redpath] shone not a glimpse. He appeared to Diana as a fatal power, attracting her without sympathy, benevolently overcoming: one of those good men, strong men, who subdue and do not kindle. The enthralment revolted a nature capable of accepting subjection only by burning. . . . She could not now say she had never been loved; and a flood of tenderness rose in her bosom, swelling from springs that she had previously reproved with a desperate severity: the unhappy, unsatisfied yearning to be more than loved, to love.

In the *OED*, the first mention of *romance* as erotic is from George Bernard Shaw's 1909 play *Overruled*. My survey of nineteenth-century novels would have been impossible without the remarkable website http://victorian.lang.nagoya-u.ac.jp/concordance.html, where one can search concordances for a huge number of English-language literary works, including a number of medieval ones.

30. An excellent account of the *cantare* and Boccaccio's transformation of this popular form into a culturally more ambitious poem is provided by David Wallace, *Chaucer and the Early Writings of Boccaccio* (Cambridge: D. S. Brewer, 1985), 76–95. Wallace usefully compares the Italian *cantare* to the English metrical romance as a mediator of courtly values to a nonaristocratic audience.

not to have been asked. C. S. Lewis said that in revising the *Filostrato* Chaucer "approached his work as an 'Historial' poet contributing to the story of Troy."[31] This is certainly true, but to a degree that Lewis did not fully appreciate. Boccaccio has virtually no interest in the historical context of his narrative. As David Wallace has pointed out, when in a letter written contemporaneously he refers to the presumed Trojan source of the noble families of Italy he does so with ill-concealed disdain.[32] Chaucer, on the other hand, for all his disclaimers about his erasure of history is in fact extraordinarily diligent in both maintaining the consistency of his classical context and in reminding us of the historical significance of his narrative. The poem contains well over a hundred classical allusions, almost all of them additions to Boccaccio's poem and with the vast majority showing both an impressive range of classical learning and unusual precision. For instance, after their first night of love Boccaccio has the lovers lament the coming of day in the general terms typical of the medieval *aubade:* "But the unfriendly day drew near, as was clearly perceived by signs, which each of them cursed angrily, for it seemed to them that it came much sooner than it usually came, which for a certainty grieved each of them."[33] But Chaucer has Troilus lament in terms specific to his cultural moment:

> Quod Troilus: "Allas, now am I war
> That Pirous and tho swifte steedes thre,
> Which that drawen forth the sonnes char,
> Han gone som bipath in dispit of me;
> Thus maketh it so soone day to be;
> And for the sonne hym hasteth to rise,
> Ne shal I nevere don hym sacrifise. (3.1702–8)

Troilus not only invokes the name of one of the four horses that pull the chariot of the sun—almost every scribe stumbled over *Pirous,* the Englished version of Pyrois—but he also refers, here as throughout the poem, to the pagan rites, and especially Troilus's devotion to Apollo, that the Christian narrator will later reject with righteous indignation.[34]

---

31. C. S. Lewis, "What Chaucer Really Did to *Il Filostrato,*" *Essays and Studies* 17 (1932): 56–75; repr. in *Chaucer Criticism, vol. 2: Troilus and Criseyde and the Minor Poems,* ed. Richard J. Schoeck and Jerome Taylor (Notre Dame, IN: University of Notre Dame Press, 1961), 19.
32. Wallace, *Chaucer and the Early Works of Boccaccio,* 176 n. 59.
33. *Il Filostrato,* ed. Vincenzo Pernicone, trans. Robert P. Roberts and Anna Bruni Seldis (New York: Garland Publishing, 1986), 168.
34. In his edition Windeatt points out that this description is found in *Metamorphoses* 2.153–54; for scribal stumbles, see the list of variants Windeatt provides.

Another, even more pointed instance, is when Chaucer inserts an entire, elaborate episode at Deiphoebus's house to allow Troilus and Criseyde to meet for the first time. The fictitious pretext for this meeting is that a man named Poliphete is, according to Pandarus, threatening Criseyde with some kind of legal action, and Pandarus is enlisting Deiphoebus and Troilus to come to her aid. When Pandarus informs Criseyde of Poliphete's threat, she replies that she would not care about him except that he is friends with Aeneas and Antenor. These two are, as we know, the Trojans who will betray the city to the Greeks; and the name Poliphete derives not from medieval versions of the Troy story but from Virgil's "Polyphoetes [or Polyboetes] sacred to Ceres" in *Aeneid* 6, where he is one of the fallen Trojans whom Aeneas sees in the underworld. There Polyphoetes is linked with a group Virgil calls "tris Antenoridas"—the three Antenorians—Glaucus, Medon and Thersilochus. In short, Chaucer had good reason to think that the "false Poliphete," as Pandarus calls him, was an associate of Antenor, and that the conspiracy Pandarus fabricates against Criseyde is later to be enacted in a darker, less fictive form.[35]

This kind of historical siting is characteristic of *Troilus and Criseyde*. And throughout the poem the world of Troy presses in on the local enclave that the lovers try to construct from their passion until it finally collapses. But the question remains: does the little disaster of the love affair (romance) explain the larger disaster of the destruction of the city (history)? At first sight, the answer appears straightforward. The word *trouthe*—which means in the first instance fidelity to a commitment or principle, a value modern English characterizes by the words "loyalty" and "integrity"—appears in the poem, in its various grammatical forms, over a hundred times, and almost always as an addition to the *Filostrato*. Occasionally it is used as a conventional, almost unthinking oath—Pandarus is especially fond of swearing "by my trouthe"—yet as the poem proceeds even these casual usages come to bear a weightier significance. "To trusten som wight is a preve / Of trouth" (1.690–91), Pandarus says early in the poem to Troilus, and then later tells Criseyde that she will be saved from Poliphete's machinations "bi thi feyth in trouthe" (2.1503).[36] A bit later Pandarus reminds Criseyde that she has her "trouthe y-plight" (3.782) to Troilus, and she later confirms her commitment to Troilus himself:

---

35. Servius' gloss to this passage says that "multi supra dictos accipiunt quod fals[os] esse Homerus docet, qui eos commemorat."

36. As Windeatt points out, "Pandarus's words echo Christ's in Luke 8.48 and 18.42" (*Troilus & Criseyde: A New Edition*, 233 *ad loc.*). The anachronism of this allusion makes the echo all the more relevant to Chaucer's audience.

> And I emforth my connyng and my might
> Have, and ay shal, how sore that me smerte,
> Ben to yow trewe and hool with al myn herte;
> And dredeles that shal be founde at preve. (3.999–1002)

"Have here my trouthe" (3.1111), she later says to Troilus, and he later replies, "Beth to me trewe, or ellis were it routhe, / For I am thyn, by god and by my trouthe" (3.1511–12). After the Trojans have decided to exchange Criseyde for Antenor, when Pandarus suggests to Troilus that he seek out a new lady, he replies angrily, "syn I have trouthe hire hight, / I wol nat ben untrewe for no wight" (4.445–46). And as Criseyde prepares to leave Troy, after promising to return, Troilus begs her to have "vertue of youre trouthe" (4.1491). Criseyde promises in turn not to be "untrewe" (4.1617)—a promise that is all the more poignant when she tells Troilus—in a radical revision of what Chaucer found in the *Filostrato*—that she fell in love with him because she saw in him "moral vertue grounded upon trouthe" (4.1672).

Of course Criseyde *is* untrue, despite Troilus's epistolary pleas "that she wol come ageyn and holde hire trouthe" (5.1585). The significance of this failure is made explicit in a line that Chaucer not only adds to his source but has Troilus say twice: "Who shal now trowe on any othes mo?" (5.1263, 5.1681). That this lament can be applied both to the love affair and the fall of the city is clear—and there is no reason to doubt that Chaucer meant his audience to respond to this rather straightforward moral lesson. If Laomedon had paid Neptune and Apollo; if Jason and Hercules had been granted the hospitality they had a right to expect; if Jason had been true to Medea; if vengeance had not been taken on Troy by the treacherous abduction of Hesione; if the next act of revenge had not been the seduction of the unfaithful wife Helen; if Achilles had not tricked Hector into an ambush; if Paris had not used Achilles' love for Polyxena to render him vulnerable; if Aeneas and Antenor had not broken faith with their countrymen; if Ulysses had not betrayed Penelope with Circe, bearing the son Telegonus who would ultimately kill him; and so on and so on. All of these actions—including those of the self-destructive Thebans whose history preceded the Trojan War, and whom Chaucer never lets us forget through some of his most extensive additions to Boccaccio—can be understood as failures of *trouthe*.[37]

Moreover, as Richard Green has shown, in the fourteenth century *trouthe* came to include the meaning "reality," as in "the truth of things."[38] And in

---

37. I have stressed the degree to which Chaucer saturates his poem with allusions to the story of Thebes, and the meaning of such allusions, in *Chaucer and the Subject of History*, 129–36 and *passim*.
38. Richard Firth Green, *A Crisis of Truth: Literature and Law in Ricardian England* (Philadelphia:

Troilus and Criseyde we are encouraged throughout to see the narrator as being *true* to the history he is recounting, however much he might wish to avoid its ultimate unhappiness. He invokes Clio, the muse of history, at the beginning of Book 2 (and in Book 3, Calliope, the muse of heroic poetry[39]); reminds us that if we don't understand someone's behavior that the story took place long ago, and "eech contree hath hise lawes" (2.42); and assures us no less than six times that "myn auctour shal I folwen as I konne" (2.49; see also 3.90–91, 3.575–81, 3.1196, 3.1325; 3.1817). Then, in the final book, when Criseyde admits that "now is clene ago / My name of trouthe in love for evere mo"(5.1054–55), the narrator insists not once but three times that he is following "the storie," i.e., the historical record, "trewely" (5.1037–57). And he goes on to say that "trewly . . . non auctour" (5.1086–88) tells how much time passed between Criseyde's arrival in the Greek camp and her acceptance of Diomede as her lover.

> Ne me ne list this sely womman chyde
> Ferther than *the storye* wol devyse.
> Hire name, allas, is publisshed so wyde,
> That for hir gilt it oughte ynough suffyse;
> And if I mighte excuse hir any wyse,
> For she so sory was for hir *untrouthe*,
> Y-wis, I wolde excuse hir yet for routhe. (5.1093–99)

In this single stanza Chaucer presents us with his rueful, rather awkward narrator, who will not "falsen" the history he is recounting, set against the charming heroine who does, alas, "falsen" Troilus. George Kane has said that the moral value of *trouthe* is "the principal formative concern of Chaucer's mature writing."[40] In the *Franklin's Tale* we are told that "Trouthe is the hyeste thyng that man may kepe;" the refrain of the "Balade de Bon Conseyl" is "And trouthe thee shal delivere, it is no drede." To deny the centrality of *trouthe* to *Troilus and Criseyde*, despite the rather moralistic and old-fashioned quality of such an interpretation, would be willfully perverse. And this moral seriousness, along with its historiographical interest, is what perhaps most distinguishes it from Boccaccio's poem, with what C. S.

University of Pennsylvania Press, 1999), 24–31.

39. Calliope is invoked, for instance, by Virgil (*Aeneid* 9.525) and by Statius (*Thebaid* 4.35 and 8.374), and in one of his *Sylvae* (almost certainly not known by Chaucer) Statius has Calliope predict a career that will reach its apotheosis in an epic (2.7).

40. George Kane, *The Liberating Truth: The Concept of Integrity in Chaucer's Writings*, The John Coffin Memorial Lecture, 1979 (London: Athlone Press, 1980), 12; see Green, *A Crisis of Truth*, 4.

Lewis called—rather ungenerously but not inaccurately—its "cynical Latin gallantries."[41]

Yet this reading in an odd way not only does not account for Chaucer's choice of the *Filostrato* as the vehicle for his own version of the Troy story, but actually makes the problem more difficult. If Chaucer wanted simply to explain the fall of Troy in terms of a failure of *trouthe*, why turn to a version that so assiduously avoids both historical context and moral import? For an answer I must return to my earlier comments about the vexed issue of beginnings. In this poem Chaucer wants not merely to assign a judgment to the collapse of both a love affair and a society, but to understand the meaning of that judgment. If we can say that at the start of secular history lies a great and terrible failure of *trouthe*, what is the cause of *that*? Are we just to say that humans are fallen creatures who often behave disgracefully? Or can we understand moral frailty in more precise terms? What exactly *is* the source of people's inability to behave as they know they should? And I should add here that Chaucer chooses to ask this question in a poem set in classical times precisely in order to avoid the foreclosure of the Pauline answer. In his Epistle to the Romans Paul laments that "I do not that good which I will; but the evil which I hate, that I do," explaining this self-division by invoking original sin: "Now then it is no more I that do it, but sin that dwelleth in me."[42] But this solution to the problem of wrongdoing—inevitable to the medieval Christian audience—Chaucer is careful to make unavailable to the classical world of *Troilus and Criseyde*.

Chaucer's alternative is to explore the way the love affair begins in order to explain its disastrous ending. In this he is following the lead of Benoît, whose poem is filled with the language of beginnings and endings.[43] And his account of the initiation of the love affair in Books I through III is where Chaucer makes the most extensive changes to Boccaccio's poem. In the first three books Chaucer expands the *Filostrato* by over three thousand lines, in the last two by less than a thousand.[44] What Chaucer adds to Boccaccio is a beginning to the love affair that is dauntingly complex. To be sure, Pandarus focuses only on what the narrator calls "the fyn of his entente" (3.553), and he seeks to foreclose the process by which that conclusion is to be achieved as of no interest. As he himself says to Criseyde,

---

41. Lewis, "What Chaucer Really Did to *Il Filostrato*," 75.
42. Romans 7:15–17.
43. See *Chaucer and the Subject of History*, 115–26.
44. In Book V Chaucer actually leaves out a substantial amount of Boccaccio's poem, especially Troiolo's laments for the absent Criseida, whereas in the earlier books he excludes very little of the *Filostrato*, preferring to rewrite what he finds inappropriate to his purposes.

> Nece, alwey—lo!—to the laste,
> How so it be that som men hem delite
> With subtyl art hire tales to endite,
> Yet for al that, in hire entencioun,
> Hire tale is al for som conclusioun. (2.255–59)

For him this conclusion is to bring Troilus and Criseyde to bed, after which "Pandarus hath fully his entente" (3.1582). But are the elaborate means by which that *entente* is brought to fulfillment (which occupies the first half of a very long poem) simply a form of erotic deferral, an elaborately extended foreplay?

To grant Pandarus's view interpretive authority is to reduce *Troilus and Criseyde* to the *Filostrato*. In Boccaccio's poem gestures toward a lofty idealism—compounded largely of Boethian and Dantean allusions—are undercut by a deeply misogynist cynicism. As we would expect, this cynicism is most explicitly voiced by Boccaccio's Pandaro:

> I certainly believe that every woman lives in amorous desire, and the only thing that restrains her is the fear of shame; and if for such a yearning a full remedy can properly be given, he is foolish who does not ravish her, for in my opinion the distress vexes her little. My cousin is a widow, she desires, and should she deny it I would not believe her.[45]

When Criseida shortly does deny it, Pandaro repeats his opinion with exasperation (2.112), and Criseida instantly drops the pretense: she smiles in assent (113), and in her subsequent interior monologue admits to herself and to us her desire for a consummation: "would that I were now in his sweet embrace, pressed face to face!" (117). According to the logic of Boccaccio's poem, this desire finds its inevitable moral extension in her later infidelity, motivated as it is by the "lies, deceits and betrayals" (8.18) that lurk within her. The *Filostrato* must, therefore, end with a misogynist outburst ("Giovane donna e mobile" [8.30]) qualified only by the claim that there does exist, somewhere, a "perfetta donna" (8.32) who is at once amorous and faithful. Nor are these values absent from the dramatic frame in which

---

45. The translation of this passage is not easy, but I have tried to capture as literally as possible the sense of Boccaccio's original. In this I have been helped by the translations of Robert P. Roberts; Nicholas Havely, *Chaucer's Boccaccio* (Cambridge: Boydell and Brewer, 1980); and N. E. Griffin and A. B. Myrick, eds. and trans., *Il Filostrato di Boccaccio* (Philadelphia: University of Pennsylvania Press, 1929).

Boccaccio's poem is set. Written to persuade the poet's own "donna gentil" of the intensity of his passive suffering, the poem demonstrates at the same time the poet's active power as moral arbiter and propagandist. The lady is disingenuously advised to apply to herself only those "praiseworthy things" written about Criseida and to regard the "other things" as there just for the sake of the story—a selective reading that is not only impossible but meant to be so. Should she not return to her adoring poet, runs the clear implication, "la donna gentil" is in danger of becoming known as another "Criseida villana" (8.28) through the agency of the now vengeful poet. His poem is, he tells us at the beginning, the "forma alla mia intenzione" (Proemio), and it accurately embodies the dangerous mix of emotions that women elicit from men who feel themselves to be at once amorous victims and textual masters.

I offer here only the briefest of summaries of the elaborately delicate process by which Chaucer has Criseyde come to accept Troilus. The purpose of his detailed account is to show not only that desire is experienced by Criseyde as an external force that comes upon her, but that even when it has become a part of her—when it has become *her* desire—she is unable to represent it to herself as her own. Aroused first by Pandarus's words, her feelings are intensified by the sight of Troilus returning from battle to the point where she can understand what is happening to her only as a form of almost chemical change: "Who yaf me drynke?" she says. She then retreats to a small private room, and then retreats yet further into her own mind. She debates the question of love in order, we assume, to make a deliberated decision. But the debate remains unresolved, so that what follows is a series of events (all of them of Chaucer's invention) that present desire as at once a part of and apart from the female subject who experiences it. First Criseyde overhears her lady-in-waiting Antigone sing a song that presents love as a benign mutuality. But the song alienates Criseyde's desire from itself by a double vicariousness: the song is not even Antigone's—much less Criseyde's—but that of an unnamed "goodlieste mayde / Of gret estat in al the town of Troye" (880–81). What then follows is a "lay / Of love" (921–22) sung by a nightingale in the cedar tree, a wordless song that by its allusion to Philomela images passion as a function only of the rapacious male. And finally Criseyde dreams that a bone-white eagle with his "longe clawes" (927) rends from her heart from her breast and replaces it with his own, fulfilling the promise of mutuality offered in Antigone's song but also staging the violence implicit in the nightingale's lay of love. By this point, Criseyde has, as she will later, passively say, "ben yold" (3.1210), but her accession to that yielding remains unspoken and unacknowledged. She knows and doesn't know that she desires: she has felt it, heard it, dreamt it—but has she done it or had it done to her?

Chaucer's point in having love come upon Criseyde in this unreflective, subterranean way is to suggest, I think, that the question of morality, of consciously willing and choosing, is here largely irrelevant. We cannot say Criseyde is a victim—she knows what is happening to her and allows it to happen—but neither can we say that she makes a deliberate decision. So too, Criseyde's betrayal is described so that actions again unfold with such imperceptible gradualism, and are so compounded of motives and circumstances, that the search for an explanation—"the cause whi"—is inevitably thwarted. At the conclusion of Diomede's first interview with Criseyde in her tent, "he roos and tok his leve." The passage continues:

> The brighte Venus folwede and ay taughte
> The wey ther brode Phebus down alighte;
> And Cynthea hire char-hors overraughte
> To whirle out of the Leoun, if she myghte;
> And Signifer his candels sheweth bright
> Whan that Criseyde unto hire bedde wente
> Inwith hire faders faire brighte tente,
>
> Retornyng in hire soule ay up and down
> The wordes of this sodeyn Diomede,
> His grete estat, and perel of the town,
> And that she was allone and hadde nede
> Of frendes help; and thus bygan to brede
> The cause whi, the sothe for to telle,
> That she took fully purpos for to dwelle. (5.1016–29)

The astronomical machinery represents not only the relentless passage of time—Criseyde had earlier promised Troilus she would return "Er Phebus suster, Lucina the sheene, / The Leoun passe out of this Ariete" (4.1591–92)—but also the workings of forces that operate in ways unavailable to self-reflection. As the moon leaves Leo so does Criseyde leave the lover who has just been described as "Yong, fressh, strong, and hardy as lyoun" (5.830). Venus is somehow in Diomede's train here, and she in turn dominates Phoebus Apollo: to say that love overcomes wisdom is a possible translation of the astronomical symbolism, but it is hardly adequate as an account of Criseyde's behavior. The Zodiac bears signs, but their meaning is unclear to her, an ignorance that is both the condition of her very existence and a key constitutive of her actions. Lying in bed, Criseyde "returns" Diomede's words in her mind as the heavens turn, a scene that itself returns to the night some three years before when "lay she stille and thoughte" (2.915) of Troilus' words, of Pandarus', and of Antigone's. Then she had heard the "lay / Of love" sung by the nightingale, had dreamed the dream of the eagle, and had awakened (we were prepared to believe) in love.

In staying with Diomede, Criseyde not only repeats her earlier behavior but reveals her life to be a continuous process that cannot be endowed with a precisely demarcated beginning and ending, in the sense of either a single motive or an intended goal. If it were true. as Pandarus had said, that "th'ende is every tales strengthe" (2.260), when we reach the conclusion we should be able retrospectively to evaluate the meaning of the events that have occurred: "But natheles men seyen that at the laste, / For any thyng. men shal the soothe se" (5.1639–40). Criseyde's liaison with Diomede ought to tell us what her liaison with Troilus meant: the end of her career in the poem should make clear the meaning of its beginning. But in fact, far from clarifying the enigma of her character and motivation, much less of human actions in general, Criseyde's behavior serves to compound the difficulty: her end does not gloss but replicates her beginning.

The narrator himself finds this inconclusiveness painful—or so we might judge from his last-minute attempt to suppress it. In the midst of Diomede's second and successful assault on Criseyde, he suddenly introduces into the poem portraits of the three protagonists. The presence of these portraits is sanctioned by the historiographical tradition: Dares, Benoît, and Joseph of Exeter all include similar passages in their histories, and Chaucer's version may owe some details specifically to Joseph. But the point about their late appearance in *this* version of the story is that they evade the very problem of interpretation on which Chaucer has hitherto insisted. By substituting for the detailed representation of subjectivity woodenly externalized *effictiones* ornamented with brief judgments—Diomede has the reputation of being "of tonge large" (804), Criseyde is "slydvnge of corage" (825), Troilus "trewe as stiel" (831)—the narrator suddenly implies that the relation of character to action has become self-evident. But nothing could be further from the truth: the narrative these portraits are meant to gloss mocks their oversimplifications.

We are left, then, with two choices. We can either read the poem as teaching us that historical disasters are caused by the violation of *trouthe,* or that both human actions themselves and their relation to historical events are unfathomable. Given that the poem ends in what Talbot Donaldson has called "a kind of nervous breakdown in poetry,"[46] we are entitled, I think, to conclude with the poet that no conclusion is possible. The relation of the individual to public events, of romance to history, remains enigmatic to the end.

---

46. E. Talbot Donaldson, *Speaking of Chaucer* (London: Athlone Press, 1970), 91.

twelve

The Silence of Langland's Study*
Matter, Invisibility, Instruction

D. VANCE SMITH

> ... *quam dum vestigat ratio, quasi somnia sentit* ...
> —John of Salisbury

I

Material is handled in the Middle Ages, as it probably is today, in a deeply ambivalent way. Material includes a lot: the stuff of body, but also the content of things as abstract as narrative—the matter of rhetorical and poetic invention. Plotinus argues, in fact, that matter literally is nothing, because anything we can say about it, or predicate of it, is really something else—dimension, density, color—that exists independent of, or prior to, matter.[1]

Even what we can say about matter is not matter. John of Salisbury, in his *Entheticus Maior*, an obscure text that Langland will use in the C version of *Piers Plowman*, puts it this way: matter [*hyle*], if you examine it,

> is now any substance whatever, at another
> time on the contrary the same thing is believed to be nothing;

---

* Although I was never a student of Anne Middleton's in the formal sense, I have learned more from her work about the intellectual possibilities for the study of Middle English than from almost anyone else. Even my nonmedievalist graduate students have found her work inspiring because of its attention to the consequences of literature, not just its arid reconstitution. This study of Dame Studie's social and intellectual complexity is in the spirit of her work, even if the matter falls short.

1. See Plotinus, *Ennead II*, tractate 4, trans. A. H. Armstrong, Loeb Classical Library, vol. 441 (Cambridge, MA: Harvard University Press, 1966).

when reason investigates it, it senses it as dreams,
and when you desire to lay hold of it, it soon hides like a fugitive.
Even so the ear hears that sound is absent when it hears nothing,
even so see darkness with your eyes by seeing nothing.

[Si specularis ilen, nunc est substantia quaevis,
contra nunc eadem creditur esse nihil;
quam dum vestigat ratio, quasi somnia sentit,
dumque tenere cupis, mox fugitiva latet.
Auris abesse sonum sic audit, dum nihil audit,
sic oculis tenebras cerne videndo nihil.][2]

The very matter, the content, of *Piers Plowman* behaves like this elusive *hyle:* now clear, now elusive, hiding when you most want to grasp it. John of Salisbury's beautiful phrase perfectly describes the poem's elusive matter, which emerges as if sensed only in a dream of reason.

There are important philosophical reasons, I would argue, why the poem and *hyle* operate in the same way: Langland's poem stakes a claim, on the formal level at least, to articulate what resists articulation. Its several parts, its multiple dreams, each aim for a totality that is broken and disrupted by the presence of the poem's other parts. It is a poem whose totality is made up of broken and thwarted totalities, ungraspable as a whole precisely because its formal perfection lies outside itself. In the same way that matter requires form to articulate what it is, *Piers Plowman* opens itself to myriad formal possibilities and interlocutors who aim to give the poem's matter voice and sight. Dame Studie, for instance, conceives of the poem's matter in this double sense, as both *hyle* and *hermeneia*. Like Will himself, she is conceived of as an ambivalent body, "lene of liche" (10.2)—enough to indicate embodied presence but slight enough to suggest that it is not *too* implicated in the materiality of the world. Her first speech angrily accuses Wit of wasting wisdom on fools, which she compares to throwing pearls before swine. In a shift of metaphorical register typical of the poem, Dame Studie parses this metaphor by saying that it actually refers to anyone who shows "by hir werkes" (10.13) that they would rather have "lond and lordshipe on er[th]e, / Or richesse or rentes" (10.14–15).[3] In other words, the real matter of the

---

2. John of Salisbury, *Entheticus Maior,* in *John of Salisbury's Entheticus Maior and Minor,* ed. and trans. Jan van Laarhoven (Leiden: Brill, 1987), 1:167, lines 945–50.

3. William Langland, *Piers Plowman: The B Version,* ed. George Kane and E. Talbot Donaldson, rev. ed. (1975; London: Athlone Press, 1988). All subsequent citations of the B text will be to this edition.

poem is not material in any sense comprehended by material economies, yet it is expressed in terms of a commodity, "margery perles," that could be considered one of the focal points of a system of secular valuation. The line naming the pearls is interestingly disjointed, its alliterative elements made up of an embedded Latin phrase (*nolite mittere*), an interjection ("man") and a bilingual tautology ("margery perles"). Its semantically superfluous components give it a metrically necessary form, and replicate *in parvo* the metaphysical difficulty of what Dame Studie is urging. Indeed, to use a metaphor Dame Studie herself will shortly use, it is a line that shows how complexly, and how deeply, the writing of the poem (at least as Dame Studie imagines it) is implicated in the metaphorics of weaving. This metaphor, I will argue, lies at the heart of the poem's formal imaginary and at the heart of Studie's embodiment as both a woman and one of the poem's important interlocutors.

II

The ancient association of weaving and writing reminds us that there is something about textiles that implicates texts. The limit case is Ovid's story of Philomela, who can only tell her sister Procne about the violence Tereus did to her by weaving a tapestry. It is a story of extraordinary violence, and a violence that extends to the story's silences, the cutting out of Philomela's tongue and the unexpressed identity of Philomela and Procne, both daughters taken from Pandion of Athens by Tereus, although one in marriage exchange and one by rape. That is what Ovid is silent about, and the silences of Procne and Philomela seem to locate both women not only outside speech, but also outside the regulation of an economy in which they are merely objects of another representational agenda. In the fourteenth century textiles remain women's work, and implicated more directly in economic figuration. Yet outside of narratives that happen to be written by men, there is not much that suggests that women drew as freely on textuality as they did on textiles, and representations of women and writing in narrative tend to emphasize the impossibility of women's writing and of a female economy. Writing, economy, and household all seem to be structured by a masculine homosociality.

The homosociality of the written household is typically expressed in the transactions of Gawain and Bertilak *in Sir Gawain and the Green Knight*. Their compact to exchange winnings at the end of the day, a day in which the erotic and the feral impulses of the household are challenged and reckoned with, is articulated not just as the settling of accounts at the end of the day, but as the inscribing and recording of the diet, the journal, by clerks of different household departments (the departments of, I suppose we could call them, Venus and venery). Those scenes are of course complicated by the poem's collapsing of that very household normativity, the possibility of its representation in the first place, into a libidinal circuit that is entangled with its economic circuit, consumptions that cannot be registered because they cannot be disposed of fully, a libidinal capital that remains unaccounted for, especially because of the inarticulate, one could even call it the unintelligible, body of Gawain in that poem.[4] That is, the body of Gawain is unresolved precisely because it is a feminized body, one that the poem's technology can't account for, unless to posit the negation, the canceling out, of the desirable body with the exhausted body of Morgan le Faye. Yet there is still the unresolved matter of the plot's orchestration by the women who lurk behind the scenes, and whose activities turn out to be determinative but not intelligible—that is, they are directed toward what is unexamined in the household of Arthur, to "assay the surquidrie."[5] What I would argue for is not the same kind of inscriptive work clearly performed by male clerks, the quotidian accounting of consumption and the reckoning of accounts in the anonymous, formal voice of the household officer, but a relation to the writing of the household, to its regulation, that is both more invested in it and that collapses the formal horizon of household writing. Is writing what a man would normally write to write as a man, for one's writing to subject oneself to the clerical and masculine dominion of the symbolic law of the household? As Susan Bordo argues in her work on body-image, "To reshape one's body into a male body is not to put on male power and privilege. To feel autonomous and free while harnessing body and soul to an obsessive body-practice is to serve, not transform, a social order that limits female possibilities."[6] I am going to argue that women can write, and can represent the fourteenth-century household, in ways that don't necessarily imply a

---

4. See especially Carolyn Dinshaw, "A Kiss Is Just a Kiss: Heterosexuality and Its Consolations in *Sir Gawain and the Green Knight*," *Diacritics* 24 (1994): 205–26; Geraldine Heng, "Feminine Knots and the Other *Sir Gawain and the Green Knight*," *PMLA* 106 (1991): 500–14; and Heng, "A Woman Wants: The Lady, *Gawain*, and the Forms of Seduction," *Yale Journal of Criticism* 5 (1992): 101–34.

5. For useful discussions of the poem's work of registration as a circumscription of a masculinized space of appearance, see Carolyn Dinshaw, "'Getting Medieval': *Pulp Fiction*, Gawain, Foucault," in *The Book and the Body*, ed. Dolores Warwick Frese and Katherine O'Brien O'Keeffe (Notre Dame, IN: University of Notre Dame Press, 1997), 116–63 (the material on *Gawain* does not appear in her reuse of this material in *Getting Medieval: Sexualities and Communities, Pre- and Post-Modern* [Durham, NC: Duke University Press, 1999]).

6. Susan Bordo, *Unbearable Weight: Feminism, Western Culture, and the Body* (Berkeley: University of California Press, 1993), 179.

mere capitulation to or repetition of the dictates of the gendered formularies and masculine formations of the ideal magnate household.

By making equivocal or even secondary the masculinized household machinery of representation women show us its limits, the limits of writing and of representation itself. The fourteenth-century Middle English *Emaré,* which comes from the same sources as Chaucer's *Man of Law's Tale* and John Gower's story of Constance in the *Confessio Amantis,* is woven, almost literally, around a robe made from an extraordinary piece of cloth. The cloth was originally made by the "Emir's daughter 'of hethenes,'" and represents on it the stories of Floris and Blancheflour, Ydoyne and Amadas, Tristram and Isolde, and of the nameless woman who embroiders it, the daughter of an Emir in love with a Sultan's son. In one sense, then, this cloth is made out of the material of writing:

> In that on korner made was
> Ydoyne and Amadas,
> Wyth love that was so trewe;
> For they loveden hem with honour,
> Portrayed they wer with trewe-love-flour,
> Of stones bright of hewe;
> Wyth carbunkull and safere,
> Kassydonys and onyx so clere
> Sette in golde newe,
> Deamondes and rubyes,
> And othur stones of mychyll pryse,
> And menstrellys with her glewe . . .
> In that othur corner was dyght
> Trystan and Isowde so bright,
> That seemly wer to se . . .
> In the thrydde korner, with gret honour,
> Was Florys and Dam Blawncheflour,
> As love was hem between . . .
> In the fowrthe korner was oon,
> Of Babylone the Sowdan sonne,
> The Amerayles dowghtyr hym by.
> For hys sake the cloth was wrowght;
> She loved hym in hert and thowght,
> As testymoyeth thys storye.
> The fayr mayden her byforn
> Was portrayed an unykorn,

> Wyth hys horn so hye;
> Flowres and bryddes on ylke a side,
> Wyth stones that wer sowght wyde,
> Stuffed wyth ymagerye.
> (*Emaré* lines 121–68[7])

All of these stories, including the last, are stories of catastrophic or frustrated love, love that remains as yet unwritten—the robe represents the embroiderer at the point before which her love is fulfilled, at the limit of desire, that is, in its purest condition, the impossibility of its ever being fulfilled. Emaré, who inherits the cloth after it is made into a robe, is cast adrift on the ocean after she refuses to sleep with her father. It may be the fault of the robe, which makes her seem, as the poem says, "non erthely wommon" when she puts it on, and her father decides on the spot to marry her. Constance in the Man of Law's tale spreads Christianity wherever she goes, but Emaré takes with her more tangible assets: her robe, but more important, her knowledge of sewing. It is clear, especially after the way the robe itself becomes a figure of writing, that Emaré's knowledge of textiles, which the poem calls "werke," includes "curtesye," the weaving together of the other knowledges that "werke" includes: embroidery, war, ethical actions, worthy deeds. The one domain that "werke" doesn't explicitly include is the "work" of the poem itself, unless it is implicated metaphorically.

In *Emaré* sewing is an insistently gendered kind of representation, a kind of writing that opens the wilderness, whether it is Wales or a merchant's household, to civilization, to the knowledge that comes with the presence of feminine "nurtoure." Without that forceful gendering of representation, masculine desire in *Emaré*, as the story shows us, could not be expressed, forced out, articulated, precisely because that feminine inscription of desire is so philosophically pure as to be unintelligible. It is only when Emaré's father acquires the robe, for instance, that he conceives an incestuous lust for her, a lust that is surprisingly legitimated by a papal intervention (233). That is, masculine desire can always be written even in its most unprecedented and horrifying forms, and it can be written *about*, committed to instruments that belong to a symbolic regime in which masculine desire can always be made regular by rewriting the conditions of regularity. But it is when Emaré's father has this embroidered cloth made into a robe for Emaré as soon as he receives the papal bull, that his tangled and unpleasant desire becomes a

---

7. *Emaré*, in *The Middle English Breton Lays*, ed. Anne Laskaya and Eve Salisbury (Kalamazoo, MI: Medieval Institute, 1995).

bit clearer. Emaré appears to be, within the folds of the robe, "noon erthely woman," a love object no longer falling within seven degrees of consanguinity, no longer, for that matter, falling within any kind of customary or natural prohibition. Just why the robe has this effect we never learn, except that it tends to confound men generally, debilitating particularly the sense of sight. When they look at it they "myght hyt not se/ For glistering . . . " (99–100). It disturbs scopic regimes, of course, but it also shows us the limits of desire's scopos, its target. That is, desire has no limits, and what we see unfolding in the poem is, in the debilitating, unintelligible light of the robe, merely the desire for desire. In pure light, as Hegel says, nothing is seen; in pure desire, perhaps, nothing is desired.[8] I do not want to suggest that the body, whether female or male, falls on the side of unintelligibility, the classic clerical stance toward it as contingent, mutable matter. But I am not suggesting, on the other hand, that it is caught within discourse, rendered, as Foucault put it, either useful or intelligible.[9] What I would like to suggest is that the relation between the body and its economy is a relation that always rests on its limits, a relation that is made in the movement of an economy of making that, like the material in *Emaré*, never fully expresses what is being undone and what is being made.

We see, use, appreciate material because of its economies, whether it is the largest economy of all, the time that is marked by the ceaseless generation and corruption of material, or the much more specific, literal economy of production, value and exchange. Chretien de Troyes's *Yvain*, as Eugene Vance has argued, chronicles and critiques the emergence of a sophisticated market economy alongside the romance. A famous scene in which Yvain discovers three hundred hungry and badly dressed women weaving silk cloth while a sumptuously dressed lord and lady recline on beds of silk is, Vance suggests, "a thinly veiled criticism of labor in a nascent textile industry lying just to the west of Champagne [where Chretien was born and lived] in Flanders." But this moment is not just the primal scene of economic expropriation. There is a third person in it, a girl of sixteen, who is reading a romance aloud. As Vance argues, Chretien clearly wants us to associate this particular form of consumption with the material kind we see in that scene, and to make the connection between the exploited producers of textiles and the (presumably exploited) producer of this text, with Chretien himself. But that turn is a negation of the critique with which Chretien begins. It is not

---

8. G. W. F. Hegel, *Philosophy of Nature: Encyclopedia of the Philosophical Sciences, Part II*, trans. A. V. Miller (Oxford: Oxford University Press, 2004), 89.
9. Michel Foucault, *Discipline and Punish: The Birth of the Prison*, trans. Alan Sheridan (New York: Vintage, 1979), 136.

just that this beautiful girl's reading of a romance is a kind of exploitation because it demonstrates the danger that romances blind one to real material exploitations, even if they are right in front of you. Nor is it that this oblivion, for Chretien, is "threatening," Vance says, "because she and her audience can remain so wholly unconcerned with the marvels of romance (just as they are with the silken rug) as a product woven by a real but nameless human being with compelling desires of his own."[10] The problem is that this critique itself negates the material, placing affective and intellectual labor on the same level as the exploitation of the body, and a body that is female. There are the three hundred women who work, hungry and cold, in conditions not remotely like Chretien's; but there is also the girl herself, whose alluring beauty is a sign of the desire and desirability of romances—she is both their consumer and its product. Yet she is not their producer any more than the desire she exhibits is her desire (if the God of Love were to see her, Chretien says, he would make her fall in love with no-one other than himself).[11] Chretien's economy, then, is very much an economy of writing, not surprisingly, but precisely as an economy of writing it is, even when it critiques the very expropriations that occur in formalized economies, inescapably masculinist.

III

I want to turn now to Dame Studie, not because she's a woman (even if an allegorical one) and women are associated with *materia,* but because I think she brings to a point a similar paradox about the entire poem *Piers Plowman:* it longs for, and anticipates, its own termination the more studiously it analyzes its preconditions. It is a poem that will matter most, to put it crudely, when it leaves its own inchoate, unformed matter behind. Perhaps only Anima oscillates so rapidly between materiality and abstraction and materiality, at one point telling Will "whiles I quykne the cors . . . *Anima* ich hatte" (15.23), at other points that she is *Racio* or a "spirit spechelees" when she leaves the body (15.28, 36). Although Studie is clearly a figure of learning—what she herself says tends to associate her with grammar schools and perhaps parts of the university curriculum—she is precisely embodied—lean and staring. If we didn't know that Will imagines himself this way, we would think of the Hippocratic face of death, a body almost with-

---

10. Eugene Vance, "Chrétien's *Yvain* and the Ideologies of Change and Exchange," *Yale French Studies* 70 (1986): 42–62.

11. Chrétien de Troyes, *Le Chevalier au lion (Yvain),* in *Chrétien de Troyes: Romans,* ed. and trans. David F. Hult (Paris: Lettres Gothiques-Poches, 1994), lines 5371–73.

out its anima. And almost from the start what she says is literally material, using language drawn from the work of spinning: "Wisdom and wit now is noȝt wor[th] a [risshe]/ But it be carded with coueitise" (10.17–18). We veer not only into the world of incipient industrialism, but also into the world of women's work. Even in London carding was farmed out to women, and especially in Langland's Midlands it would have been done by women in the house.[12] In Claudian's Western Roman Empire carding was associated firmly enough with women that it could be used as an insult to masculinity: "If eunuchs shall give judgment and determine laws," Claudian wrote in his invective against the mores of the Eastern Empire *In Eutropium*, "then let men card wool and live like the Amazons, confusion and licence dispossessing the order of nature."[13] What I want to consider is not entirely whether or not Dame Studie is a figure of learning, whether we mean by that partial learning or not.[14] I want to examine why Dame Studie's environment disappears into the milieu of the school so easily, why readers of the poem seem to associate her important work exclusively with the space of appearance, with the schoolroom rather than the household.

Dame Studie first appears in the poem as Wit's "wif," not an unaffiliated "public" woman like Meed (whose filiation is in every sense called into question, as a bastard, the daughter of Fals [2.24–25]). What this means is usually understood semi-allegorically, as if the ties of marriage were easier to understand than, and help to explain, the ties between *ingenium* and erudition. What strikes me about the passus, though, is how differently we might read this passus if Dame Studie's name were different, say Dame Stay-at-home. She has a surprising amount to say about households. She urges Will to cultivate the art of being a generous host, not to become "Homeliche at o[th]ere mennes houses and hatien hir owene" (10.96). She laments the general decline of the importance of the institution of the household, and of traditional practices within it:

---

12. See Marjorie Keniston McIntosh, *Working Women in English Society, 1300–1620* (Cambridge: Cambridge University Press, 2005), 211–20.

13. Claudian, *Against Eutropius*, in *Claudian*, vol. 1, trans. Maurice Platnauer, Loeb Classical Library (London: Heinemann, 1922), 2.175.

14. For recent arguments that Dame Studie represents only the elementary level of instruction in the schools, see Christopher Cannon, "Langland's Ars Grammatica," *Yearbook of Langland Studies* 22 (2008): 1–25; and James Simpson, "The Role of Scientia in *Piers Plowman*," in *Medieval Religious and Ethical Literature: Essays in Honour of G. H. Russell*, ed. Gregory Kratzman and James Simpson (Cambridge: D. S. Brewer, 1986), 49–65. Ralph Hanna has argued similarly that Imaginatif is constructed from basic elements of the trivium: "Langland's Ymaginatif: Images and the Limits of Poetry," in *Images, Idolatry, and Iconoclasm in Late Medieval England: Textuality and the Visual Image*, ed. Jeremy Dimmick, James Simpson, and Nicolette Zeeman (Oxford: Oxford University Press, 2002), 81–94. But for an argument that Dame Studie actually draws on a wide range of sources beyond the schools, see Andrew Galloway, "*Piers Plowman* and the Schools," *Yearbook of Langland Studies* 6 (1992): 89–107.

> "Elenge is þe halle, ech day in þe wike,
> Ther þe lord ne þe lady likeþ noȝt to sitte.
> Now haþ ech riche a rule to eten by hymselue
> In a pryuee parlour for pouere mennes sake,
> Or in a chambre wiþ a chymenee, and leue þe chief halle
> That was maad for meles men to eten Inne,
> And al to spare to spille that spende shal anoþer."
> (10.97–103)

She balances this pragmatic Aristotelian advice about economic circulation with specifically biblical injunctions about the operation of the hypereconomy of charity, choosing one passage that uses the household as both a literal and a spiritual arena of action. Quoting Theologie, Dame Studie says that we must do "good agein yuel" (10.204), by working for the good of everyone in general, and the good of the other members of the household of faith in particular: "*Dum tempus [est], operemur bonum ad omnes, maxime autem ad domesticos fidei*" (10.204a). And most ringingly Dame Studie endorses the lesson Tobit gives his son about the ethics of wealth management: "*Si tibi sit copia habundanter tribue; si autem exiguum, illud impertiri studi libenter*" ([If you have many riches, give generously; if you have only a little, be diligent to give willingly according to what you have] 10.89a).

The quotation from Tobit can be subordinated to the *textus* of the schools, because one of the standard texts was Matthew of Vendome's versification of it, and so it would seem to confirm suspicions that Dame Studie does not know much beyond that curriculum. But in this context Dame Studie's name takes on a meaning that is both more *and* less important than the sense that points us toward the *studium:* to "diligently practice" charity and largess, *studie libenter.*

So why does this larger environment, in which study subordinates not only rudimentary intellectual labor, but also affective and more advanced strands of intellectual labor, tend to disappear? It is partly because we tend to take the schools so seriously as a monolithic and normative structure, perhaps.[15] In reconstructing the texts used in the schools, we may be tempted to treat them as a stable canon that took the same shape and produced the

---

15. See, for example, David Herlihy, *Medieval Households* (Cambridge, MA: Harvard University Press, 1985); Christopher Woolgar, *The Great Household in Late Medieval England* (New Haven, CT: Yale University Press, 1999); Elliott Kendall, *Lordship and Literature: John Gower and the Politics of the Great Household* (Oxford: Oxford University Press, 2008). For primary records of household finances, see Christopher Woolgar, *Household Accounts from Medieval England*, 2 vols., British Academy, *Records of Social and Economic History,* New Series 17–18 (Oxford: Oxford University Press, 1991–92).

same knowledges wherever they were used. That assumption robs them of their vitality and creative force, in the same way traditional source criticism tempts us to think the real interest of a story lies in its strata of borrowings and influences. Even where the texts of the schools was determined precisely and repeated for every generation of students, we need to remember how much generative potential they possess, how exciting they could be, for each student encountering them for the first time. I would like to suggest that we should do that for the records of the household, as well. Historians have looked at the form of such records to reconstruct the normative practices of the medieval household in England, and to show the remarkable consistency of forms of household management and documentation.[16] Perhaps because such practices need to be regular and repeatable, we tend not to imagine that they could embody deliberate initiative, especially when a woman might be responsible for the work of registration.

What would a real Dame Studie look like in the archive of the household? I'd like to offer one possibility, from the fragmentary muniments of a prominent fourteenth-century family. Four fourteenth-century fragments of accounts kept by the Catesbys of Northamptonshire for their estates survive, all written in the same hand.[17] The earliest of these, written in 1380–81, is, like the rest of them, probably a receiver's roll, the counter-roll written by the official presiding over the yearly or term accounts for the manor or manors held by a household. It is the beginning of the roll, and starts, as formularies and treatises advise, with a title spelling out the function and extent of the roll. The title tells us that it covers Michaelmas through Pentecost of 1380–81, and that it is the "Rotulus expensarum domus Johannis de Catesby."[18] That is exactly the formula one can find in every model book and in almost every other set of English accounts in the fourteenth century. But the title continues "yconomie facte per uxorem euisdem," that is, "the roll of expenses of the house of John de Catesby *and* the 'economy' "made by his wife."

There are several unusual things in that last clause. The first is that these accounts record what the roll calls an "economy," a word that does not, to my knowledge, appear in any English account formularies or in other household accounts. One of the most commonly copied sample accounts, for instance, is almost identical to the Catesby's, except for the word "economy": "Rotulus expensarum domini Radulphi Comitis Staffordie de monibus bonis receptis et expen[sis] fact[um] per Johannem Brouleye Clericum

---

16. See especially Woolgar, *Household Accounts*.
17. Kew, The National Archives [hereafter TNA], E 101/510/21 and E 101/511/15.
18. TNA E 101/510/21 mem. 1.

hospicii dicti Domini."[19] The word "economia" has a wide range of senses in the fourteenth century, but its only appearance in this specific context is in the title of one copy of Walter of Henley's *Husbandry*, which refers to it as a "Carmen . . . quod vocatur Yconomia sive Housbundria."[20] I know of no other uses of the word "yconomia" in this specific context, and in a place like the Catesby accounts it is an unusual and somewhat recondite word. It is possible that "yconomia" is simply a synonym for husbandry here, and that the title distinguishes between expenses for the house and for the farm. But the roll itself does not make that distinction: expenses for the two appear together with no discrimination made between the two sites of expenditure. Further, the account includes income from manorial rents, so it is not just an expense account. The expenses in the title would apply just to the expenditures of the *domus*, and "yconome" would modify "Rotulus" rather than "expensarum": "Roll of the economy and expenses of the household of John Catesby." I would argue that *yconomia* here means something broader than husbandry: the broader economic regulation of the entire household.[21] At any rate, the roll itself records the broad economic activity of a large enterprise made up of several manors.

This record of the work of consumption and registration for a large household is subordinated under the name of John de Catesby, whose titular dominion also indicates that this is probably not a record of the expenses and the economy that his wife incurs or regulates. I think it means that his wife made the roll, not that she spent all the money. Later in this account she refers to wine bought for or consumed by "patre meo."[22] Her apparent work on this account is one example of a number of records written by her and John, both obviously highly literate and educated administrators of their own property. John was in fact a man of law, learned and sophisticated enough that his opponents in a lawsuit complained of the "subtiles et cautyles qe le dit Johan ad en la ley."[23] A number of documents from this

---

19. London, British Library, MS Harley 4971, fol. 27.
20. See Dorothy Oschinski, ed., *Walter of Henley and Other Treatises on Estate Management and Accounting* (Oxford: Clarendon Press, 1971), 40. The word in this sense appears in copies of Palladius' *De re rustica* and most commonly refers to what Nicholas Oresme glosses elsewhere as the "art ou industrie de teles choses [appartenants a un hostel ou a une maison] bien ordonees et bien disposes." Quoted in Claire Richter Sherman, *Imaging Aristotle: Verbal and Visual Representation in Fourteenth-Century France* (Berkeley: University of California Press, 1995), 286.
21. A valuation, also in Latin, of Catesby manors from five years later than this account, in 1385, uses the term "husbondria" rather than "yconomie": J. R. Birrell, "The *Status Maneriorum* of John Catesby, 1385 and 1386," in *Dugdale Society Miscellany I*, ed. R. Bearman, Publications of the Dugdale Society 31 (Oxford: Dugdale Society, 1977), 25.
22. TNA E 101/510/21 mem. 2.
23. Printed in J. B. Post, "Courts, Councils, and Arbitrators in the Ladbroke Manor Dispute,"

lawsuit survive, apparently in John's own hand—he refers to himself in the first person several times, and a petition in the same hand is clearly a draft.[24] John also kept Status Maneriorum accounts, which are unique examples for a small secular estate, and are another indication of the unusually strong documentary interests of his household.[25] The innovativeness of these accounts suggests that the Catesby household was unusually sophisticated in thinking about economic matters, and reached for unprecedented ways of representing them. But John's wife's involvement in administration and record-keeping is even more unusual. Her hand also appears in several documents from the lawsuit, including drafts of the final legal opinion, full narratives of the case, and a transcript of witness's statements from Coventry. She was apparently deeply involved in the case, not just John's amanuensis.[26]

The assumption that administrative matters in the medieval household are run by, recorded by, and for the benefit of, the men in it runs deep. The historian and former archivist at the Public Records Office who edited the two Status Maneriorum accounts and the lawsuit documents, J. B. Post, says that the rolls of John's household expenses and the economy made by his wife are "headed with unintentional irony."[27] I suppose what he means is that "yconomie" suggests "economizing," and that, since this is a roll of expenses, John's wife has pretty much failed to economize. Even if this heading isn't ironic, and I don't think it is, it suggests that accounting does more than simply list anonymous expenditures and the various things you happen to have to use or to own. The distinction between "expenses" and "economy" suggests that an "economy" might be different from the business of recording what the household spends, that it is something like the unregistered, as-yet-unwritten business of dwelling in the household, the habits and practices that are recorded after the fact by the tallying of expenses and consumptions. This woman, the wife of John Catesby, makes the economy by living it before it is written. And unlike a mere clerk, she is implicated in the economy of the household directly and pervasively. The account is, in a real and immediate sense, the economy of her own life, the making not just of that economy but of the self that writes it. In a deeper, and materially more important sense, this woman does make the economy of the household. The wife of John de Catesby was Emma Cranford, who brought with

---

in *Medieval Legal Records Edited in Memory of C. A. F. Meekings*, ed. R. F. Hunnisett and J. B. Post (London: H. M. Stationery Office, 1978), 332.

    24. See Post, "Courts, Councils, and Arbitrators," 298.
    25. See Birrell, "The *Status Maneriorum* of John Catesby," 18–19.
    26. Post, "Courts, Councils, and Arbitrators," 299.
    27. Post, "Courts, Councils, and Arbitrators," 299.

her to the marriage several of the manors that made up the Catesby's wealth, particularly the manor of Ashby St. Ledger, which became their principal residence.[28]

That is yet another reason why the heading of that account wouldn't be ironic, because a lot of John Catesby's wealth was Emma's. Rather than drain the household accounts, she contributed substantially to them, at least by bringing manors with annual rents with her when she married John. But I would argue that she contributed to the household accounts in another substantial way. Emma probably kept accounts because of the manors that came with her, manors that established the Catesby family as one of the more important Northamptonshire families. John Catesby emerged after the marriage, at least according to charters, as an important ecclesiastical patron, making grants to a number of foundations. After John died in 1405, Emma's name, along with that of her sons John and Robert, appears almost as frequently. It is likely that Emma had been as interested in ecclesiastical endowments during her husband's life, but that her own interests and involvement are obscured by the nominal control of their property by her husband, indeed by the customary masculine control of the name of the household.[29]

But the names that appear in Emma's own accounts show that it is she who controls the household in a direct and literal way. This 1380 receiver's account is the counter-roll, the register of account drawn up to reconcile and record the returns from all of the Catesby manors and the expenses for the household as a whole for that term. It is made in the form of an indenture, the other part of which was presumably held by the man who collected the manorial rents and presented them and the accounting to Emma, a man named here as William Capellanus, William the Chaplain. Emma's account also names him in the list of those receiving a stipend from the household, the large sum of 26 s. 8d. By comparison, the next largest stipend is 10s.

William is not just an itinerant cleric, who traveled around compiling accounts for large households; he has persistent and very close ties to the Catesby household. A fragment of an undated account, also in Emma's hand, lists the stipend paid to William as 20s., but also lists bread worth 16s 6d.

---

28. The Catesby family is best known for Emma's and John's great-grandson William Catesby, who is the Catesby in Shakespeare's *Richard III*, and for Robert Catesby, William's direct descendant, who instigated the Gunpowder Plot. The Catesby accounts are part of the muniments called into Chancery in the wake of the Plot.

29. There is no definitive study of the fourteenth-century Catesbys and Cranfords, but useful articles are N. W. Alcock, "The Catesbys in Coventry: A Medieval Estate and Its Archives," *Midland History* 15 (1990): 1–36; Post, "Courts, Councils, and Arbitrators"; Birrell, "The *Status Maneriorum* of John Catesby," 15–28.

"empto," bought for or consumed by, William "et sociis," his associates.[30] As his identification as "capellanus" suggests, William may have belonged at this point to one of several local ecclesiastical or monastic foundations, from the college church at Ashby St. Ledger itself to the alien priory of Everdon, about eight miles away, a church where a "William Haukyns" is listed together with two other chaplains on a charter of enfeoffment at the end of the century.[31] It is possible that William and his socii are responsible for one of the most unusual features of the accounts that Emma records with him: they are written on paper, the only example I know of where paper is used this early in a private English household (this is in 1380). The watermark on the paper matches paper made in Rouen in the fourteenth century, and it may be that the alien priory at Everdon acquired the paper from the parent monastery in Normandy. Most of the surviving examples of the use of paper in fourteenth-century England come either from coastal towns and ports or from monasteries and colleges, where it is used, as at Merton College, exclusively for the keeping of accounts.

By the end of the century, William's work and his place in the stipendiary accounts of the Catesby household had been taken over by another man, William Brok. He first shows up on a receiver's roll written by Emma recording the receipt of manorial incomes, from 14 manors, excluding Ashby, totaling 84l. 4s. 4d. It is sewn to a two-membrane account also written by Emma, which covers expenses for the year from Michaelmas 1392 to Michaelmas 1393. Written less systematically than Emma's other account from 1380, it may be the running record on which expenses were recorded as they were incurred. Its title, though, tells us that it is a comprehensive fiscal view of the household in every sense, from the *familia* to the *domus*. It does not describe itself, as the previous account does, in terms of documentary form, as a roll recording the expense and economy of John of Catesby's household. This one says "Expensum noui edificii & iconomie & aliorum necessarium facit [*sic*] per Emmam vxorem Johannis De Catesby," "the expense for the new building and the economy and other necessaries made by Emma, the wife of John de Catesby." Not only is she named here in her own right, but this account gives us a further glimpse into the pedagogical edification of her household, also. As I have suggested, the household did not exactly lack for clerks when things needed to be written and accounts needed to be drawn up. It kept several in the household permanently: William Haukyn, William Brok (col-

---

30. "Empto" technically means "bought," but in many English account books of the period expenditures are a valuation of goods consumed in the household. See Woolgar, *Household Accounts from Medieval England*, 1:40.

31. Berkeley Castle Muniments C/2/2/14 (GC4127).

lector of manorial rents in 1390 and rector of nearby Barton Seagrave), and other unnamed clerks like William Capellanus's *socii*. So what is surprising is the entry for the teaching of young John Catesby in 1392/3, not at the local school, nor by the local schoolmaster, but by a woman named Margaret Islip, who was paid 6s 8d. "per doctrinam" of the 13-year-old "Johanne de Catesby."

She is not Dame Studie, nor was meant to be. But between them Emma and Margaret demonstrate the gravitational pull of the household precisely in the jurisdiction of study. Even further evidence of the study of texts in Emma's household is the set of brasses she probably commissioned for herself and her husband after he died in 1405 (she lived until at least 1414). Rather than the usual text "ici gyst" or "orate pro . . . " around the margins of the image, each brass quotes one half of a responsory from the second nocturne of the office of the dead: "Domine secundum actum meum noli me iudicare nichil dignum in conspectu tuo egi" continuing in the second scroll "Ideo deprecor maiestatem tuam ut tu deus deleas iniquitatem meam" ("Lord, do not judge me according to my deeds, for I have done nothing worthy in your sight" "therefore I pray your majesty that you, O God, will erase my iniquity"). As with quotations from *Piers Plowman*, we are left wondering who is speaking. Whose are "*my*" acts? "*My*" iniquities? What does it mean that Emma's brass is the one that makes the semi-syllogistic petition for the erasure of sins, and in such a perdurable form? And how much of the context of these words are we supposed to remember?

The reading for which this is the responsory seems so apt in this case, when the responsory is used to frame the bodies of husband and wife, that it must have been part of the commemorative scheme as it was originally imagined. It is a reading from Book 19 of Job (verses 20–27): "Have pity on me, have pity on me, O you my friends, for the hand of God has touched me! Why do you, like God, pursue me? Why are you not satisfied with my flesh? Oh that my words were written! Oh that they were inscribed in a book! Oh that with an iron pen and lead they were graven in the rock forever!" It seems more haunting to have to remember these words while we look at words that are graven forever, and to realize that all that is left is the petition, the cry for grace.

IV

All that *Piers Plowman* leaves us with, too, is a cry for grace at the end, an inarticulate and inchoate cry that is unanswered. This ending beyond the capacity of the poem's considerable linguistic resources reiterates the paradox of the figure of Studie, whose very being is pervaded by something preverbal or even below the threshold of speech. A look from her silences Wit; she says a lot about the futility of study, and in the B version comes within hailing range of the rug-pulling garrulousness of Chaucer's Manciple. Which is to say that she undercuts what she urges, an appropriate, well-mannered respect in the face of superior knowledge; not a *recte loquendi*, but a *recte tacendi*. Unlike grammar, however, the urging of *recte loquendi* can't have positive rules; it can't merely be the opposite of suitable discourse or the choice of precisely the right solecism. So what rules does *recte tacendi* follow? Here in this passus it is, as it should be, the rules constraining what is not in front of us: the body. Wit falls silent when Dame Studie gives him a look; Will knows because of Wit's gestures that he, but not Wit, may speak.

Similarly, Imaginatyf tells Will he ought to fall silent in the face of knowledge: "you would have been a philosopher if you had remained silent; I have often regretted speaking, but never regretted staying silent" (*"Philosophus esses si tacuisses; & alibi: Locutum me aliquando penituit, tacuisse nunquam"* [C 13.224a / B 11.416a]). Imaginatyf is quoting here from Boethius and Cato's distichs, texts straight from the schools, and we have to wonder, as Ralph Hanna has urged us to do, what exactly Imaginatyf means by being philosophical, because his orbit is so constrained by the authorities not of advanced speculation but of elementary instruction.

Dame Studie, in comparison, ranges across the field of knowledge, from elementary grammar to arcane subjects. She first gives us a list of authorities—"Aristotle and o[th]ere mo to argue" (10.179) and emphasizes in particular the "Logyk" she has taught Scripture (10.176). This brief and specialized curriculum sounds suspiciously like the curriculum that John of Salisbury says is swamping the traditional curriculum of the schools: the new kind of scholar, he says sardonically, "praises Aristotle alone, he scorns Cicero . . . logic alone pleases [*logica sola placet*]."[32] Yet Studie next describes her role as a very traditional pedagogue, beating grammar into students with a birch (10.177–78), and finally as the founder of necromantic sciences, "folk to deceyve" (10.215). Her epistemic domain, in other words, stretches from the basic discipline of linguistic rectitude, grammar, to the deceptive arts of alchemy and geomancy. "Study" itself is an unstable and ambiguous practice, the pursuit of which does not guarantee the truth of things. Nor does it encompass a stable disciplinary orbit. Her examples and objects of cri-

---

32. John of Salisbury, *Entheticus Maior*, 113.

tique extend far beyond the classroom, shaped as much by the court and the household as by the schoolroom.

The C text revision of the poem in fact deletes a reference to that metonym of the entire elementary curriculum, the *Disticha Catonis,* or what Studie in the B text disparagingly calls the "Catons kennyng" of clerks (10.194). Indeed, in the B text Studie cites as an example of the deficiency of that kind of knowledge a distich that seemingly endorses deception, the beguiling of art with art. The site of knowledge in the C text, in other words, rests less securely on the already destabilized foundation of the classical curriculum. Knowledge and rectitude are impeached at least as strongly by the demands of the household. Scattered throughout Studie's discourse are references to animal husbandry (don't cast pearls before swine who already have "hawes at wille" [B 10.10]), the eleemosynary obligations of the table in a wealthy household to the beggars at its gate (B 10.58), and the talk that follows the minstrels at a meal when they are "stille" (B 10.52). More protractedly Studie complains about the deformation of the traditional household by new practices:

> Eleng is the halle, ech day in the wike,
> Ther the lord ne the lady liketh noght to sitte.
> Now hath ech riche a rule—to eten by hymselve
> In a pryvee parlor for povere mennes sake,
> Or in a chamber with a chymenee, and leve the chief halle
> That was maad for meles, men to eten inne,
> And al to spare to spille that spende shal another.
> (B 10.96–102)

This complaint is Studie's most specific and pointed, and suggests the importance to her of the household as a site of both misrule and of potential rectitude. Even the excision of this passage in the C text underscores this importance. Replacing the entire passage, and a subsequent criticism of the idle theological speculation that goes on over the banquet table, is a more abstract but global critique of household practices: lords only want, says Dame Studie, to hear how they might "leest goed spene" (C 11.75) and the only wit that matters is what "of wynnynge soune" (C 11.77). The focus of critique, in other words, moves from the kinds of comportment that enable charity to the governing principle of household economics, of "wynnynge."

The other important site of critique in Studie's discourse is the law court. We already know that the law court is a bad place from the opening passus of the poem, over which Fals, Wrong, and Lady Meed preside. And that is ostensibly the reason Langland steers us away from this impasse by beginning the C version of the Studie passus with a quotation that leaves us in no doubt about the bad faith implicit in such eloquence. The B text's general complaint at the start of the Studie passus concerns anyone who "can construe deceits and conspire wronges . . . and . . . lette þe truthe" (10.19–20). In the C text the complaint is precisely focused on the law: whoever can do all this *and* "coveite" will be "cleped into consayle" (C 11.18). This refinement, if we can call it that, is underpinned by a new quotation in the C text: "*Qui sapiunt nugas & crim[ina] lege vocantur; / Qui recte sapient lex iubet ire foras*" ("Those who know about trifles and slander are called in by the law; those who are truly wise the law commands to go out/ to go forth" [C 11.18a–18b]). The source of this quotation is part of the play of intellectual reference, and of sites of knowledge, in this passus. It comes from one of John of Salisbury's lesser works, the *Entheticus Maior*, in a section that has extraordinary resonance for *Piers*, concerning the scandals, vanities and *nugae* of the court, and of lawyers in particular.[33] The following section concerns the obligations of households to extend hospitality, and these two sections on the depredations of English culture are preceded by a long analysis of the failures of contemporary education to appreciate the *auctores*, part of which I have already quoted. Indeed, the whole of the *Entheticus Maior*, which spans John of Salisbury's own career from a student in Paris to a member of the curia at Canterbury, with its fluid associations of social, political, and academic sites of interest, is startlingly like Dame Studie's discourse, and if the evidence did not suggest that Langland came across the *Entheticus Maior* late in the career of the poem, it would appear to be a specifically literary antecedent.[34] My point is that Studie steps out of the schoolroom and

---

33. The *Entheticus Maior*, also known as the *Entheticus de Dogmate Philosophorum*, survives in three complete medieval copies, one of them produced at St. Albans and owned by Richard de Bury. There are at least three extracts or digests of it, and they appear with John of Salisbury's better-known works, the *Policraticus* or the *Metalogicon*. The *Entheticus Minor*, also called the *Entheticus in Policraticum*, usually appears as an introductory poem with the *Policraticus*. It is largely an extract of Part Three of the *Entheticus Maior*, which concerns court and curia. See Laarhoven, 1:25–35, 71–75.

34. Its ramshackle, stop-and-start structure contains a remarkably large range of topics and modes, including a discussion about grammar and morality, grace, causality, fortune, the classics, philosophy, the order of the sciences, and scripture in the first 450 lines; a meandering description of classical philosophers; and a satirical portrait of English institutions under King Stephen (mostly) that reads much like passus 3 and 4 of the B text, which also includes a complaint about the danger of a country that has a youthful king (lines 1464–65). One of the three surviving manuscripts of the *Entheticus* is contained in a miscellany of texts about the kinds of knowledge that Studie mentions: Cambridge, University Library, MS Mm ii 18, a fourteenth-century compilation that includes, among others, a text of the *Consolation of Philosophy*, texts on algebra, strategy, geometry, astronomy, epigrams attributed to Martial, and excerpts from Macrobius's *Saturnalia*, Ovid, Gospel commentaries, Gerald of Wales's *Topographia Hiberniae*, and John of Salisbury's *Metalogicon*. Miscellanies like this are

the household in the C-Text to quote from a relatively arcane philosophical text—indeed, one about the difficulties of philosophical speech—to suggest that the site of *recte loquendi* lies not there, nor in the court, nor in the household, but simply "foras," "outside."

It is here, I think, that the passage's importance for an understanding of Langland's literary imaginary comes into focus. Studie's discourse is a systematic exposure of the tractability, indeed the unsettling contingency, of traditional kinds of literary and intellectual matter. To step outside them is not to discard them altogether, but to take their practices to new sites of knowledge, especially the baffling one Studie calls love. This movement is the inverse of one that Chaucer makes in his career, according to Anne Middleton, in taking the forms of decorous 'luf-talkyng,' in her words, "*out of court*" in the *Canterbury Tales*.[35] Langland's, or Studie's, calling out of court of the truly wise in order to pursue the science of love would seem to thwart the very purpose of study itself, to acquire and use technical practices in a circumscribed domain. And yet these practices are no longer sufficient, even when used as a means to critique their importance, as with the distich whose ultimate point is not to heed the advice of distichs. In other words, the passage also concerns the problem that Langland voices so sharply in the C text autobiographical passage about the practice and form that will legitimate— or more precisely *not deligitimate*—the poem. Its quest for true wisdom calls it forth on the way to love, yet places it outside the secure domain of traditional discursive practices.

Like the narrators in the *Canterbury Tales* whom Middleton refers to as "new men," defined by their "literary conduct, rather than objective social status," Studie gives traditional forms of knowledge and narration a new ethical purpose.[36] Indeed, her B text discourse initially imagines these forms of knowledge as recalcitrantly embodied, "Plato," "Aristotle," a spanking Grammar, or as objects insistently materialized, like a book or a "forcere" full of "fibiches" (B 10.211). In cutting out what was starting to become an encyclopedic catalogue of the kinds of matter that could be objects of study, Langland takes Studie out of the anti-intellectual impasse in which she finds herself in the B text, and indeed out of the impasse in which a woman is seen to be caught within highly tractable matter. It is not so much that Langland's silence in the C text about how to classify improper knowledge

---

probably what Studie has in mind when she talks about the various disciplines she teaches—measurement, theology, astronomy, and geometry (B 10.179–207).

35. Anne Middleton, "Chaucer's 'New Men' and the Good of Literature in the *Canterbury Tales*," in *Literature and Society*, ed. Edward Said (Baltimore: Johns Hopkins University Press, 1980), 40.

36. Middleton, "Chaucer's 'New Men' and the Good of Literature," 16.

encourages us to look ahead to further forms of knowing—to Clergie, to Scripture, etc. It is that the silences *of and in* the space of appearance—the court, the schoolroom, the household—are where we find love, the only possible response to theology, or at least where we know we are no longer being deluded by mere art.

thirteen

Voice and Public Interiorities
Chaucer, Orpheus, Machaut

DAVID LAWTON

"A voice neither universal nor personal ... a common voice"

Whatever happened to voice? Critical use of the term is often diffident, and as far from standardized as any critical term can be. Paul Zumthor's comment in 1983 remains true: "It is strange that, among all the institutionalized disciplines, there is not yet a science of voice. Let us hope that one is forthcoming."[1] It is unlikely to be a science. The term voice itself appears more often than not in inverted commas, in order perhaps to distinguish literary voice from actual, physical voice (a not unproblematic distinction); but we have no such compunction about inverted commas in our use of the term "body." And, as with body, the definitions implied by the use of "voice" are many and various. I suspect that a certain reticence about voice in Anglo-Saxon contexts still lingers from the suspicion that "voice" is an unreconstructed leftover from New Criticism. I believe that New Criticism is strong and still relevant in the area of voice; but in truth the term has since been much reconstructed, especially by scholars working in European languages: such as Zumthor himself, Barthes on the "grain of the voice,"[2]

---

1. Paul Zumthor, *Oral Poetry: An Introduction*, trans. Kathleen Murphy-Judy (Minneapolis: University of Minnesota Press, 1983), 4.

2. Roland Barthes, "The Grain of the Voice" (1972), in *Image, Music, Text*, trans. Stephen Heath (New York: Hill and Wang, 1978), 179–89.

Mladen Dolar on voice as the Lacanian *objet petit a*,[3] and Adriana Cavarero's work on a philosophy of vocal expression.[4] I would argue that voice is among the most productive terms we have for understanding literature; that our experience of reading and writing literature is crucially bound up with questions of voice; and that the literary history of voice, though divided into episodes each important enough to seem like new beginnings, is continuous from the medieval period, specifically from the new medieval voicing of literature composed in the vernacular languages. A longer perspective would also be valuable: both biblical and classical texts are central to medieval practices of voicing, but as a prehistory that is drawn upon and remodeled when medieval writers come to narrate the vernacular. A continuous history of voice in English and other European literatures needs to begin with the medieval, and with the function of voicing in producing what I have called public interiorities.[5]

The subject of this essay is therefore the interrelation between voice and "public," the latter defined both as public life of and in institutions, alongside their practices of written record, and also as the common European literary heritage of classic texts that offer models for vernacular voicing. I shall focus here on the Ovidian, and two of the three shaping figures of the artist in the *Metamorphoses:* in reverse order of importance, Pygmalion and Orpheus. Together with the third such figure, Narcissus, they insistently relate voice (Orpheus's song, Pygmalion's prayer, Echo) and image (Eurydice's specter, Pygmalion's statue, Narcissus's reflection). In medieval grammatical theory, the complementarity of voice and image is fulfilled in letters themselves. This is the science that Chaucer cheerfully twists in glossing the appearance of images in the Houses of Fame and Rumor:

> Whan any speche ycomen is
> Up to the palais, anoonright
> It waxeth like the same wight
> Which that the word in erthe spak,
> Be it clothed red or blak,
> And so wereth his liknesse
> That spak the word, that thou wilt gesse
> That it the same body be,

---

3. Mladen Dolar, *A Voice and Nothing More* (Cambridge, MA: MIT Press, 2006).

4. Adriana Cavarero, *For More Than One Voice: Toward a Philosophy of Vocal Expression,* trans. Paul A. Kottman (Stanford, CA: Stanford University Press, 2005). I have also been much instructed by Steven Connor's history of ventriloquism, *Dumbstruck* (Oxford: Oxford University Press, 2000).

5. David Lawton, "Voice after Arundel," in *After Arundel,* ed. Vincent Gillespie and Kantik Ghosh (Turnhout: Brepols, 2011), 133–54.

Man or womman, he or she.
And is nat this a wonder thing?
(*House of Fame* 1074–83)⁶

This is the eagle's adaptation of stock passages in Boethius' *De Musica* and, most obviously, Donatus on the "multiplicacioun of soun": speche, or word, or voice, is *aer ictus,* ayr ybroken, a series of ripples that in the *House of Fame* turns at the last into visual images, likenesses. The eagle's explanation upends Donatus' focus on the written form of utterance, letters, which are supposedly the images of sounds, and takes a huge, surreal step backwards from the utterance to its maker. Voice and image are identical, but alienated from one another. These voice-images here are like the dead in Homer's underworld: as Proust describes memory, "real without being present, ideal without being abstract." But their language is that of the living, coming not only from literature, the international and the classic, as in the House of Fame, but also from new social institutions, as in the House of Rumor, whose voices are pushing their way into literature for the very first time—guild, parliament, bills, the government offices of Chancery and Privy Seal, the shared interiorities of devotion and commonplace book.

A range of historical meanings is relevant to a study of late medieval voice. The concept is spread across several classical terms, with the human voice distinguished from the sounds of musical instruments but then often explained in terms of one type of instrument or another (percussion or string).⁷ Voice is almost nothing, in one musically derived definition *aer ictus,* or like starlight; we perceive it as it dissipates, having already left a body. Yet, as Elaine Scarry reminds us, body and voice "are among the most elementary and least metaphorical categories we have."⁸ This does not make voice an easy subject. For Clement of Alexandria, according to Peter Brown, it was "the most delicate instrument of all . . . Greek and Near Eastern ears had a sensitivity to the human voice that takes some mental effort if the modern Anglo-Saxon imagination is to recapture it."⁹ For Aristotle in *De*

---

6. Quotations from *The Riverside Chaucer,* gen. ed. Larry Benson, 3rd ed. (Boston: Houghton Mifflin, 1987).

7. Charles Burnett, "Sound and Its Perception in the Middle Ages," in *The Second Sense: Studies in Hearing and Musical Judgment from Antiquity to the Seventeenth Century,* ed. Charles Burnett, Michael Fend, and Penelope Gouk (London: Warburg Institute, 1991), 43–69.

8. Elaine Scarry, *The Body in Pain: The Making and Unmaking of the World* (Oxford: Oxford University Press, 1987), 182.

9. Peter Brown, *The Body and Society: Men, Women, and Sexual Renunciation in Early Christianity* (New York: Columbia University Press, 1988), 126.

Anima, the voice proceeds from the soul (as air, as spirit); it is the outward form of the imagination. And so voice is both a signature, "I," singularity, and a clear marker of difference, "not I," multiplicity (so both Many and One). It sometimes operates as a trace, the mere presumption of a body, as in the standard use of *vox* to mean text, the already spoken or written. So voice has to do crucially with translation and interpretation; intertextuality, or "intervocality";[10] performance and the memory or potential of performance (Zumthor clearly had in mind a notion of scribal performance as voicing when he coined the term *mouvance*); a dialectic of presence and absence; the subject; words not always fully inhabited by a speaker. Medieval readers are trained in voice. Culturally standard modes of reading—in schooling, in religious practice—do in fact extend an invitation to their readers to inhabit, or try, the voices of the texts they read. I think here of Jody Enders's work on rhetorical *actio;*[11] of Marjorie Curry Woods's account of the pedagogical uses of rape in Pamphilus and Galatea;[12] of Anne Astell's account of the Song of Songs, where readers are asked alternately to occupy, or audition for, the roles of both Bride and Bridegroom;[13] and Matthew Parker's program for reading the Psalms: "Whoever taketh this book in his hand here reputeth and thinketh all words he readeth (except the words of prophecy) to be his very own words spoken in his own person."[14] Impersonation begins at home. And if one emblem for the cultivation of voice is, as in the last example, David, his classical counterpart is Orpheus—whose inevitable association with voice is signaled in the received etymology of his name as Oraia-Phone, Consummate Voice.[15] To conceptualize voice is at once to think of Orpheus. It is true for *sonus,* music in general (ninth-century attempts at musical notation worked with a stave that represented Orpheus's lyre),[16] and for *vox,* that special music of the human voice.

---

10. The term is Paul Zumthor's, *La lettre et la voix* (Paris: Seuil, 1987), 161.

11. Jody Enders, *Rhetoric and the Origins of Medieval Drama* (Ithaca, NY: Cornell University Press, 1992).

12. Marjorie Curry Woods, "Rape and the Pedagogical Rhetoric of Sexual Violence," in *Criticism and Dissent in the Middle Ages,* ed. Rita Copeland (Cambridge: Cambridge University Press, 1996), 56–86.

13. Ann W. Astell, *The Song of Songs in the Middle Ages* (Ithaca, NY: Cornell University Press, 1990), especially chap. 7.

14. Matthew Parker, *The Whole Psalter Translated into English Metre* (London, 1567), quoted in James Simpson, *Burning to Read: English Fundamentalism and its Reformation Opponents* (Cambridge, MA: Harvard University Press, 2007), 163–64.

15. John Block Friedman, *Orpheus in the Middle Ages* (Cambridge, MA: Harvard University Press, 1970), 89.

16. I am grateful to Christopher Page for pointing this out to me, and to the Middle English seminar at the University of Cambridge, in which I read the first version of this paper in January 2009.

In thinking through the relation of literary voice to literary (and political) public, the single most helpful resource is Anne Middleton's groundbreaking essay, published in 1978, on "The Idea of Public Poetry in the Reign of Richard II."[17] The voice delineated in the essay is one that articulates shared values of its community. Middleton argues that "public poetry" is to be defined not by its subject but by its relation to its audience; indeed, she claims, its subject is that relation itself. A useful analogy might be with Erasmus's *Adages*, which anthologizes many hundreds of *sententiae* that are the common property of Erasmus and his public, collected under the rubric "Friends hold all things in common" (the title of Kathy Eden's study).[18] Yet this community of shared sentence is not altogether inclusive—it's actually defined precisely by the knowledge of the sentences it presumes; and the anthologizer stakes an uncommon claim to something like intellectual property in the act of representing it. Middleton's account of public Ricardian poetry is to be supplemented by her slightly later distinction between a text's audience, which is actual, and its public, which it imagines;[19] there is normally a shortfall between the two. One might call that shortfall, in Huizinga's sense, playful. The voice of public poetry speaks "as if to the entire community, not to a coterie or patron" (98). The transparency Middleton ascribes to it is, as she clearly shows, factitious, part of its own self-fashioning. Nor is it a single voice, since, like Erasmus's *Adages*, it is composed of many hundreds of antecedent sentences. But it is a voice: for Langland and Gower, "a voice neither universal nor personal but a "middel wei" between the two, a common voice," that—it sounds rather Jeffersonian—of "an enlightened citizen among peers" (114).

Given this hallmark, it is perhaps troubling that Middleton is adamant in excluding Chaucer from "the idea of public poetry," except, as she says, intermittently and by indirect discourse. She has good reason for this, since she sees Chaucer addressing a narrower public of "new men," but I would be worried by an implication that one cannot be both public and indirect—someone ought to tell politicians—and, more, that Chaucer's multiple voices disqualify him from enlightened citizenship. I suspect against its will, the essay contributes to a long history of Chaucerian exceptionalism. In 1982 it marked, and added impetus to, a necessary movement of the field away from a Chaucer or even "Age of Chaucer" center; at the time, the "reign

---

17. *Speculum* 53 (1978): 94–114.
18. Kathy Eden, *Friends Hold All Things in Common: Tradition, Intellectual Property, and the "Adages" of Erasmus* (New Haven, CT: Yale University Press, 2001).
19. Anne Middleton, "The Audience and Public of *Piers Plowman*," in *Middle English Alliterative Poetry and Its Literary Background*, ed. David Lawton (Cambridge: D. S. Brewer, 1982), 101–23, 147–53.

of Richard II," following Burrow's *Ricardian Poetry*, was a more capacious alternative.[20] Middleton was concerned to decenter Chaucer from the literary history of the long fifteenth century, and her impulse was in that sense profoundly just. Large as Chaucer looms, experimentation with voice occurs in very different forms outside his work, and continues after him, and sometimes in spite of him, in a fifteenth century whose innovative multivocality is still inadequately recognized. Middleton's was a necessary move in opening up the fertile review of the fifteenth century that has occupied much of the intervening generation, yet one that came dangerously close to quarantining Chaucer as anomalous. (In a changed critical climate I risk an equal and opposite danger here, by centering a discussion of voice on Chaucer.) The effect of the quarantining was compounded when in criticism contemporary with and after Middleton's, Bakhtin entered the equation and, in what I see as a radical misunderstanding of his work, much fifteenth-century poetry is cast as "monologic" in contrast to Chaucer's "dialogic."[21] In fact, the voice that presents itself as single and transparent and the voices that flaunt themselves as many are both multiple, the one more heterogeneous than it pretends to be, if only in consequence of the sentences that help compose it, the other operating its diversity from a staple, surprisingly less variable, stylistic repertoire (many voices from a much smaller range of styles). This is a formal mathematics of voice that applies both to Chaucer and to poets who come after him such as Hoccleve, Lydgate, and Skelton.

Middleton's essay did much to re-energize voice as a critical category in medieval studies that could be recuperated—as, for her and most others, *persona* could not be[22]—from the New Criticism. In the intervening years, voice has been theorized, as already mentioned; it has been historicized, as for example in the work of Emily Steiner on the idea of the commune[23] and Matthew Giancarlo's fine recent study of literature and parliament,[24] which

---

20. J. A. Burrow, *Ricardian Poetry: Chaucer, Gower, Langland, and the "Gawain" Poet* (New Haven, CT: Yale University Press, 1971).

21. I argue the point about Bakhtin in "English Literary Voices, 1350–1500," in *The Cambridge Companion to Medieval English Culture*, ed. Andrew Galloway (Cambridge: Cambridge University Press, 2011), 238–39.

22. Middleton, "Audience and Public," 109: "The problem of the *persona* virtually disappears if we take these voices seriously." I have tried to maintain both terms, as in my essays "Skelton's Use of Persona," *Essays in Criticism* (1980): 9–28, and "The Subject of *Piers Plowman*," *Yearbook of Langland Studies* 1 (1987): 1–30.

23. Emily Steiner, "Commonalty and Literary Form in the 1370s and 1380s," *New Medieval Literatures* 6 (2003): 199–222; see also her *Documentary Culture and the Making of Medieval English Literature* (Cambridge: Cambridge University Press, 2003).

24. Matthew Giancarlo, *Parliament and Literature in Late Medieval England* (Cambridge: Cambridge University Press, 2007).

puts voices at the center of both artistic and political representation; it has been textualized, as in the work of Mary Carruthers (I think here of her insistence that an *auctor* is a text, not a person);[25] it has been essentialized, as in some gender studies. These form a range of critical perspectives in which voice passes between text and reader, between poet and public. Mindful of Katherine Zieman's fine work, and her claim that "Chaucer articulates the literary through a conceptualization of 'voice,'"[26] I would like to reposition Chaucer in this landscape—as a public poet, and a poet concerned with voice.

"real without being present, ideal without being abstract"

First, a new definition is in order. The term voice itself has a long prehistory, latterly too caught up in battles between speech and writing, presence and absence, and from ancient times in a state of complex tension between the physical voice and the word's more abstract, sometimes apparently more idealized or even metaphorical, meanings as breath or spirit. What do I mean by voice? I begin with a much later turning point in the history of voice: *In Search of Lost Time*. Proust's Narrator makes western literature's aboriginal, and surely its most portentous, telephone call. Since no words are better than Proust's, and there is no hubris greater than the illusion that one can summarize his prose, I shall give his account very largely in his own words. It occurs at an early moment in what are not yet mass communications, when the telephone is almost impossibly new-fangled and very few families have them in their homes. In order to receive the call from his grandmother, the Narrator is taken by his friend Saint-Loup to the post office at Doncières, where at a pre-arranged time he is connected manually by an operator. His grandmother's purpose is to persuade him to stay on in Normandy with Saint-Loup for the good of his health rather than return to her in Paris (and so she conceals from him her own serious illness). After initial difficulty,

> I spoke, and after a few seconds of silence I suddenly heard the voice I mistakenly thought I knew so well, for until then, whenever my grandmother had talked with me, I had always followed what she was saying on the open score of her face, in which her eyes were so predominant; but today what I was hearing for the first time was her actual voice. And because the propor-

---

25. Mary Carruthers, *The Book of Memory*, 2nd ed. (Cambridge: Cambridge University Press, 2008), 190–91.
26. Katherine Zieman, "Chaucer's *Voys*," *Representations* 60 (1997): 70–91 (71).

tions of that voice seemed different the minute it was isolated, reaching me on its own in this way, unaccompanied by the facial features, I was aware for the first time how affectionate that voice was; . . . and with it alone beside me, experienced without the mask of her face, I noticed for the first time how pain had cracked it in the course of a lifetime.

But was it solely the voice, heard in isolation, that created the new impression that tore at my heart? Not at all: it was, rather, that the isolation of the voice was like a symbol, an evocation, a direct consequence of another isolation, that of my grandmother, separated from me for the first time. . . . By telling me to stay, my grandmother filled me with an anxious, desperate desire to return home. The freedom she was now granting me . . . suddenly seemed as painful as the sort of freedom I might experience after her death (when I would still love her and she would have abandoned me forever). I cried out, "Grandmother! Grandmother!," and I wanted to kiss her; but all that I had beside me was her voice, a ghost as bodiless as the one that would perhaps come back and visit me when my grandmother was dead. "Speak to me"; then, suddenly, I ceased to hear the voice, and was left even more alone. My grandmother could no longer hear me, was no longer in communication with me; we had ceased to be in contact, to be audible to each other; I continued to call her, groping in the darkness, with the feeling that calls from her must be going astray . . . I felt as though it were already a beloved ghost that I had just allowed to disappear into the world of shadows, and standing there alone in front of the telephone, I went on vainly calling, "Grandmother! Grandmother!" like the abandoned Orpheus repeating the name of his dead wife.[27]

The invocation of Orpheus and Eurydice here spells out the figure that has structured Proust's entire account: that of the underworld visit. At the beginning of the call,

As soon as our call has rung out, in the darkness peopled with apparitions to which our ears alone are opened, a shred of sound—an abstract sound—the sound of distance suppressed—and the voice of the dear one speaks to us . . .

The dear ones, the voices of the dear ones speaking, are with us. But how far away they are! . . . A real presence, the voice that seems so close—but is in fact miles away! But it is also a foreglimpse of an eternal separa-

---

27. I quote the translation of Proust by Mark Treharne, *The Guermantes Way* (New York: Viking, 2004), 128–30.

tion! Many times, as I listened in this way without seeing the woman who spoke to me from so far, I have felt that the voice was crying out to me from depths from which it would never emerge again, and I have experienced the anxiety that was one day to take hold of me when a voice would return like this (alone and no longer part of a body I was never to see again) to murmur in my ear words I would dearly like to have kissed as they passed from lips forever turned to dust.

Proust's language here (poignantly and pointedly, for the Narrator's grandmother is modeled on Proust's mother) casts the voice as the image of Odysseus's mother in the underworld visit of *Odyssey* Book XI: it may look real, but when you try to embrace it, there is nothing but air. Proust's did not invent the connection between this underworld image and the voice; it has a long and powerful history. As already seen, Chaucer employs it in his much more upbeat version of an otherworld journey, the *House of Fame,* when in the House of Rumor the space is crammed with apparent bodies that are, in fact, only the airy projection of the speaker of words on earth—that is to say, voices. It is hard to appreciate the sheer imaginative energy of this association when we are so used to skype and satellite transmission, but it is such imaginings—for Chaucer, scientific at least as much as literary—that eventually enable the invention of the telephone.

Indeed, there is a lesson in the cultural specificity of the Proust passage. The extraordinary strangeness of the telephone experience there, the textbook alienation, is almost lost to us in our own culture, surrounded as we are by people announcing to unseen interlocutors that the plane has just landed or the bus is three minutes late—people narrating themselves by cellphone; though aspects of Proust's Narrator's experience will still appear familiar to those of us old enough to recall phone calls between Britain and Australia thirty or more years ago, where one battled the void of time-lag and the sussuration of electronic high surf. As a medievalist, though, I do not make use of postmedieval examples (as here) in order to be "transhistorical," whatever that is, but rather to make the point about cultural specificity, here about the historically fluctuating nature of our relation to voice. We can just about recover some aspects of the Proustian, but we have real historical difficulty imagining the impact of older forms of technology, such as that of writing in a previously mainly oral culture—though I think that Proust's account of the telephone call allows us to glimpse some sort of spectral, empathetic analogy.

How many voices do we hear in Proust's account? The Narrator, in past and (fictitious) present, the constantly moving time of the text in reading; the grandmother, both as she is heard on the telephone and as she is recollected, these being different; the operator; Saint-Loup as the albeit silent entrepreneur; white noise; the Orpheus myth; and the babble of ghosts in the Homeric underworld—voice here is plural, never singular. Yet it is plural in rather a singular way: the experience that the reader is made to undergo, of overhearing a private phone call from one end, enacts Paul Valéry's brilliant term for literature itself, *monodialogue*.[28]

Are these voices we hear real or ideal? We know that Proust's text addresses and radically transforms his life experience, but in unpredictable ways: his mother turns into the grandmother; two separate places turn into Combray; the Narrator himself turns preposterously heterosexual. Voicing here becomes a process of disembodiment and mythical reincorporation, the world of the text itself a fantastic underworld. The experience of hearing his grandmother's voice convinces the Narrator that he has lost her: she is both there and not there. One can pun prettily and long on presence and absence without getting to the core of this uncanny voice without a face. When the Narrator next sees his grandmother, he sees a sick, red-faced old stranger: the voice without a face is more real than the old body, but only because loss is a process, not an instant. When the grandmother is disconnected, her voice lost, she is committed irrevocably to memory. Voice here is therefore akin to memory itself, "real without being present, ideal without being abstract."[29] So her voice is as wrongly real as a voice without a face can be; it is also, in its unrepeatable sweetness, ideal, an ideality sustained in a kind of desperate dialogue at a level that makes it mythical. These are the qualities that I would attribute to literary voice—beyond presence and absence, beyond even public and private, both ideal and real, both embodied and phantasmal. Above all, such voices are voices in reproduction, simultaneously themselves and not themselves: reproduction and reproducibility are at the core of literary voice, and alienate it from the physical, even, as here, cruelly, from the mortal.

As often in Proust, this is a self-defining moment: the air is thick with questions about what art can possibly do. No wonder that the account concludes with Orpheus. The image is a resonant one throughout Proust's work, as a figure of apprenticeship, writing as singing, and as a figure of lost love, doomed before it starts by the myth it re-enacts. Falling in love in Proust

---

28. Paul Valéry, *Cahiers 1894–1914*, ed. Nicole Celeyrette-Pietri and Judith Robinson (Paris: Gallimard, 1987), 1:196, 242; and see William Marx, "The Dialogues and *Mon Faust*: The Inner Politics of Thought," in *Reading Paul Valéry: The Universe in Mind*, ed. Paul Gifford (Cambridge: Cambridge University Press, 1999), 155–64; and Christine M. Crow, *Paul Valéry and the Poetry of Voice* (Cambridge: Cambridge University Press, 1982), 45.

29. The translation is Richard Howard's: Gilles Deleuze, *Proust and Signs* (Minneapolis: University of Minnesota Press, 2000), 58.

is always the Orphic search for the lost Eurydice. It links the Narrator with Swann, who searches for Odette at night in the cafes of the Bois de Boulogne and is approached by prostitutes on the street: "Anxiously he clutched at all these dim forms, as though, among the phantoms of the dead, in the realms of darkness, he had been searching for Eurydice."[30] The image is echoed when the ageing Narrator describes revisiting the Bois in 1913 and sees the women of his past acquaintance, as they pass by, as the ghosts of their former selves. His art is an underworld, a place of phantoms, and for that very reason an art of the voice, of voices, the figure for which is Orpheus.

"Is that your los?"

And so to Chaucer, for whom these same associations hold true. In the *Book of the Duchess,* the dreamer follows a little dog into a grove in the forest, and there he finds the Man in Black singing of his grief at his wife's death, surrounded by wild beasts with his back against a great oak. This is of course exactly how Ovid describes Orpheus. The landscape is Augustan, and it is Augustus—the Emperor Octavian—who can be heard hunting afar. And the dreamer has been reading one of the two great Augustan poets, Ovid, whose Ceyx and Alcyon story is retold, minus the metamorphosis that alone motivates it in Ovid, to demonstrate the dreamer's prior sleeplessness and absolute lack of feeling. The Black he encounters is his tutelary opposite; the dreamer overhears him when, as he thinks, he is without human company, lament the death of his wife White. It is an intercalated lyric, and an accomplished one: Black sings or recites a formal *planh* that breaks the couplet rhyme scheme of the poem. There follows the dreamer's conversation with Black, at the end of which the hitherto insensate dreamer expresses the feeling of which he has been incapable, compassion, and does so in a rhyme, *routhe/trouthe,* that is to become a signature of Chaucer's poetic career at its most serious or contentious moments:

> "She is deed." "Nay!" "Yis, by my trouthe."
> "Is that your los? By God, it is routhe."
> (1309–10)

---

30. Here and in subsequent references (by volume and page) I have preferred the translation of Moncrieff and Kilmartin, revised D. J. Enright: Marcel Proust, *In Search of Lost Time* (New York: Modern Library, 1992), 1:326. I have always consulted the original French, *À la recherche du temps perdu* (Paris: Quarto Gallimard, 1999).

The conversation ends at dusk when "this kyng," whom I take to be not Black but the Emperor Octavian, returns to his castle and the poem punningly pays tribute to John of Gaunt, Earl of Richmond, who has lost his wife Blanche—a loss that is clearly the occasion, but not in my view the ostensible subject, of the poem.

I think I may have the first to argue the key point here, that "this kyng" does not signify John of Gaunt (for all that he was later able, albeit implausibly, to style himself "King of Castile") but rather the Emperor Augustus—in which case the Man in Black does not return to the home comforts of some Yorkshire castle but remains separated from the dreamer's real time by more than a millennium in the darkest of Ovidian dark woods.[31] It is the dreamer who changes, rediscovering the power of feeling, not Black, who cannot bear the grief that in this poem he must not only endure but embody, "for Y am Sorwe, and Sorwe is Y" (597). It seemed to me then as now that given this heavily Ovidian text, and given Chaucer's consuming interest in all things Augustan, both Ovidian and Virgilian, there can be no mistaking the primacy of the classical reference or what it means, that the bereaved Man in Black is a figure of Orpheus. The point has since been rediscovered by Jane Chance, who reads the *Book of the Duchess* in terms of underworld descents by heroes or heroines of classical literature—the men Hercules, Theseus and Orpheus, and the women, as Chance would argue Alcyone herself and certainly Alcestis—before deciding on Orpheus as the key term: "A group of underworld references piled one atop another by the Black Knight mourning behind his oak tree type him as an Orpheus in his grief."[32] She also compares Orpheus' loss, incidentally, to Daedalus's loss of Icarus, thus aligning the key mythological references of three out of four of Chaucer's major dream visions: Orpheus in *Book of the Duchess,* Daedalus and the labyrinth in *House of Fame,* Alcestis in *Legend of Good Women.*

All this does not occur in the context of some sort of nightmarish Joycean pubcrawl, in which the consciousness of the focalizing subject is suborned by authorial intertextuality, but rather in the context of a dream landscape whose Augustan reference could hardly be more clearly articulated by the poet. Moreover, the Ovidian reference, and the marking of Black as Orpheus, are considerably more forceful and concerted than the elegant but last-minute and formally anagrammatic tribute to John of Gaunt, the loss of whose wife is the occasion but not the direct subject of the whole Orphic schema. If this has not been stressed in the criticism, that can only be because the

---

31. David Lawton, *Chaucer's Narrators* (Cambridge: D. S. Brewer, 1985), 48–57.
32. Jane Chance, *The Mythographic Chaucer: The Fabulation of Sexual Politics* (Minneapolis: University of Minnesota Press, 1994), 28.

criticism has remained loyal to the notion of the poem as a consolation; and that, to my mind misconceived, commitment determines Chance's mythographic reading of the Orpheus allusion, which she sees, without discussion, as entirely moral, Boethian or indeed Boccacian: it's time Orpheus gave up his enervating attachment to lost earthly objects (so much for wives) and gave himself to thoughts of heaven. This is certainly an available reading, but it is not, as we'll see, an inevitable one. Nor am I convinced that it is Chaucer's. Unless the Man in Black is John of Gaunt, and as John of Gaunt is then the "king" who returns to Richmond castle—neither of which, in my view, is textually defensible—there is no sign in Chaucer's poem of any commendation of transcendence. On the contrary, Black's grief is as irresoluble as his poetry is consummate, like Orpheus. The dreamer is the lucky one, able to bond with a homosocial rather than a heterosexual mentor, and by virtue of the role, and compliment, the poem confers upon him—as perhaps within the circle of John of Gaunt, but assuredly as Orpheus's apprentice.

It is the power of Sorrow that the apprentice learns. We need to deepen the notion of Chaucer we have inherited as the great comic poet. Black is desolate, Troilus is inconsolable, Troilus and Arcite die, good women mostly perish, the Griselda story and others show Chaucer drawn to the theme of torture, three of four certainly Chaucerian extant prose texts and the lost *De Miseria Humanae Conditionis* are about how to bear the damage that life inflicts upon us, and, if the Retractions are correctly placed, Chaucer's career ends on a note of bitter renunciation. The odd fabliau provides welcome relief. It may be true in other ways that Chaucer "lacks high seriousness"—as, say, Samuel Beckett does in the face of human abjection. Life is too serious for tragedy. For all Chaucer's reputation in and for comedy, which criticism has ceaselessly repeated from Dryden to, say, John Bowers,[33] his real transgression is that he is the unsentimental poet of human pain and suffering and loss, unmatched in this by any English contemporary or European peer, and often without transcendence:

> His spirit changed hous and wente ther,
> As I cam nevere, I can nat tellen where;
> Therfore I stinte—I nam no divinistre;
> Of soules finde I nat in this registre.
> (*Knight's Tale*, 2809–12)

---

33. John Bowers, *Chaucer and Langland: The Antagonistic Tradition* (Notre Dame, IN: University of Notre Dame Press, 2007), takes Matthew Arnold's view of Chaucer to its limit and casts the comic Chaucer as the beginning of a dominant literary tradition of jocular Englishness.

It is not the case that Chaucer always eschews the transcendent, though it is a peculiarity that when he resorts to it—as in the Prioress's Tale or the very end of *Troilus*—his voice sounds most exceptionally unlike a "common voice." Yet he has an extraordinary capacity to stick determinedly with the reality of human pain—not, most likely, in denial of the divine, but as if to recognize a horizon between the two. Such a capacity marks Chaucer as being just as much a public poet as any of his less Ovidian contemporaries. If, as the Orpheus story teaches us, even love is the harbinger of intolerable suffering, so that Chaucer's work addresses equally those who would win and those who have lost their chess game with Fortune, then no theme, sadly, speaks to more people. Being Orpheus' apprentice is nothing if not a public project.

It maps onto a mythological program—Alcestis, Theseus, Daedalus: the connection helps us see why Chaucer's labyrinth is a *labor-intus,* and corresponds to the cup of sorrows that the poet as a *homo dolorosus* must drink (*House of Fame,* 1878–80: Orpheus as Christ?). To follow the mythography just one step further is to find references all in the same place linking Orpheus to Tantalus, Sisyphus, Ixion, and the Furies—all, for example, formative (with Orpheus's mother Calliope) in the frame of the *Troilus.* The path of Orpheus is a serious vocation, leading Chaucer into prose translation, the *Boece,* as well as poetry. Boethius's *Consolation* provides the textual place just cited in Book III meter 12 and, together with Ovid, is Chaucer's *locus classicus* for the figure of Orpheus. To read this is to inquire into the mythography, to ask what the Orpheus story means to Chaucer and whether its voices too may be multiple.

"True singing is another kind of breath"

"Happy is he who can look into the shining spring of good; happy is he who can break the heavy chains of earth." The Boethian meter opens with its contrast of heaven and hell, and then gives a summary of Orpheus' descent that equally balances the power of poetry and the power of grief. It is pity evoked by his poetry that causes the underworld to relent, with the condition only that Orpheus not look back. When he does, uniquely in Boethius, "Orpheus Eurydicem suam / uidit, perdidit, occidit."[34] Commentators differ about the reading of this line, as to whether *occidit* refers to Orpheus or

---

34. The translation cited is Friedman's; the text is that edited by J. Keith Atkinson and Anna Maria Babbi (Verona: Fiorini, 2000), IX, X.

breaks the parallelism by being the one verb of which the subject is Eurydice. In either case, we read an act of supreme compression in the haste to reach a moral. The moral is double: love cannot observe any law; and whoever, instead of raising this mind to sovereign day, "is conquered and turns his eyes into the pit of hell, looking into the inferno, loses all the excellence he has gained." If we compare Walton's translation with Chaucer's, to which, according to Ian Johnson, Walton's seeks to be corrective imitation,[35] we find Walton altogether stronger in drawing the *contemptus mundi* moral at start and end. Man must disentangle himself from "bondes of this worldly wrechidnesse," says Walton, glossing Boethius, while Chaucer sticks with "the bondes of the hevy erthe"; "Lo all that evire youre labour hath yow dight / Ye loose it when ye loken into hell," concludes Walton, forcefully enough, while Chaucer slightly softens and points the moral by concluding, if anticlimactically, with Trivet's gloss on hell, "that is to seyn, into lowe thinges of the erthe." The point is clear either way: Orpheus is undone by the trammels of worldly sensuality. But where Walton's translation tends to repudiation, Chaucer's has a flatter, sadder, renunciation. It is a note that recurs in Chaucer's treatment of human love, and it privileges the poetry, and the sorrow, over the love that occasioned it. It is as if art outgrows love. Rilke draws the moral when he reads the teaching of Orpheus: "song is *not* desire: so you taught." And again, from the third sonnet to Orpheus (I quote Don Paterson's translation):

>   Youth—
> Don't fool yourself that love unlocks this art ;
> For though love's voice might force your lips apart
>
> you must forget those sudden songs. They'll end.
> True singing is another kind of breath.
> A breath of nothing. A sigh in a god. A wind.[36]

Rilke's sonnet is another profound exploration of the Orpheus myth in terms of poetry and, particularly, in terms of voice. We should follow Chaucer in acknowledging such anachronism as a force in reading—that is, the inter-

---

35. I. R. Johnson, "Walton's Sapient Orpheus," in *The Medieval Boethius*, ed. Alastair Minnis (Cambridge: D. S. Brewer, 1987), 139–68. See also Johnson's edition of the Walton commentary in *The Idea of the Vernacular*, ed. Jocelyn Wogan-Browne, Nicholas Watson, Andrew Taylor, and Ruth Evans (University Park: Pennsylvania State University Press, 1999), 34–38. The edition of Walton used only for these few lines is *Boethius: De Consolatione Philosophiae, Translated by John Walton*, ed. Mark Science, EETS o.s. 170 (London, 1927 [1925]).

36. Don Paterson, *Orpheus* (London: Faber and Faber, 2006), 5.

vening intertexts that shape our reading from the interval between old books and ourselves. Thus Rilke, for us, properly illuminates Chaucer.

Yet the renunciation of love in favor of art can quickly become a chilly solipsism, a sort of My Last Duchess moment: it can become the scandalous version of Orpheus Jean de Meun has Genius provide, as poet-pederast. This is clearly an influential viewpoint. In an elevated poem it entirely dominates Poliziano's important *Fabula di Orfeo* in the fifteenth century, and it becomes normative in Bruce Holsinger's account of Orpheus.[37] Yet I find no trace of it in the *Book of the Duchess*. In fact, the *Book of the Duchess* bears no evident mark of Boethius either; these influences are yet to be seen, and they contribute to what I am representing as a career-long reflection on Orpheus, that is, to say on the poet's voice. Chaucer would have been aware from the start, though, of the extraordinary range of often contradictory interpretations Orpheus inspires, as poet but also as priest. He is related to Apollo and healing, but also to Dionysus and madness. As well as the austerely moralist and misogynist view of Boethius, there is the *Ovide Moralisé,* which defeats any distinction between secular and religious by reading the love of Orpheus and Eurydice in terms of the Song of Songs. There is also the much more secular romance Orpheus, complete with happy ending, which Chaucer would have known from *Sir Orfeo,* and a more general minstrel categorization which seems especially pertinent to the *dits amoureux:* Orpheus as the compiler of lyric anthologies, their highest genre being complaint, or lament.

There is no need here to give an exhaustive account of the mythography, which is readily available in Friedman's still valuable study, supplemented by Holsinger's vigorous revisionism, and collections of primary sources such as that from *Medioaevi* in 2000, *L'<Orphée> de Boèce au Moyen Age*. The most important point of contention is the value of Eurydice herself: is she worth going to hell for, and if so is she worth turning for? Is this second loss a fault on Orpheus' part, or is it inherent in Eurydice herself? There's the Platonic tradition that blames Orpheus, not only for turning but for the manner of his going to hell; unlike Alcestis, he is not prepared to do the job properly by dying, and is punished for his half-heartedness. But if Orpheus is generally seen as exemplary, what does that make Eurydice? There's some ambiguity in the Boethian meter itself, even though that initiates the more misogynist

---

37. Bruce W. Holsinger, "Orpheus in Parts: Music, Fragmentation and Remembrance," chapter 7 of his *Music, Body, and Desire in Medieval Culture* (Stanford, CA: Stanford University Press, 2001), 295–343. For the three texts of Poliziano, see the editions by Stefano Carrai (Milan: Mursia, 1988) and Antonia Tissoni Benvenuti (Padua: Editrice Antenore, 1986). On the homoerotic Orpheus of Jean de Meun, following Alanus, see Marilynn Desmond and Pamela Sheingorn, *Myth, Montage, and Visuality in Late Medieval Manuscript Culture: Christine de Pizan's Epistre Othea* (Ann Arbor: University of Michigan Press, 2003), 47.

and censorious commentary. Is she the mind, that which Orpheus seeks to draw to the upper skies, or is she the sensuality that brings it down again? Trivet and Walton agree on the latter, where Chaucer hesitates. Her death by snakebite lends itself to an overtly Christian, moralizing reading; but it is by no means inevitable or universal in the commentary traditions. For Fulgentius, Eurydice is Orpheus' equal partner: together they compose the marriage of eloquence and wisdom, of music and rhetoric. She is Orpheus' soul, or his voice—perhaps even the chthonic undervoice; and it is Orpheus' loss of her rather than the vengeful Maenads that literally tear him apart. In the traditions of commentary readily to hand Chaucer would have found not a harmonious view but multiple and conflicting voices; and it seems to me that the Orpheus story can be taken to license and originate such multiplicity. It is the irresoluble condition of the Orpheus story. It leads Poliziano in the fifteenth century to write three versions of his *Fabula di Orfeo*, albeit that he attributes it to *subitus calor:* two are lyric, varying in prosody, number of speakers, and balance between Latin and the vernacular; and the third is a full-fledged drama. It also leads Harrison Birtwistle in his superb modern opera *The Masks of Orpheus* to represent each of his three main characters (including Aristaeus) by three different means and to tell three conflicting stories: Eurydice is faithful, or not; dies or does not, is rescued or lost.[38] To be a poet in the manner of Orpheus is to be conflicted, torn and multiple, not whole but in pieces. It is an aesthetic that would instill a love of contradiction and oxymoron; poets and commentators after Ovid augment this, and for the most part do not seek to reconcile it. Such is the nature of literary voice.

I would argue, then, that the question of literary voice leads Chaucer and other medieval makers to Orpheus, where they find a myth—and reinvent it as an aesthetic program—of separation, fragmentation and division, held in suspension by the art, the over-voice, of the poet. It is, to be sure, an intellectual and rather European view of the poet's function: the parallels I find for it are in English commentary and French and Italian poets rather than in an insular poetic tradition. This does not make it an exercise in solipsism compared to the public poetry of Middleton's account. Orpheus' poetry has a profound social effect, on animals and gods as well as humans. The only person it does not help is Orpheus himself, and that is the function of sorrow: the expression of sorrow being, now as then, poetry's most evident and widespread social function. Moreover, Orpheus has the prime social func-

---

38. Harrison Birtwistle, *The Mask of Orpheus*, BBC Symphony Orchestra conducted by Andrew Davis, 1999, compact disc.

tion in the mythography of civilizer, the builder of sympathetic societies. "It is fayned that . . . Orpheus assembled the wilde beasts to come in heards to his musicke, and by that meanes made them tame, implying thereby, how by his discreete and wholesome lessons uttered in harmonie and with melodious instruments, he brought the rude and savage people to a more civil and orderly life"; "For as the workes of wisdom surpass in dignity and power the works of strength, so the labours of Orpheus surpass the labours of Hercules."[39] This might make Orpheus the prototype of a public intellectual. Certainly, his role is seen as a public role, one that does not need to "stretch" itself to accommodate difference but rather, and I think crucially, bases its civil society in multiplicity. This is hardly or self-evidently apolitical.

It is also crucial to the history of culture. There is a compelling musical analogy: Monteverdi's *Orfeo*.[40] Produced in Mantua in 1607, *Orfeo* was not the first opera (and indeed Monteverdi's name for it was not opera but melodrama: sung theater), but it is universally seen as foundational. The impetus was in sustained, coterie intellectual and aesthetic activity in Florence and other cities, involving a revaluation of the vocal relationship between music and poetry. We find a comparable rethinking at the turn of the fifteenth century, in Deschamps' emphasis in *L'Art du Dictier* that lyric poetry is natural music and does not necessarily have to be sung (to artificial music).[41] In both cases the revaluation foregrounds a single voice; and indeed the structure of Monteverdi's melodrama imitates the form of poetic collections in moving through framed narrative by way of climactic set pieces of lament. I'm inclined to suggest that Chaucer criticism might look at the interplay in Monteverdi's work between multiple voices and a single voice, for it is the reinvention of monody out of polyphony that in many ways provides the dynamism of Monteverdi's formal innovation—whereas I suspect that in Chaucer scholarship we (and I) have reached the point of overemphasizing the polyphonic. This may seem a surprisingly direct connection, but there is evidence that the development of musical forms leading to Monteverdi's

---

39. Respectively George Puttenham, *The Arte of English Poesie*, 6; Francis Bacon, "The Wisdom of the Ancients," *Philosophical Works*, 835, quoted by Robin Headlam Wells, *Shakespeare on Masculinity* (Cambridge: Cambridge University Press, 2001), 1.

40. I have closely consulted the performance by Ensemble La Venexiana, *L'Orfeo: Favola in musica, Mantua 1607,* in the 2007 Glossa edition with commentary. I have also consulted F. W. Sternfeld, "The Orpheus Myth and the Libretto of *Orfeo*," in *Claudio Monteverdi, Orfeo*, ed. John Whenham (Cambridge: Cambridge University Press, 1986), 20–34; F. W. Sternfeld, *The Birth of Opera* (Oxford: Clarendon Press, 1993); and Mark Ringer, *Opera's First Master: The Musical Dramas of Claudio Monteverdi* (Pompton Plains, NJ: Amadeus Press, 2006).

41. Eustache Deschamps, *L'art de dictier*, ed. and trans. Deborah Sinnreich-Levi (East Lansing, MI: Colleagues Press, 1994), 63–67.

opera is itself a response to literary stimuli, particularly to the interplay and complexity of voices in Petrarch's poetry that occasion new musical modes in the madrigal.

The choice of Orfeo is clearly part of a mythological program for Monteverdi, one that will lead him to Ariadne and to Ulysses (the connection between Orpheus and Ulysses is made by Boethius and repeated by Petrarch: Orpheus' tree grows in Penelope's bedchamber, and Ulysses' bow is strung with Orpheus' lyre). The performance takes place in Mantua's palazzo ducale, along from the Duke's new chamber whose ornament takes the form of the labyrinth. Moreover, Monteverdi's is one of twenty or so representations of Orpheus over as many years in proto-operatic Italian musical drama. Not only is the Orpheus myth of obvious appeal for early opera; it is also, in its emphasis on both music and voice, uniquely reflexive. "In the beginning," writes F. W. Sternfeld of Monteverdi's work, "was the myth, and the myth was Orpheus."[42] It is the case I am making about Chaucer. Why might this be? The answer takes us beyond analogy. It must be, I think, that times of great formal musical or poetic innovation entail major changes in the conceptualizing of performance and speech, in other words voice; the subject of artistic metamorphosis is voice, and the metamorphosis of voice is Ovid and Orpheus. Orpheus as voice is the hallmark of a modernism. (As it is for Birtwistle, who later turns, in separate works, to Theseus and to the Minotaur.)

Ovidian style, with its constant contrasts of tone and mood, leads Monteverdi and his librettist Struggio to the late substitution, not quite of a happy ending, as in Glück, but to a heavenly apotheosis for Orpheus, and a final pastoral dance. The very deviation from Ovid is Ovidian, a response to his quicksilver shifts in tonality, and Monteverdi refused to work on an opera of *Narciso* precisely because it did not allow such contrasts. And Ovidian mythology also enters the very form of Monteverdi's work. The great climactic lament of *Orfeo* is structured in the form of an echo—a repeated "Farewell"; and this follows Ovid's linkage, reiterated by Petrarch, between Eurydice and Echo, Orpheus and Narcissus (the mythographic connection that informs the whole of Cocteau's film *Orphée,* product of a yet later modernist revision of the legend). The linkage of the two myths is a reminder that the aesthetic is as much about seeing as about sound: voice is visual as well as verbal. To hear a voice is to imagine a body: this is where the impulse for musical drama originates. And it is something Chaucer knows very well: that is why in the *House of Fame* (1073–83) we are told that words spoken

---

42. Sternfeld, *Birth of Opera,* 3.

on earth produce the illusion of a body in the houses of Fame and Rumor. I should like to complete this rapid survey of Chaucer's modernist, Orphean aesthetic by touching on the implications voice has for vision; and that will entail looking at just one more Ovidian mythological figure, Pygmalion.

"A breath of nothing"

The connection between Pygmalion and Orpheus arises from Book X of the *Metamorphoses,* where it is Orpheus who narrates Pygmalion. It is also a commonplace in the poetry of Chaucer's European, not English, contemporaries: for example, Froissart in *Le Paradis d'Amours* (where the narrator writes of the pain love causes him, "Car jains par figure vraie / Limage pymalion," but immediately laments "Je ne sui pas orpheus");[43] and, more significantly, Petrarch, who in sonnet 135 and elsewhere takes upon himself as lover the dual identity of Orpheus and Pygmalion.[44] This may be a more fruitful connection for Chaucer than Jean de Meun, given Jean's pigeonholing of Orpheus as pederast, though Jean's reworking of Pygmalion is definitive and fully explores the myth's Ovidian ambiguities: is it a life-affirming narrative of the power of love, which brings a statue to life, or a deathly narrative of the effects of misogyny, the turning away from real women to the solipsistic construct of art?

The most sustained medieval imagining, however, of what it means for the poet to undergo secondary metamorphosis from Orpheus into Pygmalion occurs in Machaut, in *Le Voir Dit*—the master work in which Machaut sets up an extended riddle of voice. I mention it here because it returns us—in the form of paradox or oxymoron—to the central questions of truth and form with which I opened this discussion of voice. A young female poet declares her love for Machaut as master poet, as Orpheus, and the text of *Le Voir Dit* anthologizes her work as well as Machaut's own—the most monumental of intercalated lyrics. We can hardly avoid asking questions about whether she really existed, or who she was, about whose voice or how many voices we hear in "her" work.[45] Yet this is merely to play the game of Mach-

---

43. Jean Froissart, *An Anthology of Narrative and Lyric Poetry,* ed. and trans. Kristen Figg (London: Routledge, 2001), lines 1122–39.

44. Theresa Migraine-George, "Orpheus and Pygmalion as Aesthetic Paradigms in Petrarch's *Rime sparse,*" *Comparative Literature Studies* 36 (1999): 226–46.

45. Guillaume de Machaut, *Le livre dou voir dit,* ed. and trans. Daniel Leech-Wilkinson (New York: Garland, 1998). This book has an extensive discussion of the biographical question. See also Kevin Brownlee, *Poetic Identity in Guillaume de Machaut* (Madison: University of Wisconsin Press, 1984). For a different, and polemical, view, see Laurence de Looze, *Pseudo-Autobiography in the Four-*

aut's poem, and the textual evidence will be received differently in different disciplines, scholars of music and song concentrating on the discussion in the letters exchanged by Machaut and Toute-Belle of Machaut's own work, literary scholars for their part reading through irony and intertextuality. These correspond to different levels of the text, each of them real enough. In any case, the example of Proust may suggest the radical and unpredictable extent to which a writer transforms life experience, even where it forms a basis of the work. Though the woman's real name may be hidden in an acrostic anagram, she is called Toute-Belle, a screen name for a screen woman, and is characterized largely as the product of the lover's fantasizing. Indeed, Machaut does not meet her until well into the poem: she approaches him by letter, and he falls in love with the idea of one in love with him, a love pursued by a sequence of intermediaries, messengers and letters, with a degree of physical separation, such that the role of Pandarus in Chaucer's *Troilus and Criseyde* looks straightforward by comparison. The Machaut of the poem constructs her before he knows her. Jealousy is therefore the shadow of his love and requires no cause—it is the inevitable next stage in the affair between the old poet and his young admirer. The poem enters an unstable cycle of jealousy and lies, of deception and betrayal. Love is at best "reciprocal torture" (the phrase again is Proust's: V:137).

In this context, the Pygmalion references—signaled overtly by Machaut (e.g., lines 6526–27)—are disorienting, since they speak of anterior texts, not cancelling the particularity of Machaut's "true" experience but deliberately diffusing it and broadening its abstract range. As Machaut's love for Toute-Belle progressively turns into, or manifests itself, as suspicion and hatred, so Machaut progressively reinvents her, overtly assuming the role of Pygmalion—except that the fantasies he follows are negative. He takes her image (clearly described in the text, and depicted in the illuminations, as a Pygmalion-size image, large but less than life-size), and it becomes his proxy for her. He is a reverse Pygmalion, turning his woman into a statue: "We are sculptors," writes Proust (V:182). "We want to obtain of a woman a statue entirely different from the one she has presented to us." Machaut's Narrator dreams that her image has changed the colour of her dress from blue to green, and turned away her head. His response is deathly, as in Proust, whose Narrator—a good medievalist—sees in the sleeping Albertine "a dead woman . . . her sheets, wrapped around her body like a shroud, had assumed, with their elegant folds, the rigidity of stone" (V:485). Machaut's Narrator

---

teenth Century: Juan Ruiz, Guillaume de Machaut, Jean Froissart, and Geoffrey Chaucer (Gainesville: University of Florida Press, 1997).

figuratively entombs his beloved. He takes the painted image of Toute-Belle and he locks it inside his coffer, Orpheus enacting as Pygmalion Eurydice's death and descent into the pit. (The image is released by the poem's end, but the mythology overshadows the uneasy rapprochement with which the poem closes.)

Indeed, Machaut's Narrator has a further dream in which he realizes that his beloved Toute-Belle is actually Fortune, whose image is twofold, smiling and scorning, and whose pattern is always to follow exaltation with betrayal. In that Boethian sense, to blame her is irrelevant: the beloved, writes Proust (V:131), "is a sea which like Xerxes we scourge with rods in an absurd attempt to punish it for what it has engulfed." But if she is his Fortune, she is also his work, his art. When she first sends her image, Machaut's Narrator *dresses* it, though it's painted (thus supplying the third, Pygmalion's, dimension). He then writes to her that he would send her his manuscript of his collected works except that it is still being "notated"—that is, having the music added—that is, in another sense, dressed. Her image and his collected works are complementary and cognate. His jealousy and his song construct her equally, and she is imprisoned in the conventions of his prosody just as her image is confined in his coffer.

The conjunction of the two myths is, one might say, Machaut's Proustian moment, quite as shocking as the hounding to death of Albertine, modernism as little short of murder. It confronts the most uncomfortable aspect of the Orpheus myth. In the world outside opera, Orpheus *must* lose Eurydice again, for without her loss he has no subject. Since he loves his own art, she must forever be its subject, its rival and its victim. Blanchot puts it tactfully: "Eurydice is the limit of what art can attain; concealed behind a name and covered by a veil, she is the profoundly dark point towards which art, desire, death and the night all seem to lead."[46] Ultimately, as in Monteverdi, the best and the most her voice can do is to echo his in valediction. What becomes of multivocality here? It turns tyrannical. Literally, as addressed by Machaut to Toute-Belle or Orpheus to Eurydice, the only choice it offers is failure. Orpheus has so much more to offer his male admirers (such as Chaucer). Yet in this suppression the poet is knowingly self-destructive, literally torn apart by his own misogyny. So, for example, Troilus' death, or in the intertexts Pandarus', can be seen as their final act of revenge against Criseyde. (If you don't deserve me, nobody does.) One could read Chaucer's *Troilus* against both Machaut and Proust, demonstrating that the great theme of all three is

---

46. Maurice Blanchot, "The Gaze of Orpheus," in *The Gaze of Orpheus and Other Literary Essays*, trans. Lydia Davis and ed. P. Adams Sitney (Barrytown, NY: Station Hill, 1981), 99.

not love but jealousy, that Chaucer is a poet fascinated not only by pain but by torture. "I loved her," writes Proust's Narrator of Gilbertine, and therefore "I was sorry not to have had time and inspiration to insult her, to hurt her, to force her to keep some memory of me" (I:200). The voice—in Proust, in Chaucer, in Machaut—is complicated, bitter, full both of other texts and of more personalized grievance. It is a strange mixture of anger and urbanity, but no less public a voice for that. Machaut's poem in fact depends on his fame as a public figure—it is a celebrity text; and in any case misogyny has never been afraid to present itself in public as civility. It is the most disturbing of all the involutions of voice and the metamorphoses of Orpheus.

The question of truth, then, is nightmarish and disorienting. But *Le Voir Dit* is also a major public landmark in the ongoing history of negotiation between voice and music. Machaut is a true Orpheus: a composer as well as a poet. For the musicologist, this leads to a very different experience of the poem from the literary critic's, in this case as a vast and reliable archive. Not only do the *de luxe* manuscripts—those placing *Le Voir Dit* as the keystone of Machaut's massive oeuvre—contain the music for a large number of the poems; but also the correspondence in the work between Machaut and Toute-Belle, containing detailed discussion of music and setting, comprises the earliest collection of composer letters in music history. Implicitly, they support the point Deschamps will make a generation later, for not all the poems are judged to need a musical setting. In that limited sense, they are evidence of the slowly widening gap between musical and literary voice: voice moving away from music, as in opera it will eventually return (with the result that continuo is needed for narrative intelligibility). This shift is also part of the Orphic function of fourteenth-century poetry—and it serves as a reminder that Zumthor's term *mouvance* was grounded in voice rather than text, and was intended to signal not a general indeterminacy but the openness that comes from a specific reliance of text on voice. Discussions of modern textuality have often obscured this medieval sense. We would retain it by borrowing a basic musical term, and thinking of the Orphic poet's work less as a text than as a score, a work that invites performance and is completed by it (except that it is never completed, as the sequence of performance remains open and indefinite). Such transferable capacity for performance, such unstable reproducibility, is the public work of voice.

works cited

Abbreviations

CCCM   Corpus Christianorum, continuatio mediaevalis
CCSL   Corpus Christianorum, series latina
CSEL   Corpus scriptorum ecclesiasticorum latinorum
EETS   Early English Text Society
e.s.   extra series
MED   *Middle English Dictionary.* Ed. Hans Kurath, Sherman M. Kuhn, and Robert E. Lewis. 22 vols. Ann Arbor: University of Michigan Press, 1952–2001. Online edition: http://quod.lib.umich.edu/m/med/.
OED   *The Oxford English Dictionary* [electronic resource; by subscription]. 2nd ed. prepared by J. A. Simpson and E. S. C. Weiner. Oxford: Clarendon Press; New York: Oxford University Press, 1989.
o.s.   original series
PL   *Patrologiae cursus completus, series latina.* Ed. Jean-Paul Migne et al. 221 vols. Paris, 1844–55 and 1862–65.

Manuscripts

Aarau, Kantonsbibliothek, MS Wett.
Aberystwyth, National Library of Wales, MS Peniarth 392D ("Hengwrt").
Berkeley Castle Muniments C/2/2/14 (GC4127).
Cambridge: Gonville and Caius College, MS 669*/646; Jesus College, MS 24 (Q.B.7); Trinity College, MS 4 B.15.17; Trinity College, MS 0.7.7; University Library, MSS Ll.4.14, Mm.2.18.

Chambéry, Bibliothèque Municipale, MS 27.
Darmstadt, Hessische Landesbibliothek, MS 535.
Florence, Biblioteca Mediceo-Laurenziana, MS Plut. 30.24.
Karlsruhe, Badische Landesbibliothek, MS St. Peter perg. 82.
Kew, The National Archives: E 101/510/21; E 101/511/15; E 101/516/9.
London: British Library, MSS Additional 17,358, 22283 ("Simeon"); British Library, MS Arundel 83 II; British Library, MSS Cotton Titus A. XX, Cotton Vespasian B XVI, Cotton Vespasian B. XXIII; British Library, MSS Harley 4971, 2253; British Library, MS Royal 1.B.x; Wellcome Historical Medical Library, MS 49.
Manchester, John Rylands Library, MS Latin 394.
Munich, Bayerische Staatsbibliothek, MSS Clm. 8201, 11465, 16104a.
New Haven, Yale University, Beinecke Rare Book and Manuscript Library, MS 416.
Oxford: Bodleian Library, MS Laud Misc. 156; MSS Rawlinson poet. 163, Digby 86, Eng. poet. a. 1 ("Vernon"); MS Rawlinson D 328; Corpus Christi College, MS 201; St. John's College, MS 58.
Paris: Bibliothèque de l'Arsenal, MSS 1037, 1100; Bibliothèque Mazarine, MS 924; Bibliothèque Nationale, MSS lat. 3445, 3464, 3473, 14289; Bibliothèque Ste Genevieve, MS 2899.
Rome, Biblioteca Casanatense, MS 1404.
San Marino, California, Huntington Library, MS EL 26 C 9 ("Ellesmere").

Printed Primary Texts

Abailard, Peter. *Sic et Non, A Critical Edition*. Ed. Blanche B. Boyer and Richard McKeon. Chicago: University of Chicago Press, 1976–77.
[Ailred of Rievaulx]. *Aelredi Rievallensis Opera Omnia*. Ed. A. Hoste and C. H. Talbot. CCCM 1. Turnhout: Brepols, 1971.
Alain de Lille. *Anticlaudianus*. Ed. R. Bossuat. Paris: Librairie Philosophique J. Vrin, 1955.
Aristotle. *Aristotle's Theory of Poetry and Fine Art*. Trans. S. H. Butcher. 4th ed. New York: Dover, 1955.
Atkinson, J. Keith, and Anna Maria Babbi. *L'Orphée de Boèce au Moyen Âge: Traductions françaises et commentaires latins (XIIe–XVe siècles)*. Verona: Fiorini, 2000.
Augustine. *Concerning the City of God against the Pagans*. Trans. Henry Bettenson. London: Penguin Books, 1972.
―――. *Confessions*. Ed. and trans. William Watts. 2 vols. Cambridge, MA: Harvard University Press, 1999.
―――. *De civitate Dei*. Trans. William Green. 7 vols. Cambridge, MA: Harvard University Press, 1978.
―――. *De doctrina christiana*. Ed. Paul Tombeur. Turnhout: Brepols, 1982.
―――. *De sermone Domini in monte*. Ed. Almut Mutzenbecher. CCSL 35. Turnhout: Brepols, 1967.
Babington, Churchill, ed. *Polychronicon Ranulphi Higden Monachi Cestrensis together with the English translations of John Trevisa and of an Unknown Writer*. 9 vols. Rolls Series 41. London: Longman, Green; Longman, Roberts and Green, 1865–86.
Barr, Helen, ed. *The Piers Plowman Tradition*. London: J. M. Dent, 1993.

Bennett, J. A. W., and G. V. Smithers, eds. *Early Middle English Verse and Prose.* 2nd ed. Oxford: Clarendon Press, 1968.
Benoît de Sainte-Maure. *Le roman de Troie.* Ed. Léopold Constans. Paris: Firmin-Didot, 1904.
Boccaccio, Giovanni. *Il Filostrato.* Ed. Vincenzo Pernicone. Trans. Robert P. Roberts and Anna Bruni Seldis. New York: Garland Publishing, 1986.
_____. *Il Filostrato di Boccaccio.* Ed. and trans. N. E. Griffin and A. B. Myrick. Philadelphia: University of Pennsylvania Press, 1929.
_____. *Tutte le opere di Giovanni Boccaccio.* Ed. Vittore Branca. 12 vols. Milan: Arnoldo Mondadoro, 1983.
Boethius, Anicius Manlius Severinus. *De Consolatione Philosophiae, Translated by John Walton.* Ed. Mark Science. EETS o.s. 170. London, 1927 (1925).
_____. *In Isagogen Porphyrii.* Ed. Samuel Brandt. CSEL 48. Vienna: Tempsky, 1906.
_____. *The Theological Tractates and the "Consolation of Philosophy."* Ed. and trans. H. F. Tester, E. K. Rand, and S. J. Tester. Cambridge, MA: Harvard University Press, 1973.
The Book of Vices and Virtues. Ed. W. Nelson Francis. EETS 217. London: Oxford University Press, 1942.
Botschuyver, H. J., ed. *Scholia in Horatium in codicibus parisinis latinis 17897 et 8223.* Amsterdam: Bottenburg, 1942.
_____, ed. *Scholia in Horatium codicum parisinorum latinorum 7972, 7974, 7971.* Amsterdam: Bottenburg, 1935.
_____, ed. *Scholia in Horatium codicum parisinorum latinorum 10310 et 7973.* Amsterdam: Bottenburg, 1939.
Brayer, Édith, and Anne-Françoise Leurquin-Labie, eds. *La Somme le Roi par Frère Laurent.* Paris: Société des anciens textes français, 2008.
Brown, Carleton, ed. *English Lyrics of the XIIIth Century.* Oxford: Clarendon Press, 1932.
Burke, Edmund. *A Philosophical Enquiry into the Origin of Our Ideas of the Sublime and Beautiful.* London: J. Dodsley, 1767.
Chaucer, Geoffrey. *The Book of Troilus and Criseyde.* Ed. Robert Kilburn Root. Princeton, NJ: Princeton University Press, 1926.
_____. *The Riverside Chaucer.* Gen. ed. Larry Benson. 3rd ed. Boston: Houghton Mifflin, 1987.
_____. *Troilus & Criseyde: A New Edition of "The Book of Troilus."* Ed. B. A. Windeatt. London: Longman, 1984.
Chrétien de Troyes. *Romans.* Ed. and trans. David F. Hult. Paris: Lettres Gothiques-Poches, 1994.
Claudian. *Against Eutropius.* In *Claudian*, vol. 1., trans. Maurice Platnauer. Loeb Classical Library. London: Heinemann, 1922.
Colonne, Guido della. *Historia destructionis Troiae.* Ed. Nathaniel E. Griffin. Cambridge: Mediæval Academy of America, 1936.
Cursor Mundi. Ed. Richard Morris. EETS 57, 59, 62, 66, 68, 99, 101. London: K. Paul, Trench, Trübner, 1874–93.
Dan Michel's Ayenbite of Inwyt. Ed. Richard Morris. Newly collated by Pamela Gradon. EETS o.s. 23. Oxford: Oxford University Press, 1965.
Dante. *The Divine Comedy.* Ed. C. S. Singleton. Princeton, NJ: Princeton University Press, 1970.
Dartmouth Dante Project. <http://dante.dartmouth.edu/>.

Deguileville, Guillaume de. *Le pèlerinage de la vie humaine*. Ed. J. J. Stürzinger. London: Printed for the Roxburghe Club by Nichols & Sons, 1893.

———. *Pilgrimage of the Life of Man, Englisht by John Lydgate, A.D. 1426, from the French of Guillaume de Deguileville, A.D. 1330, 1355*. Ed. Frederick J. Furnivall and Katherine B. Locock. EETS e.s. 77, 83, 92. London: K. Paul, Trench, Trübner, 1899–1904.

De miseria condicionis humane. Ed. and trans. Robert E. Lewis. Athens: University of Georgia Press, 1978.

Deschamps, Eustache. *L'art de dictier*. Ed. and trans. Deborah Sinnreich-Levi. East Lansing, MI: Colleagues Press, 1994.

Devlin, Sister Mary Aquinas, ed. *The Sermons of Thomas Brinton, Bishop of Rochester (1373–1389)*. 2 vols. with continuous pagination. Camden Society, 3rd ser., 55–56. London: Offices of the Royal Historical Society, 1954.

Dictionnaire du Moyen Français (1330-1500). <http://www.atilf.fr/dmf>.

Dives and Pauper. Ed. Priscilla Heath Barnum. 2 vols. in 3. EETS 275, 280, and o.s. 323. London: Oxford University Press, 1975–2004.

du Bellay, Joachim. *Deffence et illustration de la langue françoyse*. Paris: Crozet, 1839.

Erasmus, Desiderius. *Ausgewählte Werke*. Ed. Annemarie Holborn and Hajo Holborn. Munich: Beck, 1933.

Expositio in Donatum majorem. Ed. B. Löfstedt. CCCM 40A. Turnhout: Brepols, 1977.

Faral, Edmond, ed. *Les arts poétiques du XIIe et du XIIIe siècle*. Paris: Champion, 1924.

Fellowes, Jennifer, ed. *Of Love and Chivalry: An Anthology of Middle English Romance*. London: J. M. Dent, 1993.

Friis-Jensen, Karsten, ed. "The *Ars Poetica* in Twelfth-Century France: The Horace of Matthew of Vendôme, Geoffrey of Vinsauf, and John of Garland." *Cahiers de l'Institut du Moyen Âge grec et latin* 60 (1990): 319–88.

Froissart, Jean. *An Anthology of Narrative and Lyric Poetry*. Ed. and trans. Kristen Figg. London: Routledge, 2001.

Gower, John. *The Complete Works of John Gower*. Ed. G. C. Macaulay. 4 vols. Oxford: Clarendon Press, 1899–1902.

———. *Mirour de l'Omme*. Trans. William Burton Wilson. East Lansing, MI: Colleagues Press, 1992.

Gray, Sir Thomas. *Scalacronica*. Ed. Joseph Stevenson. Edinburgh: Maitland Club, 1836.

Grosseteste, Robert. *Templum Dei*. Ed. Joseph Goering and F. A. C. Mantello. Toronto: Centre for Medieval Studies, 1984.

Haddan, A. W., and W. Stubbs, eds. *Councils and Ecclesiastical Documents Relating to Great Britain and Ireland*. 3 vols. Oxford, 1869–78. Reprint, 1974.

Horace. *Opera*. Ed. D. R. Shackleton Bailey. Stuttgart: Teubner, 1985.

———. *Satires, Epistles, and Ars poetica*. Trans. H. R. Fairclough. Cambridge, MA: Harvard University Press; London: Heinemann, 1926. Reprint, 1978.

Horace his arte of Poetrie, Epistles, and Satyrs Englished, and to the Earle of Ormounte by Tho. Drant addressed. London, 1567 [STC (2nd ed.) 13797].

Isidore of Seville. *Etymologiae sive originum*. Ed. W. M. Lindsay. Oxford: Clarendon Press, 1911.

Jerome. *De optimo genere interpretandi*. Ed. G. J. M. Bartelink. Leiden: Brill, 1980.

John of Salisbury. *Entheticus Maior and Minor*. Ed. and trans. Jan van Laarhoven. Leiden: Brill, 1987.

———. *Ioannis Saresberiensis Episcopi Cartonensis Metalogicon Libri IIII.* Ed. C. I. I. Webb. Oxford: Clarendon Press, 1929.
Johnson, Samuel. *The Letters of Samuel Johnson.* Ed. R. W. Chapman. 3 vols. Oxford: Clarendon Press, 1952.
Kant, Immanuel. *Critique of the Power of Judgment.* Ed. Paul Guyer. Trans. Paul Guyer and Eric Matthews. Cambridge: Cambridge University Press, 2000.
Keller, Otto, ed. *Pseudacronis scholia in Horatium vetustiora.* 2 vols. Leipzig: Teubner, 1902–4.
Knighton's Chronicle, 1337–1397. Ed. and trans. G. H. Martin. Oxford: Oxford University Press, 1995.
Kristensson, Gillis, ed. *John Mirk's "Instructions for Parish Priests."* Lund: Gleerup, 1974.
Landino, Cristoforo. *In Q. Horatium Flaccum commentaria.* In *Opera Q. Horatii Flacci Venusini, grammaticorum antiquiss. Heleni Acronis, et Porphirionis commentariis illustrata.* Basel: Heinrich Petri, 1555.
Langland, William. *Piers Plowman: A New Annotated Edition of the C Text.* Ed. Derek Pearsall. Exeter: University of Exeter Press, 2008.
———. *Piers Plowman: The A Version; Will's Visions of Piers Plowman and Do-well.* Ed. George Kane. London: Athlone Press, 1960.
———. *Piers Plowman: The B Version; Will's Visions of Piers Plowman, Do-well, Do-better, and Do-best.* Ed. George Kane and E. Talbot Donaldson. London: Athlone Press, 1975.
———. *Piers Plowman: The C Version; Will's Visions of Piers Plowman, Do-well, Do-better, and Do-best.* Ed. George Russell and George Kane. London: Athlone Press, 1997.
———. *Piers Plowman by William Langland: An Edition of the C-Text.* Ed. Derek Pearsall. York Medieval Texts, second series. London: Arnold, 1978.
———. *The Vision of Piers Plowman: A Critical Edition of the B-Text Based on Trinity College Cambridge Ms. B.15.17.* Ed. A. V. C. Schmidt. 2nd ed. London: J. M. Dent; Rutland, VT: Charles E. Tuttle, 1995.
———. *The Vision of William Concerning Piers the Plowman in Three Parallel Texts together with Richard the Redeless by William Langland.* 2 vols. Ed. W. W. Skeat. London: Oxford University Press, 1886.
———. *The Vision of William Concerning Piers the Plowman, together with Vita de Dowel, Dobet, et Dobest, Secundum Wit et Resoun, by William Langland, Part Three: Langland's Vision of Piers the Plowman, The Whitaker Text; or Text C.* Ed. W. W. Skeat. EETS o.s. 54. London: N. Trübner, 1873.
Laskaya, Anne, and Eve Salisbury, eds. *The Middle English Breton Lays.* Kalamazoo, MI: Medieval Institute, 1995.
Lewis, Charlton T., and Charles Short, eds. *A Latin Dictionary.* <http://www.perseus.tufts.edu/hopper/resolveform?redirect=true&lang=Latin>
Machaut, Guillaume de. *Le livre du voir dit.* Ed. Paul Imbs, Jacqueline Cerquiglini-Toulet, and Noël Musso. Paris: Librairie Générale Française, 1999.
———. *Le livre dou voir dit.* Ed. and trans. Daniel Leech-Wilkinson. New York: Garland, 1998.
Manuel pour mon fils. Ed. Pierre Riché. Trans. Bernard de Vregille and Claude Mondésert. Sources Chrétiennes 225 bis. Paris: Éditions de Cerf, 1991.
Minnis, A. J., and A. B. Scott, eds. *Medieval Literary Theory and Criticism c. 1100–c. 1375: The Commentary Tradition.* Rev. ed. Oxford: Clarendon Press, 1991.

Monteverdi, Claudio. *L'Orfeo: Favola in musica, Mantua, 1607.* Ensemble La Venexiana. Dir. Claudio Cavina. San Lorenzo de El Escorial: Glossa, 2007.
The Parlement of the Thre Ages. Ed. M. Y. Offord. EETS 246. London: Oxford University Press, 1959.
[Paulinus of Nola]. *Letters of St. Paulinus of Nola.* Ed. P. G. Walsh. Westminster, MD: Newman Press; London: Longmans, Green, 1968.
Pemberton, Caroline, ed. *Queen Elizabeth's Englishings of Boethius, "DCP" A.D. 1593, Plutarch, "De Curiosite," Horace, De Arte Poetica (part) A.D. 1598.* EETS o.s. 113. London: Kegan Paul, Trench, Trübner, 1899.
Peter the Chanter. *Verbum abbreviatum.* Ed. Monique Boutry. CCCM 196. Turnhout: Brepols, 2004.
Petrarch, Francis. *Letters of Old Age.* Trans. Aldo S. Bernardo, Saul Levin, and Reta A. Bernardo. 2 vols. Baltimore: Johns Hopkins University Press, 1992. Reprint, New York: Italica Press, 2005.
_____. *Letters on Familiar Matters.* Trans. Aldo S. Bernardo. 3 vols. Baltimore: Johns Hopkins University Press, 1982–85. Reprint, New York: Italica Press, 2005.
_____. *Lettres familières I–III / Rerum familiarum I–III.* Ed. Ugo Dotti. Trans. (in French) André Longpré. Paris: Belles Lettres, 2002.
_____. *Petrarchi Opera Omnia.* 3 vols. Basel: Henricus Petri, 1554.
_____. *Petrarch's Ascent of Mount Ventoux: The Familiaris IV, I.* Ed. Rodney Lokaj. Rome: Edizioni dell'Ateneo, 2006.
_____. *Petrarch's Testament.* Ed. and trans. Theodor E. Mommsen. Ithaca, NY: Cornell University Press, 1957.
Plotinus. *Ennead II.* Trans. A. H. Armstrong. Loeb Classical Library, vol. 441. Cambridge, MA: Harvard University Press, 1966.
Poliziano, Angelo. *L'Orfeo del Poliziano.* Ed. Antonia Tissoni Benvenuti. Padua: Editrice Antenore, 1986.
_____. *Stanze, fabula di Orfeo.* Ed. Stefano Carrai. Milan: Mursia, 1988.
Proust, Marcel. *À la recherche du temps perdu.* Paris: Quarto Gallimard, 1999.
_____. *The Guermantes Way.* Trans. Mark Treharne. New York: Viking, 2004.
_____. *In Search of Lost Time.* Trans. C. K. Scott Moncrieff and Terence Kilmartin. Rev. D. J. Enright. New York: Modern Library, 1992.
Reigny, Galand de. *Petit livres de proverbes.* Ed. Jean Chatillon, Maurice Dumontier, and Alexis Grélois. Source Chrétiennes 436. Paris: Éditions de Cerf, 1998.
[Rolle, Richard]. *Richard Rolle: Prose and Verse from MS. Longleat 29 and Related Manuscripts.* Ed. S. J. Ogilvie-Thomson. EETS o.s. 293. Cambridge: Boydell & Brewer, 1988.
Le Roman de la Rose. Ed. Armand Strubel. Paris: Librairie Générale Française, 1992.
Sandler, Lucy Freeman. *The Psalter of Robert de Lisle in the British Library.* 2nd ed. London: Harvey Miller Publishers, 1999.
Sources and Analogues of the "Canterbury Tales." Vol. 1. Ed. Robert M. Correale and Mary Hamel. Chaucer Studies 28. Cambridge: D. S. Brewer, 2002.
South, Robert. *Sermons Preached upon Several Occasions.* Philadelphia: Sorin & Ball, 1845.
Speculum Vitae: A Reading Edition. Ed. Ralph Hanna. 2 vols. EETS 331–32. Oxford: Oxford University Press, 2008.
Statutes of the Realm. 10 vols. London: Eyre and Strahan, 1810–28.
Summa virtutum de remediis anime. Ed. Siegfried Wenzel. Athens: University of Georgia Press, 1984.

Tertullian, Q. Septimius Florens. *De Carne Christi Liber: Tertullian's Treatise on the Incarnation.* Ed. and trans. Ernest Evans. London: Society for Promoting Christian Knowledge, 1956.
Thorlac Turville-Petre, ed. *Alliterative Poetry of the Later Middle Ages.* London: Routledge, 1989.
Valéry, Paul. *Cahiers 1894–1914.* Vol. 1. Ed. Nicole Celeyrette-Pietri and Judith Robinson. Paris: Gallimard, 1987.
The Vernon Manuscript: A Facsimile of Bodleian Library, Oxford, MS. Eng. poet. a.1. Intro. A. I. Doyle. Cambridge: D. S. Brewer, 1987.
Victorian Literary Studies Archive Hyper-Concordance. <http://victorian.lang.nagoya-u.ac.jp/concordance.html>.
Virgil. *Opera.* Ed. R. A. B. Mynors. Oxford: Clarendon Press, 1969.
Waldron, Ronald. "Trevisa's Original Prefaces on Translation: A Critical Edition." In *Medieval English Studies Presented to George Kane,* ed. Edward Kennedy, Ronald Waldron, and Joseph Wittig, 171–202. Cambridge: D. S. Brewer, 1988.
Walter of Henley and Other Treatises on Estate Management and Accounting. Ed. Dorothy Oschinski. Oxford: Clarendon Press, 1971.
Woolgar, Chris. *Household Accounts from Medieval England.* 2 vols. British Academy, Records of Social and Economic History, New Series 17–18. Oxford: Oxford University Press, 1991–92.
Zechmeister, J., ed. *Scholia Vindobonensia ad Horatii artem poeticam.* Vienna: C. Geroldum, 1877.

Secondary Works

Aers, David. *Community, Gender, and Individual Identity: English Writing 1360–1430.* London: Routledge, 1988.
Alcock, N. W. "The Catesbys in Coventry: A Medieval Estate and Its Archives." *Midland History* 15 (1990): 1–36.
Alford, John. *Piers Plowman: A Guide to the Quotations.* Binghamton, NY: Medieval and Renaissance Texts and Studies, 1992.
Anderson, David. *Before the Knight's Tale: Imitation of Classical Epic in Boccaccio's "Teseida."* Philadelphia: University of Pennsylvania Press, 1988.
Astell, Ann W. "Apostrophe, Prayer, and the Structure of Satire in the *Man of Law's Tale.*" *Studies in the Age of Chaucer* 13 (1991): 81–97.
―――. *The Song of Songs in the Middle Ages.* Ithaca, NY: Cornell University Press, 1990.
Baker, Joan, and Susan Signe Morrison. "The Luxury of Gender: *Piers Plowman* B 9 and the *Merchant's Tale.*" In *William Langland's "Piers Plowman": A Book of Essays,* ed. Kathleen Hewett-Smith, 41–68. New York: Routledge, 2001.
Bakhtin, Mikhail. *The Dialogic Imagination: Four Essays.* Ed. Michael Holquist. Trans. Caryl Emerson and Michael Holquist. Austin: University of Texas Press, 1982.
―――. *Problems of Dostoevsky's Poetics.* Trans. Caryl Emerson. Minneapolis: University of Minnesota Press, 1984.
Barney, Stephen A. *The Penn Commentary on Piers Plowman.* Vol. 5: *C Passus 20–22; B Passus 18–20.* Philadelphia: University of Pennsylvania Press, 2006.
―――. "The Plowshare of the Tongue: The Progress of a Symbol from the Bible to *Piers Plowman.*" *Mediaeval Studies* 35 (1973): 261–93.

———. "Troilus Bound." *Speculum* 47 (1972): 445–58.
Baron, Hans. *In Search of Florentine Civic Humanism: Essays on the Transition from Medieval to Modern Thought*. 2 vols. Princeton, NJ: Princeton University Press, 1988.
Barr, Helen. "The Relationship of *Richard the Redeless* and *Mum and the Sothsegger*: Some New Evidence." *Yearbook of Langland Studies* 4 (1990): 105–33.
———. *Signes and Sothe: Language in the "Piers Plowman" Tradition*. Cambridge: D. S. Brewer, 1994.
Barthes, Roland. *Image, Music, Text*. Trans. Stephen Heath. New York: Hill and Wang, 1978.
———. *S/Z*. Trans. Richard Howard. New York: Hill and Wang, 1974.
Baswell, Christopher. *Virgil in Medieval England: Figuring the "Aeneid" from the Twelfth Century to Chaucer*. Cambridge: Cambridge University Press, 1995.
Benson, C. David. *The History of Troy in Middle English Literature: Guido delle Colonne's "Historia Destructionis Troiae" in Medieval England*. Woodbridge, UK: D. S. Brewer, 1980.
———. "Poetic Variety in the *Man of Law's* and the *Clerk's Tales*." In *Chaucer's Religious Tales*, ed. C. David Benson and Elizabeth Robertson, 137–44. Cambridge: D. S. Brewer, 1990.
Benson, C. David, and Lynne Blanchfield. *The Manuscripts of "Piers Plowman": The B-Version*. Cambridge: D. S. Brewer, 1987.
Benson, C. David, and Barry A. Windeatt. "The Manuscript Glosses to Chaucer's *Troilus and Criseyde*." *Chaucer Review* 25 (1990): 33–53.
Benson, Larry D. *Malory's "Morte Darthur."* Cambridge, MA: Harvard University Press, 1976.
Birrell, J. R. "The *Status Maneriorum* of John Catesby, 1385 and 1386." In *Dugdale Society Miscellany I*, ed. R. Bearman, 15–28. Publications of the Dugdale Society 31. Oxford: Dugdale Society, 1977.
Birtwistle, Harrison. *The Mask of Orpheus*. BBC Symphony Orchestra conducted by Andrew Davis, 1999, compact disc.
Blamires, Alcuin. "*Mum and the Sothsegger* and Langlandian Idiom." *Neuphilologische Mitteilungen* 76 (1975): 583–604.
Blanchot, Maurice. *The Gaze of Orpheus and Other Literary Essays*. Trans. Lydia Davis. Ed. P. Adams Sitney. Barrytown, NY: Station Hill, 1981.
Bloomfield, Morton W. "Chaucer's Sense of History." *Journal of English and Germanic Philology* 51 (1952): 301–13.
———. "Distance and Predestination in *Troilus and Criseyde*." *PMLA* 72 (1957): 14–26.
———. "A Grammatical Approach to Personification Allegory." *Modern Philology* 40 (1963): 161–71.
———. "*Piers Plowman* and the Three Grades of Chastity." *Anglia* 76 (1958): 227–53.
———. *"Piers Plowman" as a Fourteenth-Century Apocalypse*. New Brunswick, NJ: Rutgers University Press, n.d. [1962].
Boas, M. "De librorum Catonianorum historia atque compositione." *Mnemosyne* 42 (1914): 17–46.
Boitani, Piero. "The 'Monk's Tale': Dante and Boccaccio." *Medium Ævum* 45 (1976): 50–69.
Bolzoni, Lina. *The Web of Images: Vernacular Preaching from Its Origins to St. Bernardino da Siena*. Trans. Carole Preston and Lisa Chien. Aldershot, UK: Ashgate, 2004.

Bordo, Susan. *Unbearable Weight: Feminism, Western Culture, and the Body.* Berkeley: University of California Press, 1993.
Borenius, Tancred. "The Cycle of Images in the Palaces and Castles of Henry III." *Journal of the Warburg and Courtauld Institutes* 6 (1943): 40–50.
Bowers, John. *Chaucer and Langland: The Antagonistic Tradition.* Notre Dame, IN: University of Notre Dame Press, 2007.
Boyle, Marjorie O'Rourke. "William Harvey's Anatomy Book and Literary Culture." *Medical History* 52 (2008): 73–91.
Breen, Katharine. *Imagining an English Reading Public, 1150–1400.* Cambridge: Cambridge University Press, 2010.
Bressie, Ramona. "A Governour Wily and Wys." *Modern Language Notes* 54 (1939): 477–90.
Brewer, Derek. "Comedy and Tragedy in *Troilus.*" In *The European Tragedy of Troilus,* ed. Piero Boitani, 95–109. Oxford: Clarendon Press, 1989.
Brink, C. O. *Horace on Poetry.* 3 vols. Cambridge: Cambridge University Press, 1963–82.
Brody, Saul N. "Making a Play for Criseyde: The Staging of Pandarus's House in Chaucer's *Troilus and Criseyde.*" *Speculum* 73 (1998): 115–40.
Brown, Peter. *The Body and Society: Men, Women, and Sexual Renunciation in Early Christianity.* New York: Columbia University Press, 1988.
Brownlee, Kevin. *Poetic Identity in Guillaume de Machaut.* Madison: University of Wisconsin Press, 1984.
Burlin, Robert B. *Chaucerian Fiction.* Princeton, NJ: Princeton University Press, 1977.
Burnett, Charles. "Sound and Its Perception in the Middle Ages." In *The Second Sense: Studies in Hearing and Musical Judgment from Antiquity to the Seventeenth Century,* ed. Charles Burnett, Michael Fend, and Penelope Gouk, 43–69. London: Warburg Institute, 1991.
Burrow, J. A. "The Action of Langland's Second Vision." *Essays in Criticism* 15 (1965): 247–68.
———. *Gestures and Looks in Medieval Narrative.* Cambridge: Cambridge University Press, 2002.
———. *The Poetry of Praise.* Cambridge: Cambridge University Press, 2008.
———. *Ricardian Poetry: Chaucer, Gower, Langland, and the "Gawain" Poet.* New Haven, CT: Yale University Press, 1971.
Buttenwieser, Hilda. "Popular Authors of the Middle Ages: The Testimony of the Manuscripts." *Speculum* 17 (1942): 50–55.
Cable, Thomas. *The English Alliterative Tradition.* Philadelphia: University of Pennsylvania Press, 1991.
Caie, Graham D. "Innocent III's *De Miseria* as a Gloss on *the Man of Law's Prologue* and *Tale.*" *Neuphilologische Mitteilungen* 100 (1999): 175–85.
Camargo, Martin. "Chaucer and the Oxford Renaissance of Anglo-Latin Rhetoric." *Studies in the Age of Chaucer* 34 (2012): 173–207.
———. "From *Liber versuum* to *Poetria nova*: The Evolution of Geoffrey of Vinsauf's Masterpiece." *Journal of Medieval Latin* 21 (2011): 1–16.
———. "The Late Fourteenth-Century Renaissance of Anglo-Latin Rhetoric." *Philosophy and Rhetoric* 45.2 (2012): 107–33.
Cannon, Christopher. *The Grounds of English Literature.* Oxford: Oxford University Press, 2004.

———. "The Invention of the Anglo-Latin Public Poetry (circa 1367–1402) and Its Prosody, Esp. in John Gower." *Mittellateinisches Jahrbuch* 39 (2004): 389–406.
———. "Langland's *Ars Grammatica*." *Yearbook of Langland Studies* 22 (2008): 1–25.
Carlson, David. *Chaucer's Jobs*. New York: Palgrave Macmillan, 2004.
Carruthers, Mary. "Allegory without the Teeth: Some Reflections on Figural Language in *Piers Plowman*." *Yearbook of Langland Studies* 19 (2005): 27–44.
———. *The Book of Memory: A Study of Memory in Medieval Culture*. Cambridge: Cambridge University Press, 1990.
———. *The Book of Memory*. 2nd ed. Cambridge: Cambridge University Press, Cambridge, 2008.
———. "Moving Images in the Mind's Eye." In *The Mind's Eye: Art and Theological Argument in the Middle Ages*, ed. Jeffrey F. Hamburger and Anne-Marie Bouché, 287–305. Princeton, NJ: Princeton Dept. of Art and Archaeology, 2006.
Catto, Jeremy. "Religion and the English Nobility in the Later Fourteenth Century." In *History and Imagination: Essays in Honor of H. R. Trevor-Roper*, ed. Hugh Lloyd-Jones, Valerie Pearl, and Blair Worden, 43–55. New York: Holmes and Meier, 1981.
Cavarero, Adriana. *For More Than One Voice: Toward a Philosophy of Vocal Expression*. Trans. Paul A. Kottman. Stanford, CA: Stanford University Press, 2005.
Cavell, Stanley. *Must We Mean What We Say?* Cambridge: Cambridge University Press, 1976.
Certeau, Michel de. *The Practice of Everyday Life*. Trans. Steven Rendall. Berkeley: University of California Press, 1984.
Chance, Jane. *The Mythographic Chaucer: The Fabulation of Sexual Politics*. Minneapolis: University of Minnesota Press, 1994.
Cloetta, Wilhelm. *Beiträge zur Literaturgeschichte des Mittelalters und der Renaissance*. Vol. 1: *Komödie and Tragödie im Mittelalter*. Halle: Niemeyer, 1890.
Clopper, Lawrence. *"Songes of Rechelesnesse": Langland and the Franciscans*. Ann Arbor: University of Michigan Press, 1997.
Connor, Steven. *Dumbstruck*. Oxford: Oxford University Press, 2000.
Cooper, Helen. "Gender and Personification in *Piers Plowman*." *Yearbook of Langland Studies* 5 (1991): 31–48.
Copeland, Rita. "Between Romans and Romantics." *Texas Studies in Literature and Language* 33 (1991): 215–24.
———. *Rhetoric, Hermeneutics, and Translation in the Middle Ages: Academic and Vernacular Texts*. Cambridge: Cambridge University Press, 1991.
Copeland, Rita, and Ineke Sluiter, eds. *Medieval Grammar and Rhetoric: Language Arts and Literary Theory, A.D. 300–1475*. Oxford: Oxford University Press, 2009.
Cornelius, Roberta. *The Figurative Castle: A Study in the Medieval Allegory of the Edifice with Especial Reference to Religious Writings*. Bryn Mawr, PA: n.p., 1930.
Cox, Virginia. "Ciceronian Rhetoric in Late Medieval Italy." In *The Rhetoric of Cicero in Its Medieval and Renaissance Commentary Tradition*. Ed. Virginia Cox and John O. Ward, 109–43. Leiden: Brill, 2006.
Crow, Christine M. *Paul Valéry and the Poetry of Voice*. Cambridge: Cambridge University Press, 1982.
Culler, Jonathan. "Introduction: Critical Paradigms." *PMLA* 125 (2010): 905–15.
———. *The Literary in Theory*. Stanford, CA: Stanford University Press, 2007.
———. *The Pursuit of Signs: Semiotics, Literature, Deconstruction*. Ithaca, NY: Cornell University Press, 1981.

Cunningham, J. V. "The Literary Form of the Prologue to *The Canterbury Tales*." *Modern Philology* 49 (1952): 172–81.
Davies, R. R. *The Revolt of Owain Glyn Dŵr*. Oxford: Oxford University Press, 1995.
Deleuze, Gilles. *Proust and Signs*. Trans. Richard Howard. Minneapolis: University of Minnesota Press, 2000.
Delisle, Leopold. "Notice sur la *Rhétorique* de Cicéron, traduite par Maitre Jean d'Antioche, MS 590 du Musée Condé." *Notices et extraits des manuscrits de la Bibliothèque Nationale* 36 (1899): 207–65.
Desmond, Marilynn, and Pamela Sheingorn. *Myth, Montage, and Visuality in Late Medieval Manuscript Culture: Christine de Pizan's Epistre Othea*. Ann Arbor: University of Michigan Press, 2003.
Dietz, David B. "*Historia* in the Commentary of Servius." *Transactions of the American Philosophical Association* 125 (1995): 61–97.
Dinshaw, Carolyn. *Chaucer's Sexual Poetics*. Madison: University of Wisconsin Press, 1989.
———. "'Getting Medieval': *Pulp Fiction*, Gawain, Foucault." In *The Book and the Body*, ed. Dolores Warwick Frese and Katherine O'Brien O'Keeffe, 116–63. Notre Dame, IN: University of Notre Dame Press, 1997.
———. *Getting Medieval: Sexualities and Communities, Pre- and Postmodern*. Durham, NC: Duke University Press, 1999.
———. "A Kiss Is Just a Kiss: Heterosexuality and Its Consolations in *Sir Gawain and the Green Knight*." *Diacritics* 24 (1994): 205–26.
Dodman, Trevor. "Hunting to Teach: Class, Pedagogy, and Maleness in *The Master of Game* and *Sir Gawain and the Green Knight*." *Exemplaria* 17 (Fall 2005): 413–44.
Dolar, Mladen. *A Voice and Nothing More*. Cambridge, MA: MIT Press, 2006.
Donaldson, E. T. "Chaucer and the Elusion of Clarity." *Essays and Studies* 25 (1972): 23–44.
———. *Speaking of Chaucer*. New York: Norton, 1970.
Doyle, A. I. "University College, Oxford, MS 97 and Its Relationship to the Simeon Manuscript (British Library Add. 22283)." In *So meny people longages and tonges: Philological Essays in Scots and Medieval English Presented to Angus McIntosh*, ed. Michael Benskin and M. L. Samuels, 265–82. Edinburgh: n.p., 1981.
Duggan, Hoyt. "Alliterative Patterning as a Basis for Emendation in Middle English Alliterative Poetry." *Studies in the Age of Chaucer* 8 (1986): 73–104.
———. "The Shape of the b-verse in Middle English Alliterative Poetry." *Speculum* 61 (1986): 564–92.
Eden, Kathy. *Friends Hold All Things in Common: Tradition, Intellectual Property, and the "Adages" of Erasmus*. New Haven, CT: Yale University Press, 2001.
Elliott, R. V. W. "The Topography of *Wynnere and Wastoure*." *English Studies* 48 (1967): 134–40.
Ellis, Roger, ed., *The Oxford History of Literary Translation in English*. Vol. 1: *To 1550*. Oxford: Oxford University Press, 2008.
Emmerson, Richard K. "'Coveitise to Konne,' 'Goddes Pryvetee,' and Will's Ambiguous Dream Experience in *Piers Plowman*." In *Suche Werkis to Werche: Essays on Piers Plowman in Honor of David C. Fowler*, ed. Míċeál Vaughan, 89–121. East Lansing, MI: Colleagues Press, 1993.
Enders, Jody. *Rhetoric and the Origins of Medieval Drama*. Ithaca, NY: Cornell University Press, 1992.

Evans, Michael. "The Geometry of Mind: Scientific Diagrams and Medieval Thought." *Architectural Association Quarterly* 12 (1980): 32–55.

———. "An Illustrated Fragment of Peraldus's 'Summa' of Vice: Harleian MS. 3244." *Journal of the Warburg and Courtauld Institutes* 45 (1982): 14–68.

Farrell, Thomas J. "The Persistence of Donaldson's Memory." *Chaucer Review* 41 (2007): 289–98.

Febvre, Lucien. "La sensibilité et l'histoire: Comment reconstituer la vie affective d'autrefois?" *Annales d'histoire sociale* 3 (1941): 5–20.

Federico, Sylvia. *New Troy: Fantasies of Empire in the Late Middle Ages*. Minneapolis: University of Minnesota Press, 2003.

Fewster, Carol. *Traditionality and Genre in Middle English Romance*. Cambridge: D. S. Brewer, 1987.

Fisher, John. *John Gower: Moral Philosopher and Friend of Chaucer*. New York: New York University Press, 1964.

Fleming, John V. *Classical Imitation and Interpretation in Chaucer's "Troilus."* Lincoln: University of Nebraska Press, 1990.

Fletcher, Alan. "Chaucer the Heretic." *Studies in the Age of Chaucer* 25 (2003): 97–98.

Fletcher, Doris. "The Lancastrian Collar of Esses: Its Origin and Transformations down the Centuries." In *The Age of Richard II*, ed. James Gillespie, 191–203. Phoenix Mill, UK: Sutton, 1997.

Foucault, Michel. *Discipline and Punish: The Birth of the Prison*. Trans. Alan Sheridan. New York: Vintage, 1979.

Fowler, Elizabeth. *Literary Character: The Human Figure in Early English Writing*. Ithaca, NY: Cornell University Press, 2003.

Fradenburg, L. O. Aranye. *Sacrifice Your Love: Psychoanalysis, Historicism, Chaucer*. Minneapolis: University of Minnesota Press, 2003.

Frank, Robert W., Jr. *"Piers Plowman" and the Scheme of Salvation*. Yale Studies in English 136. New Haven, CT: Yale University Press, 1957.

Fredborg, Margareta. *"Difficile est proprie communia dicere* (Horats, A.P. 128): Horatsfortolkningens bidrag til middelalderens poetik." *Museum Tusculanum* 40–43 (1980): 583–97.

Friedman, John Block. *Orpheus in the Middle Ages*. Cambridge, MA: Harvard University Press, 1970.

Friis-Jensen, Karsten. "Horace and the Early Writers of Arts of Poetry." In *Sprachtheorien in Spätantike und Mittelalter*, ed. Sten Ebbesen, 360–401. Tübingen: Gunter Narr Verlag, 1995.

———. "Medieval Commentaries on Horace." In *Medieval and Renaissance Scholarship*, ed. Nicholas Mann and Birger Munk Olsen, 51–73. Leiden: Brill, 1997.

Fyler, John M. *Language and the Declining World in Chaucer, Dante, and Jean de Meun*. Cambridge: Cambridge University Press, 2007.

Galloway, Andrew. "Authority." In *A Companion to Chaucer*, ed. Peter Brown, 23–39. Oxford: Blackwell, 2000.

———. "Chaucer's Quarrel with Gower, and the Origins of Bourgeois Didacticism in Fourteenth-Century London Poetry." In *Calliope's Classroom: Didactic Poetry from Antiquity to the Renaissance*, ed. Annette Harder, Geritt Reinink, and Alasdair MacDonald, 245–68. Leuven, Paris, and Dudley, VA: Peeters, 2007.

———. "The Economy of Need in Late Medieval English Literature." *Viator* 40 (2009): 309–31.

———. "Gower in His Most Learned Role and the Peasants' Revolt of 1381." *Mediaevalia* 16 (1993): 329–47.
———. "Latin England." In *Imagining a Medieval English Community*, ed. Kathryn Lavezzo, 41–95. Minneapolis: University of Minnesota Press, 2003.
———. "The Literature of 1388 and the Politics of Pity in Gower's *Confessio Amantis*." In *The Letter of the Law: Legal Practice and Literary Production in Medieval England*, ed. Emily Steiner and Candace Barrington, 67–104. Ithaca, NY: Cornell University Press, 2002.
———. *The Penn Commentary on Piers Plowman*. Vol. 1: *C Prologue-Passus 4; B Prologue-Passus 4; A Prologue-Passus 4*. Philadelphia: University of Pennsylvania Press, 2006.
———. "*Piers Plowman* and the Schools." *Yearbook of Langland Studies* 6 (1992): 89–107.
Ganim, John. *Chaucerian Theatricality*. Princeton, NJ: Princeton University Press, 1990.
Gehl, Paul. *A Moral Art: Grammar, Society, and Culture in Trecento Florence*. Ithaca, NY: Cornell University Press, 1993.
Giancarlo, Matthew. *Parliament and Literature in Late Medieval England*. Cambridge: Cambridge University Press, 2007.
Gill, Miriam. "The Role of Images in Monastic Education: The Evidence from Wall Painting in Late Medieval England." In *Medieval Monastic Education*, ed. George Ferzoco and Carolyn Muessig, 117–35. London: Leicester University Press, 2000.
Gillespie, Vincent. "From the Twelfth Century to c. 1450." In *The Cambridge History of Literary Criticism*, vol. 2: *The Middle Ages*, ed. Alastair Minnis and Ian Johnson, 145–235. Cambridge: Cambridge University Press, 2005.
Ginsberg, Warren. *The Cast of Character: The Representation of Personality in Ancient and Medieval Literature*. Toronto: University of Toronto Press, 1983.
———. *Chaucer's Italian Tradition*. Ann Arbor: University of Michigan Press, 2002.
Godden, Malcolm. *The Making of "Piers Plowman."* London: Longman, 1990.
Godefroy, Frédéric. *Dictionnaire de l'ancienne langue française et de tous ses dialectes du IXe au XVe siècle*. 10 vols. Paris, 1880–1902.
Gradon, Pamela. "Langland and the Ideology of Dissent." *Proceedings of the British Academy* 66 (1980): 179–205.
Gransden, Antonia. *Legends, Traditions, and History in Medieval England*. London; Rio Grande, OH: Hambledon Press, 1992.
Green, Richard Firth. *A Crisis of Truth: Literature and Law in Ricardian England*. Philadelphia: University of Pennsylvania Press, 1999.
Greenblatt, Stephen. "What Is the History of Literature?" *Critical Inquiry* 23 (1997): 460–81.
Griffiths, Lavinia. *Personification in "Piers Plowman."* Cambridge: D. S. Brewer, 1985.
Haahr, Joan G. "Criseyde's Inner Debate: The Dialectic of Enamorment in the *Filostrato* and the *Troilus*." *Studies in Philology* 89 (1992): 257–71.
Hames, Harvey. "The Language of Conversion: Ramon Llull's Art as a Vernacular." In *The Vulgar Tongue: Medieval and Postmedieval Vernacularity*, ed. Fiona Somerset and Nicholas Watson, 43–56. University Park: Pennsylvania State University Press, 2003.
Hamilton, George L. *The Indebtedness of Chaucer's "Troilus and Criseyde" to Guido delle Colonne's "Historia trojana."* New York: Columbia University Press, 1903.
———. "Theodolus: A Medieval Textbook." *Modern Philology* 7 (1909): 169–85.
Hanawalt, Barbara. "Men's Games, King's Deer: Poaching in Medieval England." *Journal of Medieval and Renaissance Studies* 18 (1988): 175–83.
Hanna, Ralph. "Augustinian Canons and Middle English Literature." In *The English Me-*

dieval Book: Studies in Memory of Jeremy Griffiths, ed. A. S. G. Edwards, Vincent Gillespie, and Ralph Hanna, 27–42. London: British Library, 2000.

———. "Langland's Ymaginatif: Images and the Limits of Poetry." In *Images, Idolatry, and Iconoclasm in Late Medieval England: Textuality and the Visual Image*, ed. Jeremy Dimmick, James Simpson, and Nicolette Zeeman, 81–94. Oxford: Oxford University Press, 2002.

———. *London Literature, 1300–1380*. Cambridge: Cambridge University Press, 2005.

———. "'Meddling with Makings' and Will's Work." In *Late-Medieval Religious Texts and Their Transmission: Essays in Honour of A. I. Doyle*, ed. A. J. Minnis, 85–94. York Manuscripts Conferences: Proceedings Series 3. Cambridge: D. S. Brewer, 1994.

———. "Presenting Chaucer as Author." In *Medieval Literature: Texts and Interpretation*, ed. Tim William Machan, 17–39. Binghamton, NY: Medieval and Renaissance Texts and Studies, 1991.

———. *Pursuing History: Middle English Manuscripts and Their Texts*. Stanford, CA: Stanford University Press, 1996.

———. "Robert the Ruyflare and His Companions." In *Literature and Religion in the Later Middle Ages: Philological Essays in Honor of Siegfried Wenzel*, ed. Richard G. Newhauser and John A. Alford, 81–96. Medieval and Renaissance Texts and Studies 118. Binghamton, NY: Medieval and Renaissance Texts and Studies, 1995.

———. "'Vae octuplex,' Lollard Socio-Textual Ideology, and Ricardian-Lancastrian Prose Translation." In *Criticism and Dissent in the Middle Ages*, ed. Rita Copeland, 244–63. Cambridge: Cambridge University Press, 1996.

———. "Will's Work." In *Written Work: Langland, Labor, and Authorship*, ed. Steven Justice and Kathryn Kerby-Fulton, 23–66. Philadelphia: University of Pennsylvania Press, 1997.

Hanna, Ralph, Tony Hunt, R. G. Keightley, Alastair Minnis, and Nigel F. Palmer. "Latin Commentary Tradition and Vernacular Literature." In *The Cambridge History of Literary Criticism*, vol. 2: *The Middle Ages*, ed. Alastair Minnis and Ian Johnson, 363–421. Cambridge: Cambridge University Press, 2005.

Harbert, Bruce. "Lessons from the Great Clerk: Ovid and John Gower." In *Ovid Renewed: Ovidian Influences on Literature and Art from the Middle Ages to the Twentieth Century*, ed. Charles Martindale, 83–97. Cambridge: Cambridge University Press, 1988.

Harrington, David V. "Indeterminacy in *Winner and Waster* and *The Parliament of the Three Ages*." *Chaucer Review* 20 (1986): 246–57.

Havely, Nicholas. *Chaucer's Boccaccio*. Cambridge: Boydell and Brewer, 1980.

Havens, Jill C. "A Narrative of Faith: Middle English Devotional Anthologies and Religious Practice." *Journal of the Early Book Society* 7 (2004): 67–84.

Hazelton, Richard. "Chaucer and Cato." *Speculum* 35 (1960): 357–80.

———. "The Christianization of 'Cato': The *Disticha Catonis* in the Light of Late Medieval Commentaries." *Medieval Studies* 19 (1957): 157–73.

Hegel, G. W. F. *Philosophy of Nature: Encyclopedia of the Philosophical Sciences, Part II*. Trans. A. V. Miller. Oxford: Oxford University Press, 2004.

Heng, Geraldine. "Feminine Knots and the Other *Sir Gawain and the Green Knight*." *PMLA* 106 (1991): 500–514.

———. "A Woman Wants: The Lady, *Gawain*, and the Forms of Seduction." *Yale Journal of Criticism* 5 (1992): 101–34.

Herlihy, David. *Medieval Households*. Cambridge, MA: Harvard University Press, 1985.

Herold, Christine. *Chaucer's Tragic Muse: The Paganization of Christian Tragedy.* Lewiston, NY: Edwin Mellen Press, 2003.
Herrick, Marvin T. *The Fusion of Horatian and Aristotelian Literary Criticism, 1531–1555.* Illinois Studies in Language and Literature 32. Urbana: University of Illinois Press, 1946.
Hill, John. *Chaucerian Belief: The Poetics of Reverence and Delight.* New Haven, CT: Yale University Press, 1991.
Hindley, Alan, Frederick Langley, and Brian Levy. *Old French-English Dictionary.* Cambridge: Cambridge University Press, 2000.
Holsinger, Bruce W. *Music, Body, and Desire in Medieval Culture.* Stanford, CA: Stanford University Press, 2001.
Homans, George C. *English Villagers of the Thirteenth Century.* Cambridge, MA: Harvard University Press, 1941.
Howard, Donald R. *The Idea of the "Canterbury Tales."* Berkeley and Los Angeles: University of California Press, 1976.
Hudson, Anne. "A New Look at *The Lay Folks' Catechism.*" *Viator* 16 (1985): 243–58.
———. *The Premature Reformation: Wycliffite Texts and Lollard History.* Oxford: Clarendon Press, 1988.
Huizinga, Johan. *The Autumn of the Middle Ages.* Trans. Rodney J. Payton and Ulrich Mammtzsch. Chicago: University of Chicago Press, 1996.
———. *Le déclin du Moyen-Âge.* Trans. Julia Bastin. Paris: Payot, 1938.
———. *The Waning of the Middle Ages: A Study of the Forms of Life, Thought, and Art in France and the Netherlands in the Fourteenth and Fifteenth Centuries.* Trans. F. Hopman. London: E. Arnold, 1924.
Humphreys, K. W. *The Friars' Libraries.* Corpus of British Medieval Library Catalogues. London: British Library in association with the British Academy, 1990.
Hunt, Tony. *Teaching and Learning Latin in Thirteenth-Century England.* 3 vols. Cambridge: Cambridge University Press, 1991.
Huot, Sylvia. "'Ci parle l'aucteur': The Rubrication of Voice and Authorship in 'Roman de la Rose' Manuscripts." *SubStance* 17 (1988): 42–48.
Irvine, Martin. *The Making of Textual Culture: "Grammatica" and Literary Theory, 350–1100.* Cambridge: Cambridge University Press, 1994.
Irvine, Martin, with David Thomson. "*Grammatica* and Literary Theory." In *The Cambridge History of Literary Criticism,* vol. 2: *The Middle Ages,* ed. Alastair Minnis and Ian Johnson, 15–41. Cambridge: Cambridge University Press, 2005.
Iser, Wolfgang. "Indeterminacy and the Reader's Response in Prose Fiction." In *Aspects of Narrative: Selected Papers from the English Institute,* ed. J. Hillis Miller, 1–45. New York: Columbia University Press, 1971.
Javitch, Daniel. "The Assimilation of Aristotle's *Poetics* in Sixteenth-Century Italy." In *The Cambridge History of Literary Criticism,* vol. 3, *The Renaissance,* ed. Glyn P. Norton, 53–65. Cambridge: Cambridge University Press, 1999.
Johnson, I. R. "Walton's Sapient Orpheus." In *The Medieval Boethius,* ed. Alastair Minnis, 139–68. Cambridge: D. S. Brewer, 1987.
Jordan, Robert M. "Heteroglossia and Chaucer's *Man of Law's Tale.*" In *Bakhtin and Medieval Voices,* ed. Thomas J. Farrell, 81–93. Gainesville: University Press of Florida, 1995.
Justice, Steven. "Literary History." In *Chaucer: Contemporary Approaches,* ed. David

Raybin and Susanna Fein, 195–210. University Park: Pennsylvania State University Press, 2009.
———. *Writing and Rebellion: England in 1381*. Berkeley: University of California Press, 1994.
Kane, George. *The Liberating Truth: The Concept of Integrity in Chaucer's Writings*. The John Coffin Memorial Lecture, 1979. London: Athlone Press, 1980.
Kaske, Robert E. "The Knight's Interruption of the Monk's Tale." *ELH* 24 (1957): 249–68.
———. "Langland and the *Paradisus claustralis*." *Modern Language Notes* 72 (1957): 481–83.
Kelly, Douglas. *The Arts of Poetry and Prose*. Typologie des Sources du Moyen Âge Occidental, fasc. 59. Turnhout: Brepols, 1991.
Kelly, Henry Ansgar. *Chaucerian Tragedy*. Cambridge: D. S. Brewer, 1997.
———. *Ideas and Forms of Tragedy from Aristotle to the Middle Ages*. Cambridge: Cambridge University Press, 1993.
Kendall, Elliott. *Lordship and Literature: John Gower and the Politics of the Great Household*. Oxford: Oxford University Press, 2008.
Kerby-Fulton, Katherine. *Reformist Apocalypticism and "Piers Plowman."* Cambridge: Cambridge University Press, 1990.
Kernan, Anne. "Theme and Structure in *The Parlement of the Thre Ages*." *Neuphilologische Mitteilungen* 75 (1974): 253–78.
Kiser, Lisa. "Elde and His Teaching in *The Parlement of the Thre Ages*." *Philological Quarterly* 66 (1987): 303–14.
Kittredge, George Lyman. *Chaucer and His Poetry*. Cambridge, MA: Harvard University Press, 1946.
Knapp, Peggy. *Chaucerian Aesthetics*. New York: Palgrave Macmillan, 2008.
Knowles, David. *The Religious Orders in England*. Vol. 2: *The End of the Middle Ages*. Cambridge: Cambridge University Press, 1955.
Kurose, Tamotsu. *Miniatures of the Goddess Fortune in Medieval Manuscripts*. Tokyo: Sanseido, 1977.
Kuskin, William. "Caxton's Worthies Series: The Production of Literary Culture." *ELH* 66 (1999): 511–51.
Ladd, Roger A. *Antimercantilism in Late Medieval English Literature*. New York: Palgrave Macmillan, 2010.
Lafferty, Maura K. *Walter of Châtillon's Alexandreis: Epic and the Problem of Historical Understanding*. Turnout: Brepols, 1998.
Lawler, Traugott. "Harlots' Holiness: The System of Absolution for Miswinning in the C Version of *Piers Plowman*." *Yearbook of Langland Studies* 20 (2006): 141–89.
———. "William Langland." In *The Oxford History of Literary Translation in English*, vol. 1: *To 1550*, ed. Roger Ellis, 149–59. Oxford: Oxford University Press, 2008.
Lawton, David. *Chaucer's Narrators*. Cambridge: D. S. Brewer, 1985.
———. "Donaldson and Irony." *Chaucer Review* 41 (2007): 231–39.
———. "Dullness and the Fifteenth Century." *ELH* 54 (1987): 761–99.
———. "English Literary Voices, 1350–1500." In *The Cambridge Companion to Medieval English Culture*, ed. Andrew Galloway, 237–58. Cambridge: Cambridge University Press, 2011.
———. Introduction to *Middle English Alliterative Poetry and Its Literary Background: Seven Essays*, 1–19. Ed. David Lawton. Cambridge: D. S. Brewer, 1982.

———. "Lollardy and the *Piers Plowman* Tradition." *Modern Language Review* 76 (1981): 780–93.
———. "Skelton's Use of Persona." *Essays in Criticism* (1980): 9–28.
———. "The Subject of *Piers Plowman*." *Yearbook of Langland Studies* 1 (1987): 1–30.
———. "Titus Goes Hunting and Hawking: The Poetics of Recreation and Revenge in *The Siege of Jerusalem*." In *Individuality and Achievement in Middle English Poetry*, ed. O. S. Pickering, 105–17. Cambridge: D. S. Brewer, 1997.
———. "Voice after Arundel." In *After Arundel*, ed. Vincent Gillespie and Kantik Ghosh, 133–54. Turnhout: Brepols, 2011.
Leicester, H. Marshall, Jr. "The Art of Impersonation: A General Prologue to the *Canterbury Tales*." *PMLA* 95 (1980): 213–24.
———. *The Disenchanted Self: Representing the Subject in the "Canterbury Tales."* Berkeley: University of California Press, 1990.
Levinson, Marjorie. "What Is New Formalism?" *PMLA* 122 (March 2007): 558–69.
Lewis, C. S. "What Chaucer Really Did to *Il Filostrato*." *Essays and Studies* 17 (1932): 56–75.
Lewis, C. T., and C. Short. *A Latin Dictionary*. Oxford: Clarendon Press, 1894.
Loomis, Roger Sherman. "Verses on the Nine Worthies." *Modern Philology* 15 (1917): 211–20.
Looze, Laurence de. *Pseudo-Autobiography in the Fourteenth Century: Juan Ruiz, Guillaume de Machaut, Jean Froissart, and Geoffrey Chaucer*. Gainesville: University of Florida Press, 1997.
Lowenstein, George, and Scott Ricks. "Economics (Role of Emotion in)." In *Oxford Companion to Emotion and the Affective Sciences*, ed. David Sander and Klaus R. Scherer, 131–33. Oxford: Oxford University Press, 2009.
Lowes, John Livingston. "The Date of Chaucer's *Troilus and Criseyde*." *PMLA* 23 (1908): 285–306.
MacIntire, Elizabeth Jelliffe. "French Influence on the Beginnings of English Classicism." *PMLA* 26 (1911): 496–527.
Magee, John. "The Good and Morality: *Consolatio* 2–4." In *The Cambridge Companion to Boethius*, ed. John Marenbon, 181–206. Cambridge: Cambridge University Press, 2009.
Manly, J. M. "Chaucer and the Rhetoricians." In *Chaucer Criticism: The Canterbury Tales*, ed. Richard J. Schoeck and Jerome Taylor, 268–90. Notre Dame, IN: University of Notre Dame Press, 1960.
Mann, Jill. *Chaucer and Medieval Estates Satire*. Cambridge: Cambridge University Press, 1973.
———. "Eating and Drinking in *Piers Plowman*." *Essays and Studies* n.s. 32 (1979): 26–43.
———. "'He Knew Nat Catoun': Medieval School-Texts and Middle English Literature." In *The Text in the Community: Essays on Medieval Works, Manuscripts, Authors, and Readers*, ed. Jill Mann and Maura Nolan, 41–74. Notre Dame, IN: University of Notre Dame Press, 2006.
———. "Satisfaction and Payment in Middle English Literature." *Studies in the Age of Chaucer* 5 (1983): 17–28.
Mariotti, Scevola, ed. *Orazio: Enciclopedia oraziana*. 3 vols. Rome: Istituto della Enciclopedia Italiana, 1996–98.
Martin, Jay. "Wil as Fool and Wanderer in *Piers Plowman*." *Texas Studies in Literature and Language* 3 (1962): 535–48.

Martindale, Charles, and David Hopkins, eds. *Horace Made New: Horatian Influences on British Writing from the Renaissance to the Twentieth Century.* Cambridge: Cambridge University Press, 1993.
Marvin, William. *Hunting Law and Ritual in Medieval English Literature.* Cambridge: D. S. Brewer, 2006.
———. "Slaughter and Romance: Hunting Reserves in Late Medieval England." In *Medieval Crime and Social Control,* ed. Barbara Hanawalt and David Wallace, 224–52. Minneapolis: University of Minnesota Press, 1999.
Marx, William. "The Dialogues and *Mon Faust:* The Inner Politics of Thought." In *Reading Paul Valéry: The Universe in Mind,* ed. Paul Gifford, 155–69. Cambridge: Cambridge University Press, 1999.
Matthews, David. *Writing to the King: Nation, Kingship, and Literature in England, 1250–1350.* Cambridge: Cambridge University Press, 2010.
Mazzoni, Francesco. *Saggio di un nuovo commento alla "Divina commedia": Inferno canti I–III.* Florence: Sansoni, 1967.
Mazzotta, Giuseppe. *The Worlds of Petrarch.* Durham, NC: Duke University Press, 1993.
McIntosh, Marjorie Keniston. *Working Women in English Society, 1300–1620.* Cambridge: Cambridge University Press, 2005.
McNamer, Sarah. *Affective Meditation and the Invention of Medieval Compassion.* Philadelphia: University of Pennsylvania Press, 2009.
Meech, Sanford B. "A Collection of Proverbs in Rawlinson MS D 328." *Modern Philology* 38 (1940): 113–32.
Meeuws, Marie-Benoît. "'Ora et labora': Devise bénédictine?" *Collectanea cisterciensia* 54 (1992): 193–219.
Merrilees, Brian. "Teaching Latin in French: Adaptations of Donatus' *Ars minor.*" *Fifteenth-Century Studies* 12 (1987): 87–98.
Meyer-Lee, Robert J. "The Emergence of the Literary in John Lydgate's *Life of Our Lady.*" *JEGP* 109 (2010): 322–48.
Middleton, Anne. "Acts of Vagrancy: The C-Version 'Autobiography' and the Statute of 1388." In *Written Work: Langland, Labor, and Authorship,* ed. Steven Justice and Kathryn Kerby-Fulton, 208–317. Philadelphia: University of Pennsylvania Press, 1997.
———. "Ælfric's Answerable Style: The Rhetoric of the Alliterative Prose." *Studies in Medieval Culture* 4 (1973 [1968]): 83–91.
———. "The Audience and Public of *Piers Plowman.*" In *Middle English Alliterative Poetry and Its Literary Background: Seven Essays,* ed. David Lawton, 101–23, 147–54. Cambridge: D. S. Brewer, 1982.
———. "Chaucer's 'New Men' and the Good of Literature in the *Canterbury Tales.*" In *Literature and Society,* ed. Edward Said, 15–56. Baltimore: Johns Hopkins University Press, 1980.
———. "The Clerk and His Tale: Some Literary Contexts." *Studies in the Age of Chaucer* 2 (1980): 121–50.
———. "The 'English Ways' of Ælfric's Prose." PhD diss., Harvard University, 1966.
———. "The Idea of Public Poetry in the Reign of Richard II." *Speculum* 53 (1978): 94–114.
———. "Langland's Lives: Reflections on Late-Medieval Religious and Literary Vocabulary." In *The Idea of Medieval Literature: New Essays on Chaucer and Medieval Culture*

in Honor of Donald R. Howard, ed. James M. Dean and Christian K. Zacher, 227–42. Newark, DE: University of Delaware Press, 1992.

———. "Making a Good End: John But as a Reader of *Piers Plowman.*" In *Medieval English Studies Presented to George Kane,* ed. Edward Donald Kennedy, Ronald Waldron, and Joseph S. Wittig, 243–67. Woodbridge, UK: D. S. Brewer, 1988.

———. "Medieval Studies." In *Redrawing the Boundaries: The Transformation of English and American Literary Studies,* ed. Stephen Greenblatt and Giles Gunn, 12–40. New York: Modern Language Association, 1992.

———. "Narration and the Invention of Experience: Episodic Form in *Piers Plowman.*" In *The Wisdom of Poetry: Essays in Early English Literature in Honor of Morton W. Bloomfield,* ed. Larry D. Benson and Siegfried Wenzel, 91–122. Kalamazoo, MI: Medieval Institute Publications, 1982.

———. "Two Infinites: Grammatical Metaphor in *Piers Plowman.*" *ELH* 39 (1972): 169–88.

———. "William Langland's 'Kynde Name': Authorial Signature and Social Identity in Late Fourteenth-Century England." In *Literary Practice and Social Change in Britain, 1380–1530,* ed. Lee Patterson, 15–82. Berkeley: University of California Press, 1990.

Migraine-George, Theresa. "Orpheus and Pygmalion as Aesthetic Paradigms in Petrarch's *Rime sparse.*" *Comparative Literature Studies* 36 (1999): 226–46.

Minnis, Alastair J. *Chaucer and Pagan Antiquity.* Cambridge: D. W. Brewer, 1982.

Mitchell, J. Allan. *Ethics and Eventfulness in Middle English Literature.* New York: Palgrave, 2010.

Monfrin, Jacques. "Humanisme et traductions au Moyen Âge." *Journal des savants* 148 (1963): 161–90.

Moran, Dennis V. "*The Parlement of the Thre Ages:* Meaning and Design." *Neophilologus* 62 (1978): 620–33.

Most, Glenn. "Classical Scholarship and Literary Criticism." In *The Cambridge History of Literary Criticism,* vol. 4, *The Eighteenth Century,* ed. H. B. Nisbet and Claude Rawson, 742–57. Cambridge: Cambridge University Press, 1997.

Mukherjee, Neel. "Thomas Drant's Rewriting of Horace." *Studies in English Literature 1500–1900* 40 (2000): 1–20.

Murphy, J. J. "The Arts of Poetry and Prose." In *The Cambridge History of Literary Criticism,* vol. 2: *The Middle Ages,* ed. Alastair Minnis and Ian Johnson, 42–67. Cambridge: Cambridge University Press, 2005.

Musa, Mark. "An Essay on the *Vita nuova.*" In *Dante's Vita nuova,* trans. Mark Musa. Bloomington: Indiana University Press, 1973.

Muscatine, Charles. *Chaucer and the French Tradition.* Berkeley: University of California Press, 1957.

———. "Form, Texture, and Meaning in Chaucer's Knight's Tale." *PMLA* 65 (1950): 911–29.

———. *Poetry and Crisis in the Age of Chaucer.* Notre Dame, IN: University of Notre Dame Press, 1972. Reprinted in *Medieval Literature, Style, and Culture: Essays by Charles Muscatine,* 111–38. Columbia: University of South Carolina Press, 1999.

Nagy, Piroska, and Damien Boquet, eds. *Le sujet des émotions au Moyen Âge.* Paris: Beauchesne, 2008.

Nelson, Alan. "Mechanical Wheels of Fortune, 1100–1547." *Journal of the Warburg and Courtauld Institutes* 43 (1980): 227–33.

Neuse, Richard. *Chaucer's Dante: Allegory and Epic Theater in the "Canterbury Tales."* Berkeley: University of California Press, 1991.
Newman, Barbara. *God and the Goddesses: Vision, Poetry, and Belief in the Middle Ages.* Philadelphia: University of Pennsylvania Press, 2002.
Ngai, Sianne. "Our Aesthetic Categories." *PMLA* 125 (October 2010): 948–58.
_____. *Ugly Feelings.* Cambridge, MA: Harvard University Press, 2005.
Nietzsche, Friedrich. *The Birth of Tragedy and The Genealogy of Morals.* Trans. Francis Golfing. New York: Doubleday, 1956.
Nolan, Maura. "The Fortunes of *Piers Plowman* and Its Readers." *Yearbook of Langland Studies* 20 (2006): 1–41.
_____. *John Lydgate and the Making of Public Culture.* Cambridge: Cambridge University Press, 2005.
_____. "Lydgate's Literary History: Chaucer, Gower, and Canacee." *Studies in the Age of Chaucer* 27 (2005): 59–92.
Nuttall, A. D. *Overheard by God: Fiction and Prayer in Herbert, Milton, Dante, and St. John.* London: Methuen, 1980.
Olsson, Kurt. "Grammar, Manhood, and Tears: The Curiosity of Chaucer's Monk." *Modern Philology* 76 (1978): 1–17.
Orme, Nicholas. "Medieval Hunting: Fact and Fancy." In *Chaucer's England: Literature in Historical Context,* ed. Barbara Hanawalt, 133–53. Minneapolis: University of Minnesota Press, 1992.
Orsten, Elizabeth M. "'Heaven on Earth'—Langland's Vision of Life within the Cloister." *American Benedictine Review* 21 (1970): 526–34.
Pantin, W. A. "A Medieval Collection of Latin and English Proverbs and Riddles, from the Rylands Latin MS 394." *Bulletin of the John Rylands Library* 14 (1930): 81–114.
Paterson, Don. *Orpheus.* London: Faber and Faber, 2006.
Patterson, Lee. *Chaucer and the Subject of History.* Madison: University of Wisconsin Press, 1991.
_____. "Court Politics and the Invention of Literature: The Case of Sir John Clanvowe." In *Culture and History, 1350–1600: Essays on English Communities, Identities, and Writing,* ed. David Aers, 7–42. Detroit: Wayne State University Press, 1992. Reprinted in Lee Patterson, *Acts of Recognition: Essays on Medieval Culture,* 56–83. Notre Dame, IN: University of Notre Dame Press, 2009.
_____. *Negotiating the Past: The Historical Understanding of Medieval Literature.* Madison: University of Wisconsin Press, 1987.
Paxson, James. "Gender Personified, Personification Gendered, and the Body Figuralized in *Piers Plowman.*" *Yearbook of Langland Studies* 12 (1998): 65–96.
Pearsall, Derek. "Criseyde's Choices." *Studies in the Age of Chaucer Proceedings* 2 (1986): 17–29.
_____. *The Life of Geoffrey Chaucer.* Oxford: Blackwell, 1992.
Peck, Russell. "The Careful Hunter in *The Parlement of the Thre Ages.*" *ELH* 39 (1972): 333–41.
Post, John B. "Courts, Councils, and Arbitrators in the Ladbroke Manor Dispute." In *Medieval Legal Records Edited in Memory of C. A. F. Meekings,* ed. R. F. Hunnisett and J. B. Post, 289–339. London: H. M. Stationery Office, 1978.
_____. "A Fifteenth-Century Customary of the Southwark Stews." *Journal of the Society of Archivists* 5 (1977): 418–28.

Putter, Ad. "The Poetry of 'Things' in Gower, *The Great Gatsby* and Chaucer." *SPELL: Swiss Papers in English Language and Literature* 22 (2009): 63–82.

———. "The Ways and Words of the Hunt: Notes on *Sir Gawain and the Green Knight, The Master of Game, Sir Tristrem, Pearl*, and *Saint Erkenwald.*" *Chaucer Review* 40 (2006): 354–85.

Quadlbauer, Franz. *Die antike Theorie der genera dicendi im lateinischen Mittelalter.* Vienna: Hermann Böhlaus, 1962.

Ramazani, Jahan. "Chaucer's Monk: The Poetics of Abbreviation, Aggression, and Tragedy." *Chaucer Review* 27 (1993): 260–76.

Raskolnikov, Masha. "Promising the Female, Delivering the Male: Transformations of Gender in *Piers Plowman.*" *Yearbook of Langland Studies* 19 (2005): 81–105.

Reynolds, Suzanne. *Medieval Reading: Grammar, Rhetoric, and the Classical Text.* Cambridge: Cambridge University Press, 1996.

Rickert, Edith. "Chaucer at School." *Modern Philology* 29 (1932): 257–74.

Rigg, A. G. *A History of Anglo-Latin Literature, 1066–1422.* Cambridge: Cambridge University Press, 1992.

Riis, Ole, and Linda Woodhead. *A Sociology of Religious Emotion.* Oxford: Oxford University Press, 2010.

Ringer, Mark. *Opera's First Master: The Musical Dramas of Claudio Monteverdi.* Pompton Plains, NJ: Amadeus Press, 2006.

Robertson, D. W., Jr. "Chaucerian Tragedy." *ELH* 19 (1952): 1–37.

———. *A Preface to Chaucer: Studies in Medieval Perspective.* Princeton, NJ: Princeton University Press, 1962.

Robertson, Kellie. *The Laborer's Two Bodies: Labor and the 'Work' of the Text in Medieval Britain, 1350–1500.* New York: Palgrave Macmillan, 2006.

Robins, William. "Troilus in the Gutter." In *Sacred and Profane in Chaucer and Middle English Literature: Essays in Honour of John V. Fleming*, ed. Robert Epstein and William Robins, 91–112. Toronto: University of Toronto Press, 2010.

Rosenwein, Barbara H., ed. *Anger's Past: The Social Uses of an Emotion in the Middle Ages.* Ithaca, NY: Cornell University Press, 1998.

———. *Emotional Communities in the Early Middle Ages.* Ithaca: NY: Cornell University Press, 2006.

———. "Theories of Change in the History of Emotions." In *A History of Emotions, 1200–1800*, ed. Jonas Liliequist, 7–20. Ithaca, NY: Cornell University Press, 2012.

Rowland, Beryl. "The Three Ages of *The Parlement of the Thre Ages.*" *Chaucer Review* 9 (1975): 342–52.

Salter, Elizabeth. "*Piers Plowman* and the Visual Arts." In *English and International: Studies in the Literature, Art, and Patronage of Medieval England*, ed. Derek Pearsall and Nicolette Zeeman 256–66, 340–42. Cambridge: Cambridge University Press, 1988.

Sanford, Eva Matthews. "The Uses of Classical Latin Authors in the *Libri Manuales.*" *Transactions and Proceedings of the American Philological Association* 55 (1924): 199–246.

Saunders, Corinne. "*Troilus and Criseyde:* An Overview." In *Chaucer*, ed. Corinne Saunders, 129–38. Blackwell Guides to Criticism. Oxford and Malden, MA: Blackwell, 2001.

Saxl, Fritz. "A Spiritual Encyclopedia of the Later Middle Ages." *Journal of the Warburg and Courtauld Institutes* 5 (1942): 82–134.

Scala, Elizabeth, and Sylvia Federico, eds. *The Post-Historical Middle Ages*. New York: Palgrave Macmillan, 2009.
Scanlon, Larry. *Narrative, Authority, and Power: The Medieval Exemplum and the Chaucerian Tradition*. Cambridge: Cambridge University Press, 1994.
Scarcia, Riccardo. "Elisabetta I, traduttrice dell' 'Ars Poetica.'" In *I 2000 anni dell'Ars Poetica*, 55–67. Genoa: D.AR.FI.CL.ET., 1988.
Scarry, Elaine. *The Body in Pain: The Making and Unmaking of the World*. Oxford: Oxford University Press, 1987.
———. *Dreaming by the Book*. New York: Farrar, Straus and Giroux, 1999.
Scase, Wendy. "*Dauy Dycars Dreame* and Robert Crowley's *Piers Plowman*." *Yearbook of Langland Studies* 21 (2007): 171–98.
Schibanoff, Susan. "Worlds Apart: Orientalism, Antifeminism, and Heresy in Chaucer's 'Man of Law's Tale.'" *Exemplaria* 8 (1996): 59–96.
Schmidt, A. V. C. *The Clerkly Maker: Langland's Poetic Art*. Cambridge: D. S. Brewer, 1987.
———. "Langland and Scholastic Philosophy." *Medium Ævum* 38 (1969): 134–53.
Schoeck, Richard J., and Jerome Taylor, eds. *Chaucer Criticism*, vol. 2: *Troilus and Criseyde and the Minor Poems*. Notre Dame, IN: University of Notre Dame Press, 1961.
Schroeder, Peter R. "Hidden Depths: Dialogue and Characterization in Chaucer and Malory." *PMLA* 98 (1983): 374–87.
Schwarz, W. "The Meaning of *fidus interpres* in Medieval Translation." *Journal of Theological Studies* 45 (1944): 73–78.
Sherman, Claire Richter. *Imaging Aristotle: Verbal and Visual Representation in Fourteenth-Century France*. Berkeley: University of California Press, 1995.
Shoaf, R. A. "'Unwemmed Custance': Circulation, Property, and Incest in the *Man of Law's Tale*." *Exemplaria* 2 (1990): 287–302.
Sidwell, K. C. *Reading Medieval Latin*. Cambridge: Cambridge University Press, 1995.
Simpson, James. *Burning to Read: English Fundamentalism and Its Reformation Opponents*. Cambridge, MA: Harvard University Press, 2007.
———. "The Other Book of Troy: Guido delle Colonne's *Historia destructionis Troiae* in Fourteenth- and Fifteenth-Century England." *Speculum* 73 (1998): 397–423.
———. "The Role of Scientia in *Piers Plowman*." In *Medieval Religious and Ethical Literature: Essays in Honour of G. H. Russell*, ed. Gregory Kratzman and James Simpson, 49–65. Cambridge: D. S. Brewer, 1986.
———. *Sciences and the Self in Medieval Poetry: Alan of Lille's "Anticlaudianus" and John Gower's "Confessio."* Cambridge: Cambridge University Press, 1995.
Singer, Samuel, ed. *Thesaurus proverbiorum medii aevi*. 13 vols. Berlin and New York: de Gruyter, 1995–2002.
Singleton, Charles S. *Dante's Commedia: Elements of Structure*. Baltimore: Johns Hopkins University Press, 1977.
Smith, D. Vance. *The Book of the Incipit: Beginnings in the Fourteenth Century*. Medieval Cultures 28. Minneapolis: University of Minnesota Press, 2001.
———. "Chaucer as an English Writer." In *The Yale Companion to Chaucer*, ed. Seth Lerer, 87–121. New Haven, CT: Yale University Press, 2006.
Smyser, H. M. "The Domestic Background of *Troilus and Criseyde*." *Speculum* 31 (1956): 297–315.
Somerset, Fiona, and Nicholas Watson, eds. *The Vulgar Tongue: Medieval and Postmedieval Vernacularity*. University Park: Pennsylvania State University Press, 2003.

Southern, R. W. *The Making of the Middle Ages*. New Haven, CT: Yale University Press, 1953.
Spearing, A. C. *Medieval Dream Poetry*. Cambridge: Cambridge University Press, 1976.
———. *Textual Subjectivity: The Encoding of Subjectivity in Medieval Narratives and Lyrics*. Oxford: Oxford University Press, 2005.
Steiner, Emily. "Commonalty and Literary Form in the 1370s and 1380s." *New Medieval Literatures* 6 (2003): 199–222.
———. *Documentary Culture and the Making of Medieval English Literature*. Cambridge: Cambridge University Press, 2003.
Sternfeld, F. W. *The Birth of Opera*. Oxford: Clarendon Press, 1993.
———. "The Orpheus Myth and the Libretto of *Orfeo*." In *Claudio Monteverdi, Orfeo*, ed. John Whenham, 20–34. Cambridge: Cambridge University Press, 1986.
Stillers, R. *Humanistische Deutung: Studien zu Kommentar und Literaturtheorie in der italienischen Renaissance*. Düsseldorf: Droste, 1988.
Strohm, Paul. "*Storie, Spelle, Geste, Romaunce, Tragedie:* Generic Distinctions in the Middle English Troy Narratives." *Speculum* 46 (1971): 348–59.
———. *Theory and the Premodern Text*. Minneapolis: University of Minnesota Press, 2000.
Szittya, Penn R. *The Antifraternal Tradition in Medieval Literature*. Princeton, NJ: Princeton University Press, 1986.
Tatlock, J. S. *Development and Chronology of Chaucer's Works*. London: Kegan Paul, Trench, Trübner, 1907.
Taylor, Karla. *Chaucer Reads the "Divine Comedy."* Stanford, CA: Stanford University Press, 1989.
Thompson, Phyllis Anina Nitze. "The Triumph of Poverty over Fortune: Illuminations from Boccaccio's *De Casibus Virorum Illustrium*." PhD diss., Boston University, 1994.
Thompson R. M., with Michael Gullick. *A Descriptive Catalogue of the Medieval Manuscripts in Worcester Cathedral Library*. Woodbridge, UK: D. S. Brewer, 2001.
Thomson, David. *A Descriptive Catalogue of Middle English Grammatical Treatises*. New York: Garland, 1979.
Todoroki, Yoshiaki. *An Addition to Miniatures of the Goddess Fortune in Medieval Manuscripts*. Tokyo: Seibido, 2000.
Tolkien, J. R. R., and E. V. Gordon, eds. *Sir Gawain and the Green Knight*. Rev. Norman Davis. 2nd ed. Oxford: Clarendon Press, 1967.
Trigg, Stephanie. *Congenial Souls: Reading Chaucer from Medieval to Postmodern*. Minneapolis: University of Minnesota Press, 2002.
Turville-Petre, Thorlac. "The Ages of Man in the *Parlement of the Thre Ages*." *Medium Ævum* 46 (1977): 66–76.
———. *The Alliterative Revival*. Cambridge: D. S. Brewer, 1977.
———. *England the Nation*. Oxford: Clarendon Press, 1996.
———. "The Nine Worthies in *The Parlement of the Thre Ages*." *Poetica* 11 (1979): 28–45.
Urban, Malte. *Fragments: Past and Present in Chaucer and Gower*. Bern: Peter Lang, 2008.
Vance, Eugene. "Chrétien's *Yvain* and the Ideologies of Change and Exchange." *Yale French Studies* 70 (1986): 42–62.
Van Dyke, Carolynn. *Chaucer's Agents: Cause and Representation in Chaucerian Narrative*. Madison, NJ: Fairleigh Dickinson University Press, 2005.
Waldron, R. A. "The Prologue to 'The Parlement of the Thre Ages.'" *Neuphilologische Mitteilungen* 73 (1972): 786–94.

Wallace, David. *Chaucer and the Early Writings of Boccaccio.* Cambridge: D. S. Brewer, 1985.

———. *Chaucerian Polity: Absolutist Lineages and Associational Forms in England and Italy.* Stanford, CA: Stanford University Press, 1997.

———. "Griselde before Chaucer: Love between Men, Women, and Farewell Art." In *Through a Classical Eye: Transcultural and Transhistorical Visions in Medieval English, Italian, and Latin Literature in Honour of Winthrop Wetherbee,* ed. Andrew Galloway and R. F. Yeager, 206–20. Toronto: University of Toronto Press, 2009.

Wallace, Kristine Gilmartin. "Array as Motif in the *Clerk's Tale.*" *Rice University Studies* 62 (1976): 99–110.

Warren, Michelle R. "Translation." In *Oxford Twenty-First Century Approaches to Literature: Middle English,* ed. Paul Strohm, 51–67. Oxford: Oxford University Press, 2007.

wa Thiong'o, Ngũgĩ. *Decolonising the Mind: The Politics of Language in African Literature.* Oxford: Currey, 1986.

Watson, Nicholas. "Censorship and Cultural Change in Late-Medieval England: Vernacular Theology, the Oxford Translation Debate, and Arundel's Constitutions of 1409." *Speculum* 70 (1995): 822–64.

Wells, Robin Headlam. *Shakespeare on Masculinity.* Cambridge: Cambridge University Press, 2001.

Wetherbee, Winthrop, III. *Chaucer and the Poets: An Essay on "Troilus and Criseyde."* Ithaca: Cornell University Press, 1984.

Whiting, Bartlett Jere, with the collaboration of Helen Wescott Whiting. *Proverbs, Sentences, and Proverbial Phrases from English Writings Mainly before 1500.* Cambridge, MA: Harvard University Press, 1968.

Williams, Raymond. *Marxism and Literature.* Oxford: Oxford University Press, 1977.

Wimsatt, W. K., Jr. "The Structure of the 'Concrete Universal' in Literature." *PMLA* 62 (1947): 262–80.

Windeatt, Barry. "Chaucer and the *Filostrato.*" In *Chaucer and the Italian Trecento,* ed. Piero Boitani, 163–84. Cambridge: Cambridge University Press, 1983.

———. *Oxford Guides to Chaucer: Troilus and Criseyde.* Oxford: Clarendon Press, 1992.

Wittig, Joseph S. "'Culture Wars' and the Persona in *Piers Plowman.*" *Yearbook of Langland Studies* 15 (2001): 167–95.

Wittig, Susan. *Stylistic and Narrative Structures in the Middle English Romances.* Austin: University of Texas Press, 1978.

Wogan-Browne, Jocelyn, Nicholas Watson, Andrew Taylor, and Ruth Evans, eds. *The Idea of the Vernacular.* University Park: Pennsylvania State University Press, 1999.

Woods, Marjorie Curry. *Classroom Commentaries: Teaching the "Poetria Nova" across Medieval and Renaissance Europe.* Columbus: The Ohio State University Press, 2009.

———. "Rape and the Pedagogical Rhetoric of Sexual Violence." In *Criticism and Dissent in the Middle Ages,* ed. Rita Copeland, 56–86. Cambridge: Cambridge University Press, 1996.

Woods, Marjorie Curry, and Rita Copeland. "Classroom and Confession." In *The Cambridge History of Medieval English Literature,* ed. David Wallace, 376–406. Cambridge: Cambridge University Press, 1999.

Woolgar, Christopher. *The Great Household in Late Medieval England.* New Haven, CT: Yale University Press, 1999.

Yeager, R. F. *John Gower's Poetic: The Search for the New Arion.* Cambridge: D. S. Brewer, 1990.

Young, Karl. "Chaucer's *Troilus and Criseyde* as Romance." *PMLA* 53 (1938): 38–63.

———. *The Origin and Development of the Story of Troilus and Criseyde.* London: Kegan Paul, Trench, Trübner, 1908.

Zak, Gur. *Petrarch's Humanism and the Care of the Self.* Cambridge: Cambridge University Press, 2010.

Zeeman, Elizabeth (Salter). "*Piers Plowman* and the Pilgrimage to Truth." *Essays and Studies* n.s. 11 (1958): 1–16.

Zieman, Katherine. "Chaucer's *Voys.*" *Representations* 60 (1997): 70–91.

———. *Singing the New Song: Literacy and Liturgy in Late Medieval England.* Philadelphia: University of Pennsylvania Press, 2008.

Zumthor, Paul. *La lettre et la voix.* Paris, Seuil, 1987.

———. *Oral Poetry: An Introduction.* Trans. Kathleen Murphy-Judy. Minneapolis: University of Minnesota Press, 1983.

index

Abelard, Peter, 38, 38n22
Aelred of Rievaulx, 62
Aers, David, 179n16
Alan de Lille, 14, 105, 109, 110; *Anticlaudianus,* 37, 216, 216n3; *Liber Parabolarum,* 37, 38, 41
Alcock, N. W., 276n29
Alcuin, 65
Alford, John, 5, 56n4, 664
Alighieri, Pietro, 247n10, 249
Ancrene Riwle, 129
Anderson, David, 248n13
Aquinas, St. Thomas, 154
aristocratic culture, 150 and n22, 118 and n40, 145–50, 196–213, 216–21, 253–55
Aristotle, 15, 17, 18n6, 30, 31, 136, 137, 147, 272; *De anima,* 286–87; *Poetics,* 15, 31, 154, 246–47; in *Piers Plowman,* 279, 282
Arnulf of Orleans, 247, 248n12
Astell, Ann, 86n27, 287, 287n13
Auerbach, Erich, 5
Augustine, *Confessiones,* 164–66, 165n45; *Contra Faustum,* 69; *De civitate Dei,* 240–41, 241n19; *De doctrina christiana,* 175–76, 175n10; *De sermone Domini in monte,* 62–63, 63n25; Augustinian doctrine, 75; in *Piers Plowman,* 58, 58n8
Avianus, 37, 41
Awyntrs off Arthure, 213
Ayenbite of Inwyt, 63–64, 123n2

Bacon, Francis, 301n39
Baker, Joan, 105n20
Bakhtin, Mikhail, 77, 79, 79n12, 92, 172n6, 289
Barney, Stephen, 55, 55n2, 67–68, 67n2, 133n21, 178n13, 180n18
Baron, Hans, 147, 147n16, 153–54, 154n29, 157, 157n37, 163n43
Barr, Helen, 35n3, 36, 36n6, 46n48, 52n67
Barthes, Roland, 172nn6–7, 186n31, 284, 284n1
Baswell, Christopher, 41n37
Bede, 58, 58n14, 67
Benoît de Sainte-Maure, *Le roman de Troie,* 186n32, 187, 187n33, 250, 257, 261

333

334 INDEX

Benvenuto da Imola, 59, 247n10
Benson, C. David, 86, 86n28, 93n49, 97n9, 98n7, 186n32
Benson, Larry D., 131n18
Bernard of Chartres, 40, 49
Bernard, St., 65
Bernardus Silvestris, 29, 248, 248n13
Bible, 41, 61, 63, 67, 70, 110, 118, 166, 192, 206n22, 250, 285; *specific books:* Genesis, 45, 6n32; 4 Kings, 63, 69; Tobit, 272; Job, 61–63, 67, 90, 278; Psalms, 58n8, 58n10, 67–68, 93, 137, 287; Ecclesiastes, 197; Song of Songs, 287; Isaiah, 63; Ezechiel, 72; Osee, 67; Matthew, 62–63, 69, 131, 137n27; Luke, 64, 64n29, 67, 73, 197, 254n36; John, 137; Acts, 62; Romans, 69–70, 257; 1 Corinthians, 69–70; Ephesians, 58; 1 Thessalonians, 38; Revelation, 39
Birrell, J. R., 274n21, 275n25, 276n29
Birtwistle, Harrison, 300, 300n38, 302
Blamires, Alcuin, 35, 35n3, 36n5
Blanchfield, Lynne, 98n7, 99n9
Blanchot, Maurice, 305, 305n46
Bloomfield, Morton, 59, 59n17, 60, 60n20, 105, 105n19, 187n34, 188n35
Boas, M., 37
Boccaccio, Giovanni, *Decameron,* 144, 146, 153n26, 162, 165; *De casibus virorum illustrium,* 203, 204n17, 206n22, 216n3; *Il Filostrato,* 173–74, 180n20, 186n32, 252–53, 255–59
Boethius, *Consolation of Philosophy,* 31, 61, 105, 149, 149n29, 150, 163, 164, 206n22, 216, 220, 220n7, 227n12, 230–31, 279, 297–99, 302; ideas about tragedy in, 244–47; *De Musica,* 286; *In Isagogen Porphyrii,* 17, 17n2
Boitani, Piero, 246n6
Boke of St. Albans, 199
Bolzoni, Lina, 110n25, 117n37, 117n39

Bonaventure, Saint, 66, 110
Book of Vices and Virtues, The, 122n1, 123n2
Bordo, Susan, 266, 266n6
Borenius, Tancred, 217n3
Bowers, John, 296, 296n33
Boyle, Marjorie O'Rourke, 68n37
Breen, Katharine, 156n36
Bressie, Ramona, 205n20
Brewer, Derek, 245n3
Brink, C. O., 24, 24n19, 28n28
Brinton, Thomas, *Sermons,* 59–60, 60n21
Brody, Saul N., 184n27
Brown, Peter, 286, 286n9
Brownlee, Kevin, 303n45
Bruce, Harbert, 42n40
Burke, Edmund, 226, 226n11
Burke, Kenneth, 5
Burckhardt, Jacob, 5
Burlin, Robert, 187n34
Burnett, Charles, 286n7
Burrow, J. A., 5, 7, 8n16, 137n28, 138n29, 170n2, 289, 289n20
Buttenwieser, Hilda, 28n28

Cable, Thomas, 35
Caie, Graham D., 86n27, 90, 90nn40–42
Camargo, Martin, 27–28, 27n24, 28n26, 29n30
Cannon, Christopher, 7, 8n16, 38, 38n19, 40n29, 49, 49n58, 271n14
Carlson, David, 6, 6 n11,7, 8n16
Carruthers, Mary, 100n10, 106n21, 107–10, 108n22, 110nn24–25, 290, 290n25
Cassiodorus, 58, 58n14
Castle of Perseverance, 104
Catesby family (Northamptonshire), 273–78
Catto, Jeremy, 150n22
Cavarero, Adriana, 285, 285n4
Cavell, Stanley, 171n4
Certeau, Michel de, 201–2, 201n11
Chance, Jane, 295, 295n32

chansons d'aventure, 197, 198
chansons de geste, 247n10
Chastising of God's Children, 129
Chaucer, Geoffrey: 4, 5, 6, 7, 8, 9, 10, 11, 12, 52n68, 58, 61, 65n30, 279, 285–306; and estates satire, 127n11, 130; knowledge of Geoffrey of Vinsauf, 29–30; knowledge of elementary school texts, 38; works: *Canterbury Tales,* 76–94, 215n2, 229, 239, 282; *Nun's Priest's Tale,* 29; *Man of Law's Tale,* 85–94, 267–68; *Knight's Tale,* 133, 211–12, 249, 296; *Clerk's Tale,* 140–66; *Franklin's Tale,* 256; *Monk's Tale,* 203–12, 246; *Book of the Duchess,* 213, 294–96; *House of Fame,* 79–82, 84, 137–38, 219n6, 285–86, 292, 295, 297, 302; *Legend of Good Women,* 207n24, 295; *Troilus and Criseyde,* 29, 84, 169–94, 235n18, 239, 244–62, 304–5. *See also* Langland, William
Chrétien de Troyes, 104n15, 251, 269–70, 270n11
Claudian, 271, 271n13
Cleansing of Man's Soul, 129
Clement of Alexandria, 286
Clopper, Lawrence, 66, 66n32
Cocteau, Jean, 302
Cok, John, 53
Colonne, Guido della, 186–87, 186n32, 201, 250
Connor, Steven, 285n4
Conrad of Hirsau, 29, 247
Cooper, Helen, 97n6
Copeland, Rita, 7, 36n10, 37n11, 40n31, 206, 207nn23–24, 208, 251n25
Cornelius, Roberta, 104n16
Cox, Virginia, 17n4
Crow, Christine M., 293n28
Crowned King, The, 34
Culler, Jonathan, 1n1, 7, 7n15, 10, 10n19, 88, 88n35
Cunningham, J. V., 127n11
Cursor Mundi, 104, 125

Dante (Alighieri), 11, 29, 59, 61, 180–85, 180n21, 206n22, 246, 247n10, 248–49, 258
Dares Phrygius, 201, 250, 261
Davies, R. R., 136n25
De Contemptu Mundi, 37–38
Deguileville, Guillaume de, 64, 206n22
Deleuze, Gilles, 29, 293n29
Delisle, Leopold, 17n4
De Lisle Psalter, The, 110–11, 118n40, 120
Deschamps, Eustache, 38, 198n5, 301, 301n41, 306
Desmond, Marilynn, 299n37
Dietz, David, 248n12
Dinshaw, Carolyn, 6, 6n12, 85n26, 86n27, 89n38, 187n34, 266nn4–5
Distichs of Cato, 37–40, 49, 279–80
Dives and Pauper, 154–55, 155n32
Dodman, Trevor, 199n7
Dolar, Mladen, 285, 285n3
Dolce, Lodovico, 16
Donaldson, E. T., 45–46, 76–77, 77n3, 94n53, 172n6, 180n19, 187n34, 262, 262n46
Donatus, 37, 249, 249n19, 286
Doyle, A. I., 129n16
dramatic mode: in Chaucer, 75–94, 159, 180; in *Piers Plowman,* 55, 136, 137–38; not assumed in medieval ideas of tragedy, 246–47
Drant, Thomas, 16, 17, 31–32
du Bellay, Joachim, 18, 32–33, 32n36, 33n37
du Mans, Jacques Pelletier, 16, 18
Duggan, Hoyt, 35n2

Eden, Kathy, 288, 288n18
"Edwardian" literary culture, 125, 139
Eliot, T. S., 61
Elizabeth II (queen of England), 31
Ellesmere manuscript of *The Canterbury Tales* (San Marino, California, Huntington Library, MS EL 26 C 9), 86, 86n31, 93 and n49, 94, 246n5
Elliott, R. V. W., 133n20

Emaré, 267–69
Emmerson, Richard, 77n8
Enders, Jody, 287, 287n11
Erasmus, Desiderius, 192n43, 288
estates satire, 82, 215, 217, 221–29. *See also* satire
Evans, Michael, 110nn25–26, 110n28, 111n30
Everett, Dorothy, 197

Facetus, 38
Fairclough, H. R., 20n11, 24n18
Faral, Edmond, 23n15, 26n22, 27n25, 47n51
Farrell, Thomas, 84n25, 94n53, 144n11
Febvre, Lucien, 142, 142n4
Federico, Sylvia, 7, 185n30
Fellowes, Jennifer, 252n28
Fewster, Carol, 131n18
Fisher, John, 215n2
Fleming, John, 188n35
Fletcher, Alan, 210n27
Fletcher, Doris, 150n20
formalism and literary form, 1, 3–6, 7, 10–12, 76, 82, 121–39, 146–47, 160–62, 202–6
fortune (*Fortuna*), 146, 147, 149, 150, 151, 154, 164, 196, 202, 203, 213, 213n31, 214, 215, 215n2, 216–43, 244, 245, 281n34, 297, 305
Foucault, Michel, 269, 269n9
Fowler, Elizabeth, 171n5
Fradenburg, L. O. Aranye, 205n21
Frank, Robert W., Jr., 122n1, 127
Fredborg, Margareta, 17n3
Friedman, John Block, 287n15, 299
Friis-Jensen, Karsten, 18n7, 19nn9–10, 20n11, 22n15, 23, 23n16, 25nn20–21
Froissart, Jean, 303, 303n43
Fuerre de Gadres, 200
Fyler, John, 193n44

Galandas Regniacensis, 72–73
Galloway, Andrew, 42n40, 55, 55n2, 60n21, 93n49, 143n8, 147n15, 155nn33–34, 156n36, 271n14
Ganim, John, 80n14
Gehl, Paul, 119, 119n45
Geoffrey of Vinsauf, 23, 27–30
Giancarlo, Matthew, 289, 289n24
Gill, Miriam, 116n35
Gillespie, Vincent, 36n10, 37n11, 39n25, 250n21
Ginsberg, Warren, 171n5, 180n20
Godden, Malcolm, 129n15
Gollancz, Sir Israel, 197
Goodwin, Amy, 162n42
Gower, John, 3, 7, 38, 52, 129, 143n8, 192, 205, 210n27; works: *Confessio amantis*, 6, 214, 217, 219, 267; *Mirour de l'Omme*, 11, 214–43; *Vox clamantis*, 42, 80, 214, 218
Gradon, Pamela, 129n15
Gransden, Antonia, 66n31
Gratian, 67
Gray, Sir Thomas, 250, 250n22,
Green, Richard Firth, 255, 255n38
Greenblatt, Stephen, 2, 2n2, 10
Gregory, St., 58n13, 72
Griffiths, Lavinia, 108n23
Grosseteste, Robert, 104, 115, 115n32, 251
Gullick, Michael, 37n14

Haahr, Joan, 178n13
Hames, Harvey, 96n3
Hamilton, George, 186n32
Hanawalt, Barbara, 200, 200n10
Hanna, Ralph, 4 and n5, 10, 39n27, 51n66, 96n2, 118n41, 123n3, 136n25, 192n42, 202, 246n5, 271n14, 279
Harbert, Bruce, 42n40
Harrington, David, 200n9
Havely, Nicholas, 258n45
Havens, Jill, 130n16
Hazelton, Richard, 37n15, 38, 38n18, 49n57
Hegel, G. W. F., 269
Heng, Geraldine, 266n4

Hengwrt manuscript of *The Canterbury Tales* (Aberystwyth, National Library of Wales, MS Peniarth 392D), 86n30, 93n49, 246n5
Herlihy, David, 272n15
Herold, Christine, 245n3
Herrick, Marvin T., 18n6, 30n31, 31nn32–33
Higden, Ranulph, *Polychronicon*, 50–51, 50n64, 156, 156n36. *See also* Trevisa, John
Hill, John, 143n8
Hilton, Walter, 129
Holsinger, Bruce, 299, 299n37
Homans, George, 138n29
Honorius of Autun, 73
Honorius of Marseille, 72
Horace, 37, 55, *Ars poetica,* 9, 189, 189n36, 229; medieval copies of, 28n28; scholia, 15–33, 189
Howard Psalter, the, 118n40
Howard, Donald, 193n44
Hudson, Anne, 129n14, 150n22
Hugh of St. Victor, 68
Hugh of Trimberg, 29
Huizinga, Johan, 5, 140–43, 140nn1–2, 288
Hunt, Tony, 39n24, 39n27
hunting, as literary motif, 11, 196–213
Huot, Sylvia, 94n50

Innocent III, *De miseria humane condicionis,* 86–92
Irvine, Martin, 36n10, 37n15, 42n39
Iser, Wolfgang, 172n6
Isidore of Seville, 38, 41, 42, 50–51, 53, 58, 58n14, 69, 100, 106, 189, 189n39, 247, 247n8, 248n12, 249, 250

Javitch, Daniel, 16n1, 31n32
Jean de Meun, 216
Jerome, 17, 17n2, 38, 57, 61, 65, 72, 192, 192n43
John of Garland, 23

John of Salisbury, 39, 40, 49, 62, 263–64, 263n2, 279, 279n32, 281, 281n34
Johnson, Ian R., 298, 298n35
Johnson, Samuel, 54
Jordan, Robert, 86n29
Jordan, William, friar, 133
Joseph of Exeter, 261
Justice, Steven, 3, 11, 11n20, 80n14

Kane, George, 256, 256n40
Kant, Immanuel, 226, 226n10
Kaske, Robert E., 59, 59n17, 209, 209n25, 246n4
Keightley, R. G., 39n27
Kelly, Douglas, 23n15, 36n10, 41n33–34, 49n59
Kelly, Henry Ansgar, 244n1, 245n3, 247n10, 248n12
Kendall, Elliott, 272n15
Kerby-Fulton, Katherine, 59n16
Kernan, Anne, 197n4
Kieckhefer, Richard, 115n31
Kiser, Lisa, 200n9
Kittredge, George Lyman, 75, 75n2
Knapp, Peggy, 7
Knighton, Henry, 156n35, 205n20
Knowles, David, 204, 204n19, 205n20
Kurose, Tamotsu, 216n3
Kuskin, William, 197n5

Lacanian theory, 285
Lafferty, Maura, 248n13
Lancastrian collar, 150
Landino, Cristoforo, 30
Langland, William, and *Piers Plowman,* 3, 5, 8, 9, 10, 77, 78, 82n17, 155–56, 198, 210n27, 215n2, 264, 270–72; and linguistic hybridity, 95–120; and the "*Piers Plowman* tradition," 34–53; distinctions from and similarities to the poetics of Chaucer, 83–93; relation to sources and analogues, 54–74, 121–39, 278–83

Langtoft, Pierre, 251
Lawler, Traugott, 54n1
Lawton, David, 4, 4n5, 5–6, 6n9, 35n2, 36, 36n8, 77–78, 77n7, 82, 82n19, 83, 83n20, 86, 86n51, 86n53, 94n51, 94n53, 213n31, 285n5, 289nn21–22, 295n31
Leicester, H. Marshall, Jr., 76, 76n5, 77n6, 171, 171n3
Levinson, Marjorie, 1, 1n1, 195
Lewis, C. S., 139, 253, 257, 257n41
Lewis, Robert E., 87n33
Liber Parabolarum, 37–38, 41
Lokaj, Rodney, 164n44
Longuyon, Jacques de, 197, 201
Loomis, Roger Sherman, 198n5
Looze, Laurence de, 303n45
Lowenstein, George, 143n6
Lowes, John Livingston, 189n38
Lydgate, John, 64
lyric: and Chaucer, 88, 180, 251, 294, 299–301; and Gower, 221–43; and Langland, 4–5

Machaut, Guillaume de, *Le livre du voir dit*, 216n3, 303–6, 303n45
MacIntire, Elizabeth Jelliffe, 17n5
Magee, John, 151n23
Manly, J. M., 207n24
Mann, Jill, 38, 38nn17–18, 49, 49n56, 49n60, 84n25, 137n28, 155n33, 204, 204n20
Manning, Robert, 130, 251
Martin, Jan, 77n8
Marvin, William, 198n5, 200n10
Marx, William, 293n28
Master of Game, The, 199
Matheolus, 64
Matthew of Vendôme, 23, 25–26, 272
Matthews, David, 6
Maximian, 39
Mazzoni, Francesco, 181n22
Mazzotta, Giuseppe, 145, 145n13
McIntosh, Marjorie Keniston, 271n12
McNamer, Sarah, 143n8

Meeuws, Marie-Benoît, 68n37
Meredith, George, 252n9
Merrilees, Brian, 17n4
Meyer-Lee, Robert, 8, 8n16
Middleton, Anne, 3–5, 4n4, 4n6, 5n8, 6, 8, 8n17, 10, 10n18, 11, 12, 35, 35n3, 54–55, 78, 78nn9–10, 79, 79n11, 82, 82nn17–18, 99, 99n9, 120–21, 120n46,130, 130n17, 134n22, 136n25, 139n31,144–46, 144n10, 150, 158, 182n23, 190n41, 195–96, 195n1, 198, 198n6, 211, 211n29, 214, 263n, 282, 282nn35–36, 288, 288nn17–18, 289, 289n22, 290, 300
Migraine-George, Theresa, 303n44
Minnis, Alastair, 7, 39n27, 188n35, 206
Mirk, John, 95–96, 115
Mitchell, J. Allan, 149, 149n21
Monfrin, Jacques, 17n4
Monteverdi, Claudio, 301–2, 305
Moran, Dennis, 198n5
Morrison, Susan Signe, 105n20
Morte Arthure, 213n31
Most, Glenn, 16n1
Mukherjee, Neel, 32n35
Mum and the Sothsegger. See "*Piers Plowman* tradition, the"
Murphy, J. J., 36n10
Musa, Mark, 183n24
Muscatine, Charles, 4, 4n6, 212n30, 250, 251n23

Neckham, Alexander, 248, 248n13
Nelson, Alan, 217n3
Neuse, Richard, 250n21
Newman, Barbara, 105n17
Ngai, Sianne, 10n19, 143n7
Nicholas of Worcester, 66
Nietzsche, Friedrich, 148
"Nine Worthies, The," 196–97, 200n9, 201, 203
noble culture. *See* aristocratic culture
Nolan, Maura, 3, 7, 8, 11, 202, 202n14
Northern Homilies, The, 130

INDEX   339

Nuttall, A. D., 172n7

O'Keefe, Katherine O'Brien, 195n1
Olsson, Kurt, 207n23
Oresme, Nicholas, 274n20
Orme, Nicholas, 205n20
Orsten, Elizabeth, 60, 60n1
Ovid, 265, 302

Page, Christopher, 287
Palmer, Nigel, 39n27
Pamphilus, 39
Parlement of the Thre Ages, The, 196–205, 208–10, 212–13
parliamentary discourse, 43n43, 124, 286, 289
Parker, Matthew, 287, 287n14
Paterson, Don, 298n36
Patterson, Lee, 4, 4n5, 6, 6n10, 7, 11, 75, 75n1, 76, 76nn4–5, 178n12, 185n30, 244n, 249n20, 255n37
Paulinus of Nola, 66, 68n36
Paxson, James, 105nn17–18, 106n20
Pearsall, Derek, 64n30, 71, 179n15, 189n38
Pecham, John, 66
Peck, Russell, 199, 199n8, 200n9
Peter Damian, 59, 63
Peter John Olivi, 66
Peter of Blois, 56–57, 57n7, 58–60, 70–71
Peter the Chanter, 55–56, 56n5, 59, 62–63, 62n4
Petrarch, Francis, 10, 144–66, 180, 204n17, 248, 248n14, 302, 303
Pierce the Ploughman's Crede. See "*Piers Plowman* tradition, the"
Piers Plowman. See Langland, William
"*Piers Plowman* tradition, the," 34–53
Plotinus, 263, 263n1
Poliziano, Angelo, 299–300
Post, John B., 138n30, 274n23, 275, 275n24, 275n26–27, 276n29
Prick of Conscience, The, 130

Proust, Marcel, 286, 290–93, 294n30, 304–6
Puttenham, George, 301n39
Putter, Ad, 161n41, 199n7

Quadlbauer, Franz, 23n15

Rabanus Maurus, 67
Ramazani, Jahan, 207n24
Raskolnikov, Masha, 106n20
Reigny, Galand de, 72–73
Renaut de Louhans, 247n10
Reynolds, Suzanne, 19n9, 36n10, 37n15, 39n24, 49n55
"Ricardian" literary culture, 5–6, 79, 79n13, 78, 82, 83, 92, 204n17, 288–89. *See also* "Edwardian" literary culture
Richard of St. Victor, 65
Richard the Redeless. See "*Piers Plowman* tradition, the"
Ricks, Scott, 143n6
Rickert, Edith, 37–38, 37n13
Rigg, A. G., 41n38
Riis, Ole, 143n6
Rilke, Rainer Maria, 298–99
Ringer, Mark, 301n40
Robertson, D. W., Jr., 175n10, 178n13, 245n3
Robertson, Kellie, 8, 8n16
Robins, Will, 186n32
Rolle, Richard, 124n6, 125n7, 128n12, 129, 136n26
Roman de la Rose, Le, 94, 127n11, 216, 216n3, 218, 299, 303
Rosenwein, Barbara, 142n5, 143, 143nn8–9
Rowland, Beryl, 200n9

Salter, Elizabeth, 20, 132n20, 138, 138n29
Sandler, Lucy Freeman, 110, 110n25, 110n27, 111n29, 116n33, 118n40

Sanford, Eva Matthews, 36n10
satire, 21, 59, 157. *See also* estates satire
Saunders, Corinne, 251, 251n23
Saxl, Fritz, 110n25
Scala, Elizabeth, 7
Scanlon, Larry, 209–10, 210nn27–28
Scarcia, Riccardo, 31n34
Scarry, Elaine, 183n25, 286, 286n8
Scase, Wendy, 49n61
Schibanoff, Susan, 86n27
Schmidt, A. V. C., 38n21, 64, 97n5, 98, 99n8
Schroeder, Peter, 172n7
Schwarz, W., 17n2
Seneca, 150
Servius, 247, 248, 254
Shaw, George Bernard, 252n29
Sheingorn, Pamela, 299n37
Sherman, Claire Richter, 274n20
Shoaf, R. A., 89n38, 92n45–47
Skeat, W. W., 103n19, 123–24
Simpson, James, 6, 6n12, 201, 201n11, 271n14, 287n14
Singleton, Charles, 184n28
Sir Degrevant, 197n5
Sir Ferumbras, 201
Sir Gawain and the Green Knight, 199, 213, 265–66
Smith, D. Vance, 5n7, 80n14, 83, 83n23, 84, 84n24, 85n26, 89n38–39, 92, 130n17, 133n20
Smyser, H. M., 184n27
Somerset, Fiona, 96n3
Somme le Roi, Le (Frère Laurent), 122–23, 127–28, 130–31
Song of Roland, 201
South English Legendary, 130, 139n31
South, Robert, 62, 71
Southern, R. W., 131n18
Spearing, A. C., 77–78, 77n7, 86n27, 86n29, 200n9
Speculum theologiae, 10, 108, 110–20
Speculum vitae, 10, 121–39
Spitzer, Leo, 5
Steiner, Emily, 289, 289n23
Stephen (king of England), 281
Sternfeld, F. W., 301n40, 302n42

Stillers, R., 16n1
Strohm, Paul, 6, 6n12, 251n26, 252n27
Summa virtutum de remediis anime, 64
Swift, Jonathan, 62, 71
Szittya, Penn, 137n28

Tatlock, J. S., 219n6
Taylor, Karla, 172n7, 245n3
Terence, 249
Tertullian, 65, 71–72
Theodolus, 37
Thompson, R. M., 37n14
Thompson, Phyllis Anina Nitze, 217n3
Thomson, David, 36n10, 118n43
Thoresby, John, 129
Todoroki, Yoshiaki, 216n3
tragedy, 11, 21, 90–91, 193, 196–213, 244–62, 296
Trevet, Nicholas, 245n3, 247n10, 298, 300
Trevisa, John, 50, 51, 96, 100
Trigg, Stephanie, 93n49
Turville-Petre, Thorlac, 35n2, 36, 36n9, 48n52, 125, 126n9, 200n9

Urban, Malte, 7, 7n13
Uthred de Boldon, 210n27

Valéry, Paul, 293, 293n28
Van Dyke, Carolynn, 175n9
Vance, Eugene, 269–70, 270n10
Virgil, 21–22, 29, 32–33, 37, 162–63, 173, 177, 177n11, 246–49, 254, 256, 295; as character in Dante's *Inferno*, 180–82

wa Thiong'o, Ngũgĩ, 80n15
Waldron, Ronald, 96n2, 200n9
Wallace, David, 85n26, 89nn38–39, 145–46, 146n14, 147, 147n17, 148, 148n18, 153n26, 160, 160n39, 204n17, 206n22, 252n30, 253, 253n2

Wallace, Kristine Gilmartin, 161n40
Walter of Henley, 274
Walton, Izaak, 62, 71
Walton, John, 298, 300
Ward, John O. 17n4
Warren, Michelle R., 202n12
Warton, Thomas, 54
Watson, Nicholas, 96n3, 119, 119n44, 128–29, 128n13
Wells, Robin Headlam, 301n39
Wetherbee, Winthrop, 179n14, 185n29, 250n21
Williams, Raymond, 143, 143n8
Wimsatt, W. K., Jr., 172n6
Windeatt, Barry A., 93n49, 174n8, 188n35, 189n38, 251, 251n23, 253n34, 254n36
Winner and Waster, 126, 127n11, 132n20
Wittig, Joseph, 78n8

Wittig, Susan, 131n18
Woodhead, Linda, 143n6
Woods, Marjorie Curry, 27, 27nn23–24, 28n27, 28n29, 36n10, 37n11, 287, 287n12
Woolgar, Christopher, 272n15, 273n16, 277n30

Yeager, R. F., 42, 42n40
Young, Karl, 187n32, 250, 251n23

Zak, Gur, 154, 154n30
Zeeman, Elizabeth. *See* Salter, Elizabeth
Zieman, Katherine, 83n21, 91n44, 93n48, 290, 290n26
Zumthor, Paul, 284–85, 284n1, 287, 287n10, 306

INTERVENTIONS: NEW STUDIES IN MEDIEVAL CULTURE
Ethan Knapp, Series Editor

Interventions: New Studies in Medieval Culture publishes theoretically informed work in medieval literary and cultural studies. We are interested both in studies of medieval culture and in work on the continuing importance of medieval tropes and topics in contemporary intellectual life.

Scribal Authorship and the Writing of History in Medieval England
MATTHEW FISHER

Fashioning Change: The Trope of Clothing in High- and Late-Medieval England
ANDREA DENNY-BROWN

Form and Reform: Reading across the Fifteenth Century
EDITED BY SHANNON GAYK AND KATHLEEN TONRY

How to Make a Human: Animals and Violence in the Middle Ages
KARL STEEL

Revivalist Fantasy: Alliterative Verse and Nationalist Literary History
RANDY P. SCHIFF

Inventing Womanhood: Gender and Language in Later Middle English Writing
TARA WILLIAMS

Body Against Soul: Gender and Sowlehele *in Middle English Allegory*
MASHA RASKOLNIKOV

www.ingramcontent.com/pod-product-compliance
Lightning Source LLC
Chambersburg PA
CBHW021831220426
43663CB00005B/200